CHANGE AND ARCHAEOLOGY

Change and Archaeology explores how archaeologists have historically described, interpreted, and explained change, and argues that change has been under-theorised.

The study of change is central to the discipline of archaeology, but change is complex, and this makes it challenging to write about in nuanced ways that effectively capture the nature of our world. Relational approaches offer archaeologists more scope to explore change in complex and subtle ways. *Change and Archaeology* presents a posthumanist, post-anthropocentric, new materialist approach to change. It argues that our world is constantly in the process of becoming and always on the move. By recasting change as the norm rather than the exception and distributing it between both humans and non-humans, this book offers a new theoretical framework for exploring change in the past that allows us to move beyond block-time approaches where change is located only in transitional moments and periods are characterised by blocks of stasis.

Archaeologists, scholars, anthropologists and historians interested in the theoretical frameworks we use to interpret the past will find this book a fascinating new insight into the way our world changes and evolves. The approaches presented within will be of use to anyone studying and writing about the way societies and their environs move through time.

Rachel J. Crellin is a lecturer in archaeology at the University of Leicester (UK). Her research interests centre on archaeological theory, especially new materialist, feminist, and posthumanist approaches to the past. She is also a specialist in the Neolithic and Bronze Age of Britain, Ireland, and the Isle of Man and a metalwork wear-analyst.

THEMES IN ARCHAEOLOGY

https://www.routledge.com/Themes-in-Archaeology-Series/book-series/SE0460

CHANGE AND ARCHAEOLOGY

Rachel J. Crellin

LONDON AND NEW YORK

First published 2020
by Routledge
2 Park Square, Milton Park, Abingdon, Oxon OX14 4RN

and by Routledge
52 Vanderbilt Avenue, New York, NY 10017

Routledge is an imprint of the Taylor & Francis Group, an informa business

British Library Cataloguing-in-Publication Data
A catalogue record for this book is available from the British Library

Library of Congress Cataloging-in-Publication Data
Names: Crellin, Rachel, author.
Title: Change and Archaeology / Rachel J. Crellin.
Description: London ; New York : Routledge/Taylor & Francis Group, 2020. | Series: Themes in archaeology | Includes bibliographical references and index.
Identifiers: LCCN 2019058257 (print) |
LCCN 2019058258 (ebook)
Subjects: LCSH: Archaeology--Philosophy. | Change.
Classification: LCC CC72 .C745 2020 (print) | LCC CC72 (ebook) |
DDC 930.1--dc23
LC record available at https://lccn.loc.gov/2019058257
LC ebook record available at https://lccn.loc.gov/2019058258

ISBN: 978-1-138-29254-3 (hbk)
ISBN: 978-1-138-29253-6 (pbk)
ISBN: 978-1-315-23285-0 (ebk)

Typeset in Bembo
by Taylor & Francis Books

For Mum and Dad,

who shape me and watch me change,

and Dave,

who changes with me.

CONTENTS

FIGURES

TABLE

NOTE TO READERS

This book contains a figure that shows cremated human remains from the Isle of Man dating to the Bronze Age. If you do not wish to see this image, please note it is Figure 5.2 and appears on p. 108.

ACKNOWLEDGEMENTS

It is becoming a cliché to talk about how books like these are relational assemblages just like the material discussed within. It might be a cliché, but it is accurate.

This book draws together much of my work over the last eight years. It gathers and assembles work from my PhD research on change, funded by the Isle of Man government and Newcastle University; from my early career fellowship, funded by the Leverhulme Trust and the University of Leicester; and from the first two years of my lectureship at Leicester. Matt, Molly, and Katie at Routledge, and my copy-editor Sarah Enticknap, have helped me turn my ideas into reality and have been very patient with me as I moved between jobs and houses. Additional thanks to Sarah Scoppie who patiently helped me to index the book and spot inconsistencies.

My Leverhulme Early Career Fellowship involved work with Early Bronze Age flat axes from Britain and Ireland. This included primary research at the Ashmolean Museum, Bristol Museum, the British Museum, the Great North Museum, the Manx Museum, the National Museum of Scotland, Perth Museum, the Pitt Rivers Museum, and the Yorkshire Museum. My thanks to the curators and staff at all these museums for enabling the research and for their patience and hospitality on my many visits. Staff from the Professional Services Team at Leicester handled logistics and expenses for many of these visits: I am grateful to them all for their hard work.

I am grateful to the following colleagues and friends for generously sharing images with me and granting permission for their reproduction: Jo Appleby, Jody Booze Daniels, Craig Cipolla, Marta Diaz Guardamino, Mark Gillings, Matthew Johnson, Andy Jones, and Manx National Heritage.

The cover art for the book features an image of the site-specific installation 'A million things that make your head spin' by the artist Megan Geckler at the Customs House in Sydney, Australia (2017). The photograph is by Jessica Lindsay. My thanks to both Megan and Jessica for agreeing to let me use the image.

My own thinking has benefitted from, and been challenged by, conversations with many of my wonderful colleagues: Mareike Ahlers, Emily Banfield, Huw Barton, Jo Brück, José Carvajal Lopez, Noa Corcoran-Tadd, Karina Croucher, Andrea Dolfini, Chris Fowler, Michelle Gamble, Rapha Hermann, John Robb, Amber Roy, Sarah Scott, Naoise Mac Sweeney, Andy Merrills, Nikki Rollason, Yvonne O'Dell, Marion Uckelmann, and Neil Wilkin. My thanks to them all. I am also particularly grateful to Neil Carlin, Lucy Cummings, Matt Knight, Amber Roy, and Pete Topping who shared copies of their PhD theses with me. My thanks are also due to everyone at Leicester over the past five years; they made me welcome and made the place home.

Special thanks to Andy Jones and Julian Thomas, both of whom made my viva enjoyable and were key in providing the impetus for this book. I've gained a lot from thinking assemblage with Ben Jervis and materials with Marta Diaz-Guardamino. Huge, bubbly, excitable thanks to Hannah Cobb for her patriarchy-smashing inspiration. I also want to thank the *Archaeology in Dialogue* team: Craig Cipolla, Lindsay Montgomery, Ollie Harris, and Sophie Moore. *Archaeology in Dialogue* overlapped with pulling the final chapters of this book together: the resultant chapters are much improved for happening in parallel and in conversation.

Jo Appleby, Craig Cipolla, Mark Gillings, and Alice Samson deserve extra thanks and credit for their feedback and encouragement on a range of chapters and extracts. Ollie Harris read, and commented on, the whole book in draft: he defies typology in the development of my thinking from teacher, to mentor, to colleague, to co-author, but mostly territorializing around the category friend.

Team Archaeology formed as an assemblage in 2007, they've since been de-territorialized and re-territorialized across the world both in the form of the megathread and in the form of the Barn. They provide answers to random questions, inspiration, and unshakable friendship. Luíseach Nic Eoin is always worthy of separate mention; she provided particular help with Chapter 4 as I put my toes tentatively into Palaeolithic waters and then her editorial prowess swept over chapters 1–5, improving things immeasurably: her wisdom and friendship have made this a better book.

The greatest thanks are due to my family for their love and support. My brother, Richard has improved my writing, taught me that compromise can be productive, and demonstrates the importance of keeping your focus on making a difference. My Mum and Dad have put up with my passion for the past for many years: they make everything possible. And finally, to Dave, my love and thanks, for holding me and the book together as we did our best to fall apart.

PART I

Introduction

Understanding stability is difficult, it requires explanation. How is it that monuments persist through time? How have racism and sexism become such long-term constants? Why do some communities appear to carry out the same practices over thousands of years? These things are so hard to explain because our worlds are constantly changing and so we have to explore how some things do manage to remain relatively similar.

We often choose to ignore the constant change that surrounds us. We might go to work by the same route each day, or eat our lunch at a similar time, and we probably see the same people. When someone asks us about our day we might say, "Oh, the usual". Indeed, there are some aspects of our lives that remain pretty similar to what came yesterday and what will come tomorrow. The reality, though, is that there is also a lot that changes day to day: our body chemistry will not be the same, we will have lost some old cells and gained some new ones; the news will have changed, and families and friends will have told us new things about their lives, and therefore different things might occupy our minds and shift our thoughts in different directions. People age and die, they come and go from our lives. The plants and animals we live among grow and wither. Slowly, gradually, the material culture we surround ourselves with shifts over time too: things become grubby, worn, and broken or might be fixed, recycled, or repurposed and made anew. Things do not remain the same, the world does not remain the same, and we do not remain the same. Yet rarely do we sit and think about the change that occurs all the time: it can be overwhelming. Stability is hard to explain, constant change can be hard to even contemplate.

Still, there are times of the year when we do actively reflect on change. I wrote this passage waiting to meet friends for an annual weekend we spend together. We do roughly the same thing each year: we rent a camping barn in the countryside, we go on long walks, we have dinner at the pub. Traditionally we eat the same food on the first night of the weekend: pasta with a vegetable sauce, a memento from when we first started these weekends after we graduated and had no money. As I sat and waited for the others to arrive, I thought about how much had changed: who had got a new job, moved house, or had a child. It is during these regular events, full of traditions, that at least appear the same, when we often reflect on change – the same can be said of festivals, the New Year, or birthdays. It is at times like these that losses are often hardest felt because change makes itself most apparent.

This is the minutiae of change that surrounds our day-to-day life over a time-scale of hours, days, and years. As archaeologists we often work on radically different timescales, from centuries to millennia – here things change at a different order of magnitude. Consider for example, Britain and Ireland at 3000BC, 2000BC, and 1000BC: at each interval they were very different places with different material culture, different practices, and communities with different ideas and beliefs. Our datasets encourage us to think and talk about change in different ways. We might study the rise of inequality, or the development of agriculture, or the impact of new materials. We try to describe, interpret, and explain changes. Our job is to explain how things got to be the way they were and how they went on to change. Often, we aim to wrap our explanation up with a sense of cause and effect: the arrival of metalwork led to the increasing development of inequality; the domestication of plants and animals allowed the development of monumental architecture. We also have to try to explain why some things appear, at least, not to change. We have to explain how change comes to have different tempos.

Part I of this book sets out my argument for why we need to consider how we think about change directly and what I see as the main hurdles in our current approaches. Part II reflects on our existing approaches to change. In Chapter 2 I provide a history of archaeological theory in relation to change and then go on, in chapters 3, 4, and 5, to look at the intersection of change with three key topics: time, scale, and biography. Part III reflects on the development of relational approaches and the space they offer us to write new narratives of change. In Chapter 6 I explore the work of Bruno Latour and those inspired by him to create symmetrical archaeology, alongside the concept of entanglement developed by Ian Hodder, explaining why I choose to work in a different way. In Chapter 7 I outline my own relational approach utilising assemblage theory, new materialism, and posthumanism. Chapter 8 offers an extended case study where I apply the ideas from Chapter 7 to the beginning of the Bronze Age in Britain and Ireland. Chapter 9 offers a conclusion to the book and considers future directions for research.

The study of change is at the very heart of the discipline of archaeology. In this book I argue that we often fail to theorise our approach to change and that we need to think more explicitly about how we describe, interpret, and explain change. We can write more nuanced, interesting, and impactful archaeology if we take the time to think about how we approach change and foreground it in our writing.

1

WHAT IS WRONG WITH CHANGE?

Change lies at the heart of archaeology. We study places, times, and worlds that are different from our own. We study ways of life, people, and objects different from those today. We also often study blocks of time and seek to characterise how they differ from what came before and what followed afterwards: we study how things change. Indeed, the study of change, over the very long term, is one of the defining features of our discipline. The archaeological record provides evidence for the rise and fall of empires, shifting gender relations, and long-term climatic changes over thousands of years. Despite this disciplinary centrality, I believe we have radically under-theorised how we describe, interpret, and explain change.

In this book I argue that change is constant in all materials from stone to metal, grasses to cows, and buildings to people, and that, as a result, our world is always in motion. Change cannot simply be book-ended at the start and beginning of periods; instead it is messier and more complex. This is not to deny that change happens at different speeds, from the very slow to the incredibly rapid. Nor do I suggest we need to create an undifferentiated past without moments of remarkable transformation. Instead, I show a new way for us to map and understand change.

Why foreground change?

The past 10 years has seen renewed debate about what the subject of archaeology should be (see, for example, Alberti et al., 2011; 2014; Barrett, 2016; Hodder, 2012; Nativ, 2018; Olsen, 2010; Olsen et al., 2012; Webmoor, 2007). For me one of the most convincing and important arguments comes from Severin Fowles (Alberti et al., 2011), who argues that archaeology is the discipline of the grand narrative[1]. He suggests this is "both our burden and our distinctive means of intervening in contemporary debates" (Alberti et al., 2011: 899). We have a vast past at our disposal, and it is this that Fowles argues defines archaeology, in contrast to those who would define our subject as the "discipline of things" (Olsen et al., 2012). He argues that we have the ability to talk about "ontologically loaded plotlines" from human origins to the emergence of tools. These are controversial topics where we might well find issue with how the history of humans has been written and presented, particularly in Euro-American contexts. Fowles argues that one of the most effective ways of intervening in ontological debates in the present is to "rewrite our foundational narratives of the past". What Fowles is suggesting is that unless we tackle the grand narrative, unless we try to deal with the vast sweep of changing history at our disposal, we will fail to grasp the true potential of our subject. Comfortably writing local narratives on 'safe ground', or failing to address how our world has changed and continues to change, is not going to demonstrate our wider value, nor will it allow us to reach the true political potential of the archaeological record. Moreover, as John Robb and Tim Pauketat (2013: 33) argue, it is not the case that if we do not tell the grand narratives (what they term large-scale histories) they will not be told. Rather, other people, who are not archaeologists, who have less knowledge of the nuance and complexity of the archaeological record, and always have their own political aims, will tell these stories in ways we may well object to. We have to deal with the grand narrative, the 'ontostory', and to do that effectively we have to deal with change in new ways.

We must be able to describe, interpret, and understand how change happens in ways that allow difference to emerge and we must avoid the teleological construction of plot lines, where what happens in the end serves as the explanation for how we got there. We have to be able to present the radical alterity of the past (and the present) in ways that do not assume other ways of being are less legitimate. As Julian Thomas (2004a: 235–241) highlights, opening ourselves up to the alterity of the past is an ethical move. As archaeologists we are well placed to show the diversity of ways of being that exist in the world – to offer a foil to our own modernity (or our lack of it, *sensu* Latour, 1993). This is political: it seeks to trouble and disrupt what we have come to know in the West as the 'normal' way of being and shows that other ways of being are equally real and legitimate. Taking an ethical stance, focusing on difference and alterity, defined as other ways of being, is one way in which we come to make archaeology matter more widely. Yet it also requires that we theorise change more carefully. It asks that we have a nuanced and proper understanding of the relationship between past and present that does not see the past as something separated from the present. Our world is not singular. Anthropology and archaeology demonstrate that what exists, and how those things which exist relate to each other (what we term ontology), is not universal. We need to be able to present alternative ontologies and ways of being, not as primitive, or lesser, a 'simpler' understanding awaiting the saving addition of western science, but instead as equally legitimate (see discussion in Harris and Cipolla, 2017: 173–185).

It some ways it could be seen as counter-intuitive that someone who argues for a nuanced and complex understanding of change as constant believes archaeology's greatest strength is its access to the grand narrative. Surely these two approaches are not natural partners? The grand narrative is normally about giving one overarching, usually teleological, story about how we ended up the way we are. Moreover, it is often broken down into a series of chapters that focus on specific moments of radical change that helped shape us into the 'wonderful, knowledgeable' people of today. Equally, it could be seen as unusual that I argue for the importance of both grand narrative and alterity. Is it not the case that grand narratives often end up (literally) whitewashing alterity? Some clarity is called for.

Archaeology has to deal with the grand narrative of human history because this is our biggest strength. By describing the past we are able to play a hand in working out the changing meaning of what it is to be human: a deeply political act. Returning to the quote from Severin Fowles, the grand narratives is also "our burden" (Alberti et al., 2011: 899). We do not have to rewrite the traditional grand narrative. Our stories of the human past need not be teleological, progressive, or deterministic. Nor do they need to uphold our current state of being as the crowning glory of humanity, the definition of success. The increasing attention on our climate crisis and the demonstration of the pervasive and damaging nature of human waste, like plastics, across the whole planet, demonstrate how foolhardy it is to think things are 'better than they have ever been'. Writing grand narratives does not mean writing simplistic narratives. We have to intervene in, rewrite, and engage with, the grand narrative that exists to write not a better one, but multiple, different, better ones. We must not be totalizing when we seek to intervene in the grand narrative – we need instead to highlight multiplicity, difference, and alterity. We need grand narratives not a grand narrative. Our rewriting must necessarily focus upon alterity, demonstrating that human history is not a singular correct, irreversible, progressive path through a number of defined stepping-stones to our current state. By thinking about change differently we can show that there is not just one way to be in the world and one correct way to understand the world but, rather, there are kaleidoscopes of possible, ever-shifting, diverse ways to live in the world.

Hurdles to change

I doubt that many archaeologists would argue against the importance of change to the discipline. What is perhaps more controversial about my argument is that I identify several hurdles in our current approaches to change that hinder us from writing more nuanced and complex narratives. All too often we still fall back on teleological ideas of progress, and our thinking, structured by our approach to periods and time, continues to be dominated by ideas of origins and revolutions. I argue that our explanations for change are often deterministic or anthropocentric (meaning they are human-centred). As a result, when we approach change in the archaeological record, all too often we seek a singular cause, often external to the pre-existing narrative (the arrival of a new community, the invention of a new technology, a big environmental change) that has the capacity to radically alter the world. This is, in part, because of the way we continue to operate a block-time approach where change happens at the beginning and ends of periods and where stasis dominates the middle.

Hurdle 1 – the block-time approach to change

Traditionally, archaeologists often focus on the study of periods. We like to specialise in blocks of time. These are blocks that we usually like to think we can define. We draw a box around the block of time, we define it as having a certain set of features, and we describe how these differ from the features of what came before and that which came afterwards (see Figure 1.1). What happens within the period block is often presented as relatively static and what happens at the beginning and end is necessarily dynamic. It is change that caused things to move from one way of being to another. I term this phenomenon the *block-time approach*. We might do this at differing scales, we could talk about the Bronze Age and characterise its difference from the Iron Age and consider what caused the transition between the two periods. Or, increasingly, we can work at far finer scales: the application of Bayesian statistical techniques to our radiocarbon dates allows us to present ever-finer chronological ranges allowing discussion of changes on a generational scale where we can consider how things differed between one generation and the next (see, for example, Whittle, 2018). In this model, change happens at the beginnings and ends of our periods and what happens in the middle is often presented as stasis.

There is something very satisfying about being able to define a period of time as having a certain set of characteristics, and contrast these with the following period (grasping first-year undergraduate courses without this model would be very difficult). Even more satisfying are cases where we can identify the factor that caused

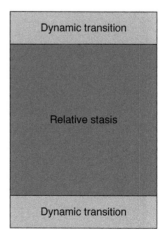

FIGURE 1.1 Block-time approach: periods of stasis and dynamic transitions
Source: R.J. Crellin.

the world to shift from being one way to another. I do not deny that there were real differences between ways of life at different points in time. For example, it would be pure fallacy to suggest that Neolithic communities did not live very different lives from Bronze Age ones. We necessarily have to start from a place where we understand what life was like at one time and how it differed at another, and perhaps the logical thing to do next is to work out how things changed from one state to the next. We have to start from this position, but we do not have to finish there.

The reality of life in a changing world is messy – communities did not spend one day being Neolithic, go to bed and then wake up the next day being Bronze Age. Lots of different things changed at once. Consider the emergence of the European Bronze Age for example, did simply having metal for the first time make a community Bronze Age? Or were they Bronze Age once they understood what metal was? Or did that happen when they knew how to make metal themselves? Or when they grasped the properties of metal? When they realised metals could be recycled? Or did being Bronze Age not have all that much to do with metal at all – was it about a different understanding of identities, or burial practices, or the development of gender relations? When we bore into the archaeological record there are many aspects of life that changed between the Neolithic and the Bronze Age, and they did not change all at once. Rather they were shifting constantly in differing ways. Considering the evidence like this it becomes clear that we cannot simply have two opposed static blocks of time, with different characteristics and a radical transition between them (see Figure 1.1). The shift between ways of life was constant and unceasing. Ultimately, creating periods of stasis interrupted by dynamic transitions sells archaeology short. We create caricatures of periods where the artist might, as it were, emphasise the nose on one cartoon and the ears on another thereby demonstrating their striking difference. Caricatures are fun, and they do tell us something about a person, but they are not the whole truth, and they are often comic. As archaeologists we have an ever-increasing ability to paint more subtle pictures. This book aims to present subtle pictures, more like the portraits in J.K. Rowling's *Harry Potter* where the subjects are never static, but free to get up, move around, and interfere in the world around them.

Chapter 2 effectively forms an extended case study of why the block-time approach sells us short. It considers the history of archaeological theory in relation to change. This is often broken down into a three-part story: culture history, processualism, and post-processualism. I consider how we can look for connections between these approaches and thereby disrupt the block-time approach by offering a more flowing narrative of change.

Hurdle 2 – progressive narratives

Progressive approaches to the study, interpretation, and explanation of change have a long history within archaeology. Bruce Trigger (2006: 97–98) suggests that the development of both progressive and evolutionary thinking in archaeology was the result of Enlightenment thinking rather than a reflection of archaeological evidence. Trigger shows how philosophers began to think in progressive and evolutionary ways that, over time, came to influence the thinking of the middle classes to believe in the inherent progress and improvement of humankind. Enlightenment thinking suggested that human progress and knowledge would continue until it reached a state of enlightened perfection (Thomas, 2004a: 28). Alternative ways of being, demonstrated by groups viewed as "technologically inferior" were understood as being examples of the primitivity through which Europeans had already progressed (Thomas, 2004a: 31). Human history thus became a story of progress from the simple to the complex and perfect via the development of human reason.

Progressive narratives are frequently linked to evolutionary thinking. Yet the understanding behind many of the progressive models of history is not based on the work of Charles Darwin (1859) but instead on his predecessor Jean-Baptiste Lamarck (1960). Lamarck argued that life evolves from simple to complex as a result of the desire of organisms to improve themselves – something he termed *vitalism*. Those creatures that did not change and improve lacked the drive to do so (there is an associated moral judgement with this). Lamarckianism suggested that characteristics were inherited by offspring and that change over time resulted in the development of new species. His model of evolution was inherently progressive, whereas Darwin's (1859) 'descent with modification' was not: there is no inherent directionality or progress in Darwinian evolution. Lamarck's ideas were adapted by Herbert Spencer (1864) who suggested that progressive development is universal as all life changes from simple to complex.

Today we can quickly spot the inherently problematic nature of such ideas, and how they have justified racism, imperialism, and the continued dominance of white western groups through this kind of thinking, yet the models that underlie them continue to influence archaeology. The idea of a teleological model of history underpins social evolutionary models such as those of Lewis Henry Morgan (1877). Morgan's model proposed universal social evolutionary stages that human societies passed through from *savagery* to *barbarism* to *civilisation*. He did not suggest they happened at the same pace everywhere, but he did argue that ultimately there was a single route to the present. Gavin Lucas (2005: 12) suggests these were the ideas, combined with Marxist thinking, that were later outlined by Gordon Childe (1942; 1951). Childe promoted evolutionary stages and combined them with agricultural and urban "revolutions", to move between these key stages in human history. Childe's ideas were later adapted by Sahlins and Service (1960) to produce their four-stage model of social complexity of *bands, tribes, chiefdoms,* and *states.*

In Lucas's (2005: 12) book on the relationship between archaeology and time he argues that the "neo-evolutionary model is the one still in use today, albeit modified (e.g. Johnson and Earle 1987), and remains the dominant paradigm of social change in the US and, to a lesser extent, in Europe". Our continued engagement with the question of agricultural and urban revolutions is inherently linked to the idea of universal, progressive models of society. Furthermore, progressive, social evolutionary tables of human history continue to feature in the basic textbooks we give to students to teach them what archaeology is and what it has achieved. A progressive table of mobile hunter-gatherers, segmentary societies, chiefdoms, and states features in Renfrew and Bahn (2016: 182, Fig 5.2) and while they caution against unthinking use, they evidently still find it a good framework, suggesting that archaeology has "to attempt to explain why some societies became more complex and others do not" (Renfrew and Bahn, 2016: 183). The implication is that some societies certainly do progress from simple to complex. One only has to look at the continuing dominance of the chiefdom model (see, for example, Kristiansen, 2018) as a way of developing more complex social units and forms of leadership to see that these kinds of progressive understandings of change (and the grand narrative) continue to dominate (for an excellent discussion of the pitfalls of this approach see Pauketat, 2007).

Hurdle 3 – teleological narratives

Progressive approaches also often result in the production of teleological narratives where our current human condition is the explanation for past change; as Clive Gamble (2007: 26) states, "the paradox of change in the past is that nothing changes unless it has significance for the present". The production of teleological narratives can be linked to the need to produce historical narratives that provide the foundations for nation states (Clark, 2003: 42).

Thomas (2004a: 233) argues that the modern world is, "absorbed with time and its irreversibility" and that as a result we have sought to distance ourselves from the so-called 'primitive past'. Time marches onwards, the past is unlike today, and it is therefore primitive. Fowles (2010) has commented on the tendency of non-western pasts to be defined by absences: the absence of a state, metallurgy, agriculture, leadership, or secular knowledge, for example, that would allow them to 'progress' along the universal model of social evolution. Gamble (2007: 22) makes a similar argument that Palaeolithic people are often defined by their differences from Neolithic farmers. Our conception of time distances us from the past and makes it 'other' and 'less than' the present (I return to concepts of time in Chapter 3).

Teleology plays another role in our broader approach to change. Today we can access news from around the world throughout the day and night via television, radio, and the internet. This globalisation of communication and news cycles is often the subject of debate regarding the nature of change in our world. We wonder whether change has ever happened so quickly and with such dramatic effect. We then look back at the past and consider the pace of change to have been far slower, less pervasive, and less significant: 'those were simpler times'. We imagine a time with less change and more stability than our ever-shifting lives today – so much so that we are happy to cleave off blocks of time and suggest that life remaining relatively similar for thousands of years. When we suggest that change was less constant or less significant in the past, we are thinking teleologically. Just as

Fowles (2010) argues that we often suggest past communities 'lack' something we have today that would make them 'like us', we also suggest they change less than we do today because they lack the things that make them 'like us'. Each time they gain one of those things that makes them 'more like us' – metal, agriculture, scientific knowledge – we grant them a rapid moment of change.

Hurdle 4 – origins and revolutions

Progressive and teleological thinking also plays a role in our continued emphasis on origins and revolutions. Gamble's (2007) book on the subject effectively highlights both their pervasiveness in archaeology and their problematic nature:

> Archaeologists will tell you that they were put on this earth to explain change. What they usually mean by that is their unflagging search for the evidence of origins; the fieldwork quest for the oldest. And once found these origin points, like well driven tent pegs, secure the ropes to explain the changes that led in the first place to the point of origin.
>
> *(Gamble, 2007: 5)*

Thomas (2004a: 233) argues that modernist thinking relies upon notions of origins and foundations, and he links the rise of antiquarianism to the need to provide origins for the emerging European nation states. New nation states ideally needed a timeless origin for their people, their rulers, and their customs in order to secure their futures. Origin-building is never apolitical as a recent *Nature Ecology and Evolution* editorial (2019) argues in response to a 2019 tweet from the Israeli prime minister Benjamin Nehtenyahu regarding aDNA research arguing that the Philistines originated in Europe (Feldman et al., 2019); talking about origins needs to be done in careful and nuanced ways.

Interest in origins spreads well beyond European nation building: many different communities around the world have long-standing interests in their origins. My critique of origins focuses on a particular kind of essentialising definition of origins where origins become associated with a 'pure', 'true', and stable version of a given phenomenon. As this book will demonstrate, there are no pure, true, or stable phenomena, rather all things are in motion. Furthermore, there are no singular origins we can associate with a given phenomenon (see Hurdle 6).

As an example, consider a discovery at the Kenyan site of Nataruk (Mirazón Lahr et al., 2016). Excavation revealed twelve articulated skeletons of hunter-gatherers from the late Pleistocene/early Holocene, ten of which showed evidence of a violent death, interpreted as a massacre. The opening paragraphs of the publication framed the story as follows:

> The origins of war are controversial. Although it is clear that intergroup violence, including intentional lethal attacks on individuals, is part of the behavioural repertoire of chimpanzees ... evolutionary explanations for human

violence have been disputed … After numerous analyses of the scarce ethnographic data, researchers remain deeply divided as to whether antagonistic
relations formed a significant element of social life in prehistory.

(Mirazón Lahr et al., 2016: 394)

The archaeological evidence of violence from Nataruk is linked to the issue of the
origins of war straight away, and we can see the authors acknowledge the con-
troversy of the research area. Furthermore, origins become linked to issues of
definition – whether chimpanzees are violent or not affects whether violence is
defined as a uniquely human trait. The University of Cambridge's own news page
used the headline "Evidence of a prehistoric massacre extends the history of warfare",[2] while newspapers ran headlines such as "World's first massacre scene?"
(Mazza, 2016). The story demonstrates the power of origins and their role in the
process of definition. Is this the earliest evidence of violence? If so, does it mean
that all humans are inherently violent? There can be no doubt that Nataruk is an
interesting and important site but linking it to the origin of violence, raises
the significance further. Doubtless there are older sites showing evidence of violence waiting to be discovered that will gain similar notoriety, displacing Nataruk
in the narrative as one of many early violence sites rather than *the* 'origin' site.

Similar to origins, revolutions index specific, singular moments that mark a radical
change of a more impressive magnitude and tempo than we see more commonly.
Gamble's (2007) argument suggests that revolutions are more of a structuring
method for telling the story of human history than a reality; he effectively shows the
'Neolithic Revolution' and the 'Human Revolution' to both be products of our
own context rather than of the archaeological evidence. The use of revolutions as a
structuring method in our narrative of change relates to our block-time approach,
where stable periods are punctuated by moments of rapid transition. Gamble (2007:
23) suggests that without revolutions as a device to explain change in the past we
tend to fall back on the notion of gradual change, something he terms future-creep.
Both revolution-based and future-creep models of change are unsatisfactory.

Gamble (2007) shows that Childe's (1942) identification of the 'Agricultural
Revolution' was a product of his own personal and political context including the
rise of nationalism in Europe. It was also a result of the evidence available at the
time: changes in tool use over the previous three million years appeared insignificant in comparison to changes that occurred at the start of the Neolithic. This was
further compounded by the then absence of radiometric dates – Childe looked at
the Neolithic as a package of changes and presumed they all happened together to
create a revolution. Today, the evidence is far more complicated and identifying
when any 'revolution' happened, or what exactly we define that as, is more complex, and arguably impossible.

Gamble (2007: 14) argues there are two contrasting approaches to revolution.
The first sees revolutions as universal stages in a progressive scheme and the second
sees them as the result of contingent factors at a particular time and place. The first
approach is the one more regularly applied to grand narratives of human history

and the second is one we might more readily associate with the call for local and specific histories that arose from post-processualism. In both cases they are broadly teleological. They form a device for cutting up history into blocks and, as argued above, they can act as a starting point, but we have the evidence to move beyond them and the ability to write more subtle and nuanced narratives of change that need not call upon the notion of a revolution.

One might well identify an apparent contradiction here between my earlier argument for the grand narrative and my argument against origins and revolutions. How can we deal with the grand narrative if we do not search for origins – be they of humanity, writing, leadership, or indeed violence? Did I not make the argument earlier that part of the importance of the grand narrative is its relationship to defining what it means to be human? How can we write a human history that does not identify some changes as having a revolutionary effect? Turning first to the issue of origins: as I've argued, the problem with an origin story is when it defines a single point in time when a given phenomenon arose. By identifying that point it then seeks to give a definition to the phenomenon itself. So we find the oldest site with evidence of violence; this allows us to define what violence is and is not – indeed there are diagnostic criteria for warfare discussed in Mirazón Lahr et al. (2016: 396), and Childe (1950) had a list of traits that identify when an Urban Revolution can be observed. Thereby we further define what humanity is or is not (inherently violent and competitive for example). The problem is twofold – the emphasis on origins suggests there is one pure, specific, singular, totalizing origin for any given phenomenon, and second, it suggests that phenomena can be defined in a single way that then remains the same through time. Yet, violence 10,000 years ago is not the same as violence 2000 years ago or even 100 years ago: violence and warfare have a changing history, they are different things at different times.

The problem with revolutions is similar. Revolution-thinking seeks some single specific moment of origin for a change: the moment of revolution. It suggests the world had one form, and then became radically different. There is clearly a link here to the problems identified earlier in the block-time approach. I am not denying that there are times of extreme change in human history, nor suggesting that some changes were not more significant than others. What I take issue with is the way revolution-thinking suggests some kind of radical, rapid, and specific moment of change. Change is more complex and messier, with multiple different processes ongoing at once and all at different tempos. It is not that there are not different tempos of change, it is rather that the notion of a revolution is unhelpful in describing, interpreting, and explaining that change.

What do I suggest in place of origins and revolutions research? We should instead trace changing histories of emergence; we should look at how violence or urbanism have emerged and changed over time. Rather than defining a singular origin point for a phenomenon we should instead acknowledge it has multiple interrelated and differing origins, in different places, at different times. We should be telling changing stories of what it means to be human rather than creating checklists of the traits that define us because those traits have always been, and will always be, shifting. I am not saying that we cannot look for the 'oldest' version of anything, just that being preoccupied with that search takes us away from telling more interesting stories.

Hurdle 5 – determinisms

The continuing influence of deterministic explanations for change links to the underlying influence of teleological thinking on our discipline. Technologically and environmentally deterministic explanations of change are inherently teleological given their directionality and links to a sense of inevitability. Determinisms remain influential when explaining change; sometimes the determinism at play is explicit and sometimes it provides an undertone to an argument. Environmental determinism often plays a role in explanations of long-term change, particularly those that focus on a scale where it seems hard to pin change onto human protagonists – in such cases, the environment, something seemingly outside of the human and occupying a global scale, often becomes the explanation for change. When we work at a larger scale it seems we need a large-scale explanation, and what larger scale is there on earth than the environment (this is explored more in Chapter 4). Technology, on the other hand, is the thing that is supposed to define our development as a species and separate us from non-humans, so what better explanation could there be for change in human history: technology is what makes us unique and changes to it are what cause the 'revolutions' in human history that led us to today.

Few archaeologists today openly embrace the technological determinism evident in the work of earlier archaeologists, but, as Tim Ingold suggests, there is still an underlying sense that technology progresses. Metal, for example, is presented as a superior and more complex technology than stone. Indeed, metallurgy is still equated with social complexity (Bray, 2012: 58; Ottaway and Roberts, 2008: 194). Craddock (1995: 32–35) talks of the "primitive" stone and antler tools used to extract metal ores – metallurgy is clearly meant to be seen as a more complex technology than the simple technology of mining. The use of terms such as 'production', 'extraction', 'factories', and 'industry' when describing early mining sites adds to the sense that they are a stepping-stone on the path towards the modern, western relationship with production. The underlying implication is that technological change progressively becomes more complex over time.

The most effective critique of both technologically and environmentally deterministic approaches to the explanation of change is that both of the terms are shorthand categories that fall apart when scrutiny is applied to them. Bruno Latour (1993), the sociologist of science and technology studies, demonstrates how the west continually carries out acts of *purification* to break the world down into specific bounded categories shaped by Cartesian dualisms, binary oppositions between two concepts such as nature and culture, or mind and matter. Environment and technology are further categories that effectively parallel nature and culture. Environmental determinism is the explanation we give when changes are beyond the human scale – when the change belongs to nature. Technological determinism is the explanation we give that centres around the human and belongs to culture. Latour (1993) demonstrates that these categories are not real as the world is always a complex network of hybrids that cannot ever be placed neatly in a single category. This is the case with change. We could identify and label something as a techno-logical cause of a given change but in reality technology is inseparable from people, animals, plants, politics, things, the climate, and our beliefs (to name but a few).

The climate crisis is devastatingly impacting on our world; it is neither an environmentally nor a technologically determined outcome. The climate crisis is not the result of either 'nature' or 'humans' but a whole host of complex and interrelated factors: capitalism, economic and political policies, the power of large corporations, reliance on electricity, and the human hunger for meat are just a few factors. Indeed, it is the monstrous hybridity of the climate crisis that makes it hard to tackle: there is no single change we can make that will solve it; we need to make many complex and interrelated changes including, most pressingly, at an ontological level in our attitude towards, and understanding of, the environment not as something we master but something we are interwoven with. This complex hybridity also links to the attitude of climate change deniers who are unhappy with placing the explanation for changes in the environment (nature in our Cartesian dualism) in the human domain (culture in our Cartesian dualism). It is not the case that we can change one thing (politics or economics, for example) and stop the climate crisis because change is so very complex and cannot be understood using simple explanatory categories.

Ingold (2000: Chapter 20) develops a critique of technological determinism along parallel lines. He argues that in many models of history there is a sense that our biology changes up to the point we become modern humans but is then somehow frozen, and what changes from that point onwards is technology and that changes to technology are then what allow humans to progress. In this argu-ment biology takes the place of nature and technology takes the place of culture in our Cartesian dualism. Ingold (2000: Chapter 20) effectively breaks down the categories of biology and technology to demonstrate that technology has a con-tinuing effect on our biology and vice versa. Suggesting that technology changes while our biology remains stable is unhelpful and inaccurate – the two develop together and are inseparable; consider, for example, the development of lactase persistence in European populations as an adaptation to the continued consump-tion of dairy products (Itan et al., 2009).

Relying on determinisms means falling back on unhelpful Cartesian categories: change is natural (environmental determinism) or it is cultural (technological determinism). These straightforward labels mask a messy reality. Environmental changes are complex: they link to human action, to technology, to politics and beliefs; they involve people, plants, animals, geology, the weather etc. We can do better than simply labelling them environmental as if it were something separate to us. Using technological determinism to explain change is perhaps even more dan-gerous because of the way it ties into an anthropocentric, progressive, and tele-ological narrative: technology makes us special and lets us triumph over nature.

Hurdle 6 – singular causation

A number of the hurdles I have outlined coalesce to create the situation where all too often our explanations of change focus on the search for a single cause located in a single moment in time. We like to be able to identify precisely what it was that made the world change and when that happened. We can see this in the search for origins of various behaviours and institutions and the column inches granted to those who find the current 'earliest' version of any phenomenon. We can also see it in identifications of revolutions as the moments when things suddenly change in momentous and irrevocable ways. The grand narrative is often written in this way – it searches for the singular origin point of a given phenomenon and the catastrophic slew of changes that result from it. These kinds of narratives are deeply satisfying: we have the cause and we can place it on a timeline. This kind of thinking is also often progressive and teleological in nature: it can produce totalizing narratives. Our habit of falling back on determinisms can also be characterised in this manner. Discussing shifting technology or climate gives us a clear cause of change. The archaeological record is complex and can be overwhelming, whereas it is satisfying to identify a simple cause-and-effect relationship and locate it at a specific moment on a timeline: we see a change in the form of settlement – we wonder what caused that – we turn to the climatic data and we find a change in rainfall levels.

Singular causation, located in a single moment, is satisfying but it does not do justice to the messy reality of the world and it does not help us write the kind of complex, nuanced grand narratives that the archaeological record captures. The political philosopher Jane Bennett (2010) has argued that we need to completely reject singular causation. With clear links to the arguments of Latour (1993) and Ingold (2000) discussed above, she argues that there are no singular agents because within any given singular agent there are really a whole series of other interwoven and interlocking factors.

What Bennett (2010: 33) refers to as billiard-ball causality is what I refer to as singular causality. She discusses the fallacy of presuming that human agency is the singular cause of anything: for her, causality is always more complex. Bennett disputes the idea that any simple body might be the sole cause of an effect. She borrows the term 'actant' from the work of Latour, who uses the word to refer to anything (human or non-human) that can have an effect (Latour, 1993). She argues that because single actants are in fact made up of many other actants we can never identify a single cause of change. A cause here is understood as a "singular, stable and masterful initiation of events" (Bennett, 2010: 33). Her argument applies equally to the identification of broader categories such as 'the environment' or 'politics' as causes. She argues instead for a radically different understanding of causality where the concepts of cause and effect fall apart: she terms this 'emergent causality' and I return to this in Chapter 7.

Change cannot be pinned on singular causes at singular moments. Agriculture was not invented in one place at one time. It emerged and re-emerged for a whole host of different reasons, in different places, at different times, and in different forms. Indeed, what we mean by agriculture is different in different places across the world and it is not the same at 5000BC as 500AD. There is no single cause to identify, nor a single, linear route to agriculture. We do not need 'always and everywhere' explanations for change in the human past – the archaeological record practically forbids it.

Hurdle 7 – anthropocentrism

Modernity has placed humans at the centre of our world (Thomas, 2004a: 225–226). They are the measure of all things and the central protagonists in history; indeed, we often refer to it as human history as if to reconfirm it is about people above all else. Bennett (2010: ix) describes humans as sitting at our "ontological apex" – they rest as a category above everything else that inhabits this world. As a result, when we approach change, we often focus on the role of humans and human agency. We seek a human explanation for change: we might think about how humans domesticated plants and animals and fail to appreciate the role that plants and animals themselves have in this process (see, for example, van der Veen, 2014). Or we might say that human desire to come together in groups led to efforts being invested into creating surplus through domestication processes, placing the human at the centre of the explanation for change. Humans are placed at the ontological apex and from there they can direct and change their own history.

There is a developing critique of our anthropocentrism in academia, and archaeology has not been exempt for this. Diverse approaches such as symmetrical archaeology (Olsen, 2007; Olsen et al., 2012; Shanks, 2007; Webmoor, 2007; Webmoor and Witmore, 2008; Witmore, 2007) and assemblage theory (Cobb and Croucher, 2014; 2020; Crellin, 2017; Fowler, 2013a,b; 2017; Hamilakis, 2017; Harris, 2014a,b; 2017; Jervis, 2016; 2018; Jones, 2012; 2017; Jones and Hamilakis, 2017) offer powerful critiques of the pervasiveness and problematic nature of anthropocentrism[3]. They do not argue that humans have no role in change or history but instead argue that we have underplayed the role of non-humans in our world and over-emphasised the importance of humans. Non-anthropocentric approaches are diverse, but all offer alternative ways of conceptualising and understanding our world (these will be discussed in much greater detail in chapters 6 and 7). They argue that humans have never acted alone in this world; they have always been deeply entangled and inseparable from non-humans and that it is time we pay non-humans their due in our narratives.

Posthumanist approaches are part of this ongoing critique of anthropocentrism. They not only critique anthropocentrism but also argue that not all humans have been represented in the 'human' category. The work of Rosi Braidotti (2013) demonstrates that existing western humanist and anthropocentric approaches have served only to elevate a certain subset of humans (white, heterosexual, males) and that women, marginalised groups, and Indigenous communities have rarely been elevated to this same position; instead they have been naturalised and othered –

removed from the category human and given a lesser role in history. Earlier, I discussed Fowles' (2010) the argument that so-called 'primitive' societies are seen as lacking key characteristics that made them 'like us'; instead they are conceived of as less-than. Posthumanist approaches try to increase the value of *all* humans *and* a diverse cast of others. These are complex and controversial theoretical waters. For now, it is important to emphasise that our anthropocentrism serves to write out a role in history for a diverse host of others, from plants, animals, materials, things, and gods, to Indigenous groups and women, in the ongoing processes of change that surround us. All too often these others are merely 'affected by' human agency that creates change rather than given a role in the process of change itself.

Case study: The Three Age System

To contextualise my critique of our approaches to change I explore the Three Age System. My discussion is not exhaustive (for excellent detailed discussions see Rowley-Conwy, 2007; Trigger, 2006: 121–138) but rather highlights the way the Three Age System can lead to a particular way of understanding change.

The Three Age System continues to dominate European pre-Roman archaeology (and is even applied beyond where it often makes little sense). By focusing upon it we can illustrate the issues of progress, origins and revolutions, teleological explanations, and determinisms. The Three Age System[4] has its origins in the work of one of the earliest archaeologists: Christian Thomsen. In 1816 Thomsen was appointed to bring order to the Danish National Collection of Antiquities so that they could be displayed in a museum. The now familiar story suggests he looked at the many artefacts from the collection not as individual objects, as had been common before, but instead arranged them into artefact assemblages, looking for objects that occurred together. His arrangement of these assemblage gave rise to the Three Age System as he showed that stone tools had first dominated and eventually been 'replaced' by bronze and then later iron. In addition, our propensity for dividing periods into Three Age Systems spreads beyond the traditional Stone, Bronze, and Iron Ages as we divide the Stone Age into the Palaeo-, Meso-, and Neolithic and the Palaeolithic into the upper, middle, and lower. For as long as authors have used the system there have been calls to reject it outright or to alter it by adding in new periods, removing periods, or placing the divides between periods elsewhere (see, for example, Bradley, 2007: 25; Cleal and Pollard, 2012: 329; Piggott, 1954: xvii). Yet, the Three Age System has remained the primary way of dividing up the European pre-Roman past; like all frameworks, it is not neutral, but acts to shape and structure our archaeological research.

The Three Age System effectively creates a block-time approach where we create periods of stability interspersed by moments of transition (or even revolution). Childe (1944) argued that it was not the case that societies in all regions of the world would pass through these transitions at the same time. He suggested that the archaeological ages might be better understood as 'technological stages' and within these there were substages (for example, he defines a Mode 0, 1, 2, and 3 for the utilisation of metal[5]). Childe suggests that all of the substages might not be present within every region, thereby allowing some space for regional diversity, but the overall pattern remains: societies must first 'master' stone tools before mastering bronze and later iron. This is an inherently progressive model of change where not only is metal seen as a more complex technology but also a functionally superior one – technology improves and triumphs in this model. Childe (1944: 9) argued that new technologies were the result of "translations of older forms" to produce "new species", linking his ideas of technological change to evolutionary and progressive thinking and thereby suggesting one technology replaces another. This scheme is of course technologically determinist: changes in technology from stone, to bronze, to iron produced concomitant changes in wider society. The technological changes are presented as progressive: we move from simple to complex technology and along the way society becomes more complex. While there is nuance in how the model was employed by Childe it was, and remains today, an inherently progressive, linear, and teleological model of change (see, for example, Lucas, 2005: 51; Griffiths, 2017; Thomas, 2004a: 67).

The Three Age System was, at its outset, progressive, rooted in origin and revolution thinking, inherently teleological (and thereby linear and unidirectional) and technologically determinist. One might argue that today we do not believe the same things about the Three Age System, or that we use it differently. Yet it is not the case that the Three Age System today simply orders the data that we have. It is not a neutral framework; rather it structures our narratives. It generates real divides between practitioners in the present, creating Neolithic specialists separate from Bronze and Iron Age ones. It also serves to separate those who study flint tools from those who study bronze and iron, and furthermore places those material specialists within certain period specialisms. This increases the divides within the subject and serves to reify and sustain a block-time approach to archaeology and thereby to our explanation of change.

Seren Griffiths (2017) explores how the way we break up time comes to shape the nature of discourse through the example of the Mesolithic-Neolithic transition. Griffiths (2017) argues that our chronological period labels do not just give sequence to the past but come to shape our arguments. She suggests that by breaking the past down into a series of successive periods we cannot deal with transition and overlap (Griffiths, 2017: 7). In the case of the Mesolithic-Neolithic transition the desire to place things under either the Mesolithic or Neolithic label is so strong that we end up ignoring the messy and complex nature of the transition when aspects of both ways of life are complexly mingled.

This same issue can be seen at play in the debate regarding the transition from the Neolithic to the Bronze Age. In some parts of Europe, such as France, Hungary, Iberia, and Italy, it is common to identify a Chalcolithic period (sometimes referred to as Copper Age or Eneolithic) to describe the time when there is evidence for early copper use but not tin-bronze alloys. Chalcolithic sites do not fit in our Three Age System block-time model, as they are neither Neolithic nor Bronze Age: the solution has been to insert another block of time. An alternative would have been instead to take the archaeological evidence at face value and understand that change is ongoing and that the emergence of metallurgy was complex, messy, and did not always follow the same path. In Britain, for example, the pattern differs from continental Europe with evidence for the use of unalloyed copper occupying a shorter timespan than elsewhere – this has resulted in a complex debate over whether or not to use the term Chalcolithic (see Allen et al., 2012).

Our chronological sequences have come to provide and shape our explanatory models (Lucas, 2005): they define the terms of the debate. As our evidence grows and the very complex and messy nature of change becomes more evident we see the models begin to fray at the edges and the nature of the intense debate about, for example, the Mesolithic-Neolithic transition (see, for example, Cummings and Harris, 2011; Sheridan, 2003; 2007; 2010; Thomas, 2004b; 2013) is a result of the failure of the structuring framework we use to deal with the complex reality of change.

Robb and Harris (2013: 91) have noted that "what is transitional depends on our analytical perspective which defines the beginning and end points between which the distance is measured". This is why a caricature approach to the past is danger-ous – we characterise block of time A (for example the Bronze Age) as having one set of characteristics and block of time B (for example the Iron Age) as having a second set of characteristics; this effectively makes the distance between these two periods appear greater and the transition thereby more marked. We predefine the important moment of change and we identify and define categories of Bronze Age and Iron Age lifeways. I do not deny that real changes occurred between 1000BC and 400BC but the way we frame the argument using the Three Age System does not allow us to write the most nuanced arguments possible about change.

Changing approaches?

Fowles is right to identify the grand narrative as both archaeology's burden and dis-tinct advantage (Alberti et al., 2011: 899). We must contest the linear, totalizing, and progressive grand narrative. We must move beyond a simplistic story of the human past because when that story is singular it whitewashes the past and promotes one way of being in and understanding the world as 'correct' at the expense of all others. In an old-fashioned grand narrative, there is little space for alterity, diversity, com-plexity, and nuance. However, it is the potential to tell long-term histories of change that makes archaeology unique and we should not shy away from it.

Many of the things that make us deeply uncomfortable when people write grand narrative-style sweeping histories result from how we approach change. When we fall back on environmental and technological determinisms, we mask complexity. If we continue to emphasise origins and revolutions and operate a block-time approach then we will continue to write histories dominated by periods of stasis punctuated by swift moments of change. Worse still, our models will continue to be incompatible with the reality of change in the world and we will sell the past short as some 'simpler, less complex' time with negative political ramifications. When we write anthropocentric historical narratives, we fail to give others their due, and those others include both the people excluded from definitions of human, and the non-humans who live entwined with us. Moreover, anthropocentric approaches let us down in the present – if we fail to address the role of non-humans, and the complex multiplicity of the things that outrage us in the present, then we stand little chance of being able to change them for the better.

By telling and constantly retelling and reshaping our stories we are offered a political opportunity – we can intervene in debates about what it means to be human, about different ways to understand the world, different ways to live alongside other people and non-humans. We need to write grand narratives that are complex and nuanced, that take on subtle data at multiple scales. We need to write grand narratives that show our world is always shifting and ever-changing in complex ways that eschew simple ideas of progress and singular causation. Archaeology has stories to tell about migration, climate change, religion, gender, and power. Ultimately, archaeology can answer the question of what it means to be human and how this is always changing. If we do not try and write better grand narratives that can intervene in the world others will.

Notes

1 Andrew Sherratt (1995) notably called for a return to archaeology as grand narrative in the 1990s.
2 http://www.cam.ac.uk/research/news/evidence-of-a-prehistoric-massacre-extends-the-history-of-warfare
3 There are equally numerous critiques of posthumanist or non-anthropocentric approaches (see, for example, Barrett, 2016; Van Dyke, 2015), which I will return to in Chapters 6 and 7.
4 Interestingly, Gamble (2007: 15) suggests that Three Age Systems of many types have a much older antiquity than that associated with the famous work of Thomsen.
5 The choice to make it 0, 1, 2 and 3 rather than 1, 2, 3 and 4 is indicative of the power of the tripart model.

Bibliography

Alberti, B., Fowles, S., Holbraad, M., Marshall, Y. and Witmore, C.L. 2011. "Worlds Otherwise": archaeology, anthropology, and ontological difference. *Current Anthropology* 52 (6): 896–912.
Alberti, B., Jones, A.M. and Pollard, J. (eds) 2014. *Archaeology after Interpretation: Returning Materials to Archaeological Theory.* Walnut Creek: Left Coast Press.
Allen, M., Gardiner, J. and Sheridan, A. (eds) 2012. *Is There a British Chalcolithic?* Oxford: Prehistoric Society and Oxbow Books.
Barrett, J. 2016. The new antiquarianism? *Antiquity* 90 (354): 1681–1686.
Bennett, J. 2010. *Vibrant Matter: A Political Ecology of Things.* London: Duke University Press.
Bradley, R. 2007. *The Prehistory of Britain and Ireland.* Cambridge: Cambridge University Press.
Braidotti, R. 2013. *The Posthuman.* London: Polity.
Bray, P. 2012. Before $_{29}$Cu became copper: tracing the recognition and invention of metalleity in Britain and Ireland during the 3rd millennium BC, in Allen, M., Gardiner, J. and Sheridan, A. (eds), *Is There a British Chalcolithic?* Oxford: Prehistoric Society and Oxbow Books: pp. 56–70.

Childe, V.G. 1942. *What Happened in History*. London: Penguin.

Childe, V.G. 1944. Archaeological ages as technological stages. *Journal of the Royal Anthropological Institute of Great Britain and Ireland* 74: 7–24.

Childe, V.G. 1950. The urban revolution. *The Town Planning Review* 21(1): 3–17.

Childe, V.G. 1951. *Social Evolution*. London: Watts.

Clark, J. 2003. *Our Shadowed Present: Modernism, Postmodernism and History*. London: Atlantic Books.

Cleal, R. and Pollard, J. 2012. The revenge of the native: monuments, material culture, burial and other practices in the third quarter of the 3rd millennium BC in Wessex, in Allen, M., Gardiner, J. and Sheridan, A. (eds), *Is There a British Chalcolithic?* Oxford: Prehistoric Society and Oxbow Books: pp. 317–332.

Cobb, H. and Croucher, K. 2014. Assembling archaeological pedagogy. A theoretical framework for valuing pedagogy in archaeological interpretation and practice. *Archaeological Dialogues* 21 (2): 197–216.

Cobb, H. and Croucher, K. 2020. *Assembling Archaeology: Teaching, Practice and Research*. Oxford: Oxford University Press.

Craddock, P. 1995. *Early Metal Mining and Production*. Washington: Smithsonian Institution Press.

Crellin, R.J. 2017. Changing assemblages: vibrant matter in burial assemblages. *Cambridge Archaeological Journal* 27(1): 111–125.

Cummings, V. and Harris, O.J.T. 2011. Animals, people and places: the continuity of hunting and gathering practices across the Mesolithic-Neolithic transition in Britain. *European Journal of Archaeology* 14: 361–392.

Darwin, C. 1859. *On the Origin of Species*. London: John Murray.

Editorial. 2019. Identity politics. *Nature Ecology and Evolution* 3: 1133.

Feldman, M., Master, D., Bianco, R., Burri, M., Stockhammer, P., Mittnik, A., Aja, A., Jeong, C. and Krause, J. 2019. Ancient DNA sheds light on the genetic origins of early Iron Age Philistines. *Scientific Advances* 5 (7): 1–10.

Fowler, C. 2013a. *The Emergent Past: A Relational Realist Archaeology of Early Bronze Age Mortuary Practices*. Oxford: Oxford University Press.

Fowler, C. 2013b. Dynamic assemblages, or the past is what endures: change and the duration of relations, in Alberti, B., Jones, A.M. and Pollard, J. (eds), *Archaeology After Interpretation: Returning Materials to Archaeological Theory*. Walnut Creek: Left Coast Press: 235–256.

Fowler, C. 2017. Relational typologies, assemblage theory and Early Bronze Age burials. *Cambridge Archaeological Journal* 27(1): 95–109.

Fowles, S. 2010. People without things, in Bille, M., Hastrup, F. and Flohr- Sørensen, T. (eds), *An Anthropology of Absence: Materializations of Transcendence and Loss*. New York: Springer: pp. 23–41.

Gamble, C. 2007. *Origins and Revolutions*. Cambridge: Cambridge University Press.

Griffiths, S. 2017. We're all cultural historians now: revolutions in understanding archaeological theory and scientific dating. *Radiocarbon* 59(6): 1347–1357.

Hamilakis, Y. 2017. Sensorial assemblages: affect, memory and temporality in assemblage thinking. *Cambridge Archaeological Journal* 27(1): 169–182.

Harris, O.J.T. 2014a. (Re)Assembling communities. *Journal of Archaeological Method and Theory* 21: 76–97.

Harris, O.J.T. 2014b. Revealing our vibrant past: science, materiality and the Neolithic, in Whittle, A. and Bickle, P. (ed), *Early Farmers: The View from Archaeology and Science*. Oxford: Proceedings of the British Academy: pp. 327–345.

Harris, O.J.T. 2017. Assemblages and scale in archaeology. *Cambridge Archaeological Journal* 27 (1): 127–139.

Harris, O.J.T. and Cipolla, C. 2017. *Archaeological Theory in the New Millennium: Introducing Current Perspectives.* London: Routledge.

Hodder, I. 2012. *Entangled: An Archaeology of the Relationships between Humans and Things.* Oxford: Wiley-Blackwell.

Ingold, T. 2000. *The Perception of the Environment: Essays in Livelihood, Dwelling and Skill.* London: Routledge.

Itan, Y., Powell, A., Beaumont, M., Burger, J. and Thomas, M. 2009. The origins of lactase persistence in Europe. *PLoS Computational Biology* 5(8): 1–13.

Jervis, B. 2016. Assemblage theory and town foundation in Medieval England. *Cambridge Archaeological Journal* 26(3): 381–395.

Jervis, B. 2018. *Assemblage Thought and Archaeology.* London: Routledge.

Johnson, A. and Earle, T. 1987. *The Evolution of Human Societies.* Stanford: Stanford University Press.

Jones, A.M. 2012. *Prehistoric Materialities: Becoming Material in Prehistoric Britain and Ireland.* Oxford: Oxford University Press.

Jones, A.M. 2017. The art of assemblage: styling Neolithic art. *Cambridge Archaeological Journal* 27(1): 85–94.

Jones, A.M. and Hamilakis, Y. 2017. Archaeology and assemblage. *Cambridge Archaeological Journal* 27(1): 77–84.

Kristiansen, K. 2018. Warfare and the political economy: Europe 1500–1100BC, in Horn, C. and Kristiansen, K. (eds), *Warfare in Bronze Age Society.* Cambridge: Cambridge University Press: 23–46.

Lamarck, J-B. 1960. *Philosophie Zoologique.* Weinheim: H.R. Engelmann.

Latour, B. 1993. *We Have Never Been Modern.* Cambridge: Harvard University Press.

Lucas, G. 2005. *An Archaeology of Time.* London: Routledge.

Mazza, E. 2016. World's first massacre scene? Scientists make grisly discovery in Kenya. *Huffington Post Uk online*: https://www.huffingtonpost.co.uk/entry/kenya-prehistoric-ma ssacre-lake-turkana_n_56a1a700e4b0d8cc10999468?guccounter=1&guce_referrer=aHR0 cHM6Ly9jb25zZW50LnlhaG9vLmNvbS8&guce_referrer_sig=AQAAACKG3jUpuL0J6 VQHLNrSJPt0x06Ehs-spID-DZJdrgrus9nounLEqCiMs23UNxLJPAFo4WnoJa–U0M76 we6gRlpcNfBgQ4aEnJBt7MLpIQUDotyFCuWT6a3pmWTgm7RSfSifWIJDJle_osqAN zbpg_sLe4vAsQcXbe5hbJkN2NX

Mirazón Lahr, M., Rivera, F., Power, R., Mounier, A., Copsey, B., Crivellaro, F., Edung, J., Maillo Fernandez, J., Kiarie, C., Lawrence, J., Leakey, A., Mbua, E., Miller, H., Muigai, A., Mukhongo, D., Van Baelen, A., Wood, R., Schwenninger, J-L., Grün, R., Achyuthan, H., Wilshaw, A. and Foley, R. 2016. Inter-group violence among early Holocene hunter-gatherers of West Turkana, Kenya. *Nature* 529 (7586): 394–398.

Morgan, L.H. 1877. *Ancient Society: Researches in the Lines of Human Progress from Savagery Through Barbarism to Civilization.* London: MacMillan and Co.

Nativ, A. 2018. On the object of archaeology. *Archaeological Dialogues* 25(1): 1–21.

Olsen, B. 2007. Keeping things at arm's length: a genealogy of symmetry. *World Archaeology* 39: 579–588.

Olsen, B. 2010. *In Defense of Things: Archaeology and the Ontology of Objects.* Plymouth: Altamira Press.

Olsen, B., Shanks, M., Webmoor, T. and Witmore, C.L. 2012. *Archaeology: The Discipline of Things.* California: University of California Press.

Ottaway, B.S. and Roberts, B. 2008. The emergence of metalworking, in Jones, A.M. (ed), *Prehistoric Europe: Theory and Practice.* Malden: Wiley-Blackwell: pp. 193–225.

Oxford English Dictionary Online. https://www.lexico.com/en

Pauketat, T. 2007. *Chiefdoms and Other Archaeological Delusions.* Plymouth: Altamira Press.

Piggott, S. 1954. *The Neolithic Cultures of the British Isles*. Cambridge: Cambridge University Press.

Renfrew, C. and Bahn, P. 2016. *Archaeology: Theories, Methods and Practice*. 7th Edition. London: Thames and Hudson.

Robb, J. and Harris, O.J.T. 2013. *The Body in History: Europe from the Palaeolithic to the Future*. Cambridge: Cambridge University Press.

Robb, J. and Pauketat, T. 2013. From moments to millennia: theorising scale and change in human history, in Robb, J. and Pauketat, T.R. (eds), 2013. *Big Histories, Human Lives*. Santa Fe: SAR Press: pp. 3–33.

Rowley-Conway, P. 2007. *From Genesis to Prehistory. The Archaeological Three Age System and its Contested Reception in Denmark, Britain and Ireland*. Oxford: Oxford University Press.

Sahlins, M. and Service, E. 1960. *Evolution and Culture*. Ann Arbor: University of Michigan Press.

Shanks, M. 2007. Symmetrical archaeology. *World Archaeology* 39(4): 589–596.

Sheridan, A. 2003. Ireland's earliest 'passage' tombs: a French connection? in Burenhult, G. and Westergaard, S. (eds), *Stones and Bones: Formal Disposal of the Dead in Atlantic Europe During the Mesolithic Neolithic Interface 6000–3000 BC*. Oxford: BAR 1201: pp. 9–26.

Sheridan, A. 2007. From Picardie to Pickering to Pencraig Hill? New information on the 'Carinated Bowl Neolithic' in northern Britain, in Whittle, A. and Cummings, V. (eds), *Going Over: The Mesolithic Neolithic Transition in North West Europe*. London: British Academy: pp. 441–492.

Sheridan, A. 2010. The Neolithization of Britain and Ireland: the 'big picture', in Finlayson, B. and Warren, G. (eds), *Landscapes in Transition*. Oxford: Oxbow: pp. 89–105.

Sherratt, A. 1995. Reviving the grand narrative: archaeology and long-term change. *Journal of European Archaeology* 3: 1–32.

Spencer, H. 1864. *The Principles of Biology*. Edinburgh: Williams and Norgate.

Thomas, J. 2004a. *Archaeology and Modernity*. London: Routledge.

Thomas, J. 2004b. Current debates on the Mesolithic–Neolithic transition in Britain and Ireland. *Documenta Praehistorica* 31: 113–130.

Thomas, J. 2013. *The Birth of Neolithic Britain: An Interpretive Account*. Oxford: Oxford University Press.

Trigger, B. 2006. *A History of Archaeological Thought*. 2nd Edition. Cambridge: Cambridge University Press.

Van der Veen, M. 2014. The materiality of plants: plant-people entanglements. *World Archaeology* 46: 799–812.

Van Dyke, R. 2015. Materiality in practice: an introduction, in Van Dyke, R. (ed), *Practicing Materiality*. Tucson: University of Arizona Press: pp. 3–32.

Webmoor, T. 2007. What about 'one more turn after the social' in archaeological reasoning? Taking things seriously. *World Archaeology* 39: 563–578.

Webmoor, T. and Witmore, C.L. 2008. Things Are Us! A commentary on human/thing relations under the banner of a 'Social Archaeology'. *Norwegian Archaeological Review* 41: 1–18.

Whittle, A. 2018. *Times of their Lives*. Oxford: Oxbow.

Witmore, C.L. 2007. Symmetrical archaeology: excerpts of a manifesto. *World Archaeology* 39: 546–562.

PART II
How do we study change?

In Chapter 1 I argued that we need to reconsider how we study change. The risk with a book like this is that while arguing for a new approach I lose sight of what we do well already. Therefore, in Part II I consider how different archaeological thinkers address change, with a two-fold aim: to support the argument of Chapter 1 and to reflect on the strengths of existing approaches.

In Chapter 2 I present a brief history of archaeological thought. I do not aim to be comprehensive (for more detail see Harris and Cipolla, 2017; Johnson, 1999; Trigger, 2006; or for an alternative see Olsen et al., 2012: 36–57) but instead focus on change[1]. Chapter 2 specifically considers how the different theoretical approaches adopted by archaeologists since the early 1900s have addressed the subject of change. In chapters 3, 4, and 5 I focus on three key themes that intersect with our approaches to change: time, scale, and biography. These chapters allow me to paint a more nuanced picture of how archaeologists describe, interpret, and explain change.

Two caveats are necessary for Part II. First, archaeological theory is vast and complex and what is presented here has a clear Euro-American bias reflecting my own context and position within the discipline. Second, one could write a whole history of archaeological thought relating to change, but my aim is to present a new approach to change as well as discussing existing thought.

When we discuss the history of archaeological theory, we often divide it up into three blocks: culture history, processualism, and post-processualism. This effectively forms something akin to a Three Age System. In the previous chapter, I discussed how this kind of sequencing framework can end up structuring debate and take on an explanatory role. When I teach archaeological theory, I conclude the lecture on culture history with a list of strengths and weaknesses of the approach, and then open the following week's lecture with a recap of the weaknesses of culture history and go on to discuss how processualists tried to address these. I adopt the same format for the transition between processualism and post-processualism. The key function of this method is to contrast the approaches, help to define them for students, and to show why ideas changed. As the course progresses, this mechanism begins to fall apart, as my students' knowledge expands and I give more detail illustrating the plurality, messiness, and complexity of approaches: Marxism does not fix functionalism's failures, phenomenology does not replace agency. The block-time approach is a foundation, but it does not provide a nuanced approach that captures the messiness and complexity of change.

Oliver Harris and Craig Cipolla (2017: 3–4) have argued that suggesting culture history, processualism, and post-processualism are a series of radical changes that replace each other (referred to as paradigm shifts) is highly problematic. It is not the case that there are no culture historians today, nor is it the case that processualists do not use the theoretical tools of culture historians. Culture history is still the dominant theoretical approach globally and an "essential part of what all archaeologists do" (Harris and Cipolla, 2017: 19). The history of archaeological thought is messy. Seren Griffiths (2017: 7) highlights how we use period names (such as Mesolithic and Neolithic) as categories into which we insert data that fits; she suggests we would do better to use them as adjectives to describe certain types of evidence, as this would allow us to deal with transition more effectively. In the same way there are aspects of archaeological thought that might be better *described* as processual or culture history rather than given strict, sequential, category labels. For example, where is Marxism best placed within an archaeological theory course? Do we teach it first as it chronologically predates culture history and was clearly influential on culture historians like Gordon Childe? Or do we teach it as part of post-processualism given its clear influence on authors like Daniel Miller, Mike Parker Pearson, Matthew Spriggs, and Chris Tilley? Placing it at the start could be misleading as it is not truly an archaeological theory but rather a theory adapted by archaeologists (as much archaeological theory is). If we teach it alongside post-processualism we risk suggesting that the Marxism of the 1980s is the same as the Marxism of the 1940s; the opposite is true if we teach it at the start. In a book about archaeology and change it would be remiss not to highlight that the culture history practiced today is different to that of the 1920s. Theories do not remain static; they change in complex ways. Yet archaeological thought does have a clear sequence to it: post-processualists were not operating in the 1920s.

Note

1 One notably absent topic is cultural evolutionary approaches; for a critical appraisal see Lewens (2015).

Bibliography

Griffiths, S. 2017. We're all culture historians now: revolutions in understanding archaeological theory and scientific dating. *Radiocarbon* 59 (5): 1347–1357.

Harris, O.J.T. and Cipolla, C. 2017. *Archaeological Theory in the New Millennium: Introducing Current Perspectives*. London: Routledge.

Johnson, M. 1999. *Archaeological Theory: An Introduction*. Oxford: Blackwell.

Lewens, T. 2015. *Cultural Evolution: Conceptual Challenges*. Oxford: Oxford University Press.

Olsen, B., Shanks, M., Webmoor, T. and Witmore, C.L. 2012. *Archaeology: The Discipline of Things*. Berkeley: University of California Press.

Trigger, B. 2006. *A History of Archaeological Thought*. 2nd Edition. Cambridge: Cambridge University Press.

2

A CHANGING HISTORY OF ARCHAEOLOGICAL THOUGHT

This chapter addresses how various theoretical approaches shape the study of change. I map a changing history of archaeological thought between the theoretical stances of culture history, the new archaeology, Marxist approaches, post-processualism, and postcolonialism. As noted in the introduction to Part II, this is not a comprehensive history and it is certainly one with a clear Euro-American bias. The chapter is structured through paired sections: the first provides an overview of the theoretical framework and how specifically it approaches change, and the second provides a more detailed case study where I bore into the detail of how different approaches describe, explain, and interpret change. Throughout I consider the relationship between the different theoretical approaches and the hurdles identified in Chapter 1.

Culture history – migrations and innovations

The definition that underlies culture history comes from the work of Edward Tylor (2010: 1), who described culture as "that complex whole which includes knowledge, belief, arts, morals, law, custom and other capabilities and habits acquired by man as a member of society". In Tylor's model culture is holistic: all people possess it. It is also learned rather than innate and as a result it is also particular to a given group. The culture in culture history is essentially a way of doing things based on a set of ideals shared by members of the same group: different cultures do things differently. Culture is something held in the mind, literally made material in material culture. For Gordon Childe (1929: v–vi) a culture was marked archaeologically by the discovery of recurring patterns of material culture that indicated the presence of a "cultural group".

In the same way that Christian Thomsen had looked for implements that occurred together in order to build the Three Age System, culture historians looked for material culture, house forms, and practices that re-occurred in order to identify past cultures.

The history in culture history refers to the placing of past cultures on chronological timescales and spatial maps. Like all theories, culture history is a product of its time: weighed down by the bulk of the material collected by antiquarians, early culture historians sought to bring order to this material and work out where and when different groups had lived. They tried to establish a chronological sequence using stratigraphic and typological relationships. Alongside creating chronological sequence goes the process of mapping where specific assemblages of recurring forms were found in order to establish the geographical spread of a given culture. Childe's famous diagrams bring order to the past – giving chronological relationships between different cultures and associating them with specific geographical areas; furthermore, they also make it possible to compare the archaeology of different regions (see Figure 2.1): they make the past less messy (Griffiths, 2017: 3).

Culture historians generally associate archaeological cultures with specific groups of people in the past, hence the Beaker people. We might be hesitant to associate objects so readily with groups of people (indeed many archaeologists reject the term 'culture' and replace it with seemingly more neutral terms such as 'community' (but see Harris, 2014a)), but we still look to place sites, objects, and practices on chronological and spatial scales with ever greater degrees of precision and accuracy (Ebersbach et al., 2017: 1). As Oliver Harris and Craig Cipolla (2017: 18) suggest, culture historians were very good at the what, where, and when of the past but were arguably less good at the why and the how, something processual archaeology responded to.

Culture historical explanations effectively rely on diffusion as the primary means of explaining change. Past cultures moved and spread, diffusing their ideas from a point of origin. Diffusion can be directly associated with migration or can focus upon the spread of an idea, innovation, or object without necessitating large-scale

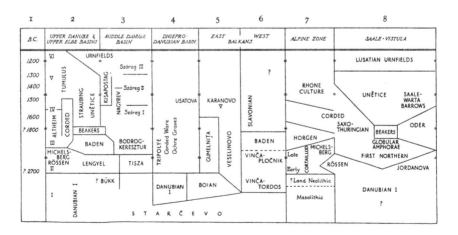

FIGURE 2.1 Childe's timetables of cultures
Source: After Childe 1957 [1925]: 345, reprinted in Harris and Cipolla, 2017: 16.

movements of people (consider for example Childe's (1930: 227) idea of the itinerant smith moving between cultural groups and thereby spreading new forms of metalwork). Behind the idea that movement (of people or things) produced change, there is an inherent idea of progress; 'better' ideas and ways of doing things would come to replace lesser ones.

Ultimately, culture history will always be about placing things in order chronologically and then locating them spatially and the process of mapping and sequencing necessarily ends up becoming part of the explanation of change. We know Beaker sherds are later than Grooved Ware in Britain and Ireland, and we know that Beaker sherds appear earlier in France and Iberia than in Britain. Therefore, the explanation for the appearance of Beaker pottery in Britain and Ireland is that Beaker people came from France and Iberia. What is not evident in this kind of explanation is why, or how, Beaker people arrived.

Another consequence of the emphasis on sequence and spread paired with the diffusion model of change is that 'origins' become a focus of attention. There is an emphasis on finding the earliest site with evidence of a given culture and then considering how it spread from that point. Postcolonial theory demonstrates the importance of considering how things might change as they spread, and the influence that Indigenous communities might have on the arrival of a 'new culture'. In culture history, this kind of nuance is missing and, as a result, change emerges as fundamentally progressive: from some pure point of origin an innovation or culture is seen to have spread and replaced pre-existing cultures. While culture historians questioned the evolutionary models of their antiquarian forebears, there is nevertheless a clear sense that the more successful innovations and cultures replace less successful ones.

Culture history is often derided as a problematic and simplistic form of archaeology but, in reality, we all stand on its foundations. We necessarily start research by working out what occurred where and when, but the framework does not allow us to consider why and how change happens. The culture historical framework, which is essentially an ordering system, becomes the explanation for change. The result is often simplistic and undertheorised: A replaces B. Culture history is the description of change. Underlying these descriptions is an inherent sense of progress and a focus on tracing origins. In culture history origins are always singular, one place at one time. In spite of this, culture history is not an example of singular causation (see Chapter 1) as there is little discussion of what actually causes changes short of referring to 'innovation'.

Case study: Childe – *Man Makes Himself*

I now explore Childe's book *Man Makes Himself*, first published in 1936, to highlight some of the nuance we lose when we lump thinkers like Childe, Glyn Daniel, Cyril Fox and Stuart Piggott, together as culture historians. Childe remains one of the most influential thinkers in archaeology because of the nature of his work: we might refer to him as the father of culture history but, truly, he is the father of the grand narrative. His books offer vast sweeping histories built upon his own detailed knowledge of archaeology. Telling the story of human history, *Man Makes Himself* is grand narrative with a clear purpose. In the preface Childe (2003) states that the book is not a manual of archaeology and nor is it concerned with the detailed arguments of specialists; instead, he argues that it is meant to be readable (we can consider it an early form of popular science). It is a political book in which he specifically rejects the concept of race (Childe, 2003: 235–236) and addresses the link between progress and biological evolution in Hitler's philosophy (2003: 2). In Chapter 1 I argued that we must address (not shy away from) the grand narrative and understand its political importance – Childe does this.

Childe makes a distinction between evolution and progress that is subtle, complex, and political. At the date of publication, people were questioning models of progress in the wake of the First World War. He does not advocate for a simple model of progress though. He argues that what we see as progress is relative and depends on our own personal situation (Childe, 2003: 2). From this position he suggests that we need a less subjective model of progress, for which he turns to science.

Childe separates evolution from progress, creating a very strict divide between culture and nature. For animals, change is the result of natural selection and evolution (Childe, 2003: 16–17). For people, change is the result of a history of progress (he defines archaeology as the study of that cultural progress (Childe, 2003: 33)). Childe describes how animals evolve as a result of gradually inherited changes over time, emphasising that these changes make creatures more or less adapted to an environment with the more adapted passing on these changes to future generations. Culture is how humans adapt to their environment and it involves intelligence, decision making, and tradition; changes in culture are faster than in natural selection and learned rather than simply inherited. Childe argues that we should measure cultural progress scientifically by linking it to an increase in reproductive success in biological terms. Cultural progress is based on human exceptionalism in this model and is clearly superior to natural history though the mechanisms behind both, and ways to assess success, share common ground.

Childe (2003: 20) defines environment very broadly arguing it is not just the climate and the landscape, but includes aspects such as food supply, predators, social traditions, customs, laws, religion, and economy. Childe is very clear that humans adapt to the environment by means of their material culture. The link here to Leslie White's (1959: 8) later idea that "culture is man's extrasomatic means of adaptation" is clear: Childe argued that material culture allows humans to adapt to an environment. This link to later processualist thinking is further strengthened when we consider his appeal in the opening pages for a "scientific attitude" to progress in unbiased and universally applicable terms (Childe, 2003: 2).

Cultural progress is also clearly linked to economic change. Childe was a committed socialist and in 1935 he visited the Soviet Union for the first time, an experience that clearly influenced this book. The core of the book is structured around a revolutionary model of history that is strongly linked to economy. Each revolution in human history brings about an economic change and a new age

(Childe, 2003: 34–36). There is also discussion of "internal contradiction" within society halting progress (Childe, 2003: 229). Childe's overall argument suggests that when the archaeologist considers the cultural whole, the technical stage of a society (Old Stone Age, New Stone Age etc.) and the state of their scientific knowledge, they can reveal the economy of the period.

Childe's arguments about evolution, progress, and difference are subtle. He rejected the idea that there are different races, believing no culture was biologically different from another and that we are all members of the same species (perhaps why he draws such a hard line between animal and human progress). Yet Childe also acknowledged that there are clear differences between living groups today. He argued that we all go through the same progressive stages but not at the same pace, suggesting that if we define these stages economically, then the Old Stone Age persists in Central Australia and Arctic America (Childe, 2003: 43–44). Childe (2003: 45) describes such groups as "contemporary savages", but argued we cannot use these populations to infer the social rules, rituals, family relationships, organisation systems, and beliefs of past populations because their culture has continued to change up to the present. He did, however, believe that studying contemporary populations could be informative about tool use and production. Today we identify this position as offensive: it ahistoricises contemporary hunter gatherers, suggesting they are less evolved and economically developed than modern westerners. Childe was, however, trying to deal with the diversity of human culture while critiquing fascism. His explanation is clearly progressive and inappropriate, but it is also subtle in a way that few culture historians are given credit for.

When we probe into a single work of Childe, undoubtedly a remarkable thinker, we see that the block-time approach to archaeological thought that divides it into three periods is problematic. Childe's thought and work is more complex than that model allows: he argues that culture is a learned means of adapting to an environment in order to increase biological success. He invokes a complicated vision of progress that attempts to be scientific rather than subjective. He promotes the use of comparative anthropology in order to understand technology. In all three of these aspects we can see clear links to later processual archaeology. This is not a simplistic case of still using the same basic techniques (typology and stratigraphy) but a complex and nuanced use of theoretical ideas. His ideas also chime, unsurprisingly given his commitment to socialism, with Marxist thinking. His views about progress and change are clearly problematic, but he addresses the grand narrative directly and uses it to critique the rise of fascism and racism.

Processual archaeology – systems and the environment

Processual archaeology, also referred to as new archaeology, is effectively a response to culture history (Johnson, 1999: 20). In trying to distance themselves from their culture historical forbears, processual archaeologists often caricatured culture history in order to both increase the distance between themselves and culture history and to thereby make the theoretical changes they were advancing appear more radical.

The two primary criticisms of culture history made by the early processualists were that culture historians failed to explain change in the past (they were accused of only ever describing and never explaining) and that they failed to make generalisations that were widely relevant (Binford, 1968; Flannery, 1967).

Processualists presented a radical new idea of what archaeology should be and what culture is. Culture was no longer viewed as something held in our heads but became something physical that could be examined. Leslie White (1959) and Julian Steward (1955), two of the founders of processual archaeology, redefined culture as the things that allowed people to adapt to their given environment in order that they might maximise energy capture; indeed for White (1959) history is the process of increasing energy capture. Cultures were defined not by ideas but instead by the environment that people were forced to adapt to. Different cultures in similar environments were considered to adapt in similar ways and could therefore be usefully compared. In this model there is no place for diffusion or migration as the external explanations for change; instead, change comes from within communities themselves.

After World War II, developing scientific techniques were beginning to be applied to archaeological questions. The result was the development of a wide spectrum of techniques and specialisms for studying archaeological remains from pot sherds to pollen grains. Alongside new techniques came developments in the theoretical underpinnings of science itself, which began to influence how archaeology was being practiced. Robert Braidwood's (1950) work at Jarmo in Iraq specifically set out to test his hypothesis that agriculture had arisen in the hilly flanks of the region. He applied a barrage of new scientific techniques from a multidisciplinary team in order to test his hypothesis. This was not just methodological innovation, it was epistemological too: the emphasis was on positivism, the argument that only things that can be proved empirically by the sciences are true. This led to an increasing emphasis on scientific neutrality, where archaeologists tried to ignore their own personal biases and be led by the archaeological evidence alone. There was also a re-alignment of aims at this time: culture historians had been collecting more and more evidence about the where and when of the archaeological record, processualists tried to deal not with the particular but with the general. Processualists aimed to hypothesis test and uncover generalising universal laws.

Lewis Binford's (1962) landmark paper 'Archaeology as Anthropology' was a significant moment in the development of archaeological thought, but it was also the culmination of a series of ideas with deeper origins stretching back at least as far as Childe. In this paper, Binford (1962) makes a bold statement about what archaeology is, redefining it, and thereby the terms of debate, by declaring that archaeology is anthropology, or it is nothing. Binford (1962) drew on work by White and Steward to argue that culture was an adaptive system and that the work of the anthropologist (and archaeologist) was to explain culture change in terms of direct cause and effect and thereby to uncover the generalising laws that underlie cultural process. The emphasis on generalising laws and rules in processualism suggests there are singular causes of change that can be located in specific singular moments. Cultural process for processualists refers to the reasons that underlie social evolutionary changes in the long term. Through recourse to anthropology Binford (1962) sought an archaeology that relied upon functionalism and systems theory, seeing culture as a complex system of parts that work together like the organs within a body to maintain stability.

Processualists, like culture historians, held underlying, if not explicit, beliefs in the progressive nature of change, believing societies progressed from simple to complex. Arguably, processualism had stronger roots in American archaeology than anywhere else and as a result the role of the Three Age System as a model for cultural evolution lessened as it was not built from, nor did it fit, the evidence from the Americas. Sahlins and Service (1960) adapted the Three Age System into their four-stage model of social complexity, where all societies progressed through different organisational structures from bands, to tribes, to chiefdoms, to states. A teleological and clearly progressive system, this model also links to the obsession with finding the universal laws that they believed underlay cultural evolution on a global scale.

Processualists work from the premise that societies can be classified into different stages of organisational complexity and that cultures are adaptive to their environment. If one can find a living population in a similar environment and at a similar level of organisational complexity to the archaeological group being studied, then that might help bridge the gap between the evidence in the archaeological record and past practice. This bridging of past and present is referred to as Middle Range Theory and led to the increasing use of ethnographic evidence to help interpret the past (referred to as ethnoarchaeology) (see, for example, Binford, 1968; 1978; 1980). Underlying this is a clear sense of a universal pattern of social evolution that makes different communities directly comparable. Change in this model is universal: all groups pass through the same process.

Processual archaeology was presented as a revolutionary new rupture, yet these ideas were not as radical as they might seem. In the previous case study, I demonstrated how Childe emphasised adaptation to the environment through material culture and the use of unbiased scientific thinking. The work of Grahame Clarke (1952) effectively combined both a culture historical approach with an emphasis on the economic and ecological relations, something that came to be of increasing importance to processualists. This blurring of boundaries is partly a product of the rhetoric, as archaeologists built archaeology anew, but it is also a product of the messy nature of change.

Case study: Flannery – *The Early Mesoamerican Village*

Kent Flannery's *The Early Mesoamerican Village* (1976) provides the next case study. The book focuses on Formative villages between 1500AD and 500BC in southern Mexico and western Guatemala. Flannery is the editor of the volume and the main author. Each chapter begins with an introduction from Flannery describing the purpose of the chapter and is followed by case studies from different areas of Mesoamerica by a variety of authors. The editorial hand is heavy, allowing the book to knit together into a coherent narrative. The volume explores both the nature of Formative-period villages and the best ways to conduct research into them.

In the opening sections of each chapter Flannery explores different research strategies through what he terms a series of "parables". The parables focus on four main characters. The first is the Great Synthesizer [sic], an older archaeologist who no longer digs but effectively summarises and assembles the work of others to write Mesoamerican history. The Real American Archaeologist is the kind of archaeologist who provides the data for the Great Synthesizer; he is presented throughout the book as 'old fashioned' and openly hostile to processualism. The third character is the Skeptical [sic] Graduate Student who is presented as a young upstart, with a religious devotion to Binford and keen to execute a more scientific archaeology. The final character is Flannery himself, who appears in the parables often to arbitrate between the characters. Flannery suggests that the Great Synthesizer, Real Mesoamerican Archaeologist, and Skeptical Graduate Student are really aspects of the personality of all Mesoamerican archaeologists. This is an effective writing technique; Flannery is able to highlight the key differences in the approaches of the Real Mesoamerican Archaeologists and the Skeptical Graduate Student through the caricatures he paints of them, therefore effectively producing distance between them. His empathetic presentation of all three characters tempers the text – he refers to the Skeptical Graduate Student as polemical and makes jokes about how zealously he adopts Binford's work, but it is also the Skeptical Graduate Student whose work he favours at the close. Flannery's parables allowed him to demonstrate how archaeology was changing at the time of writing.

The text is underlain by a clear sense of a directed history. The Formative is described as the first stepping-stone on the route towards complexity and "high civilisations" (Flannery, 1976: 2). The systems theory that underlies much of the analysis is also predicated on change from simple to complex systems (see, for example, Flannery, 1976: 162–173). The Formative villages are the origin point for the later Mesoamerican civilisations and there is a sense that understanding this origin point will allow a better grasp of what follows. Similarly, the chiefdoms model appears within the text as a means of classifying societies as part of an evolutionary stage.

The book discusses the importance of the need for a clear research strategy and, in particular, the need to design sampling strategies to produce meaningful data; this is indicative of the shift towards scientific method. There is discussion of hypothesis testing, though Flannery (1976: 8) argues that there is not enough data to allow effective hypothesis testing in this volume. In the sections that discuss regional analysis (chapters 6 and 7), the narrative is underwritten by a sense that over time villages will expand with so-called 'daughter' and 'granddaughter' populations. Flannery argues that many 'random' factors shape this process, but he still argues that underlying rules, such as the distance between settlements, affect the 'evolution' of the settlement pattern. In the discussion, though, there is little sense of what causes these settlements to expand over time, why people might leave a village to start a new one. Given the critique that new archaeologists offered of culture history it is notable that the 'rules' which affect how change occurs often eschew cause and effect.

Despite the criticism of later post-processualists about the lack of 'humanity' in processual archaeology, there are aspects of the book that come across as interpretive. There is discussion, for example, of men's and women's work areas within households; this discussion connects to post-processualism's engagement with feminism. Despite this, the text is problematic from a feminist standpoint: all the characters in the parables are male and the only role for women is as flirts who proposition the men in bars. The text also addresses the role of religion in village societies (see Flannery, 1976: Chapter 11). On balance, though, there is little sense of human agency in the book. It feels as though the villages are dots on a map rather than places where people actually lived their lives. The closing chapter is interesting from the perspective of the post-processualist critique: the final parable has all four characters discussing the draft of the book before it was sent to the publishers. The four characters all read the text differently and get different things from it. This discussion of multiple interpretations of a single text effectively foreshadowed one of the key post-processualist arguments, that texts have multiple contextual meanings.

The Early Mesoamerican Village is a landmark book that combines both debate about methodology and theory with well-worked case studies to illustrate the argument. The book rests on a progressive model of change and identifies the "rules" that govern the system and thereby shape the change within it. These rules operate at a system level, and as a result human agency and people feel absent from the text. A top-down model of change emerges where smaller units such as households are clearly part of the dataset, but when understanding change the emphasis is on the regional level. We are left with little sense of why it is that systems evolve. The argument is teleological and directed, as it is premised on an increase in complexity following the Formative period. This allows the authors to offer explanations where settlement expansion produces more complex systems that thereby need more complicated forms of leadership.

Marxism – revolutions and false consciousness

Marxist theory is a diverse body of thought that has been very influential in archaeology. Theoretical approaches that utilise Marxism are always being worked and reworked in new ways and to try and address this diversity would take a whole book (see, for example, McGuire, 1992; Miller and Tilley, 1984a; Spriggs, 1984). In this section I explore some of the differing ways in which Marxist thinking has influenced approaches to change. In the earlier case study drawn from the work of Childe, I noted how Karl Marx's notion of social change was a key influence. Marx's model of society shifting through several stages with revolutions marking the transitions between them has clear links to models such as the Three Age System and Marshall Sahlins and Elman Service's (1960) model of changing social organisation. This is hardly surprising given the influence of Lewis-Henry

Morgan's (1877) three-stage model of social evolution on Fredrick Engels' (2001) description of the progressive stages through which society had passed (primitive communism, hunter-gatherer, feudal, capitalist). These kinds of models are predicated on a gradual build-up of changes within society resulting in a moment of significant and rapid change. In these models, social changes are thoroughly entangled with economic changes: changes in the mode of production have social consequences for the organisation of labour and society more broadly.

Fundamentally, the ideas developed by Marx and Engels are about the relationship between people and things. Their ideas stress that history consisted of a series of progressive stages in which the relationships between people, things, and labour shifted over time. Marx and Engels (2018) suggested that the mode of economic production and exchange (e.g. feudal, capitalist), defines the social organisation and politics of the period. From an archaeological perspective this is an attractive theory: it is materialist, and as archaeologists we deal primarily in the material. Furthermore, it suggests that if we can grasp the nature of production then we can understand social organisation (and politics). Moreover, built into this theory is a mechanism of change. The forces of production are asserted to have an inherent tendency to grow and increase. Over time this growth serves to highlight relations of inequality between people, which causes the development of increasing contradictions and tensions between opposed social classes and ultimately leads to change. Classical Marxism of this type is inherently progressive.

Many of Marx's most famous idioms have the issues of change and history at their heart and it is a clear underlying theme across his work. For example, "The history of all hitherto existing societies is the history of class struggles" (Marx and Engels, 2018: 1). This famous quote suggests that the driver of history is the antagonism between different classes. Change is the result of the struggle for control of the means of production, and power more broadly, between opposed social classes, and this struggle will often lead to conflict. We see this concern with history and change again in the following quote: "Men make their own history, but they do not make it as they please; they do not make it under self-selected circumstances, but under circumstances existing already, given and transmitted from the past" (Marx, 2001: 7). The ability of people to shape their own history is writ large in this quotation, alongside their inability to change the nature of the circumstances they are forced to make that history within.

In Matthew Spriggs' (1984) introduction to *Marxist Perspectives in Archaeology* he (drawing on Giddens (1979: 150–153)) identifies seven ways in which Marx's materialist theory has been used, highlighting the diversity of Marxist thinking that has influenced the social sciences and humanities. Spriggs (1984: 3) suggests that theorists can adopt one or more of the approaches in a relatively flexible way. The subject of change is central to four of these approaches: Marx's ideas can be used as a "methodology for historical analysis"; or to emphasise the "significance of *labour* in the development of human society"; or they can be used as a "theory of social change stressing determination by economic factors"; or a theory that stresses the importance of class struggle to history (Spriggs, 1984: 2–3). Furthermore, another branch of Marxist thinking emphasises *praxis* theory, which explores the possibilities and limitations of what could be termed human agency and thereby the human capacity to effect change (though usually only when working as part of a larger class group). Marxist *praxis* became influential in the development of structure and agency theory, which, at its core, is about the tension between change and stability and the role of humans within this (discussed below).

Marxist thinking came to heavily influence archaeology again in the 1980s as the post-processualists critiqued the new archaeology. A key critique centred upon how processualism, drawing on functionalism, argued that societies were naturally harmonious and always seeking balance. Post-processualists disagreed, instead adopting the Marxist idea that conflict was always inherent within systems. This led to an engagement with issues such as power and ideology (Miller and Tilley, 1984a and papers therein; Spriggs, 1984 and papers therein).

These 1980s approaches are more correctly labelled as neo-Marxist as they move beyond the progressive social evolutionism and concepts of false consciousness associated with classical Marxism. This was part of why these ideas appealed to post-processualists, as they were seeking a way to escape the simple evolutionary approaches of processualism. Daniel Miller and Chris Tilley (1984b: 2), for example, critique approaches that effectively create a "league table" for societies where some achieve civilisation and others are "relegated to the lower divisions of band and chiefdom". They go on to argue that the comparison that happens in such processes is deeply judgemental and does not grant all humans the agency and volition we grant to ourselves (Miller and Tilley, 1984b: 2). Their critique is withering and reflective of the politics of post-processualism (see below). They remedy these problems by humanising the past and giving past communities "the same abilities as we credit ourselves, rather than reducing them to the passive recipients of external forces" (Miller and Tilley, 1984b: 2). Part of this process was through an engagement with both ideology and power that allowed them to demonstrate that past people had the same kinds of problems and experiences as those in the present, rather than making them seem merely to be pawns in the movement of larger forces.

In Marxist thinking, ideology is the representation of the world that the bourgeoisie make to themselves – it serves to legitimise the status quo and to make what is historically specific (and unfair) appear timeless and natural (Miller and Tilley, 1984b: 10). This is not ideology as pure doctrine but something that is made material and comes to guide everyday life and practice. The ideology of the dominant class is used to support stability; as Miller and Tilley (1984c: 148) state, ideology is always "part of attempts to produce, maintain or resist large-scale social changes, attempts which are always related to the existence of clashes of interest between different individuals and/or groups". Ideology therefore plays a key role for Marxist thinkers in the relationship between stability and change. It is ideology that acts to keep things stable. Societies are always in the process of change and stability has to be actively produced and maintained through ideology. This movement towards seeing stability as needing explanation is quite radical, as it effectively posits that change is the norm.

In the concluding chapter of *Ideology, Power and Prehistory* Miller and Tilley (1984c) reflect on the papers in the volume and consider specifically how archaeologists should approach long-term change. They identify the long timeframe of archaeology as a specific problem for the discipline, and go on to suggest that in some interpretations (one presumes processualist) the long timeframe has been used to legitimate mechanical and deterministic approaches to change (Miller and Tilley, 1984c: 147). They specifically reject universalising models of social change that could be applied in all places and to all times; instead their focus is upon the specific and contingent factors that bring about change within a given case study – they aim to focus on variability in the archaeological record and not to use this in order that they might produce generalisations (Miller and Tilley, 1984c: 148). For them, long-term change is always social change, and they argue that functionalist and adaptive approaches do not really explain change but instead describe it. This critique is notable as it was a criticism that the processualists levelled at culture historians – that they could not really explain change but rather only describe it.

Marxist approaches are vast and varied and their impact has been wide ranging and complex. Early archaeologists, such as Childe, were influenced by Marxist theory to present an understanding of the past as a series of progressive stages or phases and revolutions through which societies had to pass. This kind of thinking has had a clear influence on a variety of social evolutionary models. It was partly a desire to critique these models of change, and to critique processualism more broadly, that led to a later engagement with neo-Marxism as a way of utilising some of Marx's ideas without the need to adopt a progressive, unilinear framework. Marxist materialist philosophy appeals to many archaeologists; moreover, its direct engagement with issues of history and change made this thinking particularly influential.

Case study: Parker Pearson – inequality in Iron Age Jutland

The next case study is drawn from the work of Mike Parker Pearson in two volumes: *Marxist Perspectives in Archaeology* (Spriggs, 1984) and *Ideology, Power and Prehistory* (Miller and Tilley, 1984d). Both volumes are part of a series that emerged in the 1980s directly critiquing the new archaeology and beginning to map the shape of post-processualism (see also Hodder, 1982a). In both of Parker Pearson's papers (1984a; 1984b) he utilised Marxist theory to explore the Early Iron Age in Jutland (Denmark). Parker Pearson (1984a) seeks to revise some aspects of Marxist thinking to provide an appropriate model of social change for archaeology. He states that Marxism, as a theory of nineteenth-century capitalism, requires "rigorous modification" in order to be applicable in archaeological contexts (Parker Pearson, 1984a: 59). One example of this modification is replacing the concept of a "class" with an "interest group" (Parker Pearson, 1984a: 61).

Parker Pearson (1984a: 62) critiques models of unilinear evolution, suggesting they are not acceptable to those that study long-term change. He also criticises what he terms multilinear models (for example, Service, 1971; Steward, 1955) on the basis that they presume a causal relationship between both the environment and technology and the changing history of social relations (Parker Pearson, 1984a: 62): this is a criticism of both environmentally and technologically deterministic approaches. Instead, he focuses on social transformation and episodes of change rather than a prescriptive history of idealised changes that societies may be slotted into. He argues for a broader definition of social revolution, not just as moments of class revolt but as moments of rapid transition that result from a gradual build-up of tension (Parker Pearson, 1984a: 63). Parker Pearson (1984a) wants a history of revolutions but not progressive stages. As a result, he presents a cyclical model of change where contradictions built up, resulting in changing social orders.

The papers are both predicated on cycles of change, the dates for these periods differing slightly between the two papers. During the Nordic Bronze Age the Jutland area is argued to have been dominated by hierarchical chiefdoms that collapsed due to a shortage of bronze at the end of the period (Parker Pearson, 1984a: 65; 1984b: 72). The collapse was followed by a social revolution where "status differences were given little material expression or simply did not exist" in the Early Iron Age (Parker Pearson, 1984a: 65). Parker Pearson marshals several categories of evidence to support this interpretation, including the homogeneous nature of settlement and burial evidence. This evidence is contrasted with that from votive offerings, which are presented as increasing through the first cycle; this is suggested to be evidence that surplus wealth was being offered to the supernatural through deposition (Parker Pearson, 1984a: 66).

In the second cycle (beginning around 100–50BC) there was a shift in settlement pattern. At the site of Hodde, for example, one farmstead became much bigger than all the others, with outbuildings, additional space for cattle, and a structure interpreted as a strong room (Parker Pearson, 1984a: 66). At the same time there were shifts in burial practice; some cremation burials began to be differentiated containing burnt remains of wagons and cauldrons. Parker Pearson (1984a: 66) suggests that materials that were once being placed in votive offerings were increasingly placed in graves as offerings to the ancestors of a restricted group. From the first century AD inhumation burials emerged that Parker Pearson (1984a: 66) associates with the elite despite their relative simplicity, in contrast to cremation burials that persisted for the non-elite. He argues that elites stopped competing in conspicuous consumption through grave goods and instead emphasised the stylistic differences (i.e. inhumation vs cremation) between themselves and commoners (Parker Pearson, 1984a: 67). Evidence suggests that around 100–200AD increasing amounts of imported Roman metalwork were beginning to be deposited in the inhumation burials. Parker Pearson (1984a: 68) argues this indicates increased long-distance trade, which would have required more surplus that was more easily produced by bigger farmsteads; the result over time, he argued, was that differences between commoners and elites became more pronounced. Initially the commoners might have accepted the differences between themselves and the elites, who probably suggested they were protecting the commoners; however, over time the self-interest of the elites became clear. Around the third century AD there was a "rapid and total transformation of material culture" with a shift towards a more homogenised burial and settlement pattern, interpreted as indicative of a revolutionary change (though broadly defined), back to a model nearer to that seen at the start of the Iron Age (Parker Pearson, 1984a: 68).

Parker Pearson's (1984a; 1984b) studies of Iron Age Jutland offer a very effective example of Marxist approaches to change. Increasing production resulted in surplus and how that surplus was dealt with shifted over time to reflect a changing ideology used to sustain differences between elites and commoners. This is no harmonious system, but one where the interest groups are antagonistic, and wealth differences play a key role in the history of change. Explanations are predicated on the build-up of contradictions within society, resulting in moments of social revolution. At the outset Parker Pearson (1984a: 62–63) calls for a move beyond unilinear models of change. The model presented does this in some ways but in other respects it is predicated on continued increases in production that do appear quite directional. What is perhaps most effective about the case study is how it marshals a range of categories of archaeological evidence. This stands alongside the detailed narrative of change *within* each of his cycles that demonstrates that change is continually ongoing; stasis is even described as an "illusion" (Parker Pearson, 1984a: 61).

Interestingly, at the conclusion of one article Parker Pearson (1984b: 89) calls for systematic survey of the area to better understand settlement patterns and productive land – this is the kind of survey methodology called for by new archaeologists such as Flannery. He also suggests more work is needed on the typologies (Parker Pearson, 1984b: 89): a call for further refinement to what is essentially a culture historic technique.

Post-processual archaeology – agents of change

Post-processualism emerged out of the critique of the new archaeology. It became clear to post-processualists that making archaeology a 'hard science' was an unrealistic goal as it proved very difficult to effectively test hypotheses against archaeological data. The failure to test hypotheses effectively came in tandem with a questioning of positivism more broadly, as a number of archaeologists argued they could never be truly neutral. This led to an increasing acknowledgement that it was not possible to simply read the data without some form of interpretation. Furthermore, archaeologists began to assert that their interpretations were always affected by their own political context in the present. Many had also become concerned that the functionalist stance of the new archaeologists was very determinist, leaving no role for humans in the production of history.

The critique came from multiple directions and drew on a diverse range of thinking. Arguably, what ties these disparate themes together is their commitment to the political. Feminist critiques of archaeology (Gero and Conkey, 1991; Spector, 1991; 1993) highlighted the lack of women in both the profession and the past. As a consequence, feminist archaeologists committed to placing people, including women, back into their interpretations (see papers within Moore and Scott, 1997). As discussed above, Marxist and neo-Marxist thinking was equally influential, reinvigorating discussion of power, resistance, and ideology (Spriggs, 1984; Miller and Tilley, 1984d). Such work aimed to move beyond simple understandings of powerful chiefs ruling over pacified dupes and instead, drawing on thinkers such as Michel Foucault (1991), looked at the construction and maintenance of power and ideology and how this could be resisted and changed – again, deeply political. The third type of thinking that had particular significance for early post-processualism was structuralism and post-structuralism (Hodder, 1982a; 1982b). Structuralism encouraged archaeologists to theorise about the meaning of material culture in the lives of people. Post-structuralism came to demonstrate the multiplicity of this meaning and how different people understand and interpret meaning, both in the past and the present, in different ways as a result of their own political and personal context. Binford had wanted archaeologists to be neutral arbitrators of the past and, like the best scientists, to be free of bias; post-processualists understood this was impossible and actively embraced a position that allowed a diversity of interpretations.

Post-processualism includes a wide range of approaches. Having already addressed neo-Marxist ideas above, I focus on the theories of structure and agency as these relate most closely to the subject of change. Pierre Bourdieu's *Outline of a Theory of Practice* (1977) offered a way for archaeologists to engage with the lives of people in the past and to understand both stability and change. 'Practice' is the term used to describe what people do and how these actions come to shape broader society and history. Bourdieu's theory is non-determinist and non-universalising and sought to understand both how practice could be stable and how it changed. Bourdieu's theory developed from Marcel Mauss's (1973) concept of *habitus*. Our *habitus* consists of the inculcated daily practices that we rarely think about, but which come to shape our behaviour. A theory of *habitus* focuses on individuals and how they act in often predictable and stable ways. This creates a bottom-up approach where the action of individuals can contribute to both the maintenance of status quo and challenges to it.

There are parallels between Bourdieu's notion of *habitus* and Anthony Gidden's (1979; 1984) theory of structuration. Structuration theory considers how our unconscious daily practices are repeated unthinkingly to create and sustain social structure. The basic model suggests that agency is something possessed by humans; it is the ability to have an effect on the world we live within. Agency is not unfettered, though; rather, it is shaped by the nature of structure. Structure in this sense includes both social conventions and rules as well as the material world that shapes our actions. Human agency can act to either maintain the existing structure, or to begin to change it, while structures both constrain and enable the agency of humans in turn. In both theories there is a clear emphasis on the ability of humans to contribute to both change and stability. Rather than being subsumed by the system, as in processualist theory, humans come to take on a crucial role and we see a re-orientation of change from being something that is defined by a top-down process to something that individuals have a real hand in from the bottom-up.

The concepts of structure, agency, and practice provide theoretical tools that specifically deal with the nature of change and stability. Structure could be read simplistically as stability and agency as change, but this fails to grasp the true nature of the model. Agency both creates stability and change: one can use their agency to keep things the same or to challenge the nature of the world and change the way things are done. Equally, structure can be the thing that enables stability – the furniture that provides the frame for tradition, but it is also the thing that enables agency to produce change (Barrett, 2001). There is a tension built into this theoretical framework between the nature of change and stability.

As a result of the emphasis on structure and agency, post-processualist theory is able to directly address both change and continuity. Post-processualists broke away from earlier models where change was universal and a matter of different communities progressing through predefined stages to show how individual human action, at the small and local scale, can act to both keep things the same and to bring about change over time. Change in structure and agency is intimately entwined with stability; the two go hand in hand. Change does not come from the large scale, the regional level, or the overarching rules, but instead emerges from everyday action in a nondirectional manner.

Case study: Joyce – agency, politics and change

This case study explores the article 'The founding of Monte Albán: sacred propositions and social practices' by Arthur Joyce (2000), published in *Agency in Archaeology* (Dobres and Robb, 2000). Joyce's (2000) study of Monte Albán tracks social and political changes over hundreds of years. It also effectively builds on the work of Flannery (1976). Monte Albán is a vast site near the Mexican city of Oaxaca perched on a mountain-top overlooking three different valleys (see Figure 2.2). At 500BC Monte Albán was one of the largest and most significant developments in the Americas. The site has imposing temple complexes and vast plazas for public gathering. Monte Albán is often classified as a complex chiefdom and interpreted as presenting clear evidence for a ruling elite.

Joyce (2000) explores the development of Monte Albán in relation to the relationships between commoners and elites across the three arms of the Oaxaca valley (for a more recent re-assessment see Joyce, 2019; Carter, 2017; Winter, 2011). Earlier models explained the emergence of Monte Albán as a result of interpolity conflict (Blanton, 1978; Marcus and Flannery, 1996). These models suggested that competition between polities within the three arms of the valley and beyond created a hostile environment that led to the founding of Monte Albán in its strategic position on top of a hill at the centre of the three arms of the Oaxaca Valley. Joyce (2000: 71) suggests that the threat from other polities may have played a role in the emergence of the site, but that this model ignores the importance of changes in social practices and ideology. He utilises structure and agency to effectively demonstrate the role of human agency in change. His explanation also includes central roles for power and ideology (linking to broader post-processualist and neo-

FIGURE 2.2 Monte Albán, Mexico
Source: David Horan.

Marxist themes). He suggests that in his understanding of the "agency–structure dialectic, power is the transformative capacity of an agent to achieve an outcome which can either reproduce or change system and structure" (Joyce, 2000: 73). Joyce suggests that power is not possessed by individuals, but extends to all people even if it takes the form of passive resistance (Joyce, 2000: 73). This extension of power beyond "an elite" is part of the wider trend to shift the emphasis from top-down explanations more common among processualists to a bottom-up approach that gives back agency to "commoners".

Joyce (2000: 73) argues that in the Oaxaca valley, and Mesoamerica more broadly, there was a long-term relationship between people and the "sacred", within which sacrificial practices played a role. His argument suggests that this relationship remained central in the long term, but that specific ritual practices and the political role they played shifted and changed over time. He suggests that a covenant existed between the people and supernatural forces, where the people made sacrifices (including bloodletting and human sacrifice) in order to encourage the supernatural to maintain fertility (Joyce, 2000: 73). Commoners (Joyce's term) were able to make sacrifices to the supernatural on their own terms or they could offer goods and labour to elites who made sacrifices on their behalf. He describes this relationship as a form of contract between commoners, elites, and supernaturals that served to structure the agency of all three groups (Joyce, 2000: 74–75).

Before the foundation of Monte Albán, elites gained power through the support of commoners, which allowed them to live a different lifestyle. Commoners sacrificed their labour and possessions to the elites in order to bring them closer to the supernatural. Joyce (2000: 76) highlights that it was not simply a case of the elites having agency, rather the agency of elites was predicated on that of the commoners. Commoners could choose to make their own sacrifices and bypass the elites, or to switch their allegiance to a different elite and thereby affect the agency elites had. The commoners thereby act to structure the identity, lifestyle, and day-to-day practices of the elites.

Between 700 and 500BC there was an apparent increase in the competition between different elites in the different arms of the Valley of Oaxaca. San José Mogote, in the Etla arm of the valley, was, prior to the foundation of Monte Albán, the largest settlement. During this violent period, the main temple (building 28) on mound 1 at San José Mogote, was burnt down. Joyce (2000: 77) postulates that in response to the burning of the temple, local elites increased their demands for goods and labour from the commoners in order to rebuild. The population at San José Mogote decreased at this time and Joyce's suggestion is that commoners, faced with increasing requests for labour and goods, moved to other parts of the valley and abandoned their elites, increasing the size of other population centres elsewhere. Following the remodelling of mound 1 the first evidence for human sacrifices emerged. Joyce (2000: 78) argues that this more violent and extreme extension of pre-existing sacrificial practices was a response to the loss of power that some elites were suffering. It was these new practices of human sacrifice (represented in the *danzante* portraits) that eventually emerged and fluoresced at Monte Albán. The argument is that elite power was failing at San José Mogote and this provoked the commoners to use their agency to leave the settlement, which caused the change in the nature of ritual practice. These new ritual practices later became popular and were part of the structure materialised at Monte Albán.

Joyce's reading is a serious break from simplistic top-down chiefdom models where commoners are often presented as "dupes". Joyce's (2000: 83) argument creates a clear role for the commoners: he suggests, at least initially, they were not coerced into building the massive public constructions at Monte Albán, but rather they chose to do so and were an "active part of the political changes". By focusing on the agency of commoners Joyce (2000: 86) suggests he creates "a richer and more human-centred" narrative. He argues that the significant changes through the period were the result of relatively small and everyday struggles between elites and commoners. In his model the founding of Monte Albán was not part of some master plan to gain control of the valley but rather the result of small changes that triggered wider ones with often unintended consequences (Joyce, 2000: 87).

Joyce's argument about change is an interesting one as it centres on human agency and not just the agency of an elite. Commoners have the power, by removing their support, to change the nature of ritual practice, a change that Joyce suggested had a great many unintentional consequences. This is a model where small changes can have big effects and human agency comes to shape the nature of history but not necessarily in intended ways. The narrative offered is not progressive, teleological, or deterministic and it avoids emphasising origins and revolutions.

Postcolonial approaches

Postcolonial approaches explore the nature of continuity and change at the point of interaction between coloniser and colonised communities. Approaching the colonial encounter asks us to deal head-on with the meeting of two apparently once-distinct ways of life and consider the changes to them that occur in the wake of this encounter. There are complex links in this area to culture historical approaches: culture historians suggested one of the main mechanisms of cultural change was an encounter with a different culture that led to change either through migration or diffusion. Today, postcolonial approaches assess the meeting of different groups in a way that does not assume the superiority of the coloniser or erase all precolonial ways of life. They aim to avoid setting up a hierarchical binary relationship between coloniser and colonised, and work to acknowledge the active roles of all communities involved, while also acknowledging the differential agency and power that groups have and the oppression, damage, and violence done to the colonised.

The colonial encounter involves a significant difference in power between the colonisers and the colonised. Colonialism has been, and is often still, used to justify European imperialism (Trigger, 1984). Colonisers are presented as technologically and morally superior, and progressive narratives prevail as the culture and practices of the colonisers are presumed to replace those of the colonised – and to be gratefully received by the colonised. Progressive narratives of change and social evolutionary approaches to the non-European Other were a justification for the removal of land, rights, wealth, and independence from diverse groups. Colonial narratives serve to keenly illustrate the violence and injustice that can come in the wake of a problematic approach to change. The history of the colonial encounter and its legacy is an area where we have serious cause to be cautious when it comes to the grand narrative. Globally, history has been written from the position of the west and the colonial encounter and nature of the colonial experience has been presented in terms that have served to justify the Euro-American position (Wolf, 1982). On colonial ground the need to produce grand narratives that tackle the past in a sensitive way, which allows difference and alterity to emerge and does not do violence to Indigenous and enslaved groups, is clearer than ever: a good example of this is Chris Gosden's (2004: 22) work, which addresses a history of colonialism from 5000BC to the present and tries to "disrupt the old grand narratives", focusing on the issue of power in colonial encounters.

Early approaches to the colonial encounter (see, for example, Redfield et al. (1936) on acculturation) often sought to present this moment of change as the meeting of two clearly bounded and defined groups: coloniser and colonised. The boundary between the two groups was presented as firm and the distance between them was constructed to appear significant. Colonised groups were often presented as static and unchanging whereas coloniser history was presented as dynamic and progressive. Essentialism and generalisation within such approaches fail to appreciate nuance and subtlety, or the lived realities of the colonial experience on the ground. Narratives of change within this framework are often a case of simply examining the relationship between change and continuity as a result of the colonial encounter. All too often, even in more recent approaches, the ontologies of Indigenous groups are presented as simplistic misunderstandings of the truth, or worse, as wholly false (but see Alberti et al., 2011; Alberti and Marshall, 2009; Holbraad, 2007).

The rise of postcolonial approaches (for example, Bhabha, 1994; Said, 1978; Spivak, 1988), primarily to literature, as well as the increasing engagement of archaeologists with Indigenous groups (see, for example, Atalay, 2012; Cipolla, 2013; Cipolla et al., 2019; Colwell-Chanthaphonh and Ferguson, 2007; Silliman, 2008) has led to a range of new postcolonial approaches that address the colonial encounter in more subtle and complex ways. Contextual approaches blur the boundaries between the groups of colonisers and colonised in order that they might move beyond an essentialist approach and focus on issues of cultural continuity and transformation in the wake of the colonial encounter. Such approaches move beyond a position that presents a given practice or perspective as being either native, or European, or African, and instead appreciate the creative unpredictability of multiple and hybrid encounters, which disturb binary and essentialised identities (for example, Samson et al., 2016; Valcárcel Rojas, 2016; Voss, 2008). Drawing on practice theory and Foucauldian ideas of power (Foucault, 1991), there is often an emphasis on resistance and the agency of Indigenous groups (for example, Funari, 2003; Liebmann and Murphy, 2011, and papers therein).

Hybridity, a term drawn from the work of Homi Bhabha (1994), tries to capture how the changes that occur as a result of the colonial encounter are neither the pure imposition of the colonisers way of life, nor the maintenance of Indigenous practices, but rather a complex mix of the two: a hybrid. The changes that are presented as hybrid contain aspects from both groups melded together to create something new that cannot again be disaggregated into its component parts; the term creolisation captures the same idea (see, for example, Challis, 2012). Such ideas have been applied beyond the historic colonial encounter to, for example, understand change as a result of Phoenician colonisation of the Mediterranean (Van Dommelen, 1998; 1997; 2012) and the experience of Roman Imperialism across Europe (Mattingly, 2006; 2014; Webster, 1997; Woolf, 1997).

Postcolonial theory is an area in which concerted effort has been focused on trying to understand the nature of cultural change and stability. The models and theories that emerge focus on interaction, the tension between change and stability, and the locus of innovation and conservatism. In the wake of the colonial encounter new practices and ways of life emerge and we see examples of how traditions must change in order to be maintained over time. These approaches also demonstrate the complex ways in which difference comes to be appreciated and affects the shape of what emerges in unpredictable ways.

Case study: Cipolla – *Becoming Brothertown*

The final case study is drawn from *Becoming Brothertown* by Craig Cipolla (2013). Cipolla explores the histories and experience of the group that came to be known as the Brothertown Indians. Telling the history of a diverse group of Indigenous communities, oppressed by the reservations system and colonialism more broadly, who left their homes on the east coast of America in the 1770s and journeyed 400km north to Oneida County in central New York state in order to found a new Indigenous multicultural Christian settlement that came to be known as Brothertown (Cipolla, 2013: 2–3). The Brothertown story is one of ethnogenesis as the Narragansett, Eastern Pequot, Mashantucket Pequot, Mohegan, Montaukett, Niantic, and Tunxis came together to form a new community and identity over time in New York state. They were not to remain here though: the Brothertown community moved once more in the nineteenth century to the Fox River Valley in present-day Wisconsin. In the study Cipolla brings together documentary sources written by, to, and about the Brothertown Indians alongside cemetery surveys. The study was designed from the bottom-up in collaboration with the Brothertown community; indeed, it was their idea to carry out an above-ground study of the cemetery sites of the community (Cipolla, 2013: 50–52).

Cipolla adopts a pragmatic approach both practically and methodologically. Pragmatism, "the effect that knowledge has in the world" (Cipolla, 2013: 19), asks us what difference our work actually makes (which may be quite apart from our intentions). Working with the Brothertown Indians Cipolla (2013) allows space for multiple explanations and narratives to emerge – it is not a case of working out who (be they Indigenous, Euro-American, or other) is correct in their interpretation of the history of the area, but instead recognising that a range of alternative perspectives about the past exist and that a monolithic answer, based in a positivist understanding of knowledge, is always going to elide that in an unhelpful way. Cipolla (2013: 18–19) therefore weaves together multiple approaches and narratives working alongside the Brothertown community, being guided by their understandings of their past, as well as his own, and those of his collaborators. The result is a textured understanding of the changing history of the group. Moreover, by avoiding a strict past–present divide, Cipolla actively sought for his engagement with the Brothertown community to have impact in the present.

Brothertown practices emerge as "neither wholly native nor wholly European but a mixed response to the cultural and social pluralities of colonialism" (Cipolla, 2013: 8). The book recognises the agency and choices that Brothertown Indians made in the past (and present) and both the intended and unintended consequences of these choices, while also identifying how the reality of the colonial experience meant that the agency of the Brothertown Indians was limited and structured in very specific ways. This is not a story played out in terms of acculturation and resistance, but rather one where Brothertown Indian practice, at a community level, pragmatically sought to create and sustain the group identity and to allow them to survive the harsh realities of colonialism.

The bulk of the data discussed in the book is concerned with grave markers from the New York and Wisconsin cemeteries and how and why these change over time (Cipolla, 2013: chapters 6 and 7) (see Figure 2.3). In New York initially, Brothertown cemeteries were dominated by handmade (rather than manufactured)

FIGURE 2.3 Brothertown cemetery, Wisconsin, USA
Source: Craig Cipolla.

limestone grave markers, in some cases associated with a small mound. They were very rarely inscribed with the name of the individual who had died and as a result they provoked an engagement with the deceased as a community of ancestors (Cipolla, 2013: 114). Cipolla (2013: 115) shows that the choice to employ these seemingly simple markers was not a result of economics but of the active choices by mourners reflecting their own shared cultural identity. Practices were not static: in New York manufactured gravestones inscribed with individual names emerged over time (Cipolla, 2013: 114). This changed the nature of commemoration at these sites as people began to remember specific known individuals rather than a community of unknown ancestors. When the Brothertown Indians moved to Wisconsin these changes to practice continued in a way that increasingly emphasised individuality. Cipolla (2013: 158) identifies three shifts in practice in Wisconsin. Initially (between 1830 and 1850 AD), manufactured headstones were used to mark graves; their inscriptions emphasised the relationship between living and deceased and the event of death as a moment of loss. Between 1850 and 1880AD, the form and decoration of headstones diversified. In the third shift, headstones declined in popularity and obelisks, ledgers, and other forms became more common as inscriptions changed to commemorate the life of the deceased as an individual.

The later Brothertown cemeteries in Wisconsin became almost inseparable from the Euro-American cemeteries in the area. Cipolla (2013: 159–160) interprets this pragmatically, arguing that the changes in funerary practice allowed Euro-American communities to blur the boundaries between themselves and the Brothertown groups. This homogenisation of practice came as the Brothertown communities were seeking US citizenship in order to get land rights. They did this by showing that they were not completely like other Indigenous groups and by stressing some of the similarities between themselves and Euro-Americans. The changes to practice can be interpreted both as active attempts to shape the identity of the Brothertown group to allow them to gain citizenship and as a reflection of the situation where land rights and land ownership was tied to individuality.

Ultimately, the book asks us to move beyond dichotomous approaches to both cultural contact and colonialism and understand that the changes that occur in the wake of these processes are a "series of negotiations and continuities between colonial domination and subaltern resistance, between insiders and outsiders, and between humans and material culture" (Cipolla, 2013: 194). The text treads a careful path that allows the reader to appreciate that Brothertown communities made active and pragmatic decisions to allow them to cope, to form a community, and to persist in spite of the harsh reality of colonial life, but equally it highlights the injustices done to them and how their agency was shaped and limited by the colonial experience. The model of change is a subtle one that looks at cultural contact in a way that neither presumes the complete replacement of one way of life nor presumes that both groups enter into a cultural contact situation with equal amounts of agency. Archaeology is full of examples of cultural contact, and the rise of aDNA studies focusing on migration is placing a new emphasis on these moments of contact (see, for example, Brace et al., 2019; Olalde et al., 2018). Postcolonial approaches such as Cipolla's offer a subtle and nuanced way of theorising and understanding these situations.

This book avoids progressive, teleological, and determinist explanations, and it does not focus on revolutions. It both is and is not a book about origins. In Chapter 1 I critiqued a particular kind of origins research that I described as essentialising because it focuses on the discovery of singular, pure, and stable origins that go on to define the nature of a given phenomenon. This story of ethnogenesis is not that. The actual origins of the group take up little space; instead it is about the continually changing lives of diverse groups of people from different communities, and how to create and sustain Brothertown they continually change their practices. It is a story that shows there are not pure, singular, stable origins, but that change is messier and more complex. It is also a book that engages directly, through its recourse to pragmatism, with its own politics.

Conclusions: a changing history

When I first set out to write this chapter, I had imagined a very traditional chapter where I discussed culture history, processualism, and post-processualism in turn. It was not until later that I looked back at my draft proposal and realised what I had done was to adopt a three-part block-time approach to model the history of archaeological thought. In this chapter I have demonstrated how the various theoretical frameworks approach change differently and thereby create different narratives of the past. More importantly, I have also highlighted the complexity and messiness of our changing frameworks of archaeological thought and how, when we look closely, they demonstrate the problems of a block-time approach. Using the three-part model of archaeological theory makes it easy to teach students (and ourselves) the history of our discipline. The block-time approach both acts to exaggerate the differences between approaches and to mask the real nature of change. We hide the connections and relations between approaches in order to produce clearly defined and static categories of thought. This is both a product of history telling (i.e. how we recount the history of our discipline) and history making (i.e. the way we might position our work as 'radically new' by drawing sharp contrasts). One could accuse this text of being teleological in that it looks forward from older frameworks of archaeological thought to link them to later ones, for example, looking at the connections between Childe and processualism. This is not what I am doing; rather, by breaking down the block-time approach, I instead show the ongoing nature of change across imposed period boundaries, highlight the overlapping, connected, and relational nature of category labels, and show that with closer scrutiny these labels are found wanting. How archaeological thought has changed is complex, overlapping, and nonlinear.

At the outset I had two key aims: to critique approaches to change to support my argument in Chapter 1 and to consider the existing strengths of our approaches (i.e. what we get right). Although culture history is progressive, unilinear, and utilises simplistic models of change, it also provides the descriptive foundation that any exploration of archaeological change has to start from. We cannot accuse it of eschewing the large-scale narrative, and more importantly, in the work of Childe, we see the use of the grand narrative for a positive political purpose (arguing against racism and fascism): this is something to aspire to. An aspect of the processual critique of culture history was that it failed to explain why things change; processualism put the study of the process of change on the archaeological agenda but the emphasis on scientific methods and generalising rules led to a situation where unilinear progressive models were once again central. Moreover, determinism came to the fore as environments were seen to define cultural responses. Marxist thinking has both clear strengths and weaknesses in relation to change. Marxist archaeology is always politically engaged (whether or not one agrees with those politics) and it also places an emphasis on power. Moreover, change is at the heart of Marxist approaches; unfortunately this is often, especially in classical Marxism, portrayed as a unilinear and progressive series of changes punctuated by moments of revolution. Post-processualism reacted against the generalising rules of processualism and the result was often an emphasis on local small-scale stories. On the one hand I agree with the politically engaged critique offered by the post-processualists; however, I also feel that the theoretical shifts and political critiques of the 1980s and 90s led to a fear of engaging with the grand narrative. While this was an understandable reaction, I think the time has now come to re-engage with those debates. More usefully, the relationship between stability and change was deeply connected to debates about agency. Postcolonial approaches focus on the change that emerges in the wake of interaction; they also seek to tell and explore alternative narratives of the kind that should be pushed to the fore as we try to build new grand narratives.

Shared between all these approaches we see the different hurdles from Chapter 1: progressive narratives, a focus on origins and revolutions, teleological and determinist approaches, and an emphasis on singular causation. The one hurdle I have not mentioned is anthropocentrism. The critique of anthropocentrism in archaeology began to emerge in the mid-2000s (see, for example, Crellin, 2017; Fowler, 2013a,b; 2017; Hamilakis, 2017; Hamilakis and Jones, 2017; Harris, 2014a,b; 2017; Jervis, 2016; 2018; Jones, 2012; 2017; Olsen, 2007; Olsen et al., 2012; Shanks, 2007; Webmoor, 2007; Webmoor and Witmore, 2008; Witmore, 2007). All five theoretical approaches discussed in this chapter could be defined as anthropocentric. One might suggest that the emphasis on typology, chronology, and distribution maps in culture history effectively meant that people were often absent; however, as Braidwood (1958: 734) argues, this was certainly not true of Childe's work. There are aspects of processualism that could be viewed as non-anthropocentric as they emphasise how humans *always* use things to adapt to their environment. While Marxism is a materialist philosophy, it is also deeply anthropocentric; humans are always the core focus. The emphasis on humans and symbolism, central to post-processualism is part of what has provoked the recent rise in non-anthropocentric approaches in archaeology. In chapters 6 and 7 I explore the multiple differing critiques of anthropocentrism in depth.

Any chapter like this can only begin to scratch the surface of how we approach and theorise change in archaeology. In the chapters that follow I seek to explore our approaches to change in a more detailed way by looking at three key topics: time, scale, and biography. These three issues have significant effects on the ways we think about change. By focusing on these issues, I hope to paint a more detailed, nuanced, and subtle picture of how archaeologists theorise and interpret change in the past.

Bibliography

Alberti, B. and Marshall, Y. 2009. Animating archaeology: local theories and conceptually open-ended methodologies. *Cambridge Archaeology Journal* 19(3): 344–356.

Alberti, B., Fowles, S., Holbraad, M., Marshall, Y. and Witmore, C. 2011. "Worlds Otherwise": archaeology, anthropology, and ontological difference. *Current Anthropology* 52(6): 896–912.

Atalay, S. 2012. *Community-based Archaeology: Research With, By, and For Indigenous and Local Communities*. Berkeley: University of California Press.

Barrett, J. 2001. Agency, the duality of structure and the problem of the archaeological record, in Hodder, I. (ed), *Archaeological Theory Today*. Cambridge: Cambridge University Press: pp. 141–164.

Bhabha, H.K. 1994. *The Location of Culture*. New York: Routledge.

Binford, L. 1962. Archaeology as anthropology. *American Antiquity* 28(2): 217–225.

Binford, L. 1968. Some comments on historical versus processual archaeology. *Southwestern Journal of Anthropology* 24: 267–275.

Binford, L. 1978. *Nunamiut Ethnoarchaeology*. London: Academic Press.

Binford, L. 1980. Willow smoke and dog's tails: hunter-gatherer settlement systems and archaeological site formation. *American Antiquity* 45 (1): 4–20.

Blanton, R. 1978. *Monte Albán: Settlement Patterns at the Ancient Zapotec Capital*. New York: Academic Press.

Bourdieu, P. 1977. *Outline of a Theory of Practice*. Cambridge: Cambridge University Press.

Brace, S., Diekmann, Y., Booth, T., van Dorp, L., Faltyskova, Z., Rohland, N., Mallick, S., Olalde, I., Ferry, M., Michel, M., Oppenheimer, J., Broomandkhoshbacht, N., Stewardson, K., Matiniano, R., Walsh, S., Kayser, M., Charlton, S., Hellenthal, G., Armit, I., Schulting, R., Craig, O., Sheridan, A., Parker Pearson, M., Stringer, C., Reich, D., Thomas M. and Barnes, I. 2019. Ancient genomes indicate population replacement in Early Neolithic Britain. *Nature Ecology and Evolution 3*: 765–771.

Braidwood, R. 1950. Jarmo: a village of early farmers in Iraq. *Antiquity* 24(96): 189–195.

Braidwood, R.J. 1958. Vere Gordon Childe 1892–1957. *American Anthropologist* 60(4): 733–736.

Carter, N. 2017. Epigraphy and empire: reassessing textual evidence for Formative Zapotec imperialism. *Cambridge Archaeological Journal* 27(3): 433–450.

Challis, S. 2012. Creolisation on the nineteenth-century frontiers of southern Africa: a case study of the AmaTola 'Bushmen' in the Maloti-Drakensberg. *Journal of Southern African Studies* 38(2): 265–280.

Childe, V.G. 1929. *The Danube in Prehistory*. Oxford: Oxford University Press.

Childe, V.G. 1930. *The Bronze Age*. Cambridge: Cambridge University Press.

Childe, V.G. 2003. *Man Makes Himself*. Nottingham: Spokesman Books.

Cipolla, C. 2013. *Becoming Brothertown: Native American Ethnogenesis and Endurance in the Modern World*. Tucson: University of Arizona Press.

Cipolla, C., Quinn, J. and Levy, J. 2019. Theory in collaborative indigenous archaeology: insights from Mohegan. *American Antiquity* 84(1): 127–142.

Clarke, J.G.D. 1952. *Prehistoric Europe: The Economic Basis*. London: Methuen.

Colwell-Chanthaphonh, C. and Ferguson, T. (eds) 2007. *Collaboration in Archaeological Practice: Engaging Descendant Communities*. Walnut Creek: AltaMira.

Crellin, R.J. 2017. Changing Assemblages: vibrant matter in burial assemblages. *Cambridge Archaeological Journal* 27(1): 111–125.

Dobres, M-A. and Robb, J. 2000. *Agency in Archaeology*. London: Routledge.

Ebersbach, R., Doppler, T., Hofmann, D. and Whittle, A. 2017. No time out: scaling material diversity and change in the Alpine foreland Neolithic. *Journal of Anthropological Archaeology* 45: 1–14.

Engels, F. 2001. *The Origin of the Family, Private Property and the State*. London: The Electric Book Company.

Flannery K. 1967. Culture history versus culture process, a debate in American archaeology. *Scientific American* 217: 119–122.

Flannery, K. 1976. *The Early Mesoamerican Village: Archaeological Research Strategy for an Endangered Species*. London: Academic Press.

Foucault, M. 1991. *Discipline and Punish: The Birth of the Prison*. London: Penguin.

Fowler, C. 2013a. *The Emergent Past: A Relational Realist Archaeology of Early Bronze Age Mortuary Practices*. Oxford: Oxford University Press.

Fowler, C. 2013b. Dynamic assemblages, or the past is what endures: change and the duration of relations, in Alberti, B., Jones, A.M. and Pollard, J. (eds), *Archaeology After Interpretation: Returning Materials to Archaeological Theory*. Walnut Creek: Left Coast Press: pp. 235–256.

Fowler, C. 2017. Relational typologies, assemblage theory and Early Bronze Age burials. *Cambridge Archaeological Journal* 27(1): 95–109.

Funari, P. 2003. Conflict and the interpretation of Palmares, a Brazilian runaway polity. *Historical Archaeology* 37: 81–92.

Gero, J. and Conkey, M. (eds) 1991. *Engendering Archaeology: Women and Prehistory*. Oxford: Blackwell.

Giddens, A. 1979. *Central Problems in Social Theory: Action, Structure, and Contradiction in Social Analysis*. Berkeley: University of California Press.

Giddens, A. 1984. *The Constitution of Society: Outline of a Theory of Structuration*. Berkeley: University of California Press.

Gosden, C. 2004. *Archaeology and Colonialism: Cultural Contact from 5000 BC to the Present*. Cambridge: Cambridge University Press.

Griffiths, S. 2017. We're all culture historians now: revolutions in understanding archaeological theory and scientific dating. *Radiocarbon* 59(5): 1347–1357.

Hamilakis, Y. 2017. Sensorial assemblages: affect, memory and temporality in assemblage thinking. *Cambridge Archaeological Journal* 27(1): 169–182.

Hamilakis, Y. and Jones, A. 2017. Archaeology and assemblage. *Cambridge Archaeological Journal* 27(1): 77–84.

Harris, O.J.T. 2014a. (Re)Assembling communities. *Journal of Archaeological Method and Theory* 21: 76–97.

Harris, O.J.T. 2014b. Revealing our vibrant past: science, materiality and the Neolithic, in Whittle, A. and Bickle, P. (ed), *Early Farmers: The View from Archaeology and Science*. Oxford: Proceedings of the British Academy: pp. 327–345.

Harris, O.J.T. 2017. Assemblages and scale in archaeology. *Cambridge Archaeological Journal* 27 (1): 127–139.

Harris, O.J.T. and Cipolla, C. 2017. *Archaeological Theory in the New Millennium: Introducing Current Perspectives*. London: Routledge.

Hodder, I. 1982a (ed) *Symbolic and Structural Archaeology*. Cambridge: Cambridge University Press.

Hodder, I. 1982b. Theoretical archaeology: a reactionary view, in Hodder, I. (ed), *Symbolic and Structural Archaeology*. Cambridge: Cambridge University Press: pp. 1–16.

Holbraad, M. 2007. The power of powder: multiplicity and motion in the divinatory cosmology of Cuban Ifá, in Henare, A., Holbradd, M. and Wastell, S. (eds), *Thinking Through Things: Theorising Artefacts Ethnographically*. London: Routledge: pp. 42–56.

Jervis, B. 2016. Assemblage theory and town foundation in Medieval England. *Cambridge Archaeological Journal* 26(3): 381–395.

Jervis, B. 2018. *Assemblage Thought and Archaeology*. London: Routledge.

Johnson, M. 1999. *Archaeological Theory: An Introduction*. Oxford: Blackwell.

Jones, A.M. 2012. *Prehistoric Materialities: Becoming Material in Prehistoric Britain and Ireland*. Oxford: Oxford University Press.

Jones, A.M. 2017. The art of assemblage: styling Neolithic art. *Cambridge Archaeological Journal* 27(1): 85–94.

Joyce, A. 2000. The founding of Monte Albán: Sacred propositions and social practices, in Dobres, M.A. and Robb, J. (eds), *Agency in Archaeology*. London: Routledge: pp. 71–91.

Joyce, A. 2019. Assembling the City: Monte Albán as a Mountain of Creation and Sustenance, in Alt, S.M. and Pauketat, T. (eds), *New Materialisms and Ancient Urbanisms*. London: Routledge: pp. 65–93.

Liebmann, M. and Murphy, M. (eds) 2011. *Enduring Conquests: Rethinking the Archaeology of Resistance to Spanish Colonialism in the Americas*. Santa Fe: SAR Press.

Marcus, J. and Flannery, K. 1996. *Zapotec Civilization*. London: Thames and Hudson.

Mattingly, D. 2006. *An Imperial Possession: Britain in the Roman Empire.* London: Penguin.

Mattingly, D. 2014. *Imperialism, Power and Identity: Experiencing the Roman Empire.* Princeton: Princeton University Press.

Marx, K. 2001. *The 18th Brumaire of Louis Bonaparte.* London: The Electric Book Company.

Marx, K. and Engels, F. 2018. *The Communist Manifesto.* Minneapolis: First Avenue Editions.

Mauss, M. 1973. Techniques of the body. *Economy and Society* 2(1): 70–88.

McGuire, R. 1992. *A Marxist Archaeology.* San Diego: Academic Press.

Miller, D. and Tilley, C. (eds) 1984a. *Ideology, Power and Prehistory.* Cambridge: Cambridge University Press.

Miller, D. and Tilley, C. 1984b. Ideology, power and prehistory: an introduction, in Miller, D. and Tilley, C. (eds), *Ideology, Power and Prehistory.* Cambridge: Cambridge University Press: pp. 1–16.

Miller, D. and Tilley, C. 1984c. Ideology, power and long-term social change, in Miller, D. and Tilley, C. (eds), *Ideology, Power and Prehistory.* Cambridge: Cambridge University Press: pp. 147–152.

Miller, D. and Tilley, C. (eds) 1984d. *Ideology, Power and Prehistory.* Cambridge: Cambridge University Press.

Moore, J. and Scott, E. (eds) 1997. *Invisible People and Processes: Writing Gender and Childhood into European Archaeology.* London: Leicester University Press.

Morgan, L.H. 1877. *Ancient Society: Researches in the Lines of Human Progress from Savagery through Barbarism to Civilization.* London: MacMillan and Co.

Olalde, I. et al. 2018. The Beaker phenomenon and the genomic transformation of northwest Europe. *Nature* 555: 190.

Olsen, B. 2007. Keeping things at arm's length: a genealogy of symmetry. *World Archaeology* 39: 579–588.

Olsen, B., Shanks, M., Webmoor, T. and Witmore, C. 2012. *Archaeology: The Discipline of Things.* Berkeley: University of California Press.

Parker Pearson, M. 1984a. Social change, ideology and the archaeological record, in Spriggs, M. (ed), *Marxist Perspectives in Archaeology.* Cambridge: Cambridge University Press: pp. 59–71.

Parker Pearson, M. 1984b. Economic and ideological change: cyclical growth in the pre-state societies of Jutland, in Miller, D. and Tilley, C. (eds), *Ideology, Power and Prehistory.* Cambridge: Cambridge University Press: 69–92.

Redfield, R., Linton, R. and Herskovits, M.J. 1936. Memorandum for the study of acculturation. *American Anthropologist* 38: 149–152.

Sahlins, M. and Service, E. 1960. *Evolution and Culture.* Ann Arbor: University of Michigan Press.

Said, E. 1978. *Orientalism.* New York: Vintage.

Samson, A.V.M., Cooper, J. and Caamano-Dones, J. 2016. European visitors in native spaces: using palaeography to investigate religious dynamics in the New World. *Latin American Antiquity* 27(4): 443–461.

Service, E. 1971. *Primitive Social Organisation: An Evolutionary Perspective.* New York: Random House.

Shanks, M. 2007. Symmetrical archaeology. *World Archaeology* 39(4): 589–596.

Silliman, S. (ed) 2008. *Collaborating at the Trowel's Edge: Teaching and Learning in Indigenous Archaeology.* Tucson: University of Arizona Press.

Spector, J. 1991. What this awl means: toward a feminist archaeology, in Gero, J. and Conkey, M. (eds), *Engendering Archaeology: Women and Prehistory.* Oxford: Blackwell: pp. 388–406.

Spector, J. 1993. *What This Awl Means: Feminist Archaeology at a Wahpeton Dakota Village.* St Paul: Minnesota Historical Society Press.

Spivak, G.C. 1988. Can the subaltern speak? in Nelson, C. and Grossbery, L. (eds) *Marxism and the Interpretation of Culture.* Urbana: University of Illinois Press: pp. 271–313.

Spriggs, M. 1984. Another way of telling: Marxist perspectives in archaeology, in Spriggs, M. (ed), *Marxist Perspectives in Archaeology.* Cambridge: Cambridge University Press: pp. 1–10.

Steward, J. 1955. *Theory of Culture Change: The Methodology of Multi-linear Evolution.* Urbana: University of Illinois Press.

Trigger, B. 1984. Alternative archaeologies: nationalist, colonialist, imperialist. *Man* 19(3): 355–370.

Trigger, B. 1993. Marxism in contemporary western archaeology. *Archaeological Method and Theory* 5: 159–200.

Tylor, E.B. 2010. *Primitive Culture.* Cambridge: Cambridge University Press.

Van Dommelen, P. 1997. Colonialism and archaeology in the Mediterranean. *World Archaeology* 28(3): 305–323.

Van Dommelen, P. 1998. *On Colonial Grounds. A Comparative Study of Colonialism and Rural Settlement in First Millennium BC West Central Sardinia.* Leiden: University of Leiden.

Van Dommelen, P. 2012. Colonialism and migration in the ancient Mediterranean. *Annual Review of Anthropology* 41: 393–409.

Valcárcel Rojas, R. 2016. *Archaeology of Early Colonial Interaction at El Chorro de Maíta, Cuba.* Tuscaloosa: University Press of Florida.

Voss, B. 2008. *The Archaeology of Ethnogenesis: Race and Sexuality in Colonial San Francisco.* Berkeley: University of California Press.

Webmoor, T. 2007. What about 'one more turn after the social' in archaeological reasoning? Taking things seriously. *World Archaeology* 39: 563–578.

Webmoor, T. and Witmore, C. 2008. Things Are Us! A commentary on human/thing relations under the banner of a 'Social Archaeology'. *Norwegian Archaeological Review* 41: 1–18.

Webster, J. 1997. Necessary comparisons: a post-colonial approach to religious syncretism in the Roman provinces. *World Archaeology* 28(3): 324–338.

White, L.A. 1959. *The Evolution of Culture.* New York: McGraw-Hill.

Winter, M.C. 2011. Social memory and the origins of Monte Alban. *Ancient Mesoamerica* 22 (2): 393–409.

Witmore, C.L. 2007. Symmetrical archaeology: excerpts of a manifesto. *World Archaeology* 39: 546–562.

Wolf, E. 1982. *Europe and the People Without History.* Berkeley: University of California Press.

Woolf, G. 1997. Beyond Romans and natives. *World Archaeology* 28(3): 339–350.

3

CHANGING TIME?

In Chapter 2 I presented a history of archaeological theory specifically considering how different theoretical frameworks address change. Our standard history of archaeological thought tends to be constructed around three main periods that are often presented as radically opposed approaches (but see Harris and Cipolla, 2017). My analysis broke down this block-time approach by highlighting aspects of continuity and searching for links between the approaches. In doing so I offered a messier and more complex image of change.

In the next three chapters I extend my analysis by moving beyond a history of archaeological thought to engage with key themes that intersect with our approaches to change. These key themes are time, scale, and biography. Our approach to time, as this chapter will demonstrate, fundamentally impacts how we talk about change. In Chapter 4 I engage with the issue of scale. Archaeologists work at scales from the microscopic to the architectural and on timescales ranging from a generation to several millennia. Does the scale of our analysis, or of our timeframe, affect the way we approach change? Finally, in Chapter 5 I engage with the literature surrounding biography. Biographies are a key way we engage with history and change at a timescale that is readily comprehensible. Archaeologically the concept has been used to shape discussions of not only human biographies but also those of materials, objects, buildings, and landscapes. The aim in these three chapters is two-fold: first to map a complex history of shifting approaches to change, and second, to explore how these themes have a significant impact on the narratives of change that emerge in their wake.

Time and change

This chapter draws on the excellent and detailed account of the relationship between time and change by Gavin Lucas (2005). Lucas (2005: 2) argues that time and change are so closely related that it can be "hard to think of them apart". How we decide (and it is a decision) to conceptualise and understand time has a significant impact on the types of narratives we write about change and how we approach archaeology. In Chapter 1 I presented seven hurdles to our approach to change: block-time approaches, progressive, teleological, deterministic, and anthropocentric approaches, analyses that emphasise origins and revolutions, and narratives that utilise singular causation. These are all issues that obstruct us from writing the kinds of nuanced and complex accounts of change that more accurately capture the nature of our world. Many of these hurdles are closely linked to how we approach time. Time is usually conceived of as always moving forward, linearly, and in a single direction. Today we tend to suggest that time is universal; it is the same whether I am in Leicester, Fiji, or Mexico (though the exact time differs, there are still 60 minutes in an hour, 24 hours in a day, and time continues to flow forward at the same rate globally).

This approach to time provides the supporting framework upon which narratives of change that are progressive and teleological can develop (cf. Hamilakis, 2013: 122). Conceiving of time as flowing in a single direction, in the same way across the planet, creates an image of time as continually moving forward (with no sense that it could move backward), and this forward movement is the same in all places, at all times. In the same way, progressive narratives of change are based on a sense that time is moving ever forward and this is linked to a belief that things are necessarily thereby always improving – progressing. The link between this conception of time's ever-forward flow and teleological reasoning is also strong. One cannot go back in time: it is presented as irreversible, and the forward flow of time to the present provides the explanation for the past from which time has separated us. Time is presented as unilinear and universal, and as a result explanations of change often follow suit. Time follows the same path to the present across the earth, and as a result we *can* create narratives of change that work in the same way. A unilinear notion of time also contributes to a focus on origins and revolutions, as instances of change are placed in single moments and we trace a single path from the past to the present. Our approach to time becomes woven into our narratives of change, as this chapter will demonstrate: if we shift our approach, we necessarily begin to alter how we describe, interpret, and explain change in the past.

Time as chronology

For archaeologists, chronology is a key tool and concept. The *Oxford English Dictionary* defines chronology as the "The arrangement of events or dates in the order of their occurrence". Chronology is vital to archaeology as without it no study of the past is possible. In particular, the ability to draw comparisons across time and space in a meaningful way is predicated on our ability to identify the date of a site. Chronology is built on a particular concept of time, as universal, linear, and uniform (Lucas, 2005: 2; see also Olsen et al., 2012: 136). Time is taken to be the same globally and in the past: minutes, hours, and years may be calculated and understood as the same at 500BC and 2020AD. Moreover, the length of the units by which we measure time is standardised and linear; one calendar year is the same length whether it is measured at 10,000BC or today. We know, archaeologically, and from historical records, that different ways of dividing time are and have been dominant; the various Maya calendars, for example, are based on day counts like our own, but they have cycles of different lengths and different calendars were used to measure time for different purposes. Yet today, when we talk about chronology, we generally draw upon a single universal concept of time. Time is perceived to flow in a single direction, in a single line from the past to the present and into the future, and it may be divided up and measured in equal units.

While this approach to time is clearly necessary in order to make comparisons and talk across geographical regions and time periods (both today and in the past), it is not without consequence. As Lucas (2005) has argued, this concept of time comes to influence the kinds of narratives we write as archaeologists; moreover, it results in "impoverished interpretations of cultural change" (Lucas, 2005: 2). This is not surprising; how we think about time is ontological and deeply embedded in the west. Today our lives are, all too often, governed by diaries that map out the nature of our days, and our calendars might be shared with our colleagues to allow collaboration. We think about time as a valuable commodity: 'that is an hour of my life I won't get back'. It is something irreversible that passes in a measured and regular manner, whether we like it or not. We learn as children how long a minute lasts and how many days there are in a week; even toddlers know to ask for 'five more minutes' on the swings. This sense of time is all pervasive and highly ingrained in our lives today. As a result, when we come to think about time in the past, and about change, this way of thinking is highly influential.

By conceiving of time as linear, universal, and uniform, many of our explanations of change have taken a similar shape (Lucas, 2005: 10; 12; 115). Lewis-Henry Morgan's (1877) evolutionary scheme of social change suggests a linear, universal sequence through which all societies pass. The Three Age System (see Chapter 1) is predicated on a series of separate, irreversible periods through which all of Europe passed. Our continued engagement with origins is about fixing a single essence at a single point in time for a given phenomenon, but this does not leave space for complex causation or multilinear histories. We see this same entwining of chronology and change in the way that increasingly fine chronologies seems to demand different kinds of explanations of change, and different types of historical narratives are seen to be emerging in their wake (see, for example, Bayliss et al., 2007; this is a topic I return to in Chapter 4).

The entwined nature of archaeological explanation and the concept of time is further demonstrated when we consider the development of chronology and absolute chronology. Olsen et al. (2012: 42) show how the ordering of objects by material and type in early museums contributed to "the serial image of time moving between discrete moments". Placing cabinet after cabinet in a chronological sequence visualised a system where one way of life was separated from and then replaced by another (Olsen et al., 2012: 42): this is the same context in which the models of the past advanced by Morgan (1877) and the Three Age System began to emerge. For many antiquarians, what mattered was when, relatively, a site or object dated to, and, perhaps, depending on their perspective, how that fitted within the broad evolutionary sequence they utilised for understanding the perceived 'progress' of human history. The later development of culture history, as a way of writing the specific regional histories of various cultures, created a greater need for comparison across regions. Lucas (2005: 7) suggests this shift played a key role in the development of absolute chronologies and scientific dating methods. The model of time that archaeology adopts and the types of explanations of change offered are intimately linked.

Chronology is something we place ontologically outside the realm of human agency. We conceive of time as ticking forward in the same measured way whether or not we want it to. We universalise it despite the fact that we understand time and chronology to have emerged in a very specific context from a combination of mathematics, observations of the planets, the rotation of the earth on its axis, the orbit of the earth around the sun, and as a result of the development of factories, steam engines, and the industrial revolution (Ingold, 2000: 323–338). It is rarely seen as something over which we can exert agency and instead becomes an external container into which activity can be inserted to provide a universal way of measuring. What was once specific has, through a series of transformations and complex causation, become general and universal. This is problematic on two levels. First, it means we come to impose our own modern concepts of time onto the past; these concepts, are culturally specific (Latour, 1993) and as a result we do not necessarily do justice to our engagements with the past (Thomas, 2004). Second, as demonstrated above, they impact upon how it is that we come to approach the subject of change. 'Clock-time' emerges from how we measure time, not necessarily what time is: it is epistemological rather than ontological. While we need to retain clock-time as a way of measuring, comparing, and dating things, we do not need to understand what time is in the same terms, particularly given how clock-time links so problematically to progressive, unilinear, and directed narratives of change.

Separating past and present

Our problematic understanding of time is further complicated by our view of the archaeological record itself. While we usually posit that time is flowing ever forward in a linear and universal manner, we also often present the archaeological record itself as static and awaiting recovery. As archaeologists we cut the timeline between past and present (Lucas, 2005; Olsen et al., 2012: 137). Generally, we work from the premise that material culture buried in the ground represents the traces of actions of past communities. We posit that these traces, buried within the archaeological record, remain, broadly speaking, static from their point of burial until they are excavated. By cutting the timeline and suggesting the buried record is static, we create a gap between past and present. We then suggest this gap is the very thing that we have to use archaeological theory to overcome (see Figure 3.1).

PRESENT   PAST

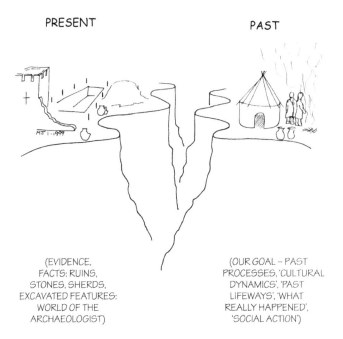

(EVIDENCE,	(OUR GOAL – PAST
FACTS: RUINS,	PROCESSES, 'CULTURAL
STONES, SHERDS,	DYNAMICS', 'PAST
EXCAVATED FEATURES:	LIFEWAYS', 'WHAT
WORLD OF THE	REALLY HAPPENED',
ARCHAEOLOGIST)	'SOCIAL ACTION')

FIGURE 3.1 The gulf between past and present
Source: Matthew Johnson (2010: 33; Fig 2.1).

Lucas (2005: 126–127) discusses the gap we create between past and present as part of what he terms the "double temporality" of archaeological materials. Archaeology rests on foundations that are concerned with discovery and excavation; it relies on the notion that something about the objects has been lost and has to be recovered by the archaeologist. Lucas (2005: 127) suggests this is reinforced by how we keep the items we excavate, these vestiges of the past, separate from the modern world. We surround archaeological sites with fences, we keep finds in specific types of boxes to further arrest the effect of time, and we present them to the public in museum cases that both act to protect the objects and separate them from us: 'do not touch'. Moreover, when we place the objects in the museum cabinet, we tend to select the best ones – the most whole, the most visually impressive – and we clean them of all traces of the period they spent buried in the earth to present them as pieces of the past brought into the present (Lucas, 2005: 127). Elsewhere Lucas (2012: 12) has argued that "what makes objects archaeological is that they are *dead*", by which he means that they are in some way separated from the living world of the present, though he is careful to show that the definition of *dead* is fuzzy and complex.

This situation arises from our ontological view of time in the west. We often present the past as thoroughly separated and different from the present: a "foreign country" (Lowenthal, 1985). Finds buried beneath the ground are seen as separate from our own world: this separation is a product of how we ontologically elevate humans.

Archaeology is that which is buried awaiting discovery by humans. As a result, the archaeological record is separated from the human sphere of action and thereby from the grasp of human agency, and we therefore consider the archaeological record to be static and unchanging (see, for example, Nativ, 2018). That which we (as humans) cannot affect is seen as separate from us. This, though, is a falsehood. The archaeological record, buried beneath the ground, continues to change from the moment of burial through excavation and beyond: no part is static. Buried archaeology interacts with and is changed by animals such as rabbits, worms, and maggots. The soil it is buried in is an incredibly vibrant material that moves physically, is the medium for various chemical reactions, and has a shifting composition. Bronze metalwork buried underground continues to corrode, its surface and shape changing over time, as its chemistry alters. Human remains decompose as flesh rots away, and the very structure of the bones themselves changes. Carbon 14 isotopes shift over time: this change is what makes carbon dating possible. Buried archaeology is not static, but continues to change; moreover, these changes are not necessarily even separate from human agency as the fertilisers we use on crops and how we manage surface water all affect the nature of the remains beneath the ground.

It was this separation of past and present that Lewis Binford (1977) sought to address with Middle Range Theory – his means of linking the "static archaeological record" with the "dynamic past processes" that created it. Middle Range Theory developed as a result of a series of debates in the 1970s primarily between Michael Schiffer and Binford about the nature of the archaeological record. Binford (1964: 425) had argued that the archaeological record was a form of "fossil record" where past behaviours were effectively "frozen"[1]. As archaeologists began to explore more scientific methodologies, Schiffer (1972) questioned whether the spatial patterning evident in the archaeological record represented the spatial patterning of activity in the past. Schiffer (1972: 156) rejected the notion that the archaeological record was a fossil record of past behaviour on the basis that it was subject to a series of transformations that effectively created biases in the record. He suggested that there was a divide between how objects were used in the past systemic context and how they came to be deposited in the archaeological context (Schiffer, 1972: 157). He created flow models that mapped how objects moved through their lifetimes in order to consider how this might bias the record at the point of recovery. By considering how materials were first procured, and then used to manufacture objects, which were then used themselves, later discarded, and then deposited as refuse, he thought about how these different processes, within what we might term today the 'biography' (see Chapter 5) of the object, would create biases in the archaeological record making it differ from the past "systemic context" (Schiffer, 1972: 158–159; Figure 1).

Schiffer continued to work on these ideas to try and better understand how the archaeological record formed. He argued that:

> The archaeological record at a site is a static, three-dimensional structure of materials existing in the present. The remains in this site have undergone

successive transformations from the time they once participated in a behavioural system to the time they are observed by the archaeologist.

(Schiffer, 1975: 838)

Schiffer (1972; 1976; 1983) has variously described the archaeological record as
"transformed" or "distorted" from the behavioural system. For Schiffer (1972: 156;
1975: 838) there were both cultural and noncultural processes that affected how the
archaeological record formed. The noncultural processes included things such as
erosion and animal burrowing, whereas the cultural processes he considered included
aspects such as how worn-out tools were discarded, the manner in which sites were
abandoned, and how the dead were buried. Schiffer and Rathje (1973) termed these
cultural processes "C-transforms" and the natural ones "N-transforms". These transformations were presented as a form of bias that had to be understood so that one
could work back to the behavioural system more accurately.

In response to the arguments put forth by Schiffer, Binford (1975) rejected his earlier use of the term 'fossil record' and began directly focusing on these issues himself.
Like Schiffer, Binford (1975; 1977) presented the archaeological record as static and (at
least in part) separated from the past processes that created it. He suggested the problem of linking static phenomena in the archaeological record with dynamic past
processes was to be solved by 'Middle Range Theory' (Binford, 1977).

There is an odd tension in the work of both Binford and Schiffer that I think
results from the way their work separates past and present and their approach to
time more broadly. In the 1975 quotation from Schiffer (above) he describes the
archaeological record as static in the first sentence and then in the second as having
gone through a series of transformations – suggesting it is not actually static. We
can see the same tension in a quotation from Binford:

> The archaeological record is a contemporary phenomenon. It is above all a
> static phenomenon. It is what remains in static form of dynamics which
> occurred in the past as well as dynamics occurring up until the present obser-
> vations are made.

(Binford, 1975: 251)

There are several things that contribute to this tension surrounding whether the
archaeological record is static or not. First, there is an issue of orientation – by
focusing on the past remains buried in the ground from a specifically archaeological
perspective (i.e. as an *archaeological* record) it becomes necessary that they identify
the ongoing changes to the record as 'distortions' rather than as part of the normal
processes of the world. It is (usually) not the case that past people set out to actively
create their own archaeology for future generations; rather, their normal activity
might effectively create archaeology. This problem becomes evident when we
consider how Schiffer (1972; 1975) suggests that the production and discard processes to which objects are subject 'bias' the archaeological record. These are not
biasing effects; these are normal everyday activities. Second, and perhaps more

importantly, their premise, that the archaeological record is static, seems to rest upon the idea, discussed above, that once things are buried they must no longer be changing. This is a product of our anthropocentrism, which posits that change is the result of the intentional action of humans. These arguments collapse if we stop creating a gulf between past and present and instead recognise that the two are connected (see, for example, Lucas, 2005; 2012; Patrik, 1985; Thomas, 1996).

Some of these points emerged as the debate between Binford (1981) and Schiffer (1985) continued in the early 1980s, as the two considered whether or not there was a 'Pompeii premise' in archaeology (i.e. that the archaeological record represents a frozen moment in time). Binford (1981) suggests that Schiffer's arguments about transformations and distortions rest upon the premise that the archaeological record is similar to Pompeii – that everything is frozen within it and then goes on to be transformed and distorted. Binford (1981: 200) argued that c–transforms are not a distortion of the archaeological record at all, but are really just examples of past action. It is not the case, Binford asserted, that by identifying the distortions and transformations that have occurred we can reveal some 'pure' archaeological record of past behaviour. Ultimately, Binford (1981: 103) argued that all cultural systems are always in the processes of entropy and renewal and are therefore not static at all. Lucas (2012) has highlighted how the work of Ascher (1961) actually prefigures much of this debate. Ascher argued that the archaeological record is not a frozen moment in time (akin to Pompeii) but is the result of a community in a process of decomposition. The formation, and persistence, of what we term the archaeological record is the result of continually ongoing processes and thereby always subject to change at a variety of differing tempos.

What does this mean for our approach to change? As Lucas (2005) has demonstrated, we archaeologists often cut the thread between past and present. This allows us to present archaeological excavations as a process of 'discovering' what was lost and our interpretations as a way of piecing together a series of puzzle pieces to understand the past. Presenting the archaeological record as 'static' further entrenches these problems. It suggests that the archaeological record is separate from the ongoing passage of time and the ongoing processes of change in the rest of the world. It is not. The archaeological record exists squarely in the present where, like the rest of the world, it is subject to constant change that emerges from the actions of a wide variety of factors from humans, to animals, to chemical reactions.

Questioning chronology

Binford and Schiffer were concerned with the issue of time and the separation of past and present, specifically in relation to the position of the archaeologist. Michael Shanks and Chris Tilley (1987a; 1987b) shifted this debate in a different direction by considering the nature of time as it was experienced by people in the past, and in particular people in the pre-industrial past. As part of the post-processual critique, Shanks and Tilley (1987a: 32; 1987b: 118–120) began to explicitly question the concept of time within archaeology, suggesting that archaeologists had a poor theoretical understanding of the nature of temporality and how it relates to experience. They argued that there are two kinds of time: the first, abstract time, is the kind of time we understand most readily in the modern west and for them it is the product of capitalism. Abstract time is exchangeable, measurable, commodified, and separable from life; it is the time measured by factory clocks and hours of labour (Shanks and Tilley, 1987a: 32; 1987b: 127–128). They contrasted abstract time with substantial time, which is the time of our lived lives, the time of practice, and the time we experience daily. Shanks and Tilley (1987a,b) suggested that chronology is a form of abstract time, whereas time is a container and a measure rather than something that is experienced. Curry and De Montmollin (1987: 2) make a similar distinction between what they term "archaeologists' time" (that of chronology) and "others' time" (that experienced by past people) and McGlade (1999) later distinguished between the human experience of time and clock time along similar lines.

Shanks and Tilley's (1987a; 1987b) critique of abstract time came from multiple directions, and they argued that abstract time was not the type of time people experienced or understood in the past. Furthermore, they argued that archaeologists were failing to see that by presenting time purely as chronology they were imposing a culturally specific version of what time is onto the past (Shanks and Tilley, 1987a: 33; 39). Chronology is a frame into which we can slot our data rather than a way in which people experienced and understood time in the past, nor is it a form of explanation. Shanks and Tilley (1987a) argued that abstract time (including chronology) is a universalising frame that produces a specific kind of history. Imposing a single model of time onto the past effectively homogenises all of humanity and fails to recognise rupture and difference across time and space (Shanks and Tilley, 1987a: 33). They suggest that the universalising and homogenising effect of chronology provided the basis for classificatory systems and evolutionary sequences of human social development that they believed should not be sustained. For Shanks and Tilley (1987a: 40), time could never be apolitical nor should it be approached as a neutral container for our data.

Their solution to this problem was to suggest that archaeology needed to explicitly theorise time as a subject. Moreover, in suggesting the inappropriate nature of abstract time, they recommended their opposed concept of substantial time. This is a form of time that is not a container but rather emerges from practice and relations. This is the time that emerges through our lived daily lives – how long it takes the kettle to boil or to write a paragraph. They also critiqued the notion of a separated past and present, with Middle Range Theory bridging the gap between them, and instead argued we should focus on "presencing", where we realise that people exist in the present and that the present is not a termination point but is itself historic (Shanks and Tilley, 1987a: 34).

There is a lot to recommend the arguments laid out by Shanks and Tilley (1987a,b). Problematically though, they establish an opposition between chronology (without which modern archaeology cannot possibly exist) and the lived experience of time that past communities had. One of the consequences of this dualism is that it actually establishes a divide between past people and present-day archaeologists (a divide that they specifically set out to question and dismantle). The debate about the nature of time as experienced versus measured plays into a series of wider dualisms and ultimately into the divide between nature and culture. For Shanks and Tilley (1987a,b) abstract time is something culturally imposed, whereas substantial time is something naturally experienced. The fallacy of this dualism becomes evident when we dwell upon it: are abstract time and chronology something we invented or something that emerges from natural phenomena? It is both: years and months do emerge from natural cycles but alternative systems of measurement can emerge from natural cycles too.

Rather than seeing these as opposed types of time, they are better understood as two of *many* ways in which time can emerge. In order to do archaeology, and to study change, we need chronology, but we also need to recognise that time emerges differently for different people across the world as a result of their experiences and conceptions of time. Time is not ultimately the same thing *always* and *everywhere* (cf. Latour, 1993). Rather than creating a dualism between abstract and substantial time we would do better to consider how both emerge together in differing ways in different contexts through the processes of change. Time in the Neolithic, for example, emerged through processes such as the time taken to knap an axe, for spring to turn to summer, for a lamb to become a sheep, or a child an adult. While we might readily identify the time taken to knap an axe as a form of what Shanks and Tilley (1987a) would term 'substantial time', classifying the time taken for the seasons to shift is more complex, as it not only involves the independent (and measurable) orbit and rotation of the earth (which we might identify as forms of abstract time), but also the more substantial 'social' recognition of a changing landscape. Equally we can consider how time emerges for us from the countdown of a stopwatch, the calculations of Bayesian analysis, or experienced as we wait for an egg to boil. Time emerges from change.

Time as experience

Shanks and Tilley's ideas effectively paved the way for the influential work of anthropologist Tim Ingold (1993; 2000) on the subject of temporality and the engagements with phenomenology by archaeologists such as Julian Thomas (1996; 2004), Chris Gosden (1994), and Tilley's own later work (1994). The turn to phenomenology in archaeology marked an attempt to escape dualisms such as nature and culture, body and mind, and subject and object, in reaction to some of the earlier theoretical emphasis on structuralism, semiosis, and symbols by post-processualists. Such work tried to eschew the dualistic thinking that characterises the proposed divide between abstract and substantial time. Moreover, it further developed the argument of Shanks and Tilley (1987a,b) that time is not a neutral container, by reacting against the notion that we can ever experience or understand time in a detached manner.

Ingold (1993) explores the relationship between archaeology and anthropology as it coalesces around the issues of time and landscape (for a re-analysis see Hicks, 2016 and responses). For our purposes his comments on time and temporality are pertinent. The paper discusses the concept of temporality as the form of time that we experience socially as we carry out tasks. Temporality is not chronology, defined as the regular system of dated intervals within which events can be placed, nor is temporality history, defined as a series of events that are dated by their occurrence within a chronology (Ingold, 1993: 157). Temporality is a form of time that is also quite different from 'clock-time' (here there are parallels with Shanks and Tilley (1987a, b) and McGlade (1999)). In clock-time "an hour is an hour, regardless of what one is doing in it, or how one feels" (Ingold, 1993: 159); clock-time is uniform, homogeneous, and quantitative. Temporality is qualitative and it is experienced; it emerges from our embodied action within the world. Ingold (1993) articulates the difference between the experience of time that passes when we are involved in a task and the nature of clock-time. He draws on anthropologist Alfred Gell (2001) to show that there is no dividing line between past and present but that time is immanent: "the present is not *marked off* from a past that it has replaced or a future that will, in turn replicate it; it rather gathers the past and future into itself" (Ingold, 2000: 160).

Both Gosden (1994) and Thomas (1996) went on to engage explicitly with phenomenology in order to reconsider the nature of time. Whereas Ingold (2000) cites Merleau-Ponty (1962), Gosden (1994) and Thomas (1996) drew primarily on the work of Heidegger (especially *Being and Time* (1962)) to understand the temporal nature of human behaviour. Heidegger (1962), in his exploration of the nature of being, argued that humans are never apart from the world, rather they are always already *thrown* in the world, existing within it and shaped by it. Temporality is not something imposed by an external measure but rather it emerges from action and practice. For Heidegger, clock-time emerges (at least partly) from humanity's experience of temporality. As Thomas says,

> human beings are fundamentally temporal. They have time written into their constitution, in that they have a past, a present and a future. This time of the world, public time or measurable clock time are abstracted from this basic temporality. The world of nature might have processes going on within it which proceed at a given rate, but no one would think to measure them in the first places if their attunement to existence were not one which was fundamentally temporal.
>
> *(Thomas, 1996: 40)*

Heidegger is specifically concerned with how human consciousness and self-awareness shape the nature of our experience. In the above quotation Thomas explains that because human existence is temporal (we know there is a past, present, and future; we know that we get older), we come to attune ourselves to the temporality of the rest of the world and to measure that temporality. In this definition abstract time is not fundamentally opposed to temporality (or what Shanks and Tilley (1987a, b) would term substantial time), but rather emerges from it and from our self-awareness. Chronology, then, can be thought of as emerging from temporality. Thomas (1996) goes on to extend temporality beyond the human to say that things have a similar temporal structure to humans because of human care.

Gosden (1994) also argues for the centrality of time to the human experience, though he develops his argument along slightly different lines. Gosden argues against the 'time as neutral container' position along multiple lines; perhaps most pertinently for our purposes, he argues for this on the basis of change:

> The view of time as external to processes of change is relatively unproblematical when applied to natural processes, but is much more dubious when applied to human history. Change which occurs in measured time is devoid of any human agency or social impetus; and it was this view of time and change which early social evolutionists, in anthropology and archaeology, adopted.
>
> *(Gosden, 1994: 3)*

Gosden says that for archaeology, understanding time as a neutral container is problematic because it leaves no space for human agency in that history, arguing that time (and space) are created by people and structure all human action (Gosden, 1994: 34). He argues that whether our behaviours are habitual or conscious, they are all recursively shaped by our past and this is how time comes to structure all our action. Drawing time and practice together in this manner allows him to move to a position where "change is endemic in human action" (Gosden, 1994: 192). He argues that there are different ways in which the past can structure, and be used to shape, the present and that these differences produced change and stability in varying ways (Gosden, 1994: 192). This is a very different position from one where time is a byword for chronology and different again from one where we temper the neutrality of chronology by opposing it to temporality.

Richard Bradley (for example, 1998; 2002) has often focused on the issue of time in archaeology. In *The Past in Prehistoric Societies* he draws upon the ideas discussed above and, through a grounding in practice theory, explores a series of archaeological examples. Bradley's work on what we might term 'past pasts' and 'past futures' explores how communities in the past, just like us today, had a sense of their own pasts and futures and that this knowledge of temporality had an effect on their practice in their present. Bradley draws on the work of Barrett (1999) to show that past communities always lived in the presence of their own past. Bradley's (2002) argument is an elegant one, and in some ways an obvious one, but it is one that as archaeologists we can easily fail to grasp. So often we spend time thinking about the past in a relatively linear way where we concern ourselves with how a site or landscape changed over time rather than thinking about how the past came to shape past presents and thereby past futures. Bradley (2002) considers how monuments came to be re-interpreted by past communities, how older objects sometimes appear in later hoards, and how past people discovered their own more ancient pasts.

The interest in the experience of time, which began in the 1980s and continued into the 1990s, could be characterised as reactionary. All the authors writing about these issues were concerned with the consequences of the relatively recent adoption of a global framework for time. Gosden (1994: 2) explains that the imposition of a singular chronological framework globally had served to highlight the difference between the multiple ways in which time is experienced in contrast to a universal model. There are many points of contact between these arguments about time but there are also differences. In Shanks and Tilley's reading there are two opposed forms of time, one that is modernist and one that is not. In contrast, Ingold (1993: 153) argues that we can have a nonmodernist form of clock-time because clock-time can be the product of any regular interval such as the rotation of the earth around the sun. For Gosden (1994) and Thomas (1996) chronology emerges from the experience of temporality we have daily as embodied beings. All these arguments emphasise a difference between measured time and lived time. For Shanks and Tilley (1987a,b) time appears to be specific to *human* experience, as though time would not emerge without people, whereas we can see the different temporalities of hills, valley, trees, and corn in Ingold's (1993) work. For Thomas (1996) and Gosden (1994) humans are fundamentally temporal beings, but temporality extends beyond humanity. Ultimately, though, it feels as though all these authors pass moral judgement on modern, abstract, measured time as differing significantly (and negatively) from the temporalities of experience. While it is true that people in the Neolithic were not ruled by hours and minutes, they did experience days and seasons – regular interval forms of time beyond their own control. Moreover, it is not true today that we experience temporality separate to clock-time (we have all watched the minutes tick down while we wait for an unwelcome appointment, or hurried them along in anticipation of a joyful occasion) – chronology and clock-time both play roles in our experience of time.

These various authors refocused the attention of archaeologists onto the experience of time in the past. John Robb and Tim Pauketat (2013: 17) argue that post-processualists and phenomenologists both "replaced the discussion of change with discussion of time" as a cultural construct. Shanks and Tilley (1987a,b) demonstrated that there were different ways to experience and understand time, and simply imposing one of our modern models on the past was inappropriate and had clear (and negative) consequences for the nature of explanations of change. The later influence of phenomenology sought to escape a position where time was purely understood as a cultural imposition but to understand how time emerged from lived action. One of the strengths of this approach is that it allows for multiple types of time to emerge.

Times multiple

Illustrating the multiple nature of time, Bradley (2002: 153–157) contrasts the archaeological techniques of field survey and stratigraphy to demonstrate the different understandings of time that emerge from them. Stratigraphical thinking is based on the premise that every layer of archaeology overlays an older layer beneath it; time is physically laid out in a vertical sequence following the geological model. By contrast those that do field survey work across a landscape horizontally and map different features from different periods – a Bronze Age barrow may divert the path of an Iron Age field boundary. In field survey times are mixed horizontally, while in stratigraphic excavation time is laid out in a linear, vertical sequence (see Figure 3.2). Bradley (2002: 155) explores how cuts and fissures into the stratigraphic sequence can make older deposits emerge and that as a result "*channels* … open between past and present". Bradley (2002: 157) ultimately argues that the conception of the past involved in landscape survey, that pasts of different ages can emerge side by side and erupt into each other, is a more accurate understanding; as he states, "times are multiple and overlapping".

There are a number of archaeologists that have written about time as multiple and nonlinear (see, for example, González-Ruibal, 2006; Hamilakis, 2013; McGlade, 1999; Olivier, 2004; 2011; Olsen et al., 2012; Webmoor and Witmore, 2008; Witmore, 2006; 2007a,b). McGlade (1999) critiques the failure of archaeologists to consider time in a nonlinear manner. He argues that archaeological techniques such as radiocarbon dating and typology only serve to further cement an understanding of time that is singular, continuous, and linear (McGlade 1999: 142–143). Part of the problem, he argues, is that having a different model of time also requires a different, and more complex, model of causality and change that allows for the interaction of multiple scales of analysis (McGlade, 1999: 141) (for discussion of scale, see Chapter 4; for discussion of causality, see Chapter 7). The argument is powerful: if our understanding of time were nonlinear, then our understanding of change might follow suit. As argued above, our singular and linear model of time has allowed the emergence of progressive and teleological models of change. If we were to replace our singular, linear model of time with a more complex and multiple one, we might also be able to unseat progressive and teleological models of change.

There is a growing interest in the work of the French philosopher Michel Serres. Serres disputes the argument that our current human condition is the summit of progress. He argues that when we place ourselves at the summit of human progress, we assume that we are more right about the world than anyone else has ever been (Serres with Latour, 1995: 48–49). Serres argues that this belief in progress rests on the linear model of time, arguing instead that we should view time as "chaotic", flowing in unpredictable and complex ways (Serres with Latour, 1995: 58). He argues that time flows, twists, and percolates, that things that are far apart can be made proximate, and old and new can be brought together, that time can be folded and crumpled. He illustrates his argument as follows:

> Consider a late-model car. It is a disparate aggregate of scientific and technical solutions dating from different periods. One can date it component by component: this part was invented at the turn of the century, another, ten years ago, and Carnot's cycle is almost two hundred years old. Not to mention that the wheel dates back to Neolithic times. The ensemble is only contemporary

FIGURE 3.2 Stratigraphy – the vertical sequencing of time (Ballanorris Iron Age house, Isle of Man) (top) and landscape – a horizontal mixture of times (Tara, Ireland) (bottom)
Source: (Top) R.J. Crellin. (Bottom) Wikicommons.

by assemblage, by its design, its finish, sometimes only by the slickness of the advertising surrounding it.

(Serres with Latour, 1995: 45)

This leads to a position where Serres argues that we always exist in multitemporal worlds where old and new are brought together and erupt into each other (see also Hamilakis, 2013: 122–124). There is a parallel here in the contrast that Bradley (2002) drew between stratigraphy and field survey. For Serres (Serres with Latour, 1995: 60–61) time and the measurement of time are two different things, and while we may measure time on a straight line, that is not how time actually is; rather it flows, percolates, and is chaotic. Serres' position on time is radical; he is happy to make things that are apparently chronological distant proximate and to see time as flowing in complex ways, viewing the world as multitemporal.

Serres' ideas have been particularly influential on the symmetrical archaeologists (see, for example, González-Ruibal, 2006; Olsen et al., 2012; Webmoor and Witmore, 2008; Witmore, 2007a,b). Symmetrical archaeology is a self-defined school of archaeological theory that advocates for a relational approach, drawing initially on the work of sociologist of science, Bruno Latour, and is explored in more depth in Chapter 6. Much symmetrical archaeology argues against a division between past and present; it argues that the world is multitemporal, and that time percolates. Alfredo González-Ruibal (2006: 111) describes how times may be mixed by writing about his experience of being in a West Ethiopian Gumuz village where, he argues, periods are mixed together as plastic beads sit alongside adzes, broken buckets, and handmade pots. He argues, therefore, that past and present are not separated. In a similar way Christopher Witmore (2007a: 556–557; see also Olsen et al., 2012: 138) has argued that the "past has not passed" by exploring how Roman roads continue to direct the flow of people and transport networks today. This argument leads to a position where the "radical chasm between past and present" (as discussed above) need no longer be maintained (Olsen et al., 2012: 138). This allows symmetrical archaeology to reach a position where time emerges from relations and the past and present are no longer separated but mixed in a multitemporal way (Olsen et al., 2012: 153). Multitemporal approaches allow us to avoid singular causation explanations as they more easily create space for multiple causation to emerge.

Serres' view of time is radical and disruptive and comes from a position that wishes to unseat both the image of the present as the pinnacle of achievement and a notion of singular truth. Operating a nonlinear view of history allows one to eschew teleological reasoning and to offer more complex narratives of the past. Seeing time as a chaotic, percolating flow with eddies and undercurrents effectively disrupts the simplistic linear modelling of change that allows problematically simple histories to emerge. It also allows authors to deconstruct the divide between past and present. In spite of this, I find the argument about multiple times advance by González-Ruibal (2006) problematic. In order to be able to identify some parts of the present as coming from the past we have to effectively cleave past and present apart once more. In my office there are objects with many different temporalities: a replica Bronze Age sword, a computer, a mug I was given as a gift eight years ago, my grandmother's engagement ring, and some Neolithic flint tools. Yet all these objects are assembled in the present and are part of the present. Yes, the engagement ring is much older, and the lithics even older still, but they are all in the present; they have persisted. It is not the case that they are 'pieces of the past' that are 'out of time'; in order to say something is 'out of time' we must first remove it from the flow of the present. This is the point I take from the Serres quotation about the motorcar: we bring many times together, but we assemble them in the present. Moreover, it is not the case that these 'older' objects that exist in the present exist unchanged; rather, the engagement ring is worn and tarnished, shaped by my own hand, and the lithics have a patina from the time spent underground. In order to persist into the present, things have to continually change (that change could be imperceptibly slow or very quick). Therefore, while I agree that time operates on multiple scales, that it emerges from action in the world, and that its flow is not best understood in a linear way, I suggest that we should avoid creating a rupture between past and present by appreciating the histories that, bring different things, animals, landscapes, and people into the present. We should aim to understand the processes of change that different archaeological remains have undergone to get them into the present rather than understanding them as vestiges of the past itself (this is discussed in more depth in chapters 6 and 7). The past and the present are connected together by the ongoing processes of change.

Conclusions

This chapter demonstrates that how we choose to understand and conceptualise time has a direct consequence for the narratives of change that we write. Unilinear, universal, and unidirectional models of time have only served to create models of history that have the same shape. Yet as archaeologists we rely on chronology (certainly a linear and directional form of time, though not necessarily universal or unilinear) as a system to be able to piece together narratives of the past and to be able to compare and contrast; without a system of chronology archaeology is unthinkable. Chronology is never neutral, but it is a key archaeological tool. Chronology emerges in the present through a series of processes from radiocarbon decay, to the seriation of pot sherds, and the Bayesian analysis of dates, but it is not the *only* way in which time emerges. There is a difference between what time is and how we measure it.

Much of the theorisation of time in archaeology reacts to the realisation that our experience of time today need not have been the experience of time that people had in the past. This is a key realisation, but it is also crucial to realise that today the measurement of hours and minutes is not in some way inauthentic but rather it emerges from our present and has come to play a role shaping our experience of time. That is not to say that our experience of time is predicated on this alone; rather it emerges from the passing of seasons, the ageing of loved ones, the ticking of a clock, the decay of plants, and the gradual erosion of the surfaces of objects. It is not the case that substantial time or temporality are in some way superior to the universal model of time; rather they are both equally valid. Nor, is it the case that the only time we can experience is 'substantial'.

Time emerges; it emerges in complex and multiple ways. It is not a neutral container for action, but neither is it best understood as a social construction. Time emerges not just from the action of people but from geological processes, chemical decay, animal ageing, and the rotation of the sun. As a result it emerges in different ways with different speeds and tempos. As archaeologists we need to avoid creating a rupture that does not exist between past and present. Separating out the past and present serves to deny the ongoing process of change that connects the two together and only serves to create a rupture that we then have to overcome. These processes of change, and time itself, operate on many differing scales, from the incredibly slow to the incredibly rapid, and it is to the relationship between time and scale that I turn in the next chapter.

Note

1 It is worth noting that geologists do not see the fossil record as frozen.

Bibliography

Ascher, R. 1961. Analogy in archaeological interpretation. *Southwestern Journal of Anthropology* 17: 317–325.
Barrett, J. 1999. The mythical landscape of the British Iron Age, in Ashmore, W. and Knapp, A. (eds), *Archaeologies of Landscape: Contemporary Perspectives*. Oxford: Blackwell: pp 253–265.
Bayliss, A., Bronk Ramsey, C., van der Plicht, J. and Whittle, A. 2007. Bradshaw and Bayes: towards a timetable for the Neolithic. *Cambridge Archaeological Journal* 17(S1): 1–28.
Binford, L. 1964. A consideration of archaeological research design. *American Antiquity* 29(4): 217–225.
Binford, L. 1975. Sampling judgement and the archaeological record, in Mueller, J. (ed), *Sampling in Archaeology*. Tucson: University of Arizona: pp. 251–257.
Binford, L. 1977. General introduction, in Binford, L. (ed), *Theory Building in Archaeology: Essays on Faunal Remains, Aquatic Resources, Spatial Analysis, and Systematic Modelling*. New York: Academic Press: pp. 1–13.
Binford, L. 1981. Behavioural archaeology and the 'Pompeii Premise'. *Journal of Anthropological Research* 37: 195–208.
Bradley, R. 1998. *The Significance of Monuments: On the Shaping of Human Experience in Neolithic and Bronze Age Europe*. London: Routledge.
Bradley, R. 2002. *The Past in Prehistoric Societies*. London: Routledge.
Curry, P. and de Montmollin, O. 1987. Time and archaeology. *Archaeological Review from Cambridge* 6(1): 2–4.
Gell, A. 2001. *The Anthropology of Time: Cultural Constructions of Temporal Maps and Images*. Oxford: Berg.
González-Ruibal, A. 2006. The past is tomorrow: towards an archaeology of the vanishing present. *Norwegian Archaeological Review* 39(2): 110–125.
Gosden, C. 1994. *Social Being and Time*. Oxford: Blackwell.
Hamilakis, Y. 2013. *Archaeology and the Senses: Human Experience, Memory and Affect*. Cambridge: Cambridge University Press.
Harris, O.J.T. and Cipolla, C. 2017. *Archaeological Theory in the New Millennium: Introducing Current Perspectives*. London: Routledge.
Heidegger, M. 1962. *Being and Time*. Oxford: Blackwell.

Hicks, D. 2016. The temporality of the landscape revisited. *Norwegian Archaeological Review* 49: 5–22.

Ingold, T. 1993. The temporality of landscape. *World Archaeology* 25(2): 152–174.

Ingold, T. 2000. *Perception of the Environment: Essays in Livelihood, Dwelling and Skill*. London: Routledge.

Johnson, M. 2010. *Archaeological Theory: An Introduction*. Malden: Wiley-Blackwell.

Latour, B. 1993. *We Have Never Been Modern*. Cambridge: Harvard University Press.

Lowenthal, D. 1985. *The Past is a Foreign Country*. Cambridge: Cambridge University Press.

Lucas, G. 2005. *An Archaeology of Time*. London: Routledge.

Lucas, G. 2012. *Understanding the Archaeological Record*. Cambridge: Cambridge University Press.

McGlade, J. 1999. The times of history: archaeology, narrative and non-linear causality, in Murray, T. (ed), *Time and Archaeology*. London: Routledge: pp. 139–163.

Merleau-Ponty, M. 1962. *The Phenomenology of Perception*. London: Routledge and Kegan Paul.

Morgan, L.H. 1877. *Ancient Society: Researches in the Lines of Human Progress from Savagery Through Barbarism to Civilization*. London: MacMillan and Co.

Nativ, A. 2018. On the object of archaeology. *Archaeological Dialogues* 25(1): 1–21.

Olivier, L. 2004. The past of the present: archaeological memory and time. *Archaeological Dialogues* 10(2): 204–213.

Olivier, L. 2011. *The Dark Abyss of Time: Archaeology and Memory*. Plymouth: Alta Mira Press.

Olsen, B., Shanks, M., Webmoor, T. and Witmore, C. 2012. *Archaeology: The Discipline of Things*. Berkeley: University of California Press.

Patrik, L. 1985. Is there an archaeological record? *Advances in Archaeological Method and Theory* 8:27–62.

Robb, J. and Pauketat, T. 2013. From moments to millennia: theorising scale and change in human history, in Robb, J. and Pauketat, T.R. (eds), *Big Histories, Human Lives*. Santa Fe: SAR Press: pp. 3–33.

Schiffer, M. 1972. Archaeological context and systemic context. *American Antiquity* 37(2): 156–165.

Schiffer, M. 1975. Archaeology as behavioural science. *American Anthropologist* 77(4): 836–848.

Schiffer, M. 1976. *Behavioural Archaeology*. New York: Academic Press.

Schiffer, M. 1983. Towards the identification of formation processes. *American Antiquity* 48 (4): 675–706.

Schiffer, M. 1985. Is there a 'Pompeii Premise' in archaeology? *Journal of Anthropological Research* 41: 18–41.

Schiffer, M. and Rathje, W. 1973. Efficient exploitation of the archaeological record: penetrating problems, inRedman, C. (ed), *Research and Theory in Current Archaeology*. New York: Wiley: pp. 169–179.

Serres, M. with Latour, B. 1995. *Conversations on Science, Culture and Time*. Ann Arbor: University of Michigan.

Shanks, M. and Tilley, C. 1987a. Abstract and substantial time. *Archaeological Review from Cambridge* 6: 32–41.

Shanks, M. and Tilley, C. 1987b. *Social Theory and Archaeology*. Cambridge: Polity.

Thomas, J. 1996. *Time, Culture and Identity*. London: Routledge.

Thomas, J. 2004. *Archaeology and Modernity*. London: Routledge.

Tilley, C. 1994. *A Phenomenology of Landscape: Places, Paths, and Monuments*. Oxford: Berg.

Webmoor, T. and Witmore, C. 2008. Things Are Us! A commentary on human/thing relations under the banner of a 'Social Archaeology'. *Norwegian Archaeological Review* 41: 1–18.

Witmore, C.L. 2006. Vision, Media, Noise and the Percolation of Time: Symmetrical Approaches to the Mediation of the Material World. *Journal of Material Culture* 11: 267–292.

Witmore, C.L. 2007a. Symmetrical archaeology: excerpts of a manifesto. *World Archaeology* 39: 546–562.

Witmore, CL.. 2007b. Landscape, time, topology: an archaeological account of the Southern Argolid, Greece, in Hicks, D., McAtackney, E. and Fairclough, G. (eds), *Envisioning Landscape: Situations and Standpoints in Archaeology and Heritage*. Walnut Creek: Left Coast Press.

4

SCALES OF CHANGE

In Chapter 3 I considered how our approaches to, and understandings of, time impact upon the study of change. I explored how a unilinear, universal, and directed model of time has supported progressive and teleological models of change. I argued that creating a gap between past and present is unhelpful as it creates problems in our analysis: when we divide past and present, we sever the ongoing processes of change. I noted that our anthropocentrism leads us to suggest, falsely, that the archaeological record is not only disconnected from the present but also static: because we place it apart from human action in the present, we presume it does not change. The chapter also explored the debates that began in the 1980s about the different ways in which time and temporality emerge and how these arguments attempted to move beyond a situation where chronology becomes explanation (though, as Robb and Pauketat (2013a: 18) have highlighted, the post-processual concern with time came at the expense of the exploration of change). In this chapter we turn our attention specifically to the issue of scale, a theme that underwrote much of the discussion in the previous chapter but deserves our direct attention now.

This chapter explores a range of approaches to scale and how these intersect with our approach to change and the politics of archaeology more broadly. I argue that when we talk about scale we either tend to oscillate between the grand and the local, or we opt for a tripart model that focuses on small, medium, and large scales. I will argue that both the dichotomous and 'nested' readings of scale are too simplistic and mask the complexity of how scales of analysis, time, and space relate to each other. I begin by exploring the politics of our scales of analysis. I then turn to studies that deal with the large scale. Archaeology's timescale is vast, with millions of years of hominin history at our disposal: how do those working in what we might term 'the deep past', at timescales that are largely incomprehensible to us today, approach the issue of change? I then move on to explore approaches that integrate scales of analysis, namely the *Annales* School and Time Perspectivism. I argue that both approaches, despite their calls for multiple scales of analysis, ultimately privilege the long term and environmental in their narrative. I then discuss the work of post-processualists who used structure and agency as a way to focus upon small scales of analysis. Shrinking the scale further, I discuss the impact that Bayesian modelling is having on our debates about scale in archaeology. Proponents suggest that Bayesian modelling can even bring an end to the concept of prehistory, allowing prehistoric archaeologists to become 'historians' (Whittle, 2018: 1; 18; Whittle et al., 2011: 911). Having thought about both forms of analysis that privilege the large and the small scales, I close the chapter by considering how different scales of analysis relate together.

In this chapter I argue that many of our debates about scale are structured by the nature–culture dualism. The nature–culture dualism is a pervasive western way of thinking that suggests that nature and culture are separate and opposed entities. As discussed in Chapter 1, dualisms do not reflect reality, but are a product of a particular (and damaging) way of thinking (Thomas, 2004). In this chapter I will explore a series of approaches to differing scales of analysis and demonstrate how they are trapped in unhelpful dualisms.

Why does scale matter?

Scale matters because it is political. We can characterise the shift from the new archaeology to post-processualism as a shift from emphasising the large to the small scale in archaeological narratives. This was a political shift. We moved from trying to understand the processes of human history at the largest and thereby, a new archaeologist would argue, most important scale of analysis, to working at a range of smaller scales down to the individual (cf. Hodder, 2000; Meskell, 1998) in order, a post-processualist would argue, to avoid believing we could speak for all people at all times. Both sides of this debate believed that their scale of analysis was the correct one and this contributed to the heated debate that emerged as different archaeologists aimed to effectively shape, and thereby define, the discipline.

John Robb and Tim Pauketat recently published an edited volume specifically focusing on the integration of what they term "big histories" with "human lives" (Robb and Pauketat, 2013b; cf. Jones, 2012: 35–36). The book focuses attention on the need to integrate the different scales of time, narratives, and data that archaeology deals with to move beyond the divisive processual vs post-processual debate about scale. Robb and Pauketat (2013a: 5; 17 and the other authors in the volume; see also, Jones, 2012: 36; Robb, 2007: 287) identify how post-processualism resulted in a turn away from large-scale analysis and an emphasis on the local as a result of a fear of determinism and the risks associated with what we can term metanarratives – over-arching, totalising, and singular explanations. Chris Gosden (2013: 207) argues that metanarratives are often written following the logic of western common sense (see also Gosden, 1994: 165): he takes the example of Darwin's 'survival of the fittest' theory and argues that it is essentially the logic of capitalism applied to all living things. Writing metanarratives and grand narratives is always loaded with risk as it is inherently political. Susan Pollock (2013: 146) parallels large-scale histories with Foucault's panopticon – the construction that surveys every person's every move. For Pollock (2013: 146) long-term histories are often teleological, masculinist, and elitist; they serve only to justify the world as it is for its winners and losers. Any large-scale history has to have a narrator, and that narrator occupies a position of power that often goes unacknowledged (Pollock, 2013: 146). Robb (2013: 31) talks about this in terms of the process of generalisation; any generalisation necessarily involves the selection of specific information and in making such choices we shape the histories we tell (and do not tell) – he argues ultimately that we all generalise and therefore we would do better to theorise this and be explicit about it.

In spite of this risk, Robb and Pauketat (2013a) argue:

> To put the matter as simply as possible: large-scale, long-term patterns exist, and if we do not deal with them well, others will deal with them badly. It is not enough to decry self-serving metanarratives of colonialism, technological progressivism, civilization, or primitivism from the safety of the ivory tower; we need to give the public other histories to think with and about.
>
> *(Robb and Pauketat, 2013a: 5)*

Pollock's (2013: 146) argument takes a different shape: we need to specifically consider why it is that we are interested in the largest scale and what we are trying to understand. She argues there is no imperative to engage with the large scale in the way that Robb and Pauketat (2013a) suggest; rather we need to consider specifically why we want to engage with it (Pollock, 2013). She argues that we might want to engage with large-scale debates so we can intervene in public discourse to offer 'better' narratives, but that if we do we must accept that we are saying our narratives are the better ones and should therefore guide future policy. From this position she argues we should not produce the coherent and comfortable long-term narrative that legitimates the present, but instead deal with the uncomfortable, focusing on the unpleasant, and considering how things could have been different. I agree with Pollock's (2013) analysis, though I do not think that means we should avoid the grand narrative. I also argue that when we focus on critiquing large-scale histories, we are effectively letting small-scale histories 'off the hook' and suggesting that they too are not powerful or political.

Change in the deep past

I focus first on large-scale narratives and approaches to change. There are few larger scales of analysis than the Palaeolithic, which spans more than two million years and makes up the bulk of human history – clearly, we cannot avoid writing long-term histories of this period. Writing narratives of change in the Palaeolithic is, however, very challenging. Taphonomy means that human remains are often partial or nonexistent, and 'settlement' evidence can be scarce. Moreover, how does one write an effective narrative of change that addresses a period so long it is hard to even imagine? Archaeologists of the following periods, like myself, often effectively ignore the Palaeolithic; we place a box around it labelled 'the deep past', marking it as different from what we do: as a result we 'Other' it. This does not serve us well, as it effectively cleaves off a large block of time as outside our analyses and reinforces a block-time approach. In addition to these problems the nature–culture dualism has heavily shaped our approaches to change in the Palaeolithic.

In Chapter 1 I argued that often when we tell origin-oriented narratives about change the underlying current of the debate is about defining what it means to be human. This is a product not just of our emphasis on origins as a means of definition, but also of the relationship between the long term and the political. Chris Gosden (1994: 169–172) has argued that our own political context influences the types of long-term narratives we write (see also Gamble, 2007: 26). For example, post-World War II political debate focused on combating racism in reaction to the holocaust, and as a result grand narratives addressed universalism, highlighting what we shared in common; similarly, the rise of feminism from the 1960s led to a critique of long-term narratives such as 'man the hunter'.

Talking about the 'deep' human past means defining what it is to be human, an inherently political act. When does *human* history begin? Authors such as Gosden (1994: 167–169) and anthropologist Tim Ingold (2000: 362–372; 373–391) have highlighted how narratives about the beginning of human history are often structured by a nature–culture divide. When archaeologists talk about the processes of change for humans we generally refer to them as human history – whereas the processes by which other creatures change are referred to as evolution. Human history is often presented as standing outside evolution: human change is therefore presented as exceptional and ontologically distinct from that which occurs to other living things. Ingold (2000: 374) writes perceptively about how long-term narratives of human change are written as though the biological processes of evolution drove change up to the point at which our ancestors became *anatomically modern*, but that evolution stopped at that point and history took over. As Ingold (2000: 376) demonstrates, it is not the case that our biology has not change since we became *modern*, rather our bodies have continued to constantly change and evolve; the development of lactase persistence in European populations as an adaptation to the continued consumption of dairy products is an example (Itan et al., 2009).

The potency of technological determinism can be explained within this same frame. One of the ways to classically separate, and ontologically elevate, humans above other species is the idea that our use of technology makes us different from other animals. Indeed, eighteenth- and nineteenth-century evolutionary anthropologists considered how technology has become more complex over time, allowing humans an ever greater 'mastery' of nature (Ingold, 2000: 312). While much has changed since then, Ingold (2000: 366) argues that it is remarkable that many anthropologists still discuss 'simple' and 'complex' technologies. The issue of scale is pertinent here: there is an undeniable shift from simple to complex if we take the widest frame and compare early Oldowan stone choppers with Australian Aboriginal glass Kimberley points, but this is a frame where we are comparing different species and failing to consider detail. When we take the more detailed view, the simple to complex narrative falls apart in the face of the complexity of the evidence[1].

Clive Gamble's book *Origins and Revolutions* is one of the most detailed and sustained critiques of how archaeologists approach change. Gamble (2007) claims that much of our thinking about change in the deep past is structured by a place he terms 'Originsland'. Originsland is the place we look to in order to explain our present human condition; archaeologists did not invent Originsland, but they have colonised it (Gamble, 2007: 62). The Palaeolithic period provides the origin point for our discipline (Gamble and Gittins, 2004) and the landscape of our Palaeolithic Originsland is shaped by a series of concepts and values to do with what it means to be human (tool use, cognitive abilities etc.). In order that we might tell directed master narratives about human history as progress, we have to give a specific shape to Originsland to provide the basis from which we can define our species and the start point of our narrative. Originsland contains more than just the Palaeolithic though, as it is structured by two revolutions: the human revolution where we received our endowment as a species and the Neolithic revolution where we grew into civilised, sedentary citizens (Gamble, 2007: 81–82). Gamble argues the human revolution is about a change in cognition, whereas the Neolithic revolution is about social change. The revolutions that structure Originsland map neatly onto the nature–culture divide discussed above.

The use of either biological or technological change to define what it means to be human is captured in the historical debate that surrounds the issue of when we became human – often referred to as the Human Revolution (Mellars and Stringer, 1989). This debate focused on locating the moment in our evolution when we believe people in the past belong within the same identity group as ourselves. For different academics this transition (or, more commonly, revolution) occurred at different points in time, in different places – many adopted a check-list approach through which they aimed to identify whether or not a particular hominin species is sufficiently like ourselves (for example, Klein, 1995; McBrearty and Brooks, 2000; Mellars, 2005; Stringer and Andrews, 1988). Calling this transition a revolution seems foolhardy given the timescales involved. The pivot-point in the debate was whether we defined the body (and biology) as the key thing that makes us human, or whether it is cultural practice (tool making, art, and imagery) that makes us human. As Gamble (2007: 36; cf. Ingold, 2000: 373–391) argues, the term *anatomically modern human* is a hybrid term that has emerged to deal with the contradictions we find between archaeological and anatomical evidence – we find skeletal remains that suggest a body like ours but cultural practices different from our own. The term itself may now fall out of favour as research increasingly reveals the complexity of evolution and the diversity within species (Editorial, 2018). When we work at the large scale, it is clear that the divide between nature and culture clearly shapes the debate about human origins.

Gamble's detailed critique of the narratives that emerge from Originsland provides the foundation for a radical new approach. He argues for an embodied approach to technology that sees humans and the material world as deeply entangled – technology weaves together the material, social, and symbolic and plays a key role in the construction of our identities (Gamble, 2007: 158–159). This position on technology holds much in common with phenomenologically inspired approaches (there is a close parallel with some of Ingold's (2000) arguments about the relationship between technology, bodies, and skill). Relating technology back to the body allows Gamble to move beyond allowing either biology or technology (nature or culture) to structure the debate about what makes us human and which are the key revolutions in our past. Gamble is explicitly theoretical in this approach: it is not about what new data can tell us but rather about how framing the existing data differently allows a new narrative to emerge.

Another problem with this debate surrounding the 'human revolution' is that it takes the 'modern human' as a yardstick and asks how hominins at other times measure up: the comparison is always unfavourable, as they are always lacking something (cf. debates about humanism in Chapter 7). The error here is to presume that what defines a human is static and singular, rather than always changing and in process. It is the same form of debate that compares Indigenous people unfavourably to colonisers, who are presented as more civilised and thereby more human, and compares women unfavourably to men, who are presented as more rational and intelligent. We would do better to steer away from attempting to define an origin point for humans as it serves to devalue diversity within and between species and suggests that there is some static, essential form of humanity. Such criteria might be helpful with issues of definition, but they are always also damaging. Instead we should focus on painting detailed, nuanced, and changing histories of what it means to be human.

The *Annales* school and archaeology

The issue of integrating the broad sweep of history into narratives that also make space for the lives of past communities has been a perennial problem for archaeologists. How do we tell stories that demonstrate patterns of changing technology over thousands of years yet also leave space for moments, revealed in the archaeological record, such as the sharpening of an axe prior to deposition in a hoard? Jan Harding (2005: 91) suggests there have been two contrasting approaches to this issue: one is to draw inspiration from historians and the other is to draw inspiration from anthropologists. This section explores first the ideas of *Annales* School historians and the related time perspectivism, both approaches that seek to integrate scales of analysis, but, as we shall see, often conclude with the large-scale dominating explanation.

The *Annales* School is most readily associated with the work of Fernand Braudel. Braudel (1972) and his fellow *Annales* historians argue that there are different layers to history which operate at differing temporalities and scales: the short-term *événement* of history (or what we might term events), the medium-term *conjonctures* of structural history, and the *longue durée* of geographical time. The *longue durée* consists primarily of the changes that occur to the environment, which are slow changes that stand somewhat outside the influence of people. The medium term consists of structural changes to society, the economy, and the rise and fall of states and civilisations; here patterns emerge over centuries. In contrast, the short-term *événement* is most readily associated with the daily lives of individuals. These three different layers operate contemporaneously and are always in contact. The different layers have different temporal rhythms to them and as a result produce different types of history. The *longue durée's* emphasis on the environment mean that it effectively focuses on nature, while the *événement* and *conjonctures* scales focus upon human culture and history.

The ideas of Braudel have influenced a range of archaeologists and most especially those who work in the Mediterranean, which was one of the main focuses of Braudel's own work (see, for example, Barker, 1995; Bintliff, 1991; Knapp, 1992). The particular influence of Braudel's ideas in the 1990s was a product of their potential to bring together processualists and post-processualists by combining both the long-term processes of history and the short-term reality of experienced life (Harding, 2005: 92). Harding (2005) also suggests the absence of explicit theoretical models within the *Annales* framework was also appealing to some in the wake of the heated theoretical debates of the 1980s.

The long-term influence of the *Annales* approach has, however, been limited, as it has attracted a significant amount of critique.[2] The most common critique argues that the *longue durée* tends to dominate historical explanation, leaving little space for human agency (see, for example, Barker, 1995: 3; McGlade, 1999: 146; Thomas, 1996: 36). Braudel (1972: 1244) himself commented that "the long run always wins in the end". While the initial appeal of the *Annales* School might have been as a way past the processual vs post-processual antagonism, the environmental determinism associated with the *longue durée* clearly posed a challenge to many post-processualists. Harding's (2005: 95) analysis goes further and argues that the emphasis on the long term results in historical and structural processes effectively existing outside, and separate from, history and agency. This issue was further compounded by what archaeologists saw as Braudel's failure to interweave the different scales of analysis effectively (Barker, 1995: 3; Robb and Pauketat, 2013: 12). McGlade (1999: 147) argues that there is also a failure to understand that the different layers include within them differing (and multiple) temporalities and rates of change. Robb and Pauketat (2013a: 12) have recently shifted the direction of the critique once more, arguing that the *Annales* School rests upon a simplistic nature–culture dichotomy where the long-term environment is placed outside historical and cultural factors.

Time perspectivism

Many archaeologists view Geoff Bailey's (1981; 1987; 2007) work on time perspectivism as drawing upon the *Annales* School (for example, Bintliff, 1991;

Harding, 2005) though Bailey himself disagrees, arguing that while there are points of contact between the two, they are actually rather different. Bailey (1987:17; 2007) states that time perspectivism is a way of working specifically designed for archaeologists. His early definition[3] of time perspectivism defines it as: "the belief that differing timescales bring into focus different features of behaviour, requiring different sorts of explanatory principles" (Bailey, 1981: 103). He argues that multiple timescales exist and that different timescales bring into focus differing processes that require different types of archaeological questions and concepts (Bailey, 1987: 7). Rather than being a simple identification of the existence of different timescales Bailey is directly concerned with the nature of archaeological evidence. He argues that his work on time perspectivism was provoked by three factors: first, the coarse temporal resolution of archaeological data; second, the idea that the great time depth available to archaeologists might make processes visible that do not appear at smaller scales; and third, that the boundary between past and present was arbitrary (Bailey, 2007: 199). The basic argument suggests that the fragmentary nature of archaeological data, the poor nature of the chronological control we have over that data (i.e. that our dates for events can have ±100 year date ranges), and the time depth at our disposal means that the theories and methods of anthropology and history are inappropriate for archaeological analysis. Instead archaeology requires a different way of working that reflects the nature of archaeological evidence; furthermore, the nature of our evidence directly affects the types of questions we are able to ask about the past (Bailey, 2007: 199). Bailey (1987: 16) argues for a complex relationship between the different timescales and scales of analysis available to archaeologists; he suggests processes at any one scale cannot be "reduced to, or deduced from" processes at other scales.

The 'perspective' in time perspectivism emphasises the need to reject an egocentric view of the past where we understand it from the location of the present (Bailey, 1987: 6; 2007: 202). Instead, the argument is that the past looks different and is distorted in different ways from different perspectives. We are asked to view the past not only on multiple timescales but also from various positions (Bailey, 1987: 6). Bailey (2007: 210–211) considers the example of mountain and hill erosion processes in Greece; he looks at how the scale of the data being examined reveals different causal relationships. At one scale of analysis we relate these erosion processes to changes in the overgrazing of goats and overcultivation of the land, whereas if we take a longer timescale, and look back into the Palaeolithic, erosion events on an even grander scale are obvious, and these cannot be related to goats and agriculture. One could see this, once again, as a nature–culture divide where, when the timescale expands, nature governs change.

Bailey (2007) suggests that time perspectivism is best implemented through analysis of the palimpsest nature of the material world. Palimpsests were originally documents that were worked and reworked in such a way as to erase some of their earlier text. Bailey (2007: 203–209) builds a strong case, by bringing together definitions of multiple types of palimpsest, that all archaeological evidence is a palimpsest. This includes traditional readings of sites where the final use erases earlier uses; sites where many sequential uses merge together in a manner that makes them inseparable; spatial palimpsests, sites that bring together objects from multiple periods to form temporal palimpsests; and even a reworking of the concept of object biography as effectively forming a palimpsest of meaning. The many different types of archaeological palimpsests require different types of research questions, which should be suited to the scales at which they operate and the nature of the data within them.

We can critique time perspectivism, like the *Annales* approach, for being environmentally determinist. For Bailey (2007) this is another misunderstanding of time perspectivism and he argues that it is not environmentally determinist. He suggests that some of the reaction against the approach is because determinism is effectively an affront to our identity as humans with free will: people do not want to believe that there are processes going on beyond their consciousness over which they have no control (Bailey, 2007: 214). Lucas (2005: 47–48) has argued that Bailey conflates the timespan of archaeology with the chronological resolution of the data – it is not the case that we cannot see fine-grained chronological resolution in the past. As a result, Lucas argues that we do not need to confine ourselves to models of change that focus upon large timescales. Lucas (2005: 47–49) further criticises time perspectivism for its emphasis on chronological time as opposed to 'narrative' or 'real' time. Similarly, Harding (2005: 88) suggests both the *Annales* and time perspectivism approaches are disconnected from any sense of temporality and the social context in which time gains its meaning. Both the *Annales* approach and time perspectivism have failed to gain sustained traction as approaches to writing change (particularly outside the Mediterranean), though it is not uncommon to see people refer to the *longue durée* across archaeologies drawing upon different theoretical perspectives. From my perspective, what both the *Annales* and time perspectivism approaches share is that they effectively separate natural and cultural processes as different types of change; the reality is that these two kinds of change are always interwoven. More troublingly, the resulting narratives often feel environmentally deterministic.

On the interplay between structure and event

Shifting the focus from larger-scale analytical frameworks drawn from history we now consider smaller-scale analytical frameworks more influenced by anthropologists. The influence of anthropology on archaeology has arguably been greater than that of history, most especially in the Americas, whereas archaeology sits firmly within the four-field, but also more broadly as a result of post-processualism (see, for example, Alberti et al., 2011; Garrow and Yarrow, 2010; Gosden, 1999). Ethnographic fieldwork involves long-term participant observation, but anthropology's long-term is archaeology's instant. As a result, there are very few anthropological studies that deal with change over the long term that archaeologists can draw upon. Those that do focus on change are often what, to archaeological eyes at least, appears to be rapid change through processes like colonialism and modernity (Robb, 2007: 292). For archaeologists working over the longer term, rapid change certainly has an effect but there are also slower processes of change at play that have wide-ranging effects: for example, Robb (2007: 292) describes how within the context of a small village a 1 per cent increase in birth rate would be unremarkable or unrecognised within an ethnographic timescale, but over the course of 70 years it could double a population.

The concepts of structure and agency were introduced in Chapter 2, but here we consider the approach in more depth and its relationship to scale. Agency can be used to change (or maintain) the structures that people live within and those structures act to enable (and restrain) the effects of agency (for a review see Robb, 2010). Harding (2005: 89) suggests that debates about agency have played out at two opposed scales; he contrasts Ian Hodder's (1990) *The Domestication of Europe* with John Barrett's (1994) *Fragments from Antiquity* to illustrate his point. Hodder's (1990) work, focusing on the long-term development of social institutions across Europe, emphasises the power of the structure rather than the individual event, whereas Barrett's (1994) discussion of changing social relations and practices in Neolithic and Bronze Age Britain focuses on the power of routine, event, and agency, which act to create structure. Effectively these are two different models of writing history: top-down and bottom-up (see McGlade, 1999: 147–148).

As post-processualist thinking around agency and structure continued to develop, the focus shifted towards the increasing use of bottom-up approaches that emphasised the role of individual actions in the shaping of structure. Gosden (1994), focusing on long-term change, outlines an approach that draws upon what he terms "acts". Gosden (1994: 15–16) argues that all acts contain links to other acts, separated from them in time and space: for example, when we choose to either repeat practice or alter practice we are always making a reference to other acts in different times and places.[4] Gosden also argues that our acts are structured by longer-term frameworks of which we are less consciously aware, including the shape of landscapes and historically specific forms of relationships. Gosden (1994: 17) appears to be indirectly referencing the effect of the *longue durée* on the shorter term but overall the focus remains on how our acts form networks of action. This is an approach that places the locus of change within short-term acts associated with human agency but tries to leave space for longer-term processes too.

Robb (2007) takes a related approach in *The Early Mediterranean Village*. He argues for a multiscalar approach to unravelling change across the Neolithic in the Mediterranean. Robb (2007: 287) specifically suggests that we lack the concepts to bridge the gap between ethnographic timeframes and archaeological ones. He is an advocate for understanding the world through a dialectic between individual choices and the conditions within which people live. Despite this he argues that the key scale for understanding the historical workings of practice is not decades and nor is it millennia, but is instead in "the order of a few centuries" (Robb, 2007: 294). He argues that at such a scale change is a mix of innovation and transition, which at times will appear inseparable. Robb argues (2007: 294–295; 322; see also, Robb, 2013; Robb and Harris, 2013) against the idea that we can identify simplistic or monocausational explanations for any particular set of changes in the archaeological record (a position I share; see chapters 1 and 7). The result is that dividing the past into neat periods, with a before and after and a clear transition, becomes impossible – this effectively rejects block-time approaches. While Robb (2007) clearly advocates for the importance of individual agency as an engine of change *and* stability, he is arguing for a longer timeframe of analysis to allow us to effectively study changes in the archaeological record.

In *The Body in History* (Robb and Harris, 2013) we can see the further development of these ideas. The book tells the long-term history of the human body in Europe from the Palaeolithic to the present day, structured through chapters addressing different archaeological periods. The result is a staged narrative, but the authors argue strongly in the closing chapter that "change happened through ongoing tinkering with variations possible within the inherited repertoire" (Robb and Harris, 2013: 218) – we might express this as agency within structure. This is demonstrated in the detail – one of the key examples of this draws upon Sørensen and Rebay-Salisbury's (2008) study of the Austrian Bronze Age cemetery site of Pitten, spanning a time when burial practices shifted from inhumation to cremation. This is undoubtedly a significant and major change, and if we zoom out we can use this to separate out the flow of change into two periods – one characterised by inhumation, the other by cremation. This is often discussed within Bronze Age studies as representing a shift in religious beliefs and thereby understandings of the body (see, for example, Harding, 1994: 130–132), yet the analysis of 235 burials from Pitten dating from 1600–1350BC that evidence both practices shows the complexity and messiness of this process of change. The analysis demonstrates the variety in practice throughout this process and suggests the inhumation–cremation divide may have been less important than the divide between whether one was buried *in* the ground or *on* the ground surface with a mound built over them. Harris et al. (2013: 90–91) argue that cremation was not necessarily viewed as radically different from inhumation as the processes through which both types of burial were produced actually had a great many similarities and points of contact; for example, cremated bodies were often buried in the same ways as inhumations (see also Appleby, 2013). This use of fine-grained detail allows the authors to move beyond a simple model that 'inhumation replaced cremation as the dominant rite' and show instead a messy process of change, where small changes in the repertoire of what was possible resulted in what, when we zoom out, appears to be a marked transition between two different forms of practice.

Harding (2005), in his work on scale discussed earlier, develops an approach with some similarities and some key divergences. Having critiqued *Annales* approaches he chooses to focus on how "complex networks of mnemonic and anticipatory relations are played out as part of specific social practices" (Harding, 2005: 97). In this call to the mnemonic and the anticipatory we can see links to Gosden's (1994) arguments that acts fold within them past acts and the sense of a future and Robb's (2007; see also Robb and Harris, 2013) argument about making choices within existing conditions. The thinking diverges though as Harding (2005: 97–98) advocates for models of causality as a means of creating a "meaningful and coherent narrative", the implication being that if we do not explore causality, what emerges is a directionless and incoherent series of events. Harding (2005: 97–98) argues that we should be tracing the genealogies of specific social entities and institutions, looking to identify their point of departure, process of change, and point of completion. This is a very different, problem-oriented approach that would certainly give shape and direction to our narratives, as it is clear that if we trace the genealogies of institutions we would have to make specific choices about what we focus on and what we leave aside. Tracing the descent of institutions could clearly be a powerful theoretical and political tool, but the suggestion that given phenomena have clear emergence and completion points is questionable.

Approaches that focus on structure and agency specifically aimed to put the people back into the past. Their focus was on peopling the past with humans whose lives we could relate to. A simplistic analysis presents this as a swing away from large-scale narratives, often driven by 'nature' towards smaller-scale narratives, driven by 'culture'. This is, on many levels, an unfair characterisation, as we can clearly see in the work of those such as Gosden (1994), Harding (2005), and Robb (2007) a concern to integrate both the larger scale as well as the human level. Robb and Harris's (2013) work on the human body shows it is possible to use an approach grounded in ideas of structure and agency to tell long-term histories. Structure and agency offer a way of integrating scales of analysis, though I do think that we more readily associate structure with long-term human institutions than we do with what we might term 'natural processes'.

Changing time scales: Bayesian analysis

We shift scale once more to consider the emergent calls for a more fine-grained scale of analysis than structure and agency. Bayesian statistical analysis (a mathematical technique applied in a range of fields) is an increasingly common way of modelling date ranges to include 'prior beliefs' (things we already know) about the material under study. The result is usually a reduction in the date range allowing analysis at the generational scale when applied to radiocarbon dates (see Bayliss et al., 2011: 19–21). Bayesian analysis has been referred to as the fourth radiocarbon revolution (Bayliss, 2009; Bronk Ramsey, 2008; Griffiths, 2017) due to the impact it is having on our understanding of the chronological sequence of the past. Within the European Neolithic particularly, the remodelling of dates is opening the door to more detailed understandings of the sequence of events (see, for example Whitehouse et al., 2014; Whittle et al., 2011; Whittle, 2018). Proponents of Bayesian analysis argue that the ability to model dates in this manner calls for a whole new way of writing the past (see, for example, Griffiths, 2017; Whittle, 2018; Whittle et al., 2008; 2011).

Those at the forefront of this field of research are not just arguing for Bayesian analysis because it results in more precise, detailed, and shorter-term chronologies, but are making wider, and indeed theoretical, arguments about the need for Bayesian modelling as a corrective to our current narratives. Alasdair Whittle

et al. (2008: 65) argue that post-processualism struggles to talk about both gen-
erational-scale analyses as well as more long-term histories, suggesting that unless
archaeologists have some special access to fine-grained chronologies (for example,
through text or excellent dendrochronology, citing Foxhall (2000) and Van Dyke
(2004) as examples), they tend to ignore the short term. Whittle et al. (2011: 1)
describe the current narratives of prehistory as "fuzzy" as a result of the lack of
fine-grained dating evidence; they suggest this results in a "smearing" of change
so that what might really be rapid and dramatic change is smeared over centuries.
Whittle (2018: 248) argues that archaeologists have come to rely on generalisation. As a result, focusing upon the long term has become the default for pre-
historians and produces gradual models of change that Whittle et al. (2011: 910)
most readily link to the environment, in contrast to the shorter-term *social* history
they call for. Their rallying cry is for detail to overcome generalisation (Whittle et
al., 2008: 66).

What then does Bayesian analysis offer us? Bayliss et al. (2017: 1174) argue that
the precise chronologies that emerge from Bayesian modelling allow us to "characterise the timing and duration of different types of phenomena, and then to
combine these into a much more differentiated narrative than previously available".
Across multiple publications those working on two big Bayesian dating projects,
Gathering Time – focusing on the start of the Neolithic in Britain – and *Times of
their Lives* – focusing on European Neolithic chronologies – call for the demonstration of more complex and messy patterns of change (see, for example, Bayliss et
al., 2017; Ebersbach et al., 2017; Griffiths, 2017; Hoffman et al., 2017; Whittle,
2018; Whittle et al., 2011). The argument is that the detail that emerges from
Bayesian modelling allows us to tell stories on a generational scale, which disrupts
the "fuzzy" broad-brush-strokes narrative we have been writing to date. Whittle
(2018: 247) argues that he works at multiple timescales, and while he sees no particular scale (or combination of scales) as correct he finds the generational scale to
be the "most illuminating" as it allows him to see actions over a lifetime and piece
together long-term change. Bayesian analysis is suggested to provide the data we
need to explore agency and the choices of individuals and communities in real
detail (Whittle et al., 2011: 4). With such dates at our disposal, timing and tempo
emerge in new ways – the order of events and speed of events become obvious
from within the "smear" of prehistory. For those advocates of the approach,
sequence reveals causation.

Whittle et al. (2011: 911) argue that Bayesian dating will allow us to "abolish"
prehistory as a term and move beyond the need to talk of the *longue durée*. Instead,
they argue that the

> possibility of multiple narratives, of the unfoldings of changes of fortune, and
> of all the 'retentions and protentions' along the sliding line of time, must be
> faced by archaeologists concerned with the deep past as much as by historians
> of more recent periods.
>
> *(Whittle et al., 2011: 911)*

Various authors have also suggested that the development of new, more detailed, Bayesian-derived, histories stand in opposition to, or are incompatible with, the recent relational turn in archaeological theory (discussed in chapters 6 and 7) (Drașovean et al., 2017; Ebersbach et al., 2017: 13; Hoffman et al., 2016; Whittle, 2018: 145–150). Ebersbach et al. (2017: 13) and Drașovean et al. (2017: 637) both argue against the adoption of relational frameworks on the basis that such theories extend agency beyond the human. Their arguments suggest that Bayesian analysis has finally given us the chance to write detailed histories of human agency and therefore "we do not want to surrender the opportunity to write detailed histories ... detailed narratives with plot driven by people – just when these begin to come within our grasp" (Drașovean et al., 2017: 637). This is an interesting turn in the debate: for proponents of relational and posthumanist theories, as we shall see in chapters 6 and 7, agency has never been limited to humans alone, so whether or not our chronologies are detailed holds little bearing on their critique.

This call to reject relational theories highlights the shape of their argument more broadly. This is not just about encouraging more people to do Bayesian modelling, it is about defining the theoretical shape of future archaeology. Rejecting the *longue durée* is the rejection of gradual, environmentally driven changes. What those advocating for a generational scale want to emphasise is the intimate, human, short-term tempo of change, which they label as 'history' (as opposed to prehistory). There is an underlying distinction in their arguments between change driven by humans being rapid and short term and change driven by the environment being more gradual. These two forms of change are presented as ontologically distinct and it is clear they believe that one is more appropriately the subject of (a clearly anthropocentric) archaeology. The problem is that this is a false divide as it is not the case that all small-scale change is human and all large-scale change is environmental, these two cannot be pulled apart. Plants, climate, animals, and landscapes all influence people and people influence them. It is not possible to separate out 'natural' and 'cultural' changes. It is also not possible to say which of these is the more important or more powerful driver of change. Rather, natural and cultural changes are thoroughly entangled at every scale. The call for an emphasis on the short term not only has the false divide between nature and culture at its heart, it is also anthropocentric. It suggests that what matters is human change, change brought about by human social worlds. This not only ignores the active roles played in the world by plants, animals, materials, and climate, but also suggests that humans are separate from these changes, which they are not. Whittle (2018: 247) and I share a view that change is dynamic and constant, but while I do not deny the exciting and important effect of Bayesian analysis upon our chronologies, I find their theoretical arguments problematic (I return to this topic in Chapter 7).

Small, medium, or large?

One of the most interesting aspects of the debate about scale, from my perspective, is how the scale of a given phenomenon (temporal or geographical) is a matter of perspective. On the one hand we have those arguing we have not dealt with the largest scale (see for example, Bailey, 2007; Robb, 2007; Robb and Pauketat, 2013) and, on the other hand, those saying we have focused on the large scale to the detriment of the small scale (Foxhall, 2000; Whittle et al., 2011), and within this debate what counts as small or large is not settled. Much of the debate seems to revolve around a sense of small-scale analysis being opposed to large scale. In this schema the small scale is characterised by a high level of detail and complexity, and an emphasis upon the human, whereas the large scale is characterised by general-isations, a lack of detail, and an emphasis upon the environment.

Into this debate we sometimes see an additional medium scale added: Robb's (2007) centuries model provides one example of this. What this medium scale consists of varies – we could think about the way that individual burials or objects can be analysed in microscopic detail to form the smallest scale of analysis and how this integrates with site- or assemblage-level analysis, which can be further inte-grated to create a regional picture. Lesley McFadyen (2008: 307) argues that in such examples different scales of analysis are treated like Russian dolls, nesting into each other (see Figure 4.1). Such an understanding of scale suggests that we can either analyse top-down or bottom-up as one scale drives another. The small scale defines the shape of the larger ones, or the larger scale effectively defines what is possible at the smallest scales: is it the largest or the smallest doll that defines the shape of the nest?

In recent years an alternative approach has begun to emerge that rejects the argument that there is a correct scale of analysis. Robb and Harris (2013: 222) talk

FIGURE 4.1 Russian dolls
Source: Julie and Philip Crellin.

about how a "clear picture at one scale decomposes into a ragged, heterogeneous mass of pixels when seen from closer up, which then calls the larger picture into question". It is not the case that the image at any one scale is the 'correct' one. Privileging any one scale of analysis over the others is reductionist (Harris, 2017; Robb and Harris, 2013; Robb and Pauketat, 2013). Instead of seeing the scales as ontologically distinct, where any one scale drives another, we can instead observe how different scales are always folded together in complex ways (Crellin, 2017; Harris, 2017: 128; Jones, 2012: 70; McFadyen, 2008: 307; Robb and Harris, 2013; Robb and Pauketat, 2013). As McFadyen (2008: 307) argues, all entities simultaneously operate at multiple scales. In this chapter I have argued that much of the debate about whether small or large scales of analysis are best is shaped by the nature–culture dualism. As Bruno Latour (1993) has demonstrated, nature and culture are really thoroughly entwined and inseparable, as are the multiple scales of analysis discussed in this chapter.

Laurent Olivier (1999) discusses the Iron Age Hochdorf burial as an eloquent example of how multiple scales (both geographical and temporal) are folded together in complex ways. This burial is commonly referred to as a 'princely' or 'chieftan' burial due to the wealth and scale of the burial: grave goods included a bronze sofa on which the deceased was placed, as well as a wheeled cart, jewellery, dress fittings, drinking horns, and tools. Olivier argues that within what we might see as the 'closed' scale of the grave assemblage there are actually multiple scales operating: some of the grave goods might have belonged to the deceased, others were created for the grave, some of the objects show signs of repair indicating they had pre-existing histories before they were placed into the grave, and each of these differing scales is folded into the scale of analysis that is the grave context (Olivier, 1999: 122; 125). Moreover, the production of the grave might have occurred over a few days, but it also draws upon longer traditions spread across a larger geographical scale of what defines a burial and ontologies regarding the dead (Oliver, 1999: 32). In examples like this we can see how different scales are constantly mixed together and cannot (or perhaps should not) necessarily be pulled apart and easily classified as small, medium, or large.

Recognising the multiscalar nature of our world is emerging as a key theme as archaeologists seek to move beyond approaches that rely upon either opposed scales of small versus large, or a nested tripart system. Yet, as Robb and Pauketat (2013: 19) note, recognising multiple scales is not the same as understanding the various historical processes that operate at them. The call for multiplicity needs to extend beyond scale. Gosden (2013: 166) notes that when we look at questions that concern all of humanity (what we might take to be the biggest scale of analysis), these should not be about the "search for a single truth, a single set of principles or an unchanging essence". *The Body in History* (Robb and Harris, 2013), a book that is certainly large in scale, traces complex and overlapping patterns of change. By homing in on the detail the authors are able to write history at the largest scale without the need to present a singular reductive narrative. This book is grand narrative in scale but deals with the complexity and contradiction we might be more used to seeing emerge in small-scale local narratives. This ties into their approach that actively rejected a single narrative and instead showed the multiplicity of understandings of the body that existed at any one moment in time (see also Harris and Robb, 2012). Gosden (1994: 166) has also argued that working on a large scale does not mean writing a simple sequence or reducing the variety of human experience to a single narrative. Robb and Harris (2013) demonstrate how we can achieve grand narratives that show the complexity and multiplicity of understandings and ontologies that can, and do, exist in our world. This is achieved through the effective integration of detailed, smaller-scale, fine-grained narratives, which, when stitched together, produce an overarching narrative that revels in (rather than denies) multiplicity, variation, and contradiction.

There is no single correct scale to work at, nor does any single scale hold control over the others. Equally, it is not the case that the images we create as we zoom out on our data are any more or less correct than those we create when we zoom in.

Conclusion

Scale is a deeply political issue. Whether we choose to work at scales that are microscopic or those that stretch across continents and millennia, the scales we adopt affect the narratives of change we construct. As we shall see in Chapter 8, I might look down a microscope at tiny traces of wear on a bronze axe that were created by minutes of use, I then take this microscopic data and use it to construct narratives of change than span across centuries or even millennia. I argued in Chapter 1 that we need to reject determinist, singular, and teleological narratives of change. Working at the largest scales of analysis comes with risks and we need to be careful to make sure that we are not writing large-scale narratives of change that simply legitimise the current state of affairs and thereby entrench elitist and masculinist narratives. Yet at the same time we cannot simply ignore the grand narrative; rather we must become narrators that are thoughtful and political in the stories that they tell.

Much of the tension and debate about scale emerges from the belief that there is a correct scale at which to work and that our scales of analysis, like nature and culture, are separable. Should we focus on the grand narrative of processualism or the individual story of post-processualism? Should our stories focus on the role of the environment and *long durée* or the agency of the individual within a given moment? Is structure or event more powerful? Is it nature or culture? These debates take us in the wrong direction as there is no single correct scale of analysis at which archaeologists should work, nor is it possible to truly pull the deeply entangled scales of analysis apart.

When it comes to scale, our desire seems to be for neatness. We wish to box different processes as working at different scales and temporalities. We want the environment to exist at the large scale, and the decisions of an individual to be small scale. We like to be able to stack our scales as though they were McFadyen's (2008) nested dolls, tidying them away. The reality, though, is far messier:

processes work across these different scales; actions and agency are not confined by them. Our scales fold together; change at one leads to change at another, but not in a simplistic or linear way; rather, the process is complex. What is a perfectly clear and neat image at one scale is a ragged mess at another. In Chapter 5 we turn our attention to biography: a subject that might appear to operate on the small scale, but, as this chapter has shown the reality is never that simple.

Notes

1 Thanks to Luíseach Nic Eoin for her insightful comments, which highlighted this to me.
2 Olivier (2006) offers an important counterpoint to the Anglo-American critique of Braudel's thinking and argues that the *Annales* School has been interpreted and understood differently (though he does not say incorrectly) by Anglo-Americans than it has been by French scholars.
3 In his 2007 article Bailey identifies four different but complimentary definitions of time perspectivism.
4 Andrew Jones (2012: 100–5) makes a similar argument about citational practice and change, specifically in the process of making, which I utilise in Chapter 8.

Bibliography

Alberti, B., Fowles, S., Holbraad, M., Marshall, Y. and Witmore, C. 2011. "Worlds Otherwise": archaeology, anthropology, and ontological difference. *Current Anthropology* 52(6): 896–912.
Appleby, J. 2013. Temporality and the Transition to Cremation in the Late Third Millennium to Mid Second Millennium BC in Britain. *Cambridge Archaeological Journal* 23(1): 83–97.
Bailey, G. 1981. Concepts, time scales and explanations in economic prehistory, in Sheridan, A. and Bailey, G. (eds), *Economic Archaeology*. Oxford: BAR international series: pp. 97–117.
Bailey, G. 1987. Breaking the barrier. *Archaeological Review from Cambridge* 6(1): 5–20.
Bailey, G. 2007. Time perspectives, palimpsest and the archaeology of time. *Journal of Anthropological Archaeology* 26: 198–223.
Barker, G. 1995. *A Mediterranean Valley*. Leicester: Leicester University Press.
Barrett, J. 1994. *Fragments from Antiquity*. London: Wiley-Blackwell.
Bayliss, A. 2009. Rolling out the revolution: using radiocarbon dating in archaeology. *Radiocarbon* 51(1): 123–147.
Bayliss, A., Healy, F., Whittle, A. and Cooney, G. 2011. Neolithic narratives: British and Irish enclosures in their timescapes, in Whittle, A., Healy, F. and Bayliss, A. (eds), *Gathering Time: Dating the Early Neolithic Enclosures of Southern Britain and Ireland*. Oxford: Oxbow Books: pp. 682–847.
Bayliss, A., Marshall, P., Richards, C., and Whittle, A. 2017. Islands of history: the Late Neolithic timescape of Orkney. *Antiquity* 91: 1171–1188.
Bintliff, J. (ed) 1991. *The Annales School and Archaeology*. Leicester: Leicester University Press.
Braudel, F. 1972. *The Mediterranean and the Mediterranean World at the Time of Philip II*. London: Continuum.
Bronk Ramsey, C. 2008. Radiocarbon dating: revolutions in understanding. *Archaeometry* 50 (2): 249–275.

Crellin, R.J. 2017. Changing assemblages: vibrant matter in burial assemblages. *Cambridge Archaeological Journal* 27(1): 111–125.

Draşovean, F., Schier, W., Bayliss, A., Gaydarska, B. and Whittle, A. 2017. The lives of houses: duration, context and history at Neolithic Uivar, Romania. *European Journal of Archaeology* 20(4): 636–662.

Ebersbach, R., Doppler, T., Hofmann, D. and Whittle, A. 2017. No time out: scaling material diversity and change in the Alpine foreland Neolithic. *Journal of Anthropological Archaeology* 45: 1–14.

Editorial. 2018. Knowing ourselves. *Nature Ecology and Evolution* 2: 1517–1518.

Foxhall, L. 2000. The running sands of time: archaeology and the short-term. *World Archaeology* 31(3): 484–498.

Gamble, C. 2007. *Origins and Revolutions*. Cambridge: Cambridge University Press.

Gamble, C. and Gittins, E. 2004. Social archaeology and origins research: a Palaeolithic perspective, in Meskell, L. and Preucell, R. (eds), *A Companion to Social Archaeology*. Blackwell, Oxford: 96–118.

Garrow, D. and Yarrow, T. 2010. *Archaeology and Anthropology: Understanding Similarity, Exploring Difference*. Oxford: Oxbow Books.

Gosden, C. 1994. *Social Being and Time*. London: Wiley-Blackwell.

Gosden, C. 1999. *Archaeology and Anthropology: A Changing Relationship*. London: Routledge.

Gosden, C. 2013. Long-term history: a short response, in Robb, J. and Paukatet, T.R. (eds), *Big Histories, Human Lives*. Santa Fe: SAR Press: 207–214.

Griffiths, S. 2017. We're all cultural historians now: revolutions in understanding archaeological theory and scientific dating. *Radiocarbon* 59(6): 1347–1357.

Harding, A. 1994. Reformation in barbarian Europe 1300–1600 BC, in Cunliffe, B. (ed), *The Oxford Illustrated History of Prehistoric Europe*. Oxford: Oxford University Press: 304–335.

Harding, J. 2005. Rethinking the great divide: a reply to Thomas, Olivier and Murray. *Norwegian Archaeological Review* 39(1): 88–97.

Harris, O.J.T. 2017. Assemblages and scale in archaeology. *Cambridge Archaeological Journal* 27(1): 127–139.

Harris, O.J.T. and Robb, J.E. 2012. Multiple ontologies and the problem of the body in history. *American Anthropologist* 114(4): 668–679.

Harris, O.J.T., Rebay-Salisbury, K., Robb, J. and Stig Sørensen, M. 2013. The body in its social context, in Robb, J. and Harris, O.J.T., *Body in history: Europe from the Palaeolithic to the future*. Cambridge: Cambridge University Press: pp.64–97.

Hodder, I. 1990. *Domestication of Europe*. London: Willey-Blackwell.

Hodder, I. 2000. Agency and Individuals in long-term processes, in Dobres, M.-A.. and Robb, J. (eds), *Agency in Archaeology*. London: Routledge: pp. 21–33.

Hoffman, D., Ebersbach, R., Doppler, T. and Whittle, A. 2017. The life and times of the house: multi-scalar perspectives on settlement from the Neolithic of the northern Alpine foreland. *European Journal of Archaeology* 19(4): 596–630.

Ingold, T. 2000. *The Perception of the Environment: Essays in Livelihood, Dwelling and Skill*. London: Routledge.

Itan, Y., Powell, A., Beaumont M., Burger, J. and Thomas, M. 2009. The origins of lactase persistence in Europe. *PLoS Computational Biology* 5(8): 1–13.

Jones, A. M. 2012. *Prehistoric Materialities: Becoming Material in Prehistoric Britain and Ireland*. Oxford: Oxford University Press.

Klein, R. 1995. Anatomy, behavior, and modern human origins. *Journal of World Prehistory* 9: 167–198.

Knapp, B. (ed) 1992. *Archaeology, Annales, and Ethnohistory: New Directions in Archaeology.* Cambridge: Cambridge University Press.

Latour, B. 1993. *We Have Never Been Modern.* Cambridge: Harvard University Press.

Lucas, G. 2005. *An Archaeology of Time.* London: Routledge.

McBrearty, S. and Brooks, A. 2000. The revolution that wasn't: a new interpretation of the origin of modern humans. *Journal of Human Evolution* 39: 453–563.

McFadyen, L. 2008. Building and architecture as landscape practice, in David, B. and Thomas, J. (eds), *Handbook of Landscape Archaeology.* Walnut Creek: Left Coast Press: pp. 307–314.

McGlade, J. 1999. The times of history: archaeology, narrative and non-linear causality, in Murray, T. (ed), *Time and Archaeology.* London: Routledge: pp. 139–163.

Mellars, P. 2005. The impossible coincidence: a single-species model for the origins of modern human behaviour in Europe. *Evolutionary Anthropology* 14: 12–27.

Mellars, P. and Stringer, C. (eds) 1989. *The Human Revolution: behavioural and biological perspectives on the origins of modern humans.* Edinburgh: Edinburgh University Press.

Meskell, L. 1998. Intimate archaeologies: the case of Kha ad Merit. *World Archaeology* 29(3): 363–379.

Olivier, L. 1999. The Hochdorf 'princely' grave and the question of the nature of archaeological funerary assemblages, in Murray, T. (ed), *Time and Archaeology.* London: Routledge: pp. 109–138.

Olivier, L. 2006. The greatest harmony is born of differences. *Norwegian Archaeological Review* 39: 89–93.

Pollock, S. 2013. Commensality, public sphere and handlungsräume in Ancient Mesopotamia, in Robb, J. and Pauketat, T.R. (eds), *Big Histories, Human Lives.* Santa Fe: SAR Press: pp. 145–170.

Robb, J. 2007. *The Early Mediterranean Village: Agency, Material Culture and Social Chance in Neolithic Italy.* Cambridge: Cambridge University Press.

Robb, J. 2010. Beyond agency. *World Archaeology* 42 (4): 493–520.

Robb, J. 2013. History in the body: the scale of belief, in Robb, J. and Pauketat, T.R. (eds), 2013. *Big Histories, Human Lives.* Santa Fe: SAR Press: pp. 77–99.

Robb, J. and Harris, O.J.T. 2013. *The Body in History: Europe from the Palaeolithic to the Future.* Cambridge: Cambridge University Press.

Robb, J. and Pauketat, T.R. 2013a. From moments to millennia: theorizing scale and change in human history, in Robb, J. and Pauketat, T.R. (eds), *Big Histories, Human Lives.* Santa Fe: SAR Press: pp. 3–34.

Robb, J. and Pauketat, T.R. (eds) 2013b. *Big Histories, Human Lives.* Santa Fe: SAR Press.

Sørensen, M.L.S. and Rebay, K. 2008. Interpreting the body: burial practices at the Middle Bronze Age cemetery at Pitten. *Archaeologia Austriaca* 89: 153–175.

Stringer, C. and Andrews, P. 1988. Genetic and fossil evidence for the origin of modern humans. *Science* 239: 1263–1268.

Thomas, J. 1996. *Time, Culture and Identity: An Interpretive Archaeology.* London: Routledge.

Thomas, J. 2004. *Archaeology and modernity.* London: Routledge.

Van Dyke, R. 2004. Memory, meaning and masonry: the Late Bonito Chacoan landscape. *American Antiquity* 69: 413–431.

Whitehouse, N., Schulting, R., McClatchie, M., Barratt, P., McLaughlin, T., Bogaard, A., College, S., Marchant, R. and Gaffrey, J. 2014. Neolithic agriculture on the European western frontier: the boom and bust of early farming in Ireland. *Journal of Archaeological Science* 51: 181–205.

Whittle, A. 2018. *Times of Their Lives.* Oxford: Oxbow.

Whittle, A., Bayliss, A. and Healy, F. 2008. The timing and tempo of change; examples from the fourth millennium cal BC in Southern England. *Cambridge Archaeological Journal* 18: 65–70.

Whittle, A., Healy, F. and Bayliss, A. 2011. *Gathering Time: Dating the Early Neolithic Enclosures of Southern Britain and Ireland*. Oxford: Oxbow Books.

5

CHANGING PEOPLE AND THINGS

In the previous chapter I focused on the relationship between scale and change. I dwelled upon the political nature of scale and explored a number of different approaches to scale utilised by archaeologists. I argued that the nature–culture dualism often plays a structuring role in debates about the 'correct' scale of analysis. In the main, I considered what we might characterise as relatively large scales of analysis. In this chapter I focus specifically on how both people and things are always changing at smaller scales. In Chapter 1 I argued that change is always ongoing in the world; in this chapter I illustrate the constant motion of our world, by investigating smaller scales of analysis. By recognising that change is constant we can begin to move beyond block-time approaches and eschew revolution thinking.

I begin by exploring how our bodies are always changing. Before we are born our bodies grow and change in the womb. This change continues throughout our lives as the muscle fibres of our bodies shift in shape and size, the neurons in our brains gain and lose connections, and our DNA accumulates mutations. By focusing our attention on how bodies grow and age I demonstrate that the human body is always in motion. I then turn our attention to things and how they change, from the wear that develops upon them, to the ways they break, or might be recycled. As things move through different contexts, their meanings, functions, and uses change too. I explore the concept of object biography as a means of tracing the changing histories of things. I consider how the object biography concept has been implemented and adapted by archaeologists to think about change.

As archaeologists we perhaps most readily associate the study of changing bodies with osteologists or perhaps bioarchaeologists, whereas those studying changing things might be material culture specialists (for wider discussion, see Sofaer, 2006: 1–3). In the previous chapter I discussed the problematic nature of approaches that separate natural or biological processes of change from human or social ones. In this chapter I build on this to show how changing people and things are thoroughly entwined. I start by thinking about how people and things change separately, but argue, at the conclusion, that they are thoroughly relationally entangled and together form part of a world in constant motion.

The power of biography

Biographical approaches are popular in archaeology. For some they provide a methodology to shape the research process; for others they provide a metaphor to illustrate change; and for others they are a narrative device. Archaeologists might explore the biographies of skeletons (osteobiographies) (Robb, 2002), or those of monuments in the landscape (Gillings and Pollard, 1999), or of things (Gosden and Marshall, 1999; Joy, 2009). All of these different approaches are addressed in detail below. What follows is a discussion of why the concept of biography has become so powerful within archaeology. Generally, biographies follow a model that transitions from birth, to childhood, through adult life, to ageing, and death (for a discussion of the nature of biography, see Burström, 2014). This story is often told in a staged manner where we cleave apart chunks of the narrative, like the chapters in a book. Significant moments are selected to break the story down and what emerges is the kind of block-time approach discussed and critiqued in Chapter 1.

The success of the object biography, as both theory and method, builds upon a series of earlier processual approaches to tracing change. The seeds of an object biographical approach were evident in Michael Schiffer's (1972, 1975) early work, discussed in Chapter 3, on the formation processes of the archaeological record, where he considered the different routes through which things come to be deposited. Schiffer (2005a,b) has more recently developed a life-history approach with links to both his earlier work and object biography.

Researchers who focus on technology have also played a key role in the development of biographical approaches. For those who study lithics, ceramics, metals, and other materials, it is common to unpick the *chaîne opératoire* of an object, or try to source the materials used to make it. The *chaîne opératoire* concept, developed by André Leroi-Gourhan (1964), focused on the technical sequence of stages involved in production. Reworkings of the concept by both Marcia-Anne Dobres (2000) and Pierre Lemonnier (1989) highlight how production processes are not just technological but have social aspects and come to shape people too. The technique has begun to be applied beyond technology specialists: Jo Appleby (2013), for example, uses it to explore the processes that produce mortuary contexts (see Figure 5.1). One of the advantages of the *chaîne opératoire* is how it opens up past processes revealing their complexity. Appleby (2013) elegantly demonstrates how we can work back from a mortuary context to explore the many processes and steps that produced it and thereby effectively enliven a relatively static context to show the effort, agency, and actions that created it.

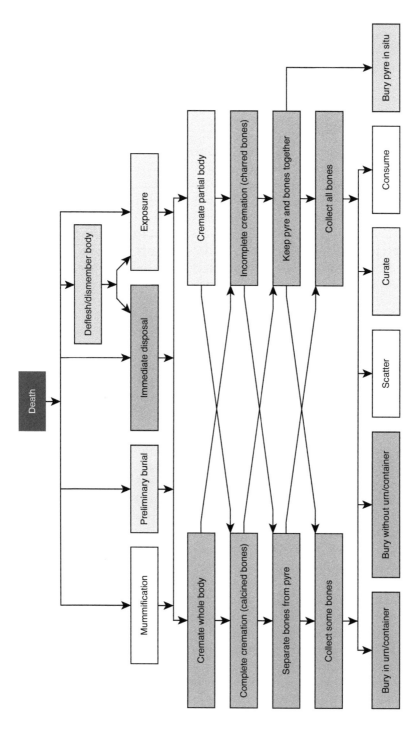

FIGURE 5.1 *Chaîne opératoire* for mortuary practices that include cremation
Source: Jo Appleby (2013; Fig. 2).

For those who study technology the *chaîne opératoire* might be combined with wear-analysis to reveal the use-life of a given object. Wear and residue analysts look for micro- and macroscopic traces of past use on the surfaces of objects, and even the residues trapped within them (see, for example, Dolfini and Crellin, 2016; Semenov, 1964; Torrence and Barton, 2006; Van Gijn, 2010). These traces allow analysts to discover how tools and objects were used, on what surfaces they were worked, and how they were repaired and reused. For such specialists, the biography offers a ready metaphor to explain their work to others. Jody Joy (2009: 542) describes *chaîne opératoire*, use-life, and biography as related concepts.

Why is it that biography has become so powerful and popular? It has a clear utility for materials specialists, allowing them to communicate the minutiae of hours spent staring down a microscope or analysing compositional data into an effective narrative for the nonspecialist. The biographical approach is very effective for data that focus on individual people and objects. For some, perhaps, the draw could be that it takes them away from the controversial issues of the grand narrative. John Robb (2013: 78) has argued that there is often an implicit sense that the human scale is the 'correct' scale of analysis because humans are the focus of archaeology. We see this in the work of Ian Hodder (2000) and Lynn Meskell (1998), who both suggest that we should focus upon the lives of individuals. Telling biographies, though, is not without politics: biographies today might be written to reveal a little-known figure, promote the achievements of a celebrated individual, to reveal the 'real' celebrity we think we know, or to simply line the coffers of the author. Biographies are always written from a certain perspective, with a powerful author who shapes the story. Moreover, choosing to focus upon biography at the expense of focusing on a different scale of analysis is, in and of itself, a clearly political choice. Focusing on the human, the biographical, is far from apolitical as any biography of a member of a royal family or government demonstrates.

While all these factors combine to result in the continued popularity of the biographical approach, I believe a major aspect of its success is rooted in its anthropocentrism. The biographical approach is inherently anthropocentric, seeking to explore and describe change in direct relation to how we understand our own changing human lives – human lives are the benchmark for change. As I have argued, the world is in constant motion and change occurs at scales varying from the very slow to the very quick: we define this speed in relation to our own human perceptions of tempo. There are changes we can see with the naked eye, those revealed by stop-frame recording over days, months, and years, and those that are so imperceptibly slow that we more readily note them as consequences that play out over the very long term. Biography provides a useful anthropocentric metaphor to aid the discussion of change at different scales and tempos. While it allows us to reach beyond the human to consider how objects, landscapes, and monuments might change, it does so by bringing all these different forms of change into a human frame of reference. It brings change that might be imperceptibly slow, dizzyingly fast, or radically different from our own experience into a frame we can readily grasp.

People change

Biographies are an effective way of thinking about how people change through their lives. In the sections that follow I consider how our physical bodies change and how archaeologists create human biographies from both material culture and skeletal remains.

We all have bodies that change, though our attitude to this is complex and contradictory. Joanna Sofaer (2006: 56–57) has argued that our biological bodies may often be more readily associated with the nature side of the nature–culture binary and as a result they may be presented as static and constant, as opposed to culture, which is presented as ever-changing and dynamic. Ageing as a process continues to be seen negatively, with the old both feminised and infantilised in the west (Gowland, 2017: 241). Appleby (2018) has argued that our failure to consider ageing archaeologically is a product of both the methodological difficulties in ageing older skeletons and our own 'ambivalent' attitude towards ageing. Furthermore, she suggests there is a moral problem with the study of ageing in that we try to avoid seeing it as "a necessarily negative process, whilst at the same time acknowledging the fact of bodily decline" (Appleby, 2018: 146). Addressing our changing bodies means confronting our own ageing processes and our feelings about them.

Sofaer (2006: 56) elegantly demonstrates how our skeletons are always changing – our bones grow and change with age, they respond to stress, exercise, disease, activity, and their very structure is under constant renewal: cortical bone, the hard outer layer, has a mean age of 20 years, whereas cancellous bone, the internal spongy bone, is usually 1–4 years old. It is not just our skeletons that are constantly changing, but the rest of our bodies too: they are moulded and changed by the lives we live. The material property that allows bodies to be moulded and changed is referred to as plasticity – this is different from acclimatisation (short-term adaptive responses) and evolution (genetic changes over the long term) (Sofaer, 2006: 70–71; see also Agarwal, 2016). We can think about how our bodies adapt to archaeological excavation as a form of plasticity – different from acclimatisation or evolution. Our bodies respond to the worlds within which they exist from conception and beyond death.

For osteologists, the body's plasticity provides them with much of their data. They cannot at present look at the tiny daily changes that go on in response to what we eat, the air we breathe, or the others we live alongside.[1] They can, though, look at the shape and structure of skeletal remains to begin to unpick the life of the deceased. Sexing a skeleton relies upon the changes that a body undergoes through puberty to go from the skeleton of a child who cannot be identified as male or female to an adult for whom this might be possible (see, for example, White and Folkens, 2005). Ageing a skeleton relies upon our knowledge of the changes that occur to our bodies throughout life (see, for example, Miles, 1963). Our ability to identify pathologies has its foundation in how our bones respond to some illnesses and diseases (see, for example, Roberts and Manchester, 2010; Waldron, 2009), as well as our daily activities and the objects, plants, and animals we live alongside. Osteologists can reveal the lives of the deceased precisely because we have bodies that change.

Analyses of skeletons can allow the construction of an osteobiography. Robb (2002: 155) has argued that biographical narratives are grounded within bodily changes *and* how biological changes come to be socialised. Osteobiographies can be characterised as commonly working at two different scales. They might be used to tell us about the culturally normative biography for a particular community (see, for example, Robb, 2002; Saul and Saul, 1989). In such examples the emphasis is upon defining categories and types of people based on their relative age and relating these groups to a coherent life narrative (Robb, 2002: 160). By bringing the normative life path for an individual within a given community into focus it also becomes possible to speak about those who have unusual biographies. Alternatively, osteobiographies can focus upon revealing the biographies of individuals, often those with somewhat exceptional or unusual biographies (see, for example, Hawkey, 1998; Knüsel et al., 2010; Matczak and Kozlowski, 2017; Robb, 2009; Stodder and Palkovich, 2012). Matczak and Koslowski (2017: 126), for example, define osteobiography as "a cultural narrative, based on osteological evidence and cultural context, which tells the story of the personal experience of an individual". In their work they explore the unusual lives of two Medieval Polish women, one with leprosy, the other with gigantism. At both scales osteobiography highlights how our bodies change over the course of our lives and how this is accounted for, adapted to, and understood by the communities we live within.

Our fleshy bodies and, importantly for osteologists, skeletons change through the course of our lives. As Rebecca Gowland (2017: 239) states: "the skeleton does not represent a snapshot in time, but rather a selective accumulation of life experience which impact upon the chemical and morphological structure of the bones". Changes to both the body, and the skeleton encased within, occur as a variety of processes at a range of scales. Importantly for archaeology, some of these changes leave material traces on the skeleton.

Changing lifecycles and life course

Alongside osteobiographies there is a related field of research that focuses upon the lifecycle or life course (defined below). In a special issue of *World Archaeology* Roberta Gilchrist (2000: 325) argued that our archaeological narratives remain static as they tend to focus on single moments in the lives of past people rather than considering their changing life histories. This is a common accusation to level at archaeology – that we need to take static contexts, be they burials, pots, or sites, and use them to produce detailed and changing narratives, or perhaps biographies. It should be clear from the discussion above that our skeletons are far from static, and, as I've argued in Chapter 3, seeing the archaeological context as static is an error that only serves to create an unhelpful rupture where we suggest the buried past is static and associate change with human action in the present alone.

Lifecycle and life-course approaches focus on how human ageing, from birth, through childhood, into young adulthood, and older years, is marked and understood socially. For Gilchrist (2000: 325) the lifecycle offers a way of integrating "the human body with natural and culture cycles, and highlights the place of age in constructing personal and social identities". Lynn Meskell (2000), for example, considered the different lifecycles of men and women in ancient Egypt. Rosemary Joyce (2000) drew on the work of Judith Butler (1993) to consider how different gendered roles were literally inscribed on the bodies of young Aztec children as they aged. The lifecycle approaches of archaeologists such as Meskell (2000) and Joyce (2000) differ from the osteological approach discussed above – they are not about the chronological ageing of bodies but about the social experience of ageing and the creation of different aged identities.

Sofaer Derevenski (2000) provides an elegant example of the role of material culture in the experience of the lifecycle. She focuses on the use of copper in the production of aged and gendered social identities in the Carpathian Basin during the Copper Age. Sofaer Derevesnki (2000: 392–394) carefully brings together the anthropological ageing and sexing of the skeletons with analyses of grave goods and mortuary contexts from the site of Tiszapolgár-Basatanya in Hungary to reveal a series of age-gender stages. Sofaer Derevenski (2000: 390) specifically links the material properties of copper items found in the grave to their role within the creation of social identities. Copper is a highly malleable material that can be reshaped, reused, and recycled. The highly malleable properties of copper are paralleled with the plasticity of the human body – just as humans change shape and form over their lifetime, copper can also be reshaped. Copper arm rings were worn by men aged between 5 and 25 (Sofaer Derevenski, 2000: 398–399). The particular form of the arm rings meant that they were adjustable in size. Sofaer argues that the bodies of these young men and their arm rings grew together. At age 25 the arm rings appear to no longer have been worn; Sofaer Derevenski (2000: 398) suggests they were removed as men reached skeletal maturity to indicate their change in status. In this model, age was not just something chronologically marked upon the body, it was culturally constructed and experienced.

Sofaer Derevenski's (2000) paper combines multiple scales of change as she explores not only how different aged and gendered identity categories were created but also how this changed through time. The creation of aged and gendered identities appears to have its roots in Late Neolithic practices in the region. Rather than arguing that metal production flourishes as a result of its technological superiority, Sofaer Derevenski (2000: 390) links the expansion of metal working in the Copper Age with the continued production of complex gendered and aged identities. She argues that the hiatus in metalworking that occurred at the end of the Copper Age in this region related to a reconfiguration of how identities were produced, which meant that metal objects were no longer needed for the same purpose (Sofaer Derevenski, 2000: 390). This is a nuanced and complex paper that combines osteological analyses with grave contexts and material culture. It demonstrates how changing and ageing bodies were understood in relation to identity. The link Sofaer Derevenski (2000) builds between these processes and the larger historical changes in metalworking practices in the regions is a neat one, allowing her to place the individual identities and bodies of the deceased within a larger historical narrative.

The concept of the life course is defined in opposition to that of the lifespan. The lifespan focuses upon the series of sequential stages through which people pass from birth to death; it is presented by Gilchrist (2012) as universal and biologically determinist. In contrast the sociological concept of the life course is a "social institution that is culturally constructed, with particular meanings attached to stages of life and the transitions between them" (Gilchrist, 2012: 2). The lifespan is broken into stages whereas the life course focuses upon a continuum of change. Gilchrist (2012) contrasts biological concepts of ageing, the lifecycle, and lifespan with the culturally constructed understandings of this, which are the focus of the life-course approach; this effectively separates out biological (natural) change from social (cultural) changes.

Gilchrist's (2012) book *Medieval Life* offers a detailed account of the differing ways in which people age. A fascinating aspect of the book focuses on how growing up was understood in the Medieval context. Young people had extended adolescences, receiving social rites of puberty into their 20s – meaning maturity was achieved more slowly than today (Gilchrist, 2012: 42). Skeletal analysis inter-estingly parallels what we might otherwise suggest to have been a cultural under-standing of the process of becoming adult: it appears that due to poor nutrition the onset of puberty was delayed and that, comparatively, young people had an extended period of juvenile growth that is evident in their skeletons (Gilchrist, 2012: 66). Rites of passage played a key role in this ageing process and were often associated with changes in clothing, literally making the transition visible (Gilchrist, 2012: 91–97): for example, young women wore their hair loose and their head uncovered once they reached puberty and might wear flower crowns to festivals. Marriage was 'delayed' as young people often left to work in a town or chose to stay in the country as servants around the ages of 12–14; for males this might have been followed by an apprenticeship, during which they were forbidden to marry and when membership of an age cohort and a guild was established. This is a rich and highly textured book that brings to light the detail of how the bodies and lives of medieval people changed as they aged. It is a book that squarely meets the challenge of talking about how people change as they age. The biggest weakness is the book's reliance upon, and opposition of, nature and culture in relation to change, and it is to this that I now turn.

Fifty is the new thirty?

Life-course and life-history approaches have historically focused upon the cultural experience and reaction to how our bodies change through time. They explore social categories of identity and cultural understandings of change. Biological and chronological ageing in these approaches can (though it need not) be treated as inevitable and naturalised, whereas the cultural experience of this process and social reaction to it can be treated as something particular, of interest to the archaeologist or anthropologist, as opposed to the biologist. Sofaer Derevenski (2000: 390), for example, has described ageing as "both universal and culturally specific in its social and material expression". Similarly, Robb (2002: 161) has commented upon the challenge that mixing skeletal and cultural ages poses for analysts. He argues that processes such as growth, illness, ageing, and death have universally recognisable material consequences that are incorporated into cultural understandings.

The principles of ageing and sexing skeletons have been based upon the idea that human remains are "universal, concrete and essentially biological phenomena" (Sofaer, 2006: 23) – learning how the teeth of a child look different from the teeth of an adult in a reference collection from medieval England allows one to identify adults and children in the Inca period in South America. It might seem that working out the sex and age of a skeleton is simply a matter of understanding universal biological processes. Yet the processes of ageing and the experience of different genders are increasingly revealed to be highly variable and complex. Studies considering the menopause, a key gendered and aged experience, show that not just the experience but also the symptoms of the menopause vary cross-culturally (see, for example, Anderson et al., 2004; Jones et al., 2012). While the menopause is commonly causatively linked to hormonal (read biological) changes, the vastly differing experiences of it indicate that the contributing factors are far more complex. Jones et al. (2012: 5) refer to the menopause as 'biocultural', as genetics, social factors, environment, individual experience, and culture all affect its nature. Work like this has led to increasing consideration of what Margaret Lock (1993) termed 'local biologies' to refer to "the manner in which biological and social processes are permanently entangled throughout life" (Lock, 2017: 8) and thereby recognises the local and specific nature of biological changes. More recently, the rise of epigenetic studies (which consider changes to gene expression that are not caused by changes to the genetic code), has led Jörg Niewöhner (2011) to develop his concept of the "embedded body" to recognise how our bodies are affected by the contexts we live within. Such approaches show that our biologies are complex and culturally embedded. A shift is arguably underway from seeing the body as biological and natural to a more complex view that eschews dualisms (see Lock, 2017); for example Appleby (2019) has combined these ideas with osteobiography in a paper that argues we should see bone as in a continual process of change.

This tension between the cultural and the biological, or natural, continues to exert some influence when it comes to the study of our bodies. The body has historically existed in a strange position in debates about change; it is the location of stable biology waiting to be enlivened by fickle cultural interpretations or it has a changing materiality that allows the construction of complex social categories. The ways our bodies change are both presented as obvious and as something that is constantly downplayed and denied. What is biological and what is cultural, what is static and what is shifting, and what is universal and what is particularistic is increasingly revealed to be complex and messy. This messiness reveals the inherent problems in dualistic thinking. It is not helpful to think of our bodies either as natural or cultural, nor to approach them as some kind of mixture of the two, especially not a mixture where one side of the equation is seen as ontologically elevated above the other. The reality is that our bodies collapse the nature–culture divide, highlighting it for what it is: a highly problematic way of understanding the world and, for the purposes of this book, a hurdle to our approach to change.

Plasticity, the property that means our bodies change and react in response to our world, provides an elegant means through which to problematise and then break down the nature–culture dualism. Plasticity is about how we respond to the world, be that, for example, changes in the environment, changes in the foods we eat, or changes in the activities we do. Our bodies are not a site of pure nature waiting to be interpreted by the cultural world, rather they are influenced by, and fully embedded within, the world (Niewöhner, 2011; Robb and Harris, 2013). It is not the case that our bodies age and change in a universal way whether we live in Japan or Britain, or we were born in 1987AD or 2000BC. Even when we are newly born we are a messy hybrid of the things we might call nature (growing in the womb, following developmental stages, etc) and the things we might call culture (whether our mothers have access to the 'right type' of food, whether we are exposed to tobacco smoke, etc) (Agarwal, 2016; Gowland, 2015). Whether or not parents can conceive is not down to biology alone but a product of environment, wealth, history, genetics; the rapidly expanding market for pre-conception supplements, fertility treatment, and IVF is testament to the complex messy combination of factors that contribute to the emergence of a new life. Focusing on plasticity collapses the nature–culture divide – there is no body that is purely natural or precultural, as all bodies exist within worlds full of other people, animals, plants, materials, and ways of being to which they respond, and as a result of which, they are always changing.

Consider the work of the new materialist Jane Bennett (2010: 39–51), who has explored how the food we ingest changes our bodies and the worlds we live in. She illustrates how fats have been shown to alter the moods and brains of humans, as well as their more commonly cited effects on the size and composition of their bodies. Bennett (2010: 41) considers research demonstrating a link between omega-3 fatty acids and changes in behaviour. The bodies she describes are always changing in response to food; such bodies eschew labelling as natural or cultural and are messy hybrids. As Bennett (2010: 49) argues, "in the eating encounter, all bodies are shown to be but temporary congealments of a materiality that is a process of becoming" – our bodies are always on the move.

The interpretive challenge of the ever-changing body extends beyond the experience of life itself. In contrast to the wriggling, shifting, fidgeting bodies that inhabit our day-to-day lives, the bodies we encounter as archaeologists appear still, dead, and lifeless, and we call upon the expertise of osteologists to re-animate their bones to reveal the changing histories encapsulated within them (Sofaer, 2006: 32). Sofaer (2006: 62) argues that "the living body is regarded as a person but as soon as the transition to death is made, the body becomes an object". This is not a state-ment that I necessarily agree with – sitting by the body of a recently deceased loved one certainly feels different from sitting with an object. From an archae-ological perspective, skeletons are certainly treated differently from other finds on archaeological sites, and we record them and excavate them following specific protocols (Buikstra and Ubelaker, 1994) because of their clear links to past dead humans and our own anthropocentrism (see Figure 5.2). For me, dead bodies occupy a hybrid position: they are neither an object like any other pot sherd or flint, nor are they treated with the same ontological elevation as a breathing person. In Chapter 3 I argued that we create an interpretive problem when we remove the archaeological record from the flow of time. While it is most certainly the case that the 'process of death' (McDonald, 2017) marks a significant transition, it is not the case that it transforms active materials into static ones: change continues to happen. As organs fail to function and cell production ceases, other processes of change begin: flesh rots, bacteria act, muscles break down, and the composition of bones begins to shift. Our bodies are constantly changing, and though that change is of a different character in the living than the dead, both types of body are nevertheless in motion.

FIGURE 5.2 Crowd of people around a Bronze Age cremation excavation at Cronk
Guckley, Berk Farm, Isle of Man
Source: Jody Booze Daniels.

Object biographies

In this next section I shift focus to consider how the concept of biography has been used to explore how objects change. The concept of the *cultural biography of objects* came to archaeology from the work of Igor Kopytoff (1986) in an edited volume exploring commodities and exchange practices (Appadurai, 1986). Kopytoff's (1986) argument suggested that things (and commodities specifically) are subject to change so their meaning cannot only be understood at a single point in time. They move through production, exchange, and consumption processes, all of which change their function, meaning, and relationship with people; Kopytoff parallels this changing history with how the lives of people change. He argues, therefore, that just as we employ biography as a tool to narrate the histories of people, so too, we can employ it to narrate the lives of things: "in doing the biography of a thing, one would ask questions similar to those one asks about people" (Kopytoff, 1986: 66).

Kopytoff's original argument has been adapted and modified by numerous authors to explore how both people and objects change. Janet Hoskins (1998; see also 2006), for example, has used objects as a way of investigating the biographies of people, arguing that our social being is determined by our relationships with objects. Hoskin's ideas have been further recast by Jane Webster, Louise Tolson, and Richard Carlton (2014), who use artefacts to elicit oral histories from communities, finding the objects themselves to be effective 'interviewers'. Chris Gosden and Yvonne Marshall (1999; and papers therein) argue that human and object histories inform each other: as "people and objects gather time, movement and change, they are constantly transformed, and these transformations of person and object are tied up with each other" (Gosden and Marshall, 1999: 169). They argue that the meanings of objects change as they move through exchange networks, as they are caught up in social interactions, and that for long-lived objects their biographies shift as they persist through time (Gosden and Marshall, 1999). Gosden and Marshall (1999: 170) focus on how an object biography, rather than the earlier processual notion of use-life, allows an exploration of the shifting and multiple *meanings* that might be invested into an object over time as a result of 'social' action.

Two key early examples from the themed issue of *World Archaeology* edited by Gosden and Marshall illustrate these different approaches: Nick Saunders (1999) discusses the movement of pearls across the Atlantic, and Mark Gillings and Joshua Pollard (1999) explore a single stone from the Late Neolithic henge of Avebury in the UK (see Figure 5.3). Saunders' (1999) paper focuses on how as pearls moved from Indigenous to colonial social contexts, their meanings and values changed. For the Amerindians pearls were valuable because of their appearance as a material that glitters and shines, which evoked for them cosmic power (Saunders, 1999: 243). As pearls were moved across the Atlantic between the fifteenth and seventeenth centuries, their value became a product of their rarity, exotic origin, flawless appearance, and colour – and over time – their association with fashion and wealth (Saunders, 1999: 253). For Saunders, the meanings of pearls change as a result of a

FIGURE 5.3 Stone 4, Avebury, UK
Source: Mark Gillings.

shift of context; for Gillings and Pollard (1999) the mechanism is quite different. They focus on a single stone from Avebury and how its meaning has shifted, without it moving or being exchanged, as it persisted from the Late Neolithic to the present. The stone is static and also 'natural', yet its meaning, as they eloquently demonstrate, has shifted through time. Gillings and Pollard's (1999: 180) interpretation of the stone demonstrates that it is not simply a case of it being possible to ascribe any meaning onto the object, but rather that the material composition and stone itself restrict what is possible, and they go on to offer an early reference to material agency.

A decade after Gosden and Marshall's (1999) paper Jody Joy (2009) offered a reassessment in the light of a wide range of publications that had adopted the approach (see, for example, Fontijn, 2002; Whitley, 2002; Woodward, 2002). Joy's paper came in the wake of the rise of material culture studies (see, for example, Miller, 2005, and papers therein; Tilley et al., 2013, and papers therein) where the object biography had continued to provide a popular way to explore the complex and interwoven relationship between people and things. Joy (2009) suggests that the biographical metaphor can be seen as limiting; he argues that objects are not restricted to single trajectories and that they might die multiple times. Therefore, he suggests, the biographical metaphor might be "convenient" but perhaps counterproductive as it restricts us from thinking about the complex and nonlinear lives objects might have (Joy, 2009: 543–544). Despite this, he advocates for the continued utility of the approach, arguing for the importance of seeing biographies as relational, a product of the different relations that exist between objects and people at different times and in different places (Joy, 2009: 545).

While Joy critiques, but ultimately retains, the concept of the object biography, Cornelius Holtorf (2002: 50) has described those using the concept as having been "infected by … [an] intellectual virus" and has even declared the death of the approach (Holtorf, 2008). Considering specifically the application of the bio-graphical model to the study of monuments, Holtorf (2008: 412) argues that our current approach to this area of study fixates on the birth and early childhood of sites as we focus attention upon their original form, construction, and meaning. What Holtorf is effectively critiquing is a focus upon origins at the expense of process and history (see also Gamble, 2007; Chapter 1). Holtorf (2008) is certainly correct to argue that, all too often, object biographies, particularly of monuments, focus on the original construction and form, effectively presenting the site as static from that moment forward. This is not a product of biography as an approach, but rather the archaeological deployment of it; indeed, in traditional biographies childhood might be underplayed in comparison to adulthood.

Holtorf also argues, convincingly, that part of the problem with object bio-graphies is that we stop the life-histories of objects at the point they end up in the ground, discounting their history from thereon (Holtorf, 2002: 54). His argument is similar to my own from Chapter 3 with regard to seeing buried archaeology as static. Holtorf's argument does not go as far as my own though, as while he sees objects as continuing to change, it is clear that he still associates that change with the action of humans: "the life histories of things do not end with deposition but continue until the present-day: activities such as discovery, recovery, analysis, interpretation, archiving, and exhibiting are taken to be processes in the lives of things too" (Holtorf, 2002: 54). In contrast, I argue that change does not come from interaction with people alone as materials are themselves ever-shifting (Chapter 3). Focusing upon monuments, Holtorf (2008) picks up this idea of continued change once more to argue that monuments persist through time as effective reminders and pieces of the past, operating in, and influencing, new pre-sents (Holtorf, 2008: 413–415). In this case, he is more readily able to demonstrate how meaning changes following 'birth' as he shows how monuments continue to be interacted with in different ways by subsequent generations after their con-struction. He goes on to argue that, as a result of this persistence, monuments show the nonlinear nature of time as parts of the past intrude into the present and thereby how the past can continue to shape the present.

Object biographies certainly foreground change and provide an effective, and readily comprehensible, narrative structure through which to discuss the changing lives of objects. What kind of change is this though? The focus tends to be upon changes in the meanings associated with objects – meanings given to objects by humans. The things themselves are not changing, rather they are being moved through contexts, performances, and/or time, and the meanings invested and inscri-bed in them by people therefore shift. This change is often presented as a series of events where we recognise specific 'life stages' to produce a block-time image of

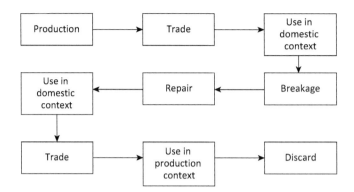

FIGURE 5.4 Generalised object biography
Source: R.J. Crellin.

change (see Figure 5.4). This staged presentation parallels the use of chapters in a biography, but, for archaeologists, it is also a product of the link between object biography and *chaîne opératoire*, an approach often depicted as a series of staged events and commonly used to write the early parts of object biographies. Holtorf (2002; 2008) is correct that all too often these are biographies that focus upon origins and production and, moreover, the common ending of a biography with death at the point of loss or burial serves to sever the flow of time and process, cutting the story short long before the end. From my perspective this creates further issues because it suggests that objects only change in the presence of humans.

Itineraries and multiples

The continued relevance of object biographies is perhaps a product of their potentially radical but contested nature. The approach laid the ground for the rise of material culture studies, demonstrating the entwined nature of people and things, as well as the argument that people have underestimated the power of objects due to their 'humility' (Miller, 2005). But where the ontological weight lies in the relationship between people and things is contentious. It is clear that in many readings (for example, Gosden and Marshall, 1999) it is humans who ascribe meaning to objects and it is as a result of interactions with humans that the meanings of objects change: the things presented in object biographies are very clearly *objects* and the humans are very clearly *subjects*. However, Michael Shanks (1998) has pushed for an alternative approach in which the relationship between people and things can be recast within a different power dynamic.

Shanks's (1998) argument is radical and was ahead of its time. He draws upon the work of Bruno Latour (1993) to argue for a symmetry between people and things by clearly rejecting the binary subject–object opposition. In this article the seeds of the later symmetrical archaeology (Olsen, 2007; Olsen et al., 2012 Shanks, 2007; Webmoor, 2007; Webmoor and Witmore, 2008; Witmore, 2007), discussed in Chapter 6, are evident. Shanks (1998: 3) argues that it is not just the meanings of things that change but that they physically alter too: they wear and they deteriorate. This change, he argues, parallels how people change as they age (Shanks, 1998: 4–5):

> Ageing and decay, basic aspects of the materiality of both people and things, are today often considered negatively. Worn out things are thought to be of no use to anyone and, when cleaned up, only of interest to a museum or collector. To be old and retired is not always to be valued and respected.
>
> *(Shanks, 1998: 5)*

By dwelling upon how our bodies deteriorate and decay, and how things, too, deteriorate and decay, Shanks (1998: 11) argues that the common lifecycles of both people and things are revealed.

Shanks' (1998) paper is one of his lesser known and cited works, arguably as a result of the radical proposition that it offers: that people and things might be considered to be equal ontologically. Richard Bradley (2002: 51; original italics) states that "there is a risk that the current emphasis on 'the cultural biographies of things' may lose sight of the fact that their main relevance to prehistoric archaeology concerns the ways in which such life histories cut across those of *particular human beings*". What Bradley (2002) is cautioning against is the decentring of the human from our research as a result of an emphasis upon the lives of objects. His argument captures some of the angst that surrounds posthumanist thinking, which we will return to in Chapter 7.

Shanks's (1998) work has begun to exert influence once more. Holtorf (2008: 243) has argued that it is an error to suggest that the identities of objects remain stable while the meanings associated with them shift: instead he asserts that the objects change too and are multiple (see also Holtorf, 2002: 54). This is a point that Shanks (1998: 14) has also made by arguing that artefacts are "a multiplicity". Andrew Jones, Marta Diaz-Guardamino and I (2016) developed this argument, suggesting that we should shift from talking about biographies to multiples. Our argument is that 'biography', as a metaphorical descriptor, "muddies our understanding of the complexities involved in the changes undergone by prehistoric artefacts" (Jones et al., 2016: 113). Nanouschka Burström (2014: 68) has argued that the idea of a biography is helpful in that it acts to structure thought and is a good tool through which to think; in contrast we ask how useful the concept truly is if artefacts might have multiple lives, die numerous times, and have lifespans that extend well beyond those of humans in length (Jones et al., 2016: 125). We take a new materialist approach that presents objects not as static things with shifting meanings imposed by humans, but instead we argue that objects too are always changing and multiple. Drawing upon the work of Anne-Marie Mol (2002) and Steve Hinchliffe (2010) we argue it is not just that objects are assigned different meanings by different people and are therefore multiple. Rather, we argue that artefacts are literally brought into being in multiple ways through different relationships involving both people and things (Jones et al., 2016: 127). We illustrate this argument using an analysis of a series of Late Neolithic plaques from the Isle of Man (see Figure 5.5). Reflectance Transformation Imaging of these slate plaques reveals that they were worked and reworked multiple times – they have been shaped, reshaped, decorated, redecorated, and even broken. These objects were always on the move, existed within multiple relationships, and were brought into being in very different and multiple ways at different times.

In a similar vein, and sharing some of the same points of critique with Jones et al. (2016), Rosemary Joyce and Susan Gillespie (2015) have introduced the idea of an object itinerary as a complement to the object biography. Joyce (2015: 22) argues that the object biography is too human-centred an approach to understand our world and that we need to understand objects on their own terms. Drawing on ideas of flow and meshwork (Ingold, 2007; 2015), the new materialisms (Bennett, 2010; Coole and Frost, 2010), and the work of Deleuze and Guattari (2014), they argue that objects are always in motion. Object itineraries are both spatial and

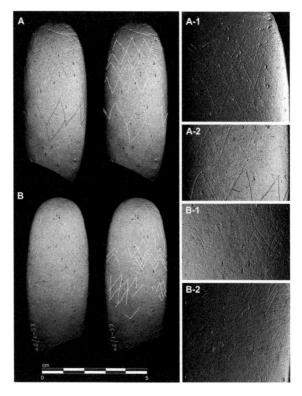

FIGURE 5.5 Annotated Reflectance Transformation Image (RTI) of Ronaldsway plaque 'e' (MNH 1965–0001/0050) from the Isle of Man. Obverse (A) and reverse (B). RTI image and annotation: Marta Diaz Guardamino
Source: © Manx National Heritage, from Jones et al., 2016: 118; Fig 3.

temporal, with "no real beginning other than where we enter them and no end since things and their extensives [representations of the object] continue to move"; they focus upon tracing the places where objects rest and how they move and circulate (Joyce and Gillespie, 2015: 3). Like others, they critique the biography metaphor for asking us to talk about multiple deaths, rebirths, zombie objects, or reincarnations to deal with the changing histories of objects following excavation (Joyce and Gillespie, 2015: 11–12). They illustrate how things continue to circulate following excavation and how these histories of circulation relate intimately to their earlier histories and are best approached as thoroughly connected. Their aim is to develop an approach that allows for the potentially long lifecycles of objects. They also make space for us to trace the movement and impact of representations of a given thing as well as the 'original' (Joyce and Gillespie, 2015: 12). Their ideas have recently been brought into explicit conversation with assemblage theory (discussed in Chapter 7) by Ben Jervis (2018).

MM RF 2014–0031 – a sword fragment from the Isle of Man

Having reflected upon both how people and objects change and the differing approaches that have been used to create narratives that seek to capture this change, I want to bring these ideas together to consider how best we might discuss a changing object. In this final section I begin to map the shape of things to come by focusing on the constant motion of a Later Bronze Age sword fragment from the Isle of Man held in the collection of the Manx Museum. I take a wide reading of the concept of motion to include both the spatial aspects, which are the focus of Joyce and Gillespie's (2015) itineraries, as well as the constant flux ongoing within both people and things (and, as chapters 6 and 7 will show, many others besides). The idea is to begin to show how we might talk about change differently in a way that eschews a biographical narrative.

The sword (see Figure 5.6) is actually a fragment of sword hilt currently located in the Manx Museum strong room but not owned by the museum. It was brought to the curator in 2014 and has been added to the museum's catalogue of registered finds as RF 2014–0031. This fragment was uncovered in 1999 while the owners were rotavating their garden; from that date onwards it was stored in a kitchen drawer until it was brought to the museum for identification.

Metalwork almost invites an approach that focuses upon narrating changing histories. The so-called lifecycle of bronze allows material specialists to discuss the *chaîne opératoire* of processes that produce such objects or to write object biographies tracing the changing history of such objects. Swords are exciting to think about in this way. We imagine their dramatic production with fire, molten alloys, and the work of an expert craftsperson. We might consider the exciting narratives of their use-life – were they brandished as weapons in anger? We might think about why communities buried these objects in the earth: were they considered to be no longer in use? Or did they continue to provide some other function? Both kinds of analyses are useful: there is much that we can learn about objects by seeking to map how they were

Break across the hilt

Lower rivet hole -
possible break?
possible corrosion?

Break across the blade

cm

0   5

FIGURE 5.6 Bronze sword fragment from the Isle of Man. Registered in the Manx
        Museum RF 2014–0031
Source: R.J. Crellin.

made, used, and deposited. On the other hand, both also limit our thinking: as I
argued above they often produce linear, singular narratives; they are anthropocentric;
they anthropomorphise objects; and they create an ontological separation between
people and things where all too often active human subjects impose social meanings
on passive objects, where people are the only source of change.

These approaches also risk isolating the sword fragment – the fragment stands
alone as the focus of the biography – but it is intimately linked to people: people
who dig up ore, people who sweat over fires smelting metals, people who might
use swords to harm others, and people who find and curate swords. Crucially, as
discussed above, these are people whose lives and physical bodies will be changed
through this interaction – changing their tolerance to heat through smelting,

developing muscles and injuries through fighting, and gaining an interest in the past accidentally while gardening! While the connections to people are manifold and clearly important, the sword fragments are also intimately linked to other-than-humans too: you cannot make a sword without fire, which might involve trees, axes, and flints. A good narrative of change surrounding this sword would bring all these things together.

Figure 5.7 shows the outline of the changing itinerary we might map for RF 2014–0031. We don't know where the sword fragment was made or whether it was made by recycling an existing object or smelting fresh ores. Metalwork wear-analysis is not particularly informative on this object either because it is highly corroded. The corrosion is almost certainly a result of the relationship between the fragment and the acidic soils of the island in which it was buried. We can, however, see that the sword, of which the fragment was once a part, has broken at least twice. One break is across the blade and the second on the hilt. The break across the blade is on a slight angle and has resulted in significant corrosion, strongly suggesting this break occurred in antiquity. The break to the hilt is a little harder to interpret as it comes at the point of the presumed second rivet hole. If this was the location of the second rivet hole then it was much expanded beyond what one would expect, and therefore it is possible that this breakage may have been the result of differential corrosion around the rivet hole resulting in the break-up and loss of material in this area (Crellin, 2017: 44). The same can be said for the lower rivet hole too.

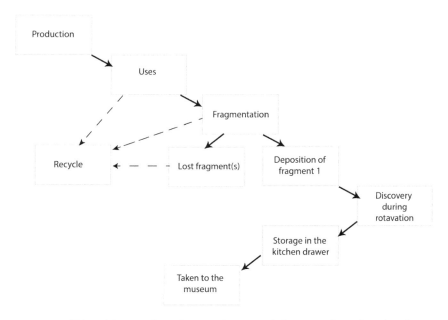

FIGURE 5.7 Object itinerary for a Bronze Age sword fragment from the Isle of Man (RF2014–0031). Solid arrows represent motion we can be certain of and dashed arrows the motion we cannot be certain of

Source: R.J. Crellin.

We can be sure that the sword the fragment was part of was broken into at least three parts and that one of the parts, the hilt, was deposited in the ground. Thousands of years later it was brought to the surface, stored in a kitchen drawer, and taken to the museum. It is now located in a strong room alongside other objects that the museum declares particularly precious. Bringing together all this information we can begin to show the changing history of the object from production, through to the museum where I eventually become a part of its story.

Mapping this story is not just a matter of tracing a simple, singular line though, because our sword fragment always exists enmeshed with other people, materials, animals, plants, places, and things at many differing scales. We might, for example, think about the other parts of the sword – were they buried elsewhere? Or recycled? Our fragment also has links beyond its physical location: photos of the object appear in lectures I have delivered, and the object's description and images appear in a publication (Crellin, 2017). Bruno Latour (1999) uses the phrase 'circulating reference' to describe how research processes allow objects and ideas to circulate beyond their physical presence. Our story is therefore not just a single line we trace, but rather a messy jumble of lines, where the object exists in multiple different forms in different places (see Figure 5.8).

There is a risk that mapping the itinerary could produce a block-time narrative of the type I critiqued in Chapter 1. This would be a narrative where human action punctuated blocks of stasis. Consider, for example, the breakage of the sword: this is a significant moment in the history of the object, one which

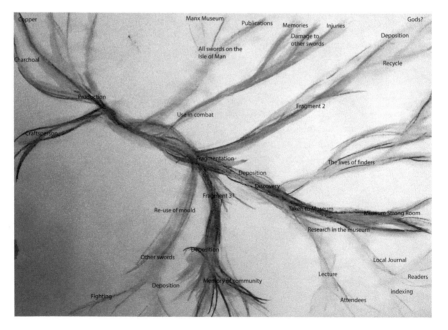

FIGURE 5.8 The complex, messy rhizome surrounding MM RF 2014–0031
Source: R.J. Crellin.

multiplies the number of narratives we can map for the object. Experimental work suggests that a breakage like this is unlikely to have happened during combat (see Crellin et al., 2018; Hermann et al., 2020) and more likely the result of deliberate action, perhaps heating the sword and using an axe to split it (Knight, 2018; 2019). The breakage of the sword is certainly a significant and important part of the history, but focusing on this alone, and telling the story in this way, continues to make humans the protagonists in the narrative and it makes the motion appear staggered. Consider how I described the sword fragment as resting in the kitchen drawer, or lying in the ground, as though it were waiting to be discovered. Such description makes the finder the key protagonist in the history, the source of change, or the meaning within the biography. But the fragment was not just lying in the ground, it was changing alongside the soil, worms, pebbles, and rainwater that interacted with it. It is during this period that the sword and the soil interacted to produce corrosion. As an analyst I look at the sword and am frustrated by how the corrosion, over which I have no control, has robbed me of the opportunity to interpret how the sword was used. The sword was not inactive in the ground; it was still in motion and its properties and potentials shifted as a result.

Here we butt up against the issue of tempo and scale. Our sword fragment is always on the move, but we tend to outline a history where this motion during burial in the ground is either ignored or plays out as insignificant. There are two reasons for this: first this motion does not directly involve humans, and second, it is a far slower motion, a motion imperceptible to the naked eye, over a timescale so vast we cannot witness it. We might say this motion is less important than the one that occurred to break the sword. We might even say it is unimportant, yet during analysis it was the corrosion motion that frustrated me the most.

We can think about the tempo of change in relation to the material properties of the sword fragment. The physical structure of a metal helps to define its properties. The strength of a metal, for example, depends on the arrangement of atoms within the crystal grains. The better aligned the atoms, the stronger the metal. In a bronze sword, atoms quiver and move within the lattice – they are always on the move, and changing the temperature of the sword changes the tempo of the motion. Considering these quivering, changing atoms and differing tempos of motion, we can begin to write an alternative type of narrative. The processes of making are not an issue of human will over material (see, for example, Conneller, 2011; Ingold, 2000; Jones, 2012). Rather, the properties of maker and metal, of tools and fire come together. For example, producing a narrow sword blade is indicative of work hardening, where the maker's hammer blows, aimed at the edge of the sword, affect the crystalline lattice of the metal: as the sword is hammered, the crystal grains become smaller and more regularly aligned. Exploiting these shifting material properties allows the maker to produce a stronger (though also more brittle) sword. Working the metal in this way changes the neurons in the craftsperson's brain, it develops their muscles in specific ways, and may even leave marks on their skeleton, thus both sword and maker emerge changed from this process. Producing more thinly bladed and sharper swords changes the kinds of action that are possible in the world, opening up new ways of being.

A sword does not stop changing after it has been made, though. The quivering atoms inside continue their motion. Corrosion stops us from being certain how the sword was used, but where it clashed with another sword, each of these blows would have re-aligned and shifted the atoms within. In some cases damage can act as a form of work-hardening, making the crystal lattice stronger; in other cases it creates weaknesses in the lattice. Wear has the ability to increase, and decrease, the tempo of motion within the sword. Damage and wear are not only the result of human action but emerge from the relationship between people, other objects, the exact alloy of the bronze, and the atoms within the sword. All these factors together produce the properties and capacities of the sword and affect the tempo of its motion. Our sword fragment was always relationally enmeshed with people and the world around it, and it was always changing, from the gathering of the ore to produce it (or the metal that was recycled to make it) up to the present and beyond as it circulates in images and print. This change is varied, of differing tempos, and had differing effects – but it is on the move nonetheless.

Conclusion

This chapter forms the beginning of a bridge towards the approaches discussed in Part III. It provided both a critical assessment of existing biographical approaches to change and also began to talk about a different way of approaching change, one that sees humans and things as deeply relationally entwined, one that asks us not to be anthropocentric in our approach, and one that argues that change (rather than stability) is the norm.

Throughout this chapter I have argued that biography has provided a way for archaeologists to address change head on. The metaphor of biography has given a methodological, theoretical, and narrative skeleton upon which different accounts of change can be hung. When we focus upon our own bodies we all too readily ignore how we age: we deny change. Biography, the lifecycle, and the life course all provide frameworks through which we can contextualise and discuss how we grow, change, and age. Research in this area highlights the material and physical nature of these changes, from changes to our bone structure, to shifts in what we might wear as we age.

Using the biographical metaphor to discuss how the surfaces of objects are modified, how they might be recycled, reused, or broken provides a metaphor to understand change of a potentially very different nature. It takes the unfamiliar changing world of things, a world of change that may be beyond our control, that may or may not be influenced by our actions, and that may perhaps be at staggeringly slow tempos and makes it familiar – like us, things age, they might break, and eventually die.

A biographical focus certainly foregrounds change and it has much to recommend it. In the work of authors like Sofaer Derevenski (2000) and Gilchrist (2012) the complex and nuanced nature of our changing lives emerges. In the work of authors like Gosden and Marshall (1999) and Joy (2009) the changing world of objects takes the spotlight – we can see that they are far from static. Their approaches could not be accused of being teleological, progressive, or evolutionary in nature; they eschew this kind of thinking through their focus on the small scale and particularistic. However, the narratives that emerge often focus on origins – consider Holtorf's (2008) analysis of approaches to monument biographies, where we all too readily focus on original meanings and fail to look at transformation over time. Many object biographies and lifecycle approaches often result in the production of staged histories with transformations akin to revolutions between them. There is also often a sense of determinism in some of these narratives: our bodies must change, age, and evolve as that is our biology, and what interests the archaeologist is how this change is culturally recognised. As I demonstrated, separating out nature/biology from culture in this way is far from helpful.

The continued popularity of biographical approaches relates to how they tackle change head on but avoid the potentially hazardous (though important) waters of the grand narrative through their focus upon the small (and often human) scale of analysis. In addition, the deeply anthropocentric nature of these approaches serves to further support their dominance. In many object biographies things are static, awaiting the enlivening hand of human agency to produce changes in the meanings ascribed to them: people are the motor of change. People are also the measure of change: the use of the term biography seeks to make change that can be radically different to that we most easily know appear familiar and understandable. When we say an object dies when it is deposited in the ground, or is buried by other-than-human processes, what we are really saying is that it is cut loose from human influence, it no longer changes, it no longer matters. The need to create stories where objects die multiple times and return as zombies shows the shortcomings of this metaphor – not everything changes like people do.

We set out from a position at the opening of this chapter where human change was perhaps most readily associated with our biology and nature and object change was cultural. As we moved through the chapter, I demonstrated the inadequacy of the nature–culture dualism for understanding the world (see also Thomas, 2004). I also illustrated how people and things are thoroughly entangled (Hodder, 2012) and produced together. As we shall go on to see, they are knotted together within a larger assemblage, including a whole host of other-than-humans, from plants and animals to materials and gods, and many others besides. All these different entities are always changing in different ways and at different tempos to produce our world-in-motion.

Note

1 Work on microstructural changes to dental enamel in mandrills has shown it may be possible to identify specific stress responses in relation to known events. In the future this technique may be applicable to humans (Lemmers, 2017).

Bibliography

Agarwal, S. 2016. Bone morphologies and histories: life course approaches in bioarchaeology. *Yearbook of Physical Anthropology, American Journal of Physical Anthropology* 159: S130–S149.

Anderson, D., Yoshizawa, T., Gollschewski, S., Atogami, F. and Courtney, M. 2004. Menopause in Australia and Japan: effects of country of residence on menopausal status and menopausal symptoms. *Climacteric* 7(2): 165–174.

Appadurai, A. 1986. Introduction: commodities and the politics of value, in Appaduarai, A. (ed), *The Social Life of Things*. Cambridge: Cambridge University Press: pp. 3–63.

Appleby, J. 2013. Temporality and the transition to cremation in the late third millennium to mid second millennium BC in Britain. *Cambridge Archaeological Journal* 23(1): 83–97.

Appleby, J. 2018. Ageing and the Body in Archaeology. *Cambridge Archaeological Journal* 28 (1): 145–163.

Appleby, J. 2019. Osteobiographies: local biologies, embedded bodies and relational persons. *Bioarchaeology International* 3(1): 32–43.

Bennett, J. 2010. *Vibrant Matter: A Political Ecology of Things*. London: Duke University Press.

Bradley, R. 2002. *The Past in Prehistoric Societies*. London: Routledge.

Buikstra, J. and Ubelaker, D. 1994. *Standards for Data Collection from Human Remains*. Fayetteville: Arkansas Archaeological Survey.

Burström, N.M. 2014. Things in the eye of the beholder: a humanistic perspective on archaeological object biographies. *Norwegian Archaeological Review* 47(1): 65–82.

Butler, J. 1993. *Bodies that Matter: On the Discursive Limits of Sex*. London: Routledge.

Conneller, C. 2011. *An Archaeology of Materials: Substantial Transformations in Early Prehistoric Europe*. London: Routledge.

Coole, D. and Frost, S. 2010. Introducing the new materialisms, in Coole, D. and Frost, S. (eds), *New Materialisms: Ontology, Agency and Politics*. Durham, NC: Duke University Press: pp. 1–43.

Crellin, R.J. 2017. Violent times? Use-wear analysis of bronze weapons from the Isle of Man. *Isle of Man Studies* XV: 26–47.

Crellin, R.J., Dolfini, A., Ucklemann, M. and Hermann, R. 2018. An experimental approach to prehistoric violence and warfare, in Dolfini, A., Crellin, R.J., Horn, C., Uckleman, M. (eds), *Prehistoric Warfare and Violence: Quantitative and Qualitative Approaches*. New York: Springer Press: pp. 279–305.

Deleuze, G. and Guattari, F. 2014. *A Thousand Plateaus: Capitalism and Schizophrenia*. London: Bloomsbury.

Dobres, M-A. 2000. *Technology and Social Agency: Outlining a Practice Framework for Archaeology*. Oxford: Blackwell.

Dolfini, A. and Crellin, R.J. 2016. Metalwork wear analysis: the loss of innocence. *Journal of Archaeological Science* 66: 78–87.

Fontijn, D. 2002. *Sacrificial Landscapes: Cultural Biographies of Persons, Objects and 'Natural' Places in the Bronze Age of the Southern Netherlands, c. 2300–2600BC*. Analecta Prahistorical Leidensia 33/34. Leiden: Sidestone Press.

Gamble, C. 2007. *Origins and Revolutions*. Cambridge: Cambridge University Press.

Gilchrist, R. 2000. Archaeological biographies: realizing human lifecycles, -courses and -histories. *World Archaeology* 31(3): 325–328.

Gilchrist, R. 2012. *Medieval Life: Archaeology and the Life Course*. Suffolk: Boydell and Brewer.

Gillings, M. and Pollard, J. 1999. Non-portable stone artefacts and contexts of meaning: the tale of Grey Whether. *World Archaeology* 31(2): 179–193.

Gosden, C. and Marshall, Y. 1999. The cultural biography of objects, *World Archaeology* 31 (2), 169–178.

Gowland, R. 2015. Entangled lives: implications of the developmental origins of health and disease hypothesis for bioarchaeology and the life course. *American Journal of Physical Anthropology* 158(4): 530–540.

Gowland, R. 2017. Growing old: biographies of disability and care in later life, in Tilley, L. and Schrenk, A. (eds), *New Developments in the Bioarchaeology of Care: Further Case Studies and Expanded Theory*. New York: Springer International: pp. 237–251.

Hawkey, D. 1998. Disability, compassion and the skeletal record: using musculoskeletal stress markers (MSM) to construct an osteobiography from early New Mexico. *International Journal of Osteoarchaeology* 8: 326–340.

Hermann, R.Crellin, R.J., Uckelmann, M., Wang, Q. and Dolfini, A. 2020. *Bronze Age Combat: An Experimental Approach*. Oxford: BAR.

Hinchliffe, S. 2010. Working with multiples: a non-representational approach to environmental issues, in Anderson, B. and Harrison, P. (eds), *Taking-Place: Non-representational Theories and Geography*. Farnham: Ashgate, pp. 303–320.

Hodder, I. 2000. Agency and individuals in long-term processes, in Dobres, M-A. and Robb, J. (eds), *Agency in Archaeology*. London: Routledge: pp. 21–33.

Hodder, I. 2012. *Entangled: An Archaeology of the Relationships between Humans and Things*. Oxford: Wiley-Blackwell.

Holtorf, C. 2002. Notes on the life-history of a pot-sherd. *Journal of Material Culture* 7: 49–71.

Holtorf, C. 2008. The life history approach to monuments. An obituary?, in Goldhahn, J. (ed), *Gropar og Monument. En vänbok till Dag Widholm*. Kalmar Studies in Archaeology iV: Kalmar: pp. 411–427.

Hoskins, J. 1998. *Biographical Objects: How Things Tell the Stories of Peoples' Lives*. London: Routledge.

Hoskins, J. 2006. Agency, objects and biography, in Tilley, C., Keane, W., Küchler, S., Rowlands, M. and Spyer, P. (eds), *Handbook of Material Culture*. London: Sage: pp. 74–85.

Ingold, T. 2000. *The Perception of the Environment: Essays in Livelihood, Dwelling and Skill*. London: Routledge.

Ingold, T. 2007. *Lines: A Brief History*. London: Routledge.

Ingold, T. 2015. *The Life of Lines*. London: Routledge.

Jervis, B. 2018. *Assemblage Thought and Archaeology*. London: Routledge.

Jones, A.M. 2012. *Prehistoric Materialities: Becoming Material in Prehistoric Britain and Ireland*. Oxford: Oxford University Press.

Jones, A.M., Diaz-Guardamino, M. and Crellin, R.J. 2016. From artefact biographies to 'multiple objects': a new analysis of the decorated plaques of the Irish Sea Region. *Norwegian Archaeological Review* 49(2): 113–133.

Jones, E.K., Jurgenson, J.R., Katzenellenbogen, J.M. and Thompson, S.C. 2012. Menopause and the influence of culture: another gap for Indigenous Australian women? *BMC Women's Health* 12: 43.

Joy, J. 2009. Reinvigorating object biography: reproducing the drama of object lives. *World Archaeology* 41(4): 540–556.

Joyce, R.A. 2000. Girling the girl and boying the boy: the production of adulthood in ancient Mesoamerica. *World Archaeology* 31: 473–483.

Joyce, R. 2015. Things in motion: itineraries of Ulua Marble Vases, in Joyce, R. and Gillespie, S.D. (eds), *Things in Motion. Object Itineraries in Anthropological Practice*. Santa Fe: SAR Press: pp. 21–38.

Joyce, R. and Gillespie, S.D. 2015. Making things out of objects that move, in Joyce, R. and Gillespie, S.D. (eds), *Things in Motion. Object Itineraries in Anthropological Practice*. Santa Fe: SAR Press: pp. 3–20.

Knight, M. 2018. *The Intentional Destruction and Deposition of Bronze Age Metalwork in South West England*. Unpublished PhD thesis, University of Exeter.

Knight, M. 2019. The deliberate destruction of Late Bronze Age socketed axeheads in Cornwall. *Cornish Archaeology* 56: 203–224.

Knüsel, C., Batt, C., Cook, G., Montgomery, J., Müldner, G., Ogden, A., Palmer, C., Stern, B., Todd, J. and Wilson, A. 2010. The identity of the St Bees Lady, Cumbria: an osteobiographical approach. *Medieval Archaeology* 54(1): 271–311.

Kopytoff, I. 1986. The cultural biography of things, in Appaduarai, A. (ed), *The Social Life of Things*. Cambridge: Cambridge University Press: pp. 64–91.

Latour, B. 1993. *We Have Never Been Modern*. Cambridge: Harvard University Press.

Latour, B. 1999. *Pandora's Hope: Essays on the Reality of Science Studies*. Cambridge: Harvard University Press.

Lemmers, S. 2017. *Stress, Life History and Dental Development: A Histological Study of Mandrills (Mandrillus sphinx)*. Unpublished PhD thesis, Durham University.

Lemonnier, P. 1989. Bark capes, arrowheads and concorde: on social representations of technology, in Hodder, I. (ed), *The Meanings of Things: Material Culture and Symbolic Expression*. London: Unwin Hyman: pp. 156–171.

Leroi-Gourhan, A. 1964. *Le geste et la parole*, vol. I: *technique et langage*. Paris: Albin Michel.

Lock, M. 1993. *Encounters with Aging: Mythologies of Menopause in Japan and North America*. Berkeley: University of California Press.

Lock, M. 2017. Recovering the body. *Annual Review of Anthropology* 46: 1–14.

Matczak, M. and Kozlowski, T. 2017. Dealing with difference: using the osteobiographies of a woman with leprosy and a woman with gigantism from Medieval Poland to identify practices of care, in Tilley, L. and Schrenk, A. (eds), *New Developments in the Bioarchaeology of Care: Further Case Studies and Expanded Theory*. New York: Springer International: pp. 125–151.

McDonald, M. 2017. The ontological turn meetings the certainty of death. *Journal of Anthropology and Medicine* 24(2): 205–220.

Meskell, L. 1998. Intimate archaeologies: the case of Kha and Merit. *World Archaeology* 29(3): 363–379.

Meskell, L. 2000. Cycles of life and death: narrative homology and archaeological realities. *World Archaeology* 31(3): 423–441.

Miles, A. 1963. Dentition in the estimation of age. *Journal of Dental Research* 42(1): 255–263.

Miller, D. 2005. Materiality: an introduction, in Miller, D. (ed), *Materiality*. Durham: Duke University Press: pp. 1–50.

Mol, A-M. 2002. *The Body Multiple. Ontology in Medical Practice*. Durham: Duke University Press.

Niewöhner, J. 2011. Epigenetics: embedded bodies and the molecularisation of biography and milieu. *BioSocieties* 6: 279–298.

Olsen, B. 2007. Keeping things at arm's length: a genealogy of symmetry. *World Archaeology* 39: 579–588.

Olsen, B., Shanks, M., Webmoor, T. and Witmore, C. 2012. *Archaeology: The Discipline of Things*. Berkeley: University of California Press.

Robb, J. 2002. Time and biography: osteobiography of the Italian Neolithic lifespan, in Hamilakis, Y., Pluciennik, M. and Tarlow, S. (eds), *Thinking Through the Body. Archaeologies of Corporeality*. New York: Springer: pp. 153–171.

Robb, J. 2009. Towards a critical Ötziography: inventing prehistoric bodies, in Lambert, H. and McDonald, M. (eds), *Social Bodies*. New York: Berghahn Books: pp. 100–127.

Robb, J. 2013. History in the body: the scale of belief, in Robb, J. and Pauketat, T.R. (eds), 2013. *Big Histories, Human Lives*. Santa Fe: SAR Press: pp. 77–99.

Robb, J. and Harris, O.J.T. 2013. *The Body in History: Europe from the Palaeolithic to the Future*. Cambridge: Cambridge University Press.

Roberts, C. and Manchester, K. 2010. *The Archaeology of Disease*. Stroud: The History Press.

Saul, F. and Saul, J. 1989. Osteobiography: a Maya example, in Iscan, M. and Kennedy, K. (eds), *Reconstruction of Life from the Skeleton*. New York: Alan R. Liss: pp. 287–301.

Saunders, N.J. 1999. Biographies of brilliance: pearls, transformations of matter and being, c. AD 1492. *World Archaeology* 31(2): 243–257.

Schiffer, M. 1972. Archaeological context and systemic context. *American Antiquity* 37(2): 156–165.

Schiffer, M. 1975. Archaeology as behavioural science. *American Anthropologist* 77(4): 836–848.

Schiffer, M. 2005a. The electric lighthouse in the nineteenth century: aid to navigation and political technology. *Technology and Culture* 46: 275–305.

Schiffer, M. 2005b. The devil is in the details: the cascade model of invention processes. *American Antiquity* 70(3): 485–502.

Semenov, S.A. 1964. *Prehistoric Technology: An Experimental Study of the Oldest Tools and Artefacts from Traces of Manufacture and Wear*. London: Cory, Adams and Mackay.

Shanks, M. 1998. The life of an artifact. *Fennoscandia Archaeologica* 15: 15–42.

Shanks, M. 2007. Symmetrical archaeology. *World Archaeology* 39(4): 589–596.

Sofaer Derevenski, J. 2000. Rings of life: the role of early metalwork in mediating the gendered life course. *World Archaeology* 31(3): 389–406.

Sofaer, J. 2006. *The Body as Material Culture: A Theoretical Osteoarchaeology*. Cambridge: Cambridge University Press.

Stodder, L. and Palkovich, M. 2012. *The Bioarchaeology of Individuals*. Gainesville: University Press of Florida.

Thomas, J. 2004. *Archaeology and Modernity*. London: Routledge.

Tilley, C., Keane, W., Kuechler, S., Rowlands, M. and Spyer, P. (eds) 2013. *Handbook of Material Culture Studies*. London: Sage.

Torrence, R. and Barton, H. 2006. *Ancient Starch Research*. London: Routledge.

Van Gijn, A.L. 2010. *Flint in Focus: Lithic Biographies in the Neolithic and Bronze Age*. Leiden: Sidestone Press.

Waldron, T. 2009. *Palaeopathology*. Cambridge: Cambridge University Press.

Webmoor, T. 2007. What about 'one more turn after the social' in archaeological reasoning? Taking things seriously. *World Archaeology* 39: 563–578.

Webmoor, T. and Witmore, C. 2008. Things Are Us! A commentary on human/thing relations under the banner of a 'Social Archaeology'. *Norwegian Archaeological Review* 41: 1–18.

Webster, J., Tolson, L. and Carlton, R. 2014. The artefact as interviewer: experimenting with oral history at the Ovenstone miners' cottages site, Northumberland. *Historical Archaeology* 48(1): 11–29.

White, T. and Folkens, P. 2005. *The Human Bone Manual*. London: Elsevier Academic Press.

Whitely, J. 2002. Objects with attitude: biographical facts and fallacies in the study of late Bronze Age and early Iron Age warrior graves. *Cambridge Archaeological Journal* 12(2): 217–232.

Witmore, C.L. 2007. Symmetrical archaeology: excerpts of a manifesto. *World Archaeology* 39: 546–562.

Woodward, A. 2002. Beads and Beakers: heirlooms and relics in the British Early Bronze Age. *Antiquity* 76: 1040–1047.

PART III

Time for a new approach to change

In Part I, I introduced the approach I have developed to describing, interpreting, and explaining change in the past. I argued that we must be bold, accepting both the opportunity (and the burden) that archaeology offers to us: it gives us a chance to help write and rewrite, define, and redefine our shared past. I argued that we have to engage with the grand narrative and offer alternative grand narratives that bring to the fore the many differing ways in which diverse communities have lived alongside each other, and how they altered and have been altered by the worlds they lived within. I argued that we have to engage with the grand narrative but we also have to do it in a way that allows alterity and diversity to rise to the fore and that stresses multiple and diverse histories rather than offering a singular, unidirectional, universal human history.

I argued that there are a number of hurdles that an effective theoretical approach to change has to overcome. We need to break away from taking a block-time approach to change where we present the past as units of relative stasis interspersed by moments of revolutionary change. Our descriptions and interpretations of change need to avoid being underwritten by progressive narratives and they must not be teleological. The present is not the apex of human achievement that we have been gradually journeying towards for all human history. We should avoid a focus on origins where the goal is to find a singular, pure, original version of a given phenomenon. We need to work towards descriptions and interpretations of change that avoid being technologically or environmentally deterministic. We also need to avoid an anthropocentric approach to change where humans are presented as the only cause or driver of change in our world. We must also avoid presenting narratives of change where a single cause, in a single moment, is given totalising explanatory weight.

In Part II I went on to discuss how archaeologists have tackled the behemoth that is change. I presented a history of archaeological thought focusing specifically on change. I then offered a more in-depth exploration of three key theoretical themes: time, scale, and biography. When the model of time that we employ is unilinear, uniform, and unidirectional, the narratives of change that emerge follow suit and thereby fall short. When we cleave the flow of time apart and divide past and present, we create interpretive problems for ourselves. In particular, when we present the buried past as static we deny the constant change that is ongoing underground and make it seem as though change only ever emerges from interaction with humans. I explored the relationship between scales of analysis and politics. There is no 'correct' scale of analysis; instead multiple scales messily fold together. When we strive for interpretive 'neatness' where our scales neatly divide, or stack like Russian dolls, we fail to reflect the reality of our world. Finally, I explored how biography has been used as a methodology, a narrative tool, and a theoretical approach to the study of change. Biographical approaches have arisen as a means of dealing with change that might otherwise be hard to grasp – our own attitudes towards ageing mean that we readily deny how we change over time. Similarly, objects change in ways that are radically different from that which we know: the biographical metaphor offers a way to describe change which is more readily familiar.

In Part III of the book I explore a range of emerging theoretical approaches. Broadly speaking, these approaches may be described as 'relational' as they focus upon the importance of the relations between people, things, animals, and plants (as well as others). Relational approaches offer a new way forward for archaeology and, as I will show, their potential for studies of change is significant. By placing an emphasis on how the relationships between different protagonists of diverse sorts bring forth the world, relational approaches avoid singular causation, revelling instead in complexity and thereby avoiding determinism. They present humans as one-of-many, where the role that other non-humans play in the world becomes part of our focus.

In Chapter 6 I address a variety of these relational approaches. I start with the work of the anthropologist, sociologist of science, and philosopher Bruno Latour. Latour's work has been incredibly influential across the humanities. I explore the application of his thinking to the problem of change and consider both its significant strengths and its weaknesses. I consider the work of the symmetrical archaeologists, inspired by Latour, who argue for a radically different view of what archaeology is and should be. I will also explore the relational 'entanglement' approach developed by Ian Hodder. Ultimately, I will argue that while these approaches allow us to avoid the hurdles identified in Chapter 1, they also have some shortcomings. In Chapter 7 I present my own approach: a new materialist, posthumanist approach to change drawing upon the Deleuzian-inspired concept of assemblage. The approach is explicitly post-anthropocentric and posthumanist, in that it advocates for an understanding of the world where we do not start from a position that sees humans as the most important actors in that world or as the measure against which all other creatures and things are seen to fall short. I utilise Jane Bennett's (2010) ideas about *vibrant matter* to present an alternative view of a world in constant motion, where change is not purely the result of human action or agency. The result is a complex and messy understanding of causation.

Chapter 8 is a lengthy case study that applies the approach outlined in Chapter 7 to the emergence of the Bronze Age in Britain and Ireland. I had originally aimed to write a far shorter case study, but, in the end, I took the time and space to offer an extended case study in the knowledge that theoretical ideas are often best illustrated through examples. The length of the case study is also a product of the nature of the approach: it is an approach that revels in detail and complexity. Finally, Chapter 9 offers a summary of my argument and a reflection on both the strengths and shortcomings of the approach I have developed.

What I hope emerges from Parts I and II is a sense that change is truly a difficult thing to talk about. It is hard to theorise, hard to describe, and very hard to explain. The combination of data that our work brings together and the geographical and chronological range of evidence at our disposal is fantastic and allows us to produce detailed narratives about our changing past. I explored case studies that told excellent, nuanced, detailed, and messy stories of change. Part III offers a potentially different approach to this most tricky of archaeological subjects. I offer this approach knowing that it can and should be further refined, but in the belief that the theoretical approaches discussed in Chapters 6 and 7 offer a radically different way to understand our world. They offer a different view of our world, with different protagonists brought into the spotlight and, importantly, they challenge our ways of thinking. The approach works to move beyond the hurdles from Chapter 1. I outline a theoretical approach that is not presented as the only way of working but rather as a way of working that I have found useful in allowing difference and alterity to emerge and which has allowed me to think differently about change, our past, and the challenges and problems we face.

Bibliography

Bennett, J. 2010. *Vibrant Matter: A Political Ecology of Things*. London: Duke University Press.

6

RELATIONAL APPROACHES

A better way to consider change?

This chapter explores a range of relational theoretical approaches that are gaining traction in archaeology. Over the past decade there have been a series of stirrings in archaeological theory, new approaches have been outlined, and there has been debate about what archaeology is (or should be) (see, for example, Alberti et al., 2011; 2014; Conneller, 2011; Fowler, 2013; Harris and Cipolla, 2017; Hodder, 2011; 2012; Ingold, 2013; Jervis, 2018; Jones, 2012; Lucas, 2012; Nativ, 2018; Olsen, 2007; 2010; Olsen et al., 2012; Shanks, 2007; Webmoor, 2007; Webmoor and Witmore, 2008; Witmore, 2007a). These new ways of thinking have been broadly termed the 'Ontological Turn' (Alberti et al., 2011) as their concern is not primarily with advocating for a new method or arguing for some under-considered aspect of the past to be brought to the fore (for example, meaning, gender etc.), but rather, what they suggest is that by changing our ontological approach, new understandings of the past can emerge. They are arguing for radically different ways of understanding how the world works, the categories we use to describe it, and what is considered to be capable of action in the world. These authors do not operate in an identical theoretical space, but much is shared between them: primarily, a concern for the relational nature of the world and a desire to explore radically alternative ontologies to our own.

Relational approaches are united by their emphasis on the need to understand things, not just in and of themselves, but as actively produced by the ever-changing relations they exist within. Relational approaches are far from homogeneous but seek to elevate the role of non-humans such as things, plants, animals, soils, rocks, places, and in some cases, beliefs and gods. Rather than concerning themselves *only* with the role of what we might term human agency in the past, these approaches seek to acknowledge the roles of a diverse cast of protagonists, including, but not limited to, humans. These diverse protagonists always emerge from highly interconnected and interdependent relations. As a result, dichotomous thinking that pits subjects against objects, or culture against nature, is inappropriate, as all things, be they human or non-human, exist in more complex and multiple relations than such thinking allows. A diverse range of metaphors for the conceptualisation of these relationships exists: for example, Latourian networks (Latour, 1993; 1999; 2005), Ian Hodder's entanglements (2011; 2012; 2016), Ingoldian meshworks (Ingold, 2011; 2015), and Deleuzian-inspired assemblages (Bennett, 2010; DeLanda, 2006; 2016). Chris Fowler (2013, 43–9) has argued that these diverse approaches are all metaphors to explore and visualise the relational nature of the world and the things that make it up. There are key differences between these relational approaches that need to be considered and, as ever, the devil (and difference) is in the detail; I will directly address this complexity at the close of the chapter.

The salient point for now is to consider what these approaches do to studies of change. Taking a relational approach has some rather radical consequences: one way to grasp this is to consider the subject–object relationship. Classically, we suggest that a subject is one who holds power and agency and is able to effect change in the world; the object is the one to whom this change is done (or done through, perhaps). So I, as a subject, am able to pick up a pen and write with it. I can use the pen to write a card filled with love to my Grandma, or I can use it to begin a feud with my neighbour – the pen is an object that I can move and control. A relational approach collapses this subject–object divide and instead considers how the pen and I are brought into being together. The pen allows me to complain to my neighbour about some petty thing, enabling me to become the kind of person who develops a feud. Or it allows me to show my Grandma how much I love her and thereby brings forth a different aspect of my character. My pen might run out of ink, or fail to write smoothly – these are all things I cannot control; at that moment, the pen is able to evoke a response from me (I might reach for an alternative, curse, or throw it in the bin). Relational approaches focus on the *relations* between things and how it is through relations that we might bring about change in the world – the pen alone cannot start a feud with my neighbour and my character means I would struggle to do it in person. Phoning or Whatsapping my Grandma will produce and demonstrate my love for her, but the time taken to hand-write a card produces a different type of relationship of a different character, with different qualities. It is a set of relationships between myself, my Grandma, the pen, a card, envelope, stamp, post office workers, and many others. Over time both the pen and I come to change: I have a lump on one of my fingers from handwriting, handwriting makes the brain work differently (James and Engelhardt, 2012), and it allows different types of relationships to emerge. Equally, the pen becomes worn and grubby, its shape shifts from how I hold it, eventually its ink is spent.

In this chapter I explore a variety of relational approaches. I start with the work of the sociologist of science Bruno Latour. Latour's ideas form our starting point for a number of reasons: they offer a readily accessible way of beginning to think in an ontologically different way; they have provided one of the main routes into this type of thinking and theory for archaeology generally; and because they were the starting point for my own journey. I will try to summarise the vast world of Latour's thinking, focusing upon his advocation for recognising the importance of things, adopting a flat ontology, and rejecting binaries. I show the utility of his thinking, but also highlight the problems that emerge from his network approach for archaeologists. I will then explore the implementation of these ideas in symmetrical archaeology and the influence of the philosopher Michel Serres and his approach to time (Serres, 1995; Serres with Latour, 1995; see also Chapter 3). Having built this foundation, I then consider the related, though different, theoretical approach of entanglement (Hodder, 2012; 2016). The aim is to demonstrate how relational approaches open the door to some radically different approaches to change.

Bruno Latour's actor network theory

Bruno Latour's primary research focuses on the anthropological study of scientists to explore how they produce knowledge about the world through their research (see, for example, Latour, 1987; 1999). This practical engagement with how science works makes him a rather unusual philosopher, as his philosophy is grounded in the study of laboratory life. Latour advances a view of the world, which the philosopher Graham Harman (2009) has come to term a metaphysics, that argues that humans are not ontologically distinct from all other things on earth. Latour argues that humans come to have effects in the world through the networks that they form around themselves. These networks are composed of both other humans and a diverse cast of non-humans.

In Latour's work, anything capable of acting in the world is termed an 'actant' (Latour, 1999: 180). The term actant is as readily applied to my pen, letter, and stamp from earlier, as it is to my Grandma and the postwoman. Actants are both things that we might traditionally label subjects and objects, and things we might label living or nonliving. Latour's use of the term actant paves the way for a different ontology to emerge where we elevate the role of non-humans to give them equal status to humans. For Latour, this acknowledges that humans act through things and entangle and enfold things into their projects.

Latour's diverse cast of actants only ever exist within relationships with other actants, which together form networks. Within a network the various actants come to depend upon and define each other. 'Actor network theory', the name most commonly used to describe Latourian thinking, makes a specific argument about the nature of agency. In the kinds of agency theory discussed in Chapter 4, agency is something we associate with humans: the woman has the agency to act. This kind of classical reading of agency is often contrasted with the anthropologist Alfred Gell's (1998) concept of 'object agency', which argues that objects can have a form of agency. Gell (1998) argued that when we stand in front of a piece of art it has the capacity to provoke a reaction in us (joy or disgust, for example) and thereby has a form of agency. This type of agency was described by Gell (1998: 20) as 'secondary agency' as he believed it derived from humans; the artist creates a particularly beautiful or grotesque painting and thereby *through* the painting is able to elicit a response from the viewer. The artwork derives its agency from a human source.[1] Latour is sometimes suggested to be an advocate for *object agency* (see, for example, Hodder, 2004: 36; Miller, 2005: 12; Robb, 2004): this is a misreading of his work (Webmoor and Witmore, 2008: 60). Latour's position on agency is that it is a quality of the relationships within networks. Actants are never capable of action on their own (no matter whether they are human or non-human); rather they come together to produce effects as part of a network: neither humans nor objects are the owners or commanders of agency. Agency is not linked to intention or consciousness (Latour, 2005: 71). Separating agency from intention allows Latour to continue to level the ontological playing field. In some interpretations of agency, it is readily linked to intention – we decide to pick up the pen. Wider readings of agency decouple it from intention because our actions in the world have effects we did not intend (Giddens, 1984: 10). Agency is not limited to intentional action and is not possessed by individuals but is a quality of relationships.

Each actant is defined by the network it exists within. Within these networks people and things (and others besides) become folded together so that they produce hybrids (Latour, 1993; 11–2). Latour (1999: 186–189) uses the example of a 'sleeping policeman' or (less elegantly) a speed bump to illustrate this hybridity – the sleeping policeman is there to slow down drivers. This is a job that could be done by a human, but instead the job can be delegated to a thing: the 'sleeping policeman'. In this way humans enfold non-humans into their projects so that they become thoroughly mixed together in networks.

Latourian networks exist at a range of scales, from the very small (such as an atom) to the very large (such as an institution like the post office). Any individual actant, when examined more closely, is always revealed to itself be a network. Consider the pen once more: it is a network of ink, metal, plastic, and rubber. Latour (1999: 183) uses the term 'blackbox' to describe a network that has stabilised in such a way as to become invisible. When my pen is working, I do not think about the ink, the plastic, the metal, the rubber: it is a blackbox. When the pen ceases to work, the parts become obvious as I change the ink cartridge or shake it to try and deliver ink to the nib. As Latour (1999: 185) states, "each of the parts inside the blackbox is itself a blackbox full of parts". Latourian networks bring into focus the multiplicity of different humans and non-humans that bring about change in our world.

Rejecting binaries and simple causation

Focusing on the relationships between multiple different actants that cause change to emerge means that Latourian networks eschew singular causation. One of the reasons relational approaches have become increasingly popular is because of their relevance to the climate crisis. The climate crisis is undoubtedly the biggest challenge that we face today. It is a challenge because there is no simple solution: stopping the proliferation of single-use plastic bottles alone will not stop the climate crisis; neither will increasing the amount we recycle, or becoming vegan. That is not to say that any of these things by themselves might not be good steps; rather the climate crisis has such a complex web of causations that combatting it has to have a very complex web of solutions. Actor network theory provides a convincing way to think about this problem (and its solutions). In Chapter 1 I discussed how the climate crisis is the result of "a whole host of complex and interrelated factors", discussing the role of corporations, electricity needs, and human hunger for meat as just some of the contributing factors. Following a Latourian approach we can see that a great many actants, both human and non-human, are enrolled in the production of the climate crisis and so the solution has to have a similar shape (this is something Latour (2017; 2018) has been explicitly thinking about in his own recent work). It is not the case that simply changing the behaviour of one individual will solve this: the change needs to be across the whole network, not just a change in human attitudes but changes in machines, things, animals, and plants too.

Binaries such as the subject and object, or material and social, have little meaning in an actor network approach. Latour (2005: 75) takes the example of having on the one hand a group of naked soldiers and officers and on the other a heap of tanks, rifles, paperwork, and uniforms. He shows that the people and the things are not opposed in a binary; rather they exist in a network to produce an army or a battle. Just as without soldiers there is no army, it is also true that without tanks, barracks, guns, missions, command rooms, and mess tents there can be no army either. Talking about the soldiers and officers as subjects opposed to the tanks and rifles as objects is a fallacy. In Chapter 5 I explored how imposing a nature–culture divide onto our studies of changing bodies was wholly unhelpful because nature and culture are so thoroughly mixed as to be indistinguishable: Latour holds the same position.

This position extends beyond mere binaries to also cover a whole series of short-hand labels such as 'politics', 'economics', 'religions', and 'the social'. In the opening pages of *We Have Never Been Modern*, Latour (1993: Chapter 1) talks about reading a newspaper: he considers how the news articles he read mixed together all kinds of different subjects in what he calls "imbroglios of science, politics, economy, law, religion, technology, fiction" (Latour 1993: 2). Considering a newspaper article on climate change, he discusses how the text jumps between the ozone layer, the chief executive officers of chemical companies, chlorofluorocarbons, heads of state, fridges, aerosols, and meteorologists. He demonstrates how our world constantly mixes all these things together, and yet we continue to try and label things in a purifying manner so that we can say something is the result of 'politics' or 'economics'. By talking about how humans and non-humans are caught up in complex and messy networks, and taking a position where agency is not located in individuals but distributed across heterogeneous networks, Latour (1993) argues that we should avoid these simple labels as well as binaries. From the perspective of change this means that singular causation also falls apart: climate change is not caused by politics, economics, or religion, it is caused by complex, messy networks of relations between humans and non-humans that eschew easy classification.

In the wake of this relational approach, the divide between culture and science also falls apart. We describe Latour as an anthropologist as his work is based on close observations of the real world where he seeks to describe and reveal how it works. That his subject is often the laboratory (Latour, 1987; 1999) raises a series of challenges to how we believe the world works. Traditional anthropologists of the early twentieth century often went to study little-known communities in remote parts of the world whose ways of life (and ontologies) were completely different to our own. Latour by contrast studied life in our own laboratories where he takes the familiar and makes it strange. In many anthropological accounts what is described is a very different way of seeing the world where, for example, shamans can become animals, or magic 'really works', and the anthropologist describes this as a set of cultural beliefs about the world. The reader is supposed to know that really people cannot become animals or that magic does not exist, as the anthropologist describes these 'false beliefs' as a cultural 'interpretation' of the world that is mistaken when compared to western science. Latour (2005: 117) wholly rejects this divide between culture and the world/nature/science. What Latour's metaphysics reveal is that none of these categories are real. There is no singular natural world onto which we place a multiplicity of cultural meanings, binaries do not help us to describe or explain the world, and there is no point in looking for simple singular causation.

The vanishing network

On the one hand, the world that emerges from actor network theory could be seen as very different to that which we traditionally know, one where microbes, petri dishes, and speedbumps all play a role in the production of knowledge and have the ability to change the world. On the other hand, it is a world that might seem familiar and perhaps align with your own experiences. The potential of Latourian thinking is significant, but, for the purposes of this book, we must consider how he approaches the topic of change.

The philosopher Harman (2009: 115) describes Latour as an occasionalist. Latour's philosophy emphasises that which exists and is real (it is therefore realist), and it focuses on relations as key to the production of everything (it is therefore relationalist). For Latour, actants are events – they are defined by their relations and the real things that happen to them; this is in contrast to a situation where we might define actants by their essence. For a philosopher of essences (such as Harman) there is some inherent, internal kernel of 'this-ness' that defines a thing; the breakfast bowl on my table has some bowl essence that means no matter whether it is upside down, the right way up, filled with breakfast, or empty, it is still a bowl. In contrast, for Latour, the bowl is defined by its relations – by being filled with breakfast it is a breakfast bowl; when used as a flower pot it is something quite different. For Latour the bowl exists within a network of relations; on the table containing porridge and a spoon, it forms part of a network. As I empty the bowl of breakfast, the network changes; indeed every time I remove a spoonful of porridge that network changes. For Latour every small change to an actant creates an entirely new network. The old network effectively vanishes, it does not persist through time, and this is why Harman (2009: 115) describes Latour as an occasionalist philosopher.

There are some significant advantages to this kind of occasionalist philosophy, especially when it comes to avoiding the hurdles defined in Chapter 1. Change becomes the norm in actor network theory: things are always changing, even as a result of small shifts within actants. This has a clear consequence for how Latour thinks about stability – stability is not just inertia but something that has to be actively produced; actants must work to keep things the same (Latour, 1999: 155). Producing stability requires the effort of "vehicles, tools, instruments, and materials" (Latour, 2005: 35). When change is the norm not the exception, it becomes harder to write block-time narratives of change and origin and revolution thinking can be easily eschewed as change is constant and ongoing. This also has a consequence for how Latour approaches time (see Chapter 3). Time is not just some kind of external container for all action, nor is it something that plods onwards as the motor of change, rather it is actively produced: "Time is not a starting point. It's not an independent force. Individual actors, for Bruno [Latour], create time by doing something irreversible" (Harman in Latour et al., 2011: 29–30).

In a Latourian model, chronological and experiential time are both real and actively produced (though in different ways); moreover, there is no one 'true' version of time that is universal. This leads to the last of the advantages of this occasionalist approach: Latour's relational realist approach and his occasionalist stance mean that he completely rejects explanations that suggest that things can be described to be true always, everywhere, never, or nowhere (Latour, 1999: 156). Consider a science experiment: we are told by the teacher that when we mix elements 'A' and 'B' there will be a resultant reaction 'C'. My experience of chemistry at school was that mixing of 'A' and 'B' rarely resulted in 'C'. The science teacher's response might be to say that I did not have all the variables controlled properly, or that I had made a mistake because the reaction between 'A' and 'B' *always* produces 'C'. Latour's position is different, he suggests that every time we carry out the science experiment it is different: different people, different equipment, different laboratory, and therefore different result. For Latour (1999: 156–157) there are not singular universal truths; rather, truth is historical, contingent, and localised. This is why he rejects explanations that claim to be always, everywhere, never, or nowhere true. His position is not relativist, or that there is no truth, but that truth is contingent and local but "nonetheless demonstrable and robust" (Alberti, 2016: 169). Every actant (whether it is a bowl, an experiment, or a person) happens at a single time in a single place – my bowl today is different from my bowl tomorrow. Such an approach allows us to completely avoid universalising and deterministic thinking.

This approach also has some significant disadvantages, however, particularly for a discipline like archaeology in which things persist through time. A single change to an actant results in the production of a whole new network, therefore actants are "perpetual[ly] perishing, since they cannot survive even the tiniest change in their properties" (Harman, 2009: 104). For Latour, things do not persist through time at all; a new network is created in response to every minor change. This denies actants both a past and a future, as actants are completely defined by their relations in a given moment, and a change in any actant in the network causes the death of that network. In such a model, how can an archaeologist expect to use an Iron Age pot sherd to help reconstruct life 2500 years ago – the pot sherd is wholly different to the one that was used in the Iron Age and the network that surrounds it has also changed.

How does Latour deal with change in his accounts? Latour approaches changing actants through the useful concepts of 'mediators', 'translations', and 'circulating references'. For Latour, mediators are actants that change the network (Harman, 2009: 15). All mediators create translations. Latour (1999: 58) argues that an entity "can remain more durable and be transported further and more quickly if it undergoes transformation at each stage". The phrasing is awkward here: things remain the same only if they are continually changed. This change and translation can be characterised by the concept of the circulating reference. A circulating reference is an actant that moves through time and space. In order to move through time and space, it has to be translated and therefore changed. Through the process of translation some aspects of the original actant are amplified and others are reduced (Latour, 1999: 70–71).

We can consider an archaeological example: the excavation of a posthole (see Figure 6.1). The materials are excavated and recorded; the context sheet (as a record) is clearly very different from the unexcavated or excavated feature. The context sheet loses something of the original soil but gains a kind of transferable and comparable description whereby it is allowed to move beyond the site back to an office. The soil samples from the fills of the posthole might be floated; the structural integrity of the soil itself is lost, but we gain a flotation record and a few bags of finds, offering an insight into what was within the soil. As the posthole circulates into a site report, the original soil, the context sheets, the analysis of the soil, and the flotation material are all lost in favour of the amplification of a few key features into a single sentence, but the role of the posthole as part of a structure is amplified into the interpretation of the site as a house. Another archaeologist reads the report and re-interprets the site not as a house but as an occupation area with fences; the posthole as part of a house is reduced and the posthole as fence is amplified. The posthole is a circulating reference: aspects of it are amplified and reduced as it is translated repeatedly; these changes make the posthole less local and specific and allow it to become part of a bigger picture (cf. Fowler, 2013).

Latour's approach has some key advantages when it comes to considering change. Change is the norm and stasis has to be explained, avoiding a situation where we characterise large blocks of time as being relatively static and locate change only in the transition at the end or the beginning. This also allows us to eschew approaches that emphasise origins and revolutions. Change is more than just the product of human agency: it is non-anthropocentric. Change cannot be considered in technologically or environmentally deterministic frames, as such simplistic labels, based on binary thinking, are dismantled by a network approach. On the other hand, it is clear that an occasionalist stance also poses a challenge to archaeologists – the vanishing networks of Latourian thinking could be considered unhelpful. The vast potential of Latourian thinking has been picked up on by one group of archaeological theorists in particular: symmetrical archaeologists.

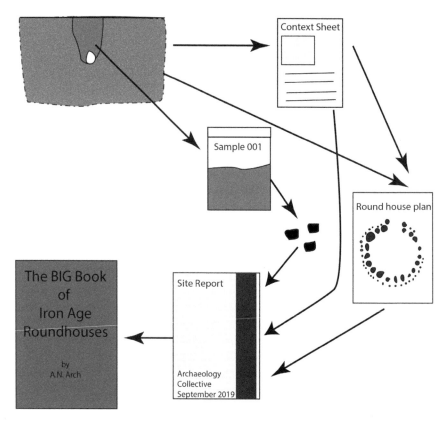

FIGURE 6.1 A posthole as a circulating reference. Each arrow represents an act of translation

Source: R.J. Crellin.

Symmetrical archaeology

Symmetrical archaeology (see Olsen, 2007; 2010; Olsen et al., 2012; Shanks, 2007; Webmoor, 2007; Webmoor and Witmore, 2008; Witmore, 2007a,b) is a self-defined school of theorists who have been deeply influenced by the work of Latour. Latour's (2005) actor network theory asks us to take a more 'symmetrical' approach to how we understand the world. His symmetry is opposed to the asymmetry we traditionally impose in an anthropocentric approach when we presume that humans are the most important protagonists in the world. This call for symmetry has been controversial, with some opponents suggesting it is about presuming humans and non-humans are the same (Barrett, 2016: 1682; Hodder, 2014; Ingold, 2011; 89–94; 2014). Latour clarifies the issue:

> ANT [actor network theory] is not, I repeat is not, the establishment of some absurd 'symmetry between humans and non-humans'. To be symmetric, for

us, simply means not to impose *a priori* some spurious asymmetry among human intentional action and a material world of causal relations.

(Latour, 2005: 76)

Advocating for symmetry is not about saying that humans and non-humans are the same but is about not presuming that the agency of humans is necessarily superior or more significant than that of non-humans.

Symmetrical archaeology launched into the archaeological consciousness in 2007 with a series of papers in *World Archaeology* (Olsen, 2007; Shanks, 2007; Webmoor, 2007; Witmore, 2007a)[2] and was further defined in the book *Archaeology the Discipline of Things* (Olsen et al., 2012). It is a clearly relational theoretical approach that draws heavily on actor network theory. In Christopher Witmore's (2007a) manifesto he presents six key slogans of the symmetrical approach:

- Archaeology begins with mixtures, not bifurcations.
- There is always a variety of agencies whether human or otherwise.
- There is more to understanding than meaning.
- Change is spawned out of fluctuating relations between entities, not of event revolutions in linear temporality.
- The past is not exclusively passed.
- Humanity begins with things.

(Witmore, 2007a: 549)

The key argument of symmetrical archaeology is that the world is a mixture not a bifurcation (see also Webmoor, 2007: 564; Webmoor and Witmore, 2008). Bifurcation is a term borrowed from Latour (1993) to capture how modern thought seeks to separate out the world into (often dualistic) categories such as people and things. This idea is explored most thoroughly in Timothy Webmoor and Witmore's 2008 article 'Things are us'. The symmetrical archaeologists argue that the world is always a mixture of people, things, places, animals, plants, etc. In some ways 'mixture' takes the place of the word 'network' in actor network theory, but in others it differs: their use of the term mixture captures how the world has always been mixed; since the first humans we have been a species that has evolved and changed alongside and with things. Things are as much a part of us as our blood, bones, and DNA. This gives rise to the final slogan – 'humanity begins with things'. As Webmoor (2007: 564) states, "humans and things cannot be artificially sieved apart, but rather must be treated as *a priori* ontologically mixed".

Their second slogan concerns agency and argues that there are a variety of agencies, including human and non-human agencies. Extending agency beyond humans seems a little like a misreading of Latour, as it suggests agency belongs to an actant rather than being a quality of relationships between them. Their third slogan deals with meaning, reading as a direct critique of post-processualism's focus upon meaning. For symmetrical archaeologists things do not just have meaning for humans, but instead they actively do things in the world and are mixed in with humans rather than being mere passive recipients of meaning.

Slogans four and five deal with change and time, and it is here that we can see the radical nature of a symmetrical approach to change. Symmetrical archaeologists actively reject technological revolutions, cultural transformations, and paradigm shifts as a way of explaining change (Witmore, 2007a: 545). Their critique of what Witmore terms the 'stratified' approach to the past was key in the development of my own thinking. They draw on the work of Gavin Lucas (2005) to argue that our approach to chronology "wraps blocks of linear temporality up into periods placed into neatly stacked boxes". This is what I term the 'block-time approach' to change in Chapter 1. From a symmetrical perspective people and things are always changing and this means that the creation of a block-time approach is always inappropriate as it creates artificial divides in the past. They advocate for a genealogical approach to tracing change as a counter to this (Olsen, 2007: 593–594; Witmore, 2007a: 546). This argument partly follows from their position on time (discussed in more detail below), which argues that the past and present cannot be separated – for them the past is not exclusively passed but continues to exist in the present.

Following Latour, the symmetrical archaeologists wholly reject dualistic thinking due to their argument that the world is a mixture. They argue that dualisms are always false and that any two things that we might oppose in a dualism are always "thoroughly mixed ontologically" (Witmore, 2007a: 546). They also critique approaches that suggest that dialectical thinking is a way of moving beyond dualistic thinking (see Figure 6.2). Dialectical approaches suggest that the two opposed parts of a dualism act to create each other. A dialectical approach, drawing on Marxism, is a crucial part of many theories of materiality (see, for example, Miller, 2005). Materiality approaches argued that we have ignored the role of things in our world and that we needed to consider them more directly (for a more detailed history see Harris and Cipolla, 2017; Olsen, 2007), which is also a key point for the symmetrical archaeologists. In the work of Daniel Miller (2005), a dialectical approach suggests that people make things, but things also act to make people. For Webmoor and Witmore (2008: 57) a dialectical is never a way to overcome a dualism because it starts with two opposed groups to begin with. Their withering critique of dialectical approaches allows them to demonstrate how their approach to things differs from, and goes beyond, materiality approaches.

As with all theories, symmetrical archaeology is not static nor monolithic, and how the approach is being thought about and implemented has changed over the last decade, leading Harris and Cipolla (2017: 138) to define two 'waves' of symmetrical archaeology. The first wave (including the early papers in *World Archaeology* and the book (Olsen et al., 2012)) clearly draws primarily on the work of Latour. More recent papers by Bjørnar Olsen and Witmore (see, for example, Olsen, 2010; Olsen and Witmore, 2015) take an approach that also draws upon the work of Harman (2009; 2016a). This has two important consequences. First, the engagement with Harman results in a shift in the definition of actants – actants are no longer purely events that are the result of their relations. Instead, actants are defined by an essence. They have certain definitional qualities that are pre-relational, qualities that

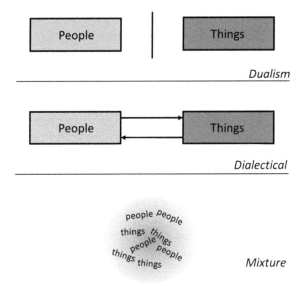

FIGURE 6.2 Dualism, dialectical, and mixture
Source: R.J. Crellin.

persist despite wider relational changes (see, for example, Olsen and Witmore, 2015: 193). The second consequence is a shift away from a focus on humans as one-of-many actants in the world to one that attempts to 'take things seriously' (cf. Webmoor, 2007), to engage with their 'otherness' and to 'decolonise' them. This feels like a progression from their early work where things always seemed to take up more of the ontological space than other non-humans. In some of the more recent symmetrical work there is little concern with the past (for example, Olsen, 2010, which does not include archaeological case studies), but an increasing focus on things alone and on ruins. Things are presented as colonised 'others' who need to be decolonised and allowed to speak (Olsen, 2003: 100), akin to the postcolonial approach to Indigenous and marginalised peoples (Harris and Cipolla, 2017: 138). Craig Cipolla (in Harris and Cipolla, 2017: 199) strongly critiques this position, arguing that to present things in the same way as Indigenous and marginalised groups does violence to the struggles through which those groups of people have gone (see also Cipolla, 2017: 225–227; Fowles, 2016). Both first- and second-wave symmetrical archaeology remain important and current.

A symmetrical approach to a Roman road

Symmetrical archaeology is often critiqued for its failure to provide developed case studies that show what the theoretical stance does to traditional archaeological accounts (Harris and Cipolla, 2017: 201). The worked examples they give often focus on specific objects (for example, Roman roads (Witmore, 2007a); the Millon

Map, and a pair of glasses (Webmoor and Witmore, 2008); ruins and abandoned buildings (Olsen, 2010; Olsen and Pétursdóttir, 2014; Pétursdóttir, 2012); and driftwood (Pétursdóttir and Olsen, 2018)) rather than traditional archaeological sites or period narratives. Their ideas, and those of Bruno Latour, have, however, been taken up by a variety of archaeologists who have applied them to more squarely archaeological case studies. Astrid Van Oyen has used actor network theory to study the role of the eponymous Roman ceramic vessels, Terra Sigilata (see, for example, Van Oyen, 2015; 2016). Ben Jervis (2014) has applied a relational Latourian approach to the study of medieval English ceramic assemblages. Peter Whitridge (2004) has used actor network theory to consider how changes to harpoon design among first millennium AD Thule whalers in the North American Arctic led to wider changes in the network of relations between people, whales, and boats.

In this section I choose to explore a symmetrical case study because it specifically highlights their approach to issues of time and change. Witmore (2006; 2007a) draws upon the example of a Roman road. Rather than seeing Roman roads as strictly 'Roman' or treating them as pieces of the past separate from today, Witmore (2006: 280; 2007a: 556) focuses on how Roman roads continue to have an effect in the present. He explores how sections of Roman roads have been used to create the modern transport network and argues therefore that they "still direct the flow of people's lives today … the past has not passed but still has action" (Witmore, 2007a: 556). In Latourian terms the original Roman road was a network of stones, broken stone, cement, and paving slabs, as well as the people and animals who walked, rode, and drove across it. This network has been translated into other forms – it might have been replaced by a medieval road, and while its material components may have changed, the original location and direction of the road have remained. Further translations transport Roman roads into the streets of today, crisscrossed by drains and high-speed internet cables, translated into concrete and tarmac. The original stones and Roman cement may now be metres below and have sewers and cable trenches dug into them, but they continue to have an effect on how people move through space in the present.

Witmore (2007a: 565) discusses how the Roman road network and contemporary transport infrastructure are made "proximate" today. For Witmore (2006; 2007a) this illustrates what he terms the percolating nature of time (discussed below) – it is not that the Roman road remains in the Roman period, rather it continues to exert influence today and is continually translated; in this way the present is a mix of times (Witmore, 2006: 280). Roman technologies as well as modern ones are made proximate. The narrative that emerges is one that clearly eschews a block-time approach to change. Here Roman things have not passed; they have agency but they have also clearly changed (been translated): the Roman road is not the street of today. This is a narrative with space for both humans and non-humans and where non-humans can be a source of change and shape action in the world as effectively as humans.

Percolating time

The example of the Roman road illustrates the central role that an alternative account of time and change has in symmetrical archaeology. In their 'manifesto' the symmetrical archaeologists state that change is "spawned out of fluctuating relations between entities, not of event revolutions in linear temporality" (Witmore, 2007a: 549). They have a very specific position on both time and change, which clearly links to the post-processual position as it rejects chronology as the only model of time and places archaeology as a subject firmly located in, and influenced by, the present. Time is not a measure, an external container, or a dimension: it is something far more complex (Witmore, 2007a: 556). Their slogan that 'the past is not passed' has two consequences. First, they argue that the past is not irrelevant but continues to exert influence and have effects in the present. Second, they see the present as a mixture of times. This argument takes its cue from their position on people and things: not only are people thoroughly mixed with things, but we are also a mix of times – technologies, objects, achievements, and knowledge from the past are all present in our world today (Webmoor, 2007: 573; Witmore, 2007a; 558). As discussed above, this allows them to squarely reject block-time narratives of change.

Symmetrical archaeologists draw heavily on the work of the philosopher Michel Serres (see for example Serres, 1995; Serres with Latour, 1995) in their understanding of time (see also Chapter 3). They draw on the link he highlights in French between the term for time and for the weather (*le temps*) to argue that time is not linear, where one block can be neatly stacked upon the next. Rather, time is turbulent: "Time is like the weather. It is full of calms, whirlwinds and chaotic fluctuations. Time percolates" (Witmore, 2007a: 556; see also Witmore, 2006: 279).

Serres (Serres with Latour, 1995) famously uses the metaphor of a handkerchief to reconsider time, suggesting that things that are far away can become close together by crumpling or folding the handkerchief. Witmore (2006: 279) takes this metaphor and makes it come alive with an archaeological twist. He argues that the timeline is the modernist image of time par excellence, where time is divided up into boxes that stack neatly in a row. He argues that if we place a timeline on a piece of paper and then fold the timeline we can make the Palaeolithic and the Iron Age proximate and therefore begin to build connections and see links between different times. This metaphor serves to illustrate how we can take a nonlinear approach to time – rather than wishing to separate time into blocks from different periods arranged in a linear chronology, we can instead look for connections between times and a different type of narrative of change can be allowed to emerge. Serres (Serres with Latour, 1995: 105) argues that we need to take a topological (rather than, for example, chronological) approach to our studies. Topology is about plotting the relations between things, looking for nodes of connection, and interaction between features that might have very differing dates.

Another key point drawn from the work of Serres (Serres with Latour, 1995: 49–50) concerns how we view the present. Serres argues that we should not believe that every period of human history constantly outstrips the previous one to produce the present as the zenith of human achievement. As Serres states, seeing the present in this way allows us to "be not only right but righter than was ever possible before" (Serres with Latour, 1995: 49). This type of thinking effectively separates the past from the present, makes the past irrelevant, and drives progressive, technologically deterministic, and teleological narratives of change. This informs the position the symmetrical archaeologists take when they state the that 'the past is not passed' and argue against a linear view of time.

Witmore (2006; 2007a,b) has applied his symmetrical approach to time and change to the study of landscape archaeology. He argues that landscapes are "polychronic" mixtures of time; they are not just, as the trope suggests, palimpsests (see Chapter 4) where past action might be erased from the landscape, decay away, or sediment into it; they are also places where distant times can become proximal (Witmore, 2006; 269; 280; 2007a: 556; 2007b: 196). It might be useful to imagine a landscape here as opposed to a section in a trench where different layers sit on top of one another in chronological sequence (see Figure 3.2). In the landscape, Bronze Age barrows might sit alongside Iron Age field systems, Neolithic henges, and medieval churches. In this way time percolates – it is gradually filtered through the landscape. Witmore (2007a: 556) argues that we actually produce time when we look at the landscape and wish to sort it out, to label one feature a Bronze Age barrow and another an Iron Age field system.

The symmetrical argument for a 'mix of times' is explored in a paper by Alfredo González-Ruibal (2006) (for a review see Lucas, 2007), where he considers ethnoarchaeology and its relationship to time and change, discussed earlier in Chapter 3. González-Ruibal argues for a symmetrical approach to overcome the "Great Divides" (by which he means dualisms); his focus is on the divide between past and present. As mentioned earlier, he discusses the experience of being in a West Ethiopian Gumuz Village and argues that a mixture of periods is present in the village (González-Ruibal, 2006: 111). He argues that attempting to pull out the 'Neolithic' from this mix of times does "violence" to the scene where ancient technologies sit alongside new ones. He goes on to argue that in these Ethiopian villages one can see an "inversion of times" as modern tractors sit abandoned in favour of wooden ploughs (González-Ruibal 2006: 114).

The arguments that are advanced by symmetrical archaeologists take a radical and critical approach to the concepts of time and change. The problems with approaches to change laid out in Chapter 1 clearly share much in common with the critique offered by archaeologists such as Witmore (2006; 2007a,b) and González-Ruibal (2006). However, I feel that their argument about percolating time is problematic. Ironically, it is only by dividing past and present that we are able to say 'this is an old technology' or this is a 'Neolithic axe'. Their attempts not to separate past and present and to see today as a 'mixture of times' are only possible by separating past and present and ignoring our own position in the scene as archaeologists who are able to state that some things might be Roman or pre-Neolithic in date. That people might still use a Neolithic adze today does not mean that the adze is a bit of the past in the present; it is clearly part of the present. Calling things 'mixtures of different times' takes a teleological view. Moreover, it brings us back to the problem of suggesting that change ceases once something becomes archaeological. The 'Neolithic' adze that is used today has changed, and continues to change, from its first use – it is not a static piece of the Neolithic. The Neolithic in 'Neolithic adze' needs to be used as an adjective not a noun; it needs to point to a changing history rather than indicating a pickled relic for whom change has been arrested. By focusing on mixture, the symmetrical archaeologists effectively move away from telling narratives that trace change through time.

Archaeology as 'material memory'

The archaeologist Laurent Olivier, particularly in his book *The Dark Abyss of Time: Archaeology and Memory* (Olivier, 2011), has had a significant impact on symmetrical archaeology, how it approaches time, and, more recently, how it understands archaeology as a discipline. Olivier (2011; see also 2004) rejects linear and unidirectional concepts of time, progressive narratives, and the idea that the past is what has passed, therefore sharing much ground with the general positions outlined by symmetrical archaeologists. Olivier (2011) builds an argument that what we study as archaeologists is not the past, but the past as it exists in the present. He argues that for things to persist through time they always have to change and as such we are not studying the past as it was (Olivier, 2011: 9); as Witmore (2014: 213) elegantly expresses, "archaeology does not deal with what was; it deals with what becomes of what was".

Olivier (2011) goes on to argue that there are many parallels between archaeology and memory. Memories exist in the present; they are discontinuous, fragmented, and as they are handed down over time, they change. The things we excavate are "memory recorded in matter" (Olivier, 2004: 204) rather than events or moments from the past (see also Lucas, 2005: 132–136 on archaeology as amnesia). As a result, he sees archaeology as more like the study of memory than history. This leads Olivier (2011: 48) to state:

> There is no way to restore the past, no way to reconstruct it, for the past *per se* never existed. It exists only as it has been shaped by what came after it and gave it its existence which is to say in a degenerated, deformed, and denatured state.
>
> (Olivier, 2011: 48)

Olivier's arguments sit well alongside symmetrical archaeology and in more recent second-wave symmetrical work it is clear that Olivier has become highly influential (in addition to Harman). Þóra Pétursdóttir (2012: 600; Olsen and Pétursdóttir, 2014) has argued that the discontinuity and fragmentation of the archaeological record are traditionally viewed as negatives. She argues that by seeing archaeology, as Olivier does, as a form of material memory (rather than as a fragmented and broken history), these negatives become less problematic as memory has absence at its very core.

The idea that archaeology excavates a kind of material memory and that the "present is a field of ruins, where past and future lie inextricably entwined, dis-membered, and crushed" (Olivier, 2011: 86) was arguably part of the spark that has led to the increasing interest of second-wave symmetrical archaeology in the study of ruins (see, for example, Olsen, 2010; Olsen and Pétursdóttir, 2014; Pétursdóttir, 2012; Witmore, 2014 and the Ruin Memories project http://ruinmemories.org/). Pétursdóttir (2012) selected an abandoned Herring station in Eyri in northwest Iceland to study because it was a neglected and crumbling ruin deserted by people. The abandoned factory, evocatively described by Pétursdóttir (2012: 578), allowed her the chance to study "how things exist, act and inflict on each other ... outside the human realm, and how they may remember ... [the] pasts in their own (alter) *native* way". In the article she explains that we could use the Eyri herring factory as a vehicle to discuss issues such as global capitalism and the rise of industrialisation, but that this fails to appreciate the ruin on its own terms and instead uses it as a means to an end (Pétursdóttir 2012: 589). While this may well be true, it also removes the opportunity to think about the roles of the objects and materials in the factory in broader narratives of change.

This work on ruins is evocative, and fascinating, but it is a very different type of archaeology. It is an archaeology that avoids the discussion of the past in many ways, and most certainly an archaeology that appears less interested in people than it is objects. Constructing narratives of the past is not the focus. Olivier's (2011) work is important and I agree with much that he has to say, particularly the point that for things to continue to exist they always have to change. However, I do think that we can still talk about the past and construct narratives about the past from archaeological evidence, despite the ways in which that evidence has undoubtedly changed and fragmented over time in order to exist in the present. I am also concerned that if we were all to abandon the study of archaeology for what it can tell us about the past (this is what seems to be suggested by authors such as Olsen, Pétursdóttir, and Witmore), this would stop us being able to talk about the kinds of histories of change this book is about. Moreover, it would not stop others continuing to talk about the past and our changing histories. I want to write narratives about the past and to produces histories of change.

Entanglements

This chapter has focused primarily on Latourian networks and how Latour's thinking has been understood by symmetrical archaeologists, as this provides a relatively easy way in to thinking relationally. To close the chapter, I explore Hodder's relational concept of entanglement (2011; 2012; 2014a; 2016; 2018) and its approach to change. Hodder's approach shares some ground with actor network theory as a result of its relational foundation, but also has some key differences, particularly because his work argues for a clear divide between humans and things. I will first outline the basics of the framework before critically evaluating the approach to change it offers.

Hodder (2012; 2016) is primarily concerned with the relationships between humans and things. He argues that things are not isolated, but always entangled in relationships with both other things and with humans (Hodder, 2012: 3). Entanglement theory suggests people and things are locked in dependencies: humans depend on things (captured in the short hand HT – where H is Human and T is thing), things depend on humans (TH), humans depend on other humans (HH), and things depend on other things (TT). Dependence and dependency are presented as a dialectic. Relations of dependence are those that are enabling, and relations of dependency are those that are constraining. Humans are caught in a "double bind, depending on things that depend on humans" (Hodder, 2012: 89). Hodder uses his shorthand to describe entanglement:

$$\text{Entanglement} = (\text{HT}) + (\text{TT}) + (\text{TH}) + (\text{HH})$$

(Hodder, 2012: 89)

What is a 'thing' in entanglement theory? Hodder (2012) initially adopted a traditional definition of things as objects drawing on Heidegger (1971). He draws a divide between things made by humans that cannot reproduce and natural things that can (Hodder, 2014: 30). However, he discusses entanglements with plants and animals, as part of the domestication process, in a way that indicates plants and animals can be things (Hodder, 2014: 29–30). In more recent work his definition seems to have broadened; for example, he argues that "ideas, thoughts, emotions, desires … institutions and bureaucracies" (Hodder, 2016: 9) are things. While what is included in the category of thing has shifted, it is clear that Hodder still draws a very firm divide between humans and the rest of the world, and he defends this separation on the basis of the human mind (Hodder, 2012: 9–10).

Human history, Hodder (2012; 2014; 2016) argues, is marked by the increasing entanglement of humans with things. For example, he contrasts the material culture of Palaeolithic, Neolithic, and present-day people to argue that there has been a clear proliferation of material things. Those things have become increasingly complex to replace, repair, and care for, and the result has been an increasing entanglement of humans and things (Hodder, 2014: 27–29). Things are always changing and breaking (Hodder, 2016: 142). This entraps humans into increasing entanglements with them as they seek to fix, stabilise, and replace things. 'Path dependency' is the term used to describe how particular practices direct us into sequences of increasing dependency (Hodder, 2016: 23–24).

Entanglement theory has clear connections to Hodder's (1990; 2000) post-processual position as he argues that we need to take a bottom-up approach where we build up from daily practice towards generalisations because this allows us to avoid essentialising and to make use of our detailed empirical analyses (Hodder, 2016:

10). He focuses on small events, at specific sites, and building up our analyses from there. Small-scale analysis can be used to answer big questions; the key is to start from the small empirical data rather than to try and answer big questions at a degree of abstraction (Hodder, 2016: 39–40; 43). Hodder's position on scale implies that he sees scale as nested (see Chapter 4).

Hodder (2016: Chapter 3) adopts a deeply relational position on causality. He argues that it is very hard to explain why things happened because the answer is always that multiple interacting causalities are at play (Hodder, 2016: 26). Searches for origins are therefore problematic because they always lead to the search for the origin of an origin (Hodder, 2016: 72). For example, considering the origin of agriculture, Hodder suggests traditional answers to this question such as 'climate change' or 'population growth' are unsatisfactory as they leave us asking 'what causes the climate change or population growth?'. The abstracted and reductive form of such answers suggests that we are researching a closed system where a single answer is possible, but the relational nature of the world means this is not the case. He argues that all "major transformations are simply the unintended consequences of the daily unfolding of human-thing entanglements" (Hodder, 2016: 40) and encourages us to search for specifics. This approach aligns with that of Latour (1993) who for the same reasons argues against shorthand labels like 'politics' or 'the environment' as explanations.

Entanglements and change

Hodder's work on entanglement marks a shift in direction theoretically, but arguably also in other ways. His more recent work is written for a popular audience (Hodder, 2018) and offers an archaeologist's perspective on human history and our future. It is political grand narrative; he discusses the climate crisis and its relationship to our increasing entanglement with things (Hodder, 2012; 2014; 2016) and the problems of inequality (Hodder, 2016, particularly Chapter 5). There are parallels to be drawn with Childe's work discussed in Chapter 2. These are books of their context, written from within late capitalism as we deal with 'throw-away culture', the proliferation of stuff, and increasing climate breakdown. There is much to admire about this work: it demonstrates the value, scope, and relevance of archaeology.

In the final chapter of *Studies in Human-Thing Entanglement* (2016) Hodder presents a critique of his own ideas by Susan Pollock, Reinhard Bernbeck, Carolin Jauss, Johannes Greger, Constance von Rüden, and Stefan Schreiber. They focus on his approach to change and describe it as progressive, determinist, reductionist, teleological (Hodder, 2016: 130–132), and universalising (Hodder, 2016: 140). They also argue that Hodder's narrative is written from the position of the successful, and therefore ignores many other possible stories about our past (Hodder, 2016: 131). Hodder responds strongly, beginning by arguing about his core thesis, that human history has been a journey towards increasing entanglement with things:

> Why do archaeologists retreat from their own observation that in the 'broad sweep of human history people have become more and more entangled in a material world they have created'? We are all aware of the dangers of social evolutionism. But is it not irresponsible to draw attention away from the one conclusion that archaeologists can readily agree on and provide evidence for, especially when the direction of that broad sweep of increasing entanglement is leading us as a species into difficulties?
>
> *(Hodder, 2016: 141)*

It is clear from Hodder's (2016: 141–150) response that he disagrees with the critics. He clearly sees his work as politically pertinent and important and argues that it is *directed* rather than progressive because he does not see the present as the pinnacle of human achievement, and takes a dark view of the increasing human contribution to global problems (Hodder, 2016: 150).

We could view Hodder's work as clearing many of the hurdles from Chapter 1. It is certainly grand narrative with political purpose.[3] He does not see his work as progressive, determinist, or teleological. His position on origins and causation, rooted in a relational perspective, holds much in common with my own and, as a result, he too rejects singular causation. Yet it is clear from the critique of his work that for some it certainly falls short. My own feelings are mixed. He is telling a very different kind of grand narrative, not one of progress but one where we are hurtling towards destruction, yet the story he is telling is distinctly singular, and we can see in the quote above it is the "broad sweep" that matters, not the multiplicity of different ways humans have existed in this world. While I do not deny that at the broad scale we see an increasing entanglement of humans and things, I wonder about what other stories are being eclipsed. The singularity of his grand narrative effectively erases alternative ways of being and ontologies surrounding things.

One way to read Hodder's work is that entanglement with things is what defines us as human. In Chapter 1 I critiqued essentialising definitions; they are static, leave no space for change, and therefore are often exclusionary. Hodder is effectively defining what it is to be human, but this definition is a shifting relationship (i.e. not static). Reflecting on the environmental crisis, Hodder (2014: 34) says we have to decide whether we want "to change what it is to be human, to become something other than ourselves". The singular nature of his narrative perhaps hurts him here, as while it is certainly clear that we need to make significant behavioural changes, it is not the case that all humans, at all times, have been locked into damaging relationships with the environment as a result of their entanglement with things. We have things to learn from both Hodder's narrative and alternative grand narratives.

His position on relational approaches is complex; he has suggested things and networks are really better seen as flows (Hodder, 2016: 9–10), holding much in common with the position I outline in Chapter 7 drawing on new materialism and assemblage thinking. However, he also suggests that entanglements are "not just networks or rhizomic flows" (Hodder, 2016: 145), arguing that they differ because of their emphasis on dependence and dependency, which means that they are not flat or symmetrical (see also Hodder and Lucas, 2017). The use of a dialectical (between dependence and dependency) explanation is a failure to overcome dualisms (cf. Webmoor and Witmore, 2008: 57) and to appreciate the complexity of the world (his use of shorthand formulas, particularly in the earlier work, certainly had a reductionist feeling). Hodder (2012: 93) has suggested, however, that he thinks the move against dualisms has gone "too far" and he is happy to draw a firm line between humans and things. My position is that one of the most positive things we could do with regard to the climate crisis would be to shift our own ontological position in relation to the environment so that we no longer see ourselves as separate from it and elevated above it. From my perspective, therefore, continuing to uphold binaries is damaging.

I also disagree with his position on ontological flatness and symmetry. Latour (2005: 76; see also Olsen and Witmore, 2015), as we saw above, argues that symmetry is about not a priori deciding to place humans in an ontologically separated position from the rest of the world. Similarly, as an assemblage theorist, I always begin from a flat ontology where I do not decide in advance who or what will emerge as powerful. Neither of these positions means that one cannot talk about hierarchies, asymmetries, or dependencies in power relations.

Hodder's (2012; 2014; 2016, 2018) work on entanglement is bold and interesting. Much of his position overlaps with my own, particularly his approach to causation and origins. This stems from the ground we share – we both operate within a relational framework and argue that things are not static. I admire the scope of his work, writing grand narrative, with political purpose, for a wider audience is no easy task. Indeed, to be able to write grand narrative that is not widely offensive is impressive and his political call for us to rethink what it means to be human is an important one (Hodder, 2014: 34). Despite this I find myself taking a different position, one that rejects dualisms and insists that we start from a place of ontological flatness. This is a position that shares more in common with Latour's actor network theory, but takes from Hodder the emphasis on writing long-term archaeological histories.

Conclusion – or why I am not symmetrical or entangled

This chapter has focused on relational approaches. Relational approaches posit that we can only understand the world and the way it changes by appreciating its deeply interconnected nature. They ask us not to study a given phenomenon (be that a pot, a person, or a cow) by itself, but instead to study it as part of a relational whole (a network, an entanglement). The different relational approaches have slightly different ontological foundations and priorities that have different consequences for how they approach change and even what they think archaeology as a discipline should be. One thing they hold in common, however, is a shared understanding that change is never simple nor the product of humans alone.

Change was at the centre of my PhD (Crellin, 2014); my initial starting point was to develop a theoretical framework that would allow me to move beyond a block-time approach. My desire to do this drew heavily on my engagement with first-wave symmetrical archaeology. I owe a great deal of my own thinking to what I have gained from an engagement with the work of Latour and the symmetrical archaeologists and, most particularly, their critiques of time and change. Why then, I imagine you might be asking, is this not a book about symmetrical archaeology?

Ultimately, there are two reasons why this book advocates for a relational approach that draws not on actor network theory but instead on the idea of assemblage (see Chapter 7). The first is to do with Latour's occasionalist stance and the second is my own desire to study the changing past. I find Latour's occasionalist stance difficult. I find it unhelpful, as an archaeologist, to work from a position where the slightest change in a network means that the network disappears. For me, things persist through time and are subject to constant change. A Neolithic pot sherd is not the same as it was 5000 years ago; its properties, potentials, and relationships have all shifted – but it does have the ability to tell us about the past because while some of its relations have clearly radically changed, altered, and even disappeared, others have remained more stable.

Second-wave symmetrical archaeology offers a solution to this problem by positing that what stays the same is the essence of the pot sherd. I do not think that a call to essences offers a solution to the problems of the 'vanishing network'. A call to essences posits a world where there is some pure and original version of a given phenomenon that can be defined in some way: here lies a route back to an *always* and *everywhere* stance where we can make statements like 'the essence or definition of the Neolithic is ….' and we can use this to create an exclusionary or universalising history. I also choose to remain squarely relational as I do not think that actants pre-exist their relations, rather I see them as emerging from them. No human has been born into this world without being already enmeshed within a web of relations with humans and non-humans, nor has any thing been made that is not enmeshed in webs of complex and diverse relations.

Latour's thinking regarding these issues has been interpreted differently by different thinkers (see Fowler and Harris, 2015). Harman (2009), as discussed, has argued that Latour is an occasionalist, where things are squarely relational, whereas Ingold (2011) has argued that for Latour objects pre-exist the relations they enter into. Ingold (2011) illustrates this with a visualisation that contrasts a network as a series of nodes joined by lines with a meshwork (his preferred metaphor) that is a series of lines from which knots might emerge. In the network the nodes (which are actants), Ingold (2011) argues, must exist first and then be connected by the lines, whereas in the meshwork the lines exist first, and thing emerge from the coagulation of lines. Chris Fowler and Oliver Harris (2015) take up these contradictory readings of Latour and ask how it is that we, as archaeologists, are to understand an archaeological site that endures through thousands of years using actor network theory if a single change to an actant produces a completely new network. They argue that there is a contradiction in Latour's work that allows it to be understood both in Harman's and Ingold's terms (Fowler and Harris, 2015: 132–133). They argue that this contradiction is productive as we need to understand both *being* and *becoming*, that is, both how actants come to exist in defined, bounded forms and how they change through time (Fowler and Harris, 2015: 144). They appeal to Latour's concepts of translation and the circulating reference (discussed above) and argue that "translations change some of the relations within a phenomenon *but not all of them at the same time*, meaning we can trace both historical change and continuity without appealing to the essence of the thing" (Fowler and Harris, 2015: 136, original emphasis). Their solution is to argue that what changes is some of the relationships that the site is enmeshed within, while other relationships remain unchanged, allowing the site to persist through time. This offers a solution to the problem of operationalising actor network theory for archaeologists. From my perspective, part of the problem here is that Latour himself is not as concerned with the processes of history as archaeologists are. I choose therefore to adopt an assemblage-based approach because it has a concern with history and change at its core.

My second reason for not adopting a symmetrical approach is that I wish to continue to study the past – a past that is not anthropocentric but still includes humans. Second-wave symmetrical archaeology seems little concerned with the study of people anymore and seems more squarely focused upon becoming 'the discipline of things'. Irene Garcia-Rovira (2015) identifies a split within the various relational approaches between the symmetrical archaeologists emphasising the study of things in themselves and those following alternativee approaches that are emphasising process and change in the past. Indeed, Olsen (2012: 25–26) has even suggested we should move away from the study of historical narratives. I have no objection to those who utilise symmetrical archaeology doing this. I find their work deeply fascinating, but I still want to write about the past, a past with space for both humans and other-than-humans to play a role in the coproduction of change. I am interested in tracing the development of institutions, ontologies, and ways of being, and I do not necessarily feel that is compatible with a symmetrical approach.

In contrast, Hodder's entanglement approach can be used to trace change in the past. I am inspired by the scope of Hodder's narrative; it is grand narrative with a political purpose. However, I find the singular nature of his narrative problematic; I think there are other stories to be told about our past that highlight different ways of living and being and I think that alterity is important and should not be eclipsed in order to tell a master story. My own relational position on causation and origins is shared with Hodder as we both reject singular origins and causation models of change. In spite of this, I do not adopt an entanglement approach because I find Hodder's use of dialecticals and retention of dualisms problematic. They serve to uphold a vision of the world where humans are separate from and ontologically elevated above the rest of the world.

I continue to be deeply influenced by actor network theory, especially when it comes to thinking about the production of knowledge and science and the practice of archaeology. Similarly, I find Hodder's work on entanglement deeply provocative. Despite this, I am more convinced by, and more engaged by, a posthumanist, new materialist approach drawing upon the concept of assemblage, and it is this which I discuss next.

Notes

1 *Art and Agency* is a complex book with internal contradictions. For discussion, see Harris and Cipolla (2017: Chapter 5).
2 Although cf. Olsen, 2003.
3 But see comments from the critics (Hodder, 2016) that suggest it is apolitical (139–40) and fatalistic (132–5).

Bibliography

Alberti, B. 2016. Archaeologies of ontology. *Annual Review of Anthropology* 45: 163–179.

Alberti, B., Fowles, S., Holbraad, M., Marshall, Y. and Witmore, C. 2011. "Worlds Otherwise": archaeology, anthropology, and ontological difference. *Current Anthropology* 52 (6): 896–912.

Alberti, B., Jones, A.M. and Pollard, J. (eds.) 2014. *Archaeology after Interpretation: Returning Materials to Archaeological Theory*. Walnut Creek: Left Coast Press.

Barrett, J. 2016. The new antiquarianism? *Antiquity* 90(354): 1681–1686.

Bennett, J. 2010. *Vibrant Matter: A Political Ecology of Things*. London: Duke University Press.

Cipolla, C. (ed) 2017. *Foreign Objects: Rethinking Indigenous Consumption in American Archaeology*. Tucson: University of Arizona Press.

Conneller, C. 2011. *An Archaeology of Materials: Substantial Transformations in Early Prehistoric Europe*. London: Routledge.

Crellin, R.J. 2014. *Changing Times: The Emergence of a Bronze Age on the Isle of Man*. Unpublished PhD thesis, Newcastle University.

DeLanda, M. 2006. *A New Philosophy of Society: Assemblage Theory and Social Complexity*. London: Continuum.

DeLanda, M. 2016. *Assemblage Theory*. Edinburgh: Edinburgh University Press.

Fowler, C. 2013. *The Emergent Past: A Relational Realist Archaeology of Early Bronze Age Mortuary Practices*. Oxford: Oxford University Press.

Fowler, C. and Harris, O.J.T. 2015. Enduring relations: exploring a paradox of new materialism. *Journal of Material Culture* 20: 127–148.

Fowles, S. 2016. The perfect subject (postcolonial object studies). *Journal of Material Culture* 21(1): 9–27.

Garcia-Rovira, I. 2015. What about us? On archaeological objects or the objects of archaeology. *Current Swedish Archaeology* 23:85–108.

Gell, A. 1998. *Art and Agency: An Anthropological Theory*. Oxford: Oxford University Press.

Giddens, A. 1984. *The Constitution of Society: Outline of a Theory of Structuration*. Berkeley: University of California Press.

González-Ruibal, A. 2006. The past is tomorrow: towards an archaeology of the vanishing present. *Norwegian Archaeological Review* 39(2): 110–125.

Harman, G. 2009. *Prince of Networks: Bruno Latour and Metaphysics*. Melbourne: Re.press.

Harman, G. 2016. *Immaterialism: Objects and Social Theory*. London: Polity Press.

Harris, O.J.T. and Cipolla, C. 2017. *Archaeological Theory in the New Millennium: Introducing Current Perspectives*. London: Routledge.

Heidegger, M. 1971. *Poetry, Language, Thought*. London: Harper.

Hodder, I. 1990. *Domestication of Europe*. Oxford: Wiley-Blackwell.

Hodder, I. 2000. Agency and individuals in long-term processes, in Dobres, M-A. and Robb, J. (eds), *Agency in Archaeology*. London: Routledge: pp.21–33.

Hodder, I. 2004. The 'social' in archaeological theory. An historical and contemporary perspective, in Meskell, L. and Preucel, R.W. (eds), *A Companion to Social Archaeology*. Oxford: Blackwell: pp. 23–42.

Hodder, I. 2011. Human–thing entanglement: towards an integrated archaeological perspective. *Journal of the Royal Anthropological Institute* 17: 154–177.

Hodder, I. 2012. *Entangled: An Archaeology of the Relationships between Humans and Things*. Oxford: Wiley-Blackwell.

Hodder, I. 2014. The entanglements of humans and things: a long-term view. *New Literary History* 45: 19–36.

Hodder, I. 2016. *Studies in Human-Thing Entanglement*. Published online under creative commons.

Hodder, I. 2018. *Where Are We Heading? The Evolution of Humans and Things*. New Haven: Yale University Press.

Ingold, T. 2011. *Being Alive: Essays in Movement, Knowledge and Description*. London: Routledge.

Ingold, T. 2013. *Making: Anthropology, Archaeology, Art and Architecture*. London: Routledge.

Ingold, T. 2014. Is there life amidst the ruins? *Journal of Contemporary Archaeology* 1(2): 29–33.

Ingold, T. 2015. *The Life of Lines*. London: Routledge.

James, K. and Engelhardt, L. 2012. The effects of handwriting experience on functional brain development in pre-literate children. *Trends in Neuroscience and Education* 1: 32–42.

Jervis, B. 2014. *Pottery and Social Life in Medieval England: Towards a Relational Approach*. Oxford: Oxbow Books.

Jervis, B. 2018. *Assemblage Thought and Archaeology*. London: Routledge.

Jones, A.M. 2012. *Prehistoric Materialities: Becoming Material in Prehistoric Britain and Ireland*. Oxford: Oxford University Press.

Latour, B. 1987. *Science in Action: How to Follow Scientists and Engineers through Society*. Cambridge: Harvard University Press.

Latour, B. 1993. *We Have Never Been Modern*. Cambridge: Harvard University Press.

Latour, B. 1999. *Pandora's Hope: Essays on the Reality of Science Studies*. Cambridge: Harvard University Press.

Latour, B. 2005. *Re-assembling the Social*. Oxford: Oxford University Press.

Latour, B. 2017. *Facing Gaia: Eight Lectures on the New Climatic Regime*. London: Polity Press.

Latour, B. 2018. *Down to Earth: Politics in the New Climatic Regime*. London: Polity Press.

Latour, B., Harman, G. and Erdelyi, P. 2011. *The Prince and the Wolf: Latour and Harman at the LSE*. Winchester: Zero Books.

Lucas, G. 2005. *An Archaeology of Time*. London: Routledge.

Lucas, G. 2007. Comments on Alfredo González-Ruibal: The past is tomorrow: towards an archaeology of the vanishing present. *Norwegian Archaeological Review* 39(2): 110–125.

Lucas, G. 2012. *Understanding the Archaeological Record*. Cambridge: Cambridge University Press.

Miller, D. 2005. Materiality: an introduction, in Miller, D. (ed), *Materiality*. Durham, NC: Duke University Press: pp. 1–50.

Nativ, A. 2018. On the object of archaeology. *Archaeological Dialogues* 25(1): 1–21.

Olivier, L. 2004. The past of the present: archaeological memory and time. *Archaeological Dialogues* 10(2): 204–213.

Olivier, L. 2011. *The Dark Abyss of Time: Archaeology and Memory*. Plymouth: Alta Mira Press.

Olsen, B. 2003. Material culture after text: remembering things. *Norwegian Archaeological Review* 36:87–104.

Olsen, B. 2007. Keeping things at arm's length: a genealogy of symmetry. *World Archaeology* 39: 579–588.

Olsen, B. 2010. *In Defense of Things: Archaeology and the Ontology of Objects*. Plymouth: Altamira Press.

Olsen, B. 2012. After interpretation: remembering archaeology. *Current Swedish Archaeology* 20: 11–34.

Olsen, B. and Pétursdóttir, þ. 2014 (eds) *Ruin Memories: Materialities, Aesthetics and the Archaeology of the Recent Past*. London: Routledge.

Olsen, B. and Witmore, C.L. 2015. Archaeology, symmetry and the ontology of things. A response to critics. *Archaeological Dialogues* 22: 187–197.

Olsen, B., Shanks, M., Webmoor, T. and Witmore, C.L. 2012. *Archaeology: The Discipline of Things*. Berkeley: University of California Press.

Pétursdóttir, þ. 2012. Small things forgotten now included or what else do things deserve? *International Journal of Historical Archaeology* 16: 577–603.

Pétursdóttir, þ. and Olsen, B. 2018. Theory adrift: The matter of archaeological theorizing. *Journal of Social Archaeology* 18(1): 97–117.

Robb, J. 2004. The extended artifact and the monumental economy: a methodology for material agency, in Demarrais, E., Gosden, C. and Renfrew, C. (eds), *Rethinking Materiality: The Engagement of Mind with the Material World*. Cambridge: McDonald Institute for Archaeological Research: pp. 131–139.

Ruin Memories project http://ruinmemories.org/ Accessed 01/08/19.

Serres, M. 1995. *Genesis*. Ann Arbor: University of Michigan Press.

Serres, M. with Latour, B. 1995. *Conversations on Science, Culture and Time*. Ann Arbor: University of Michigan Press.

Shanks, M. 2007. Symmetrical Archaeology. *World Archaeology* 39(4): 589–596.

Van Oyen, A. 2015. The Roman city as articulated through Terra Sigillata. *Oxford Journal of Archaeology* 32(3): 279–299.

Van Oyen, A. 2016. Historicising material agency: from relations to relational constellations. *Journal of Archaeological Method and Theory* 23: 354–378.

Webmoor, T. 2007. What about 'one more turn after the social' in archaeological reasoning? Taking things seriously. *World Archaeology* 39: 563–578.

Webmoor, T. and Witmore, C.L. 2008. Things Are Us! A commentary on human/thing relations under the banner of a 'Social Archaeology'. *Norwegian Archaeological Review* 41: 1–18.

Whitridge, P. 2004. Whales, harpoons, and other actors: actor-network theory and hunter-gatherer archaeology, in Crothers, G. (ed), *Hunters and Gatherers in Theory and Archaeology*. Carbondale: Center for Archaeological Investigations, Southern Illinois University: pp. 445–474.

Witmore, C.L. 2006. Vision, media, noise and the percolation of time: symmetrical approaches to the mediation of the material world. *Journal of Material Culture* 11: 267–292.

Witmore, C.L. 2007a. Symmetrical archaeology: excerpts of a manifesto. *World Archaeology* 39: 546–562.

Witmore, C.L. 2007b. Landscape, time, topology: an archaeological account of the Southern Argolid, Greece, in Hicks, D., McAtackney, E. and Fairclough, G. (eds), *Envisioning Landscape: Situations and Standpoints in Archaeology and Heritage*. Walnut Creek: Left Coast Press.

Witmore, C.L. 2014. Archaeology and the new materialisms. *Journal of Contemporary Archaeology* 1: 203–246.

7

ASSEMBLING CHANGE

In Chapter 1 I laid out a series of hurdles that impede archaeologists from studying change effectively. I argued that we need to avoid a block-time approach, writing progressive narratives, focusing on origins or revolutions, being teleological, determinist, or anthropocentric, and singular causation. In chapters 2, 3, 4, and 5 I explored the different ways in which archaeologists have described, interpreted, and explained change. I looked not only at the history of our approaches but also at the intersection of these approaches with ideas about time, scale, and biography. An effective approach to change must have a sophisticated approach to time where it is not just seen as an external container, or universal parameter. Our approach to scale needs to understand that scales do not just nest like Russian dolls, nor is there a 'correct' archaeological scale at which to work. Approaches drawing upon the idea of biography provide an effective narrative structure for change, but their anthropocentric nature and relationship with the nature–culture dichotomy are problematic. In this chapter I present the approach I have developed, which seeks to clear my hurdles from Chapter 1, develop an effective approach to time and scale, and take on the strengths of existing archaeological practices relating to change.

In the previous chapter I demonstrated the potential of a relational approach to provide a theoretical framework for the study of change. I explored the work of the sociologist of science and technology Bruno Latour and his 'actor network theory' as one potential way of working. His non-anthropocentric and relational model offers a way of overcoming issues of technological and environmental determinism, and demands we move beyond singular causation. However, his occasionalist approach to time and change, where any small change in a network produces a new network, creates problems for archaeological interpretations, which often stretch across thousands of years.

I also considered the archaeological adaptation of Latour's ideas by symmetrical archaeologists. The work of symmetrical archaeologists, and particularly Christopher Witmore (2006; 2007a,b), seeks to address many of the same issues as this book. Whereas first-wave symmetrical archaeology was arguably occasionalist through its engagement with Latour, second-wave symmetrical archaeology has abandoned Latour's occasionalism in favour of a model based on essences inspired by the work of the philosopher Graham Harman. For me, a model based on essences is not the solution to Latour's vanishing networks. The invocation of essences argues that there are parts of the world that are withdrawn, unseen, and pure. Essences are stable, unchanging, and ahistorical. I also think they risk turning our focus towards origins: the essence of a sword is this, the essence of humanity is that.

I also explored the relational approach of Ian Hodder (2011; 2012; 2014; 2016; 2018) in his work on Entanglements. Hodder is specifically thinking about how we approach change and writing impressive politically engaged grand narrative. However, unlike Hodder, I do think we need to move beyond dualisms and that we need to begin with a flat ontology.

In this chapter I lay out my own approach. It draws upon the concept of assemblage drawn from the work of the philosopher Giles Deleuze and the psychoanalyst Felix Guattari (2014) and explored and developed by the political ecologist Jane Bennett (2010) and the philosopher Manuel DeLanda (2006; 2011; 2016). I combine the concept of assemblage with a new materialist approach, drawing on Bennett's (2010) theory of vibrant matter.[1] I turned to these ideas for a number of reasons; first, because they are specifically relational; second, because they reject anthropocentrism; and finally, because they are also posthumanist. As we will see, feminist scholars are utilising these ideas as a means to question the historical definition of what it means to be human, which has focused upon white, western, straight men, and argue instead for a more diverse approach to our world (see, for example, Barad, 2003; 2007; Bennett, 2010; Braidotti 2013; 2019; Grosz, 1994; 2009). Their work is inspired by our current world: by late capitalism, by the increasing influence of machines, robots, and artificial intelligence, and by the highly mediated nature of life. For me archaeology is firmly situated in the present and the insight feminist posthumanist scholars bring to our current world is significant and inspiring, but I also find their approaches applicable and engaging for the study of the past too. These approaches are not only radically exciting and politically relevant, they also create a world where there is no space for teleological, universal, and unilinear approaches to change. Finally, new materialism and assemblage theory are theoretical approaches that have change at their very core. Thinking about change through time is not an afterthought in these theoretical frameworks but is instead central – just as it is in archaeology.

A post-anthropocentric *and* posthumanist approach

There are two key aspects to my theoretical approach. The first is that it is post-anthropocentric and the second is that it is also posthumanist. The post-anthropocentric aspect of the approach developed first following my engagement with the non-anthropocentric work of Bruno Latour (1993; 1999; 2005). The posthumanist aspect has developed more recently following my engagement with feminist critical theorists, most particularly, Rosi Braidotti (2013; 2019). In the recent archaeological (and broader) literature, the terms non-anthropocentric and posthumanist have often been elided. It is easy to see why: both terms share similar ground and the ontological re-imaginings of our world that they permit overlap at least in part. Non-anthropocentric approaches are concerned with the decentring of the human and the recognition of the key roles that non-humans have in the production of our shared world and of our human subjectivity. By contrast, post-humanist approaches are an active critique of humanism. Thereby they also seek to decentre the human, but this is coupled with a powerful critique of how the majority of our species were never included in the category 'human' to begin with. In what follows I discuss non-anthropocentrism and posthumanism in turn, aiming to show why they are often spoken of in the same breath. At the close of the chapter, as I move on to discuss the fierce critiques of both approaches that exist within archaeology, I aim to show why the political commitment of posthumanism is not only deeply necessary but also provides a response to some of the most common critiques of non-anthropocentrism. In the light of these debates I go on to explain why I no longer use the term non-anthropocentric, but instead prefer the term post-anthropocentric (see, for example, Braidotti, 2013).

Non-anthropocentric approaches argue that humans should not be seen as, nor are they, ontologically elevated above all other living and nonliving things on the planet (see, for example, Bennett, 2010; Latour, 1993; 1999; 2005). Bennett (2010: ix) describes how humans sit at the "ontological apex" in much western thinking. The conscious, sentient human, capable of action and agency in the world, is elevated above the animals with whom he (it is always a he) shares the planet and then, in turn, those animals are elevated above first plants and then the unconscious and unliving world of things and materials (see Figure 7.1). The work of Bruno Latour provides a sharp counterpoint to this anthropocentric ontology as it illustrates how things (in particular) come to completely surround, structure, shape, and impact upon our world. In the previous chapter I discussed the work of Latour at length and how he demonstrates that our world is co-constructed by the relationships between things and non-things that produce change together. In Latour's (1993; 1999; 2005) non-anthropocentric approach it is mistaken to see humans as the seat of agency and as ontologically elevated above non-humans because it is clear that non-humans play a central role in the production of the world, and it is mistaken to see agency as something possessed (either by humans or non-humans) because it is actually a product of relations.

Latour decentres the human by emphasising the non-human. The non-humans he most frequently focuses on are things. However, the calls to adopt a non-anthropocentric approach are far wider than just those that emphasise things. The feminist scholar Donna Haraway (2003) demonstrates how we as humans are deeply entangled with animals and that we both emerge together. Haraway (2003)

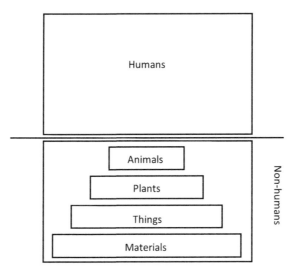

FIGURE 7.1 Ontological elevation
Source: R.J. Crellin.

shows that animals are a key part of our world, co-creating the structures we live within and producing our subjectivities. The result is a call for a multispecies understanding of our world where *Homo sapiens* are not ontologically elevated above all other living things. Similarly, the work of the anthropologist Anna Tsing (2015) focuses upon plants and fungi. Her ethnography is exactly the type of multispecies study that Haraway calls for and it demonstrates how people, plants, and mushrooms produce the world together. There are many other thinkers in different fields who have shown that our world is not produced by humans alone but emerges from the interactions and relations between humans and a diverse range of non-humans (see, for example, Banfield, 2018 on the relationship between cows and people in the Neolithic; Cipolla and Allard, 2018 on rivers and the fur trade; Overton and Hamilakis, 2013 on the role of animals more broadly; van der Veen, 2014 on plants).

The result of these non-anthropocentric studies of non-humans is an under-mining of human exceptionalism. This leads to calls for us to adopt non-anthropocentric approaches where humans are no longer ontologically elevated, nor are they seen as the lone seat of agency or the primary source of change in the world. As a result, many of those who follow non-anthropocentric approaches call for the adoption of a flat ontology (DeLanda, 2002: 51). The call for a flat ontology argues that rather than adopting a hierarchical way of understanding the place of different species, things, and materials within the world (see Figure 7.1) we should instead *start* from a place of ontological flatness where cows, pots, whiteboards, cars, brothers, and mushrooms are all capable of having an effect in the world, creating and maintaining the worlds we live in, and bringing about change. As discussed in the previous chapter, the narratives that emerge from non-anthropocentric approaches offer a radical re-imagining of our world where non-humans are elevated from their current inactive status into an active role in the world.

Non-anthropocentric approaches are about recognising the importance of the often-ignored non-humans in our world. Our humanist emphasis on human exceptionalism and uniqueness has left the many non-human others who make up our world by the wayside, incapable of effecting change, and unimportant. Posthumanist approaches are diverse, but generally focus upon a critique of human exceptionalism; the posthumanist approach I adopt is drawn primarily from the work of Braidotti (see, for example, 2013; 2019) and argues that it is not just the non-humans that we have been ignoring and presenting as passive, but also the majority of our species itself. The category of 'human' constructed by humanists was based around an idealised version of a white, western, heterosexual man (Braidotti, 2013). Those who did not fit within this category were ontologically inferior. The 'post' within posthumanist indicates that the approach exists as a radical critique of human exceptionalism. The ground is complex here; this specific posthumanist approach is not antihuman (which, as we will see, is a frequent critique of posthumanism), but instead is an approach that critiques a specific view of what it means to be human – where the category human is static and clearly bounded. This is a view rooted in Cartesian dualisms, in the ideas of reason, rights, and property, and a view where *Man* is the 'measure of all things' (Braidotti, 2013: 1–2; 13).

The work of Rosi Braidotti (2013) elegantly demonstrates that existing humanist approaches have served not to elevate all humans ontologically but actually only to elevate a certain subset of humans (white, straight, western, males) while 'others' such as women, minorities, LGBTQI+, non-westerners, and Indigenous groups have rarely been elevated to that same position. Humanism has served to consistently not only 'other' these groups but also to naturalise them (Braidotti, 2013: 15; 27–8). The human in humanism is an essentialised model of what it means to be a person. Braidotti (2013: 14, Figure 1) invokes the images of Vitruvian man in all his muscular, pure, isolated glory to represent the essentialised model of what it means to be a human at the heart of humanism. This is a man who stands above all others, alone, free from relations, the seat of his own agency, separate from the rest of the world and the messy, naturalised, and passive non-humans it contains. This 'essential' human is dehistoricised, held up as the timeless model of our species, and as the yardstick against which the majority of our species will never be positively compared. For posthumanists, our anthropocentrism and our humanism have not valued all humans equally.

Posthumanism shares ground with non-anthropocentric approaches as both critique the notion of human exceptionalism and decentre the human from our narratives (see, for example, Barad, 2003; 2007; Bennett, 2010; Braidotti, 2013; Ferrando, 2019; Grosz, 1994; 2009). Posthumanists frequently work from a flat ontology where they highlight the crucial roles of non-human things, plants, animals, and ideas in our world. It is crucial that I am clear about what a flat ontology is and is not. When I work from a flat ontology, I am not arguing that we live in a world where cars, shoes, cacti, people, and iguanas are all equally important and powerful. Nor is it about saying that in the pasts that I study pots, cremations, bronze axes, people, and seeds are all equally important or powerful. Rather, it is about saying that all these different protagonists are *equally capable* of having an effect in our world. I start from a place of ontological flatness where I do not presume *in advance* that humans (and especially white, western, heterosexual men) are going to be the most important protagonists. I do not impose an ontological hierarchy on the past because I know that our current Cartesian ontological hierarchy is a product of European Enlightenment thinking (cf. Thomas, 2004a) and is not the only way to understand the world (see Harris and Crellin, 2018 for a discussion of ontology in pre-Roman Europe). Moreover, when I consider the world around me today, I do not consider humanist and anthropocentric thinking to best capture either how the world works or to represent a politically positive way to think about my relations to those who surround me. Adopting a flat ontology is a starting point. It does not mean that one has to necessarily take a heterarchical or egalitarian approach to relations (though both are possible), nor does it mean that a hierarchy cannot emerge; instead it leaves the ground open for different ontologies to emerge.

A related point emerges when we consider the different humans and non-humans who make up the world. Non-anthropocentric approaches do not suggest that humans and non-humans are the same: jam jars and prime ministers are clearly quite different; equally jam jars and plates are also clearly different (see Dawney et al., 2017: 122). Posthumanist approaches similarly do not argue that there are no differences between all those who make up our human species: I am different from you. Rather they argue that difference is the driving force that produces humans. Instead of measuring the difference of a given thing, animal, plant, or person from an idealised and essentialised 'type' (i.e. as in humanism), these approaches choose to appreciate difference as a productive force in the emergence of both humans and non-humans (Deleuze, 2004; for an archaeological application see Bickle, 2019).

Braidotti (2013) argues that we need to be *both* posthumanist *and* post-anthropocentric (a term she uses instead of non-anthropocentric, and one I explore in more depth below); that means we need to critique human exceptionalism by appreciating both the diverse cast of non-humans who are crucial in the co-creation of our world and subjectivity, as well as critiquing how humanism has not valued all humans equally. In many ways one can think about this as an approach to a double hierarchy. Non-anthropocentric approaches critique the ontological hierarchy that *a priori* places humans above all non-humans and posthumanism critiques the ontological hierarchy that places white, straight, Euro-American men above all other humans.

New materialisms

New materialism is a theoretical approach that is relational, non-anthropocentric, and (can be) posthumanist. New materialist thinkers argue for a reconsideration of the role of materials in our world. Like Marxist materialists they argue for the

importance of the material world, but they argue for a radically different understanding of the nature of matter. This thinking emerges from the work of a range
of different scholars (particularly feminist philosophers), including Karen Barad
(2003; 2007), Jane Bennett (2010), Rosi Braidotti (2013), Manuel DeLanda (2006;
2016), Francesca Ferrando (2019), Elizabeth Grosz (1994), and Tim Ingold (2007a,
b; 2011). As with most philosophical and theoretical viewpoints, not all the thinkers agree precisely or in totality. These thinkers often draw their inspiration from
the work of Deleuze and Guattari (2014) and their thinking also draws upon both
the humanities and philosophy, as well as the increasingly complex understandings
of matter emerging from the hard sciences.

New materialist approaches reject binary oppositions that separate mind and
matter, nature and culture, animate and inanimate. Coole and Frost (2010: 8)
consider how Cartesian-Newtonian understandings of matter suggest it is static,
quantifiable, bounded, and incapable of movement without the application of
force. New materialists argue that matter is never just brute, dead, substance that is
manipulated by human agency, but instead argue it is lively, ever shifting, and full
of potential (for example, Bennett, 2010). All matter has properties and capacities
that form (and change) as a result of the relations that it is caught up within. Matter
is always changing, it is unpredictable, and uncontrollable (Gosden and Malafouris,
2015: 703). Rather than the properties of matter being a fixed and essential list
known to us through science, in new materialist thinking, properties are emergent,
immanent, and always relational. Consider bronze as a material: in school we learn
some of the properties of bronze are malleability, ductility, and its ability to conduct heat or electricity, but new materialism argues that these properties are not
essential to the material but emerge relationally. It is only through bending bronze
I learn of its ductility, it is only through holding it in my hand that conducting heat
emerges as a property (cf. Barad, 2007). Alone, in a vacuum, divorced from relations, these properties do not emerge. In the same way that Latour (1993; 1999;
2005) elevates non-humans and Haraway (2003) elevates animals, new materialists
ontologically elevate the materials from which things, people, and plants are all
made, and as with non-anthropocentric approaches, they also thereby critique
human exceptionalism.

In the Cartesian-Newtonian view of matter it acts as a blank canvas for the
application of human will. We take inert matter and, via our human agency, we
are able to bend it to our will, to design and make from it. The active human is the
master of the inert material. This understanding of the relationship between matter
and maker is often termed hylomorphic, where inert matter is formed and shaped
by human agents. The new materialist stance is not that matter is inert, but that it
too is capable of effect; as with Latour (2005: 71), agency is not held by either the
human or the material but instead emerges from relations. Matter is capable of self-
organisation without the interference of humans (DeLanda 2011). It also shifts and
changes without our interference. Ingold (2000; 2007a) provides an example from
his reflection on the process of weaving a basket, where it is clear that the material
plays a central role in the weaving process itself, almost guiding the hands of the

maker (Ingold, 2000: 339–348).[2] The process of making emerges not as the imposition of agency and will but instead as the relational coming together of maker and material with both playing an active role in the processes of making and in the outcomes (Ingold, 2000: 339–348; 2007a,b; 2011; 2012: 433; 2013; cf. Gosden and Malafouris, 2015: 704–707 on the process of pottery production).

In archaeology to date, new materialist thinking is arguably best explored in the work of Chantal Conneller (2011) and Andrew Jones (2012). Conneller (2011: 4–7) neatly illustrates how the properties and definition of materials are not fixed, by exploring the different attitudes of the Spanish conquistadors and the Incas to gold. For the Spanish the value of gold came from its purity and rarity. Purity was its key property. By contrast the value of gold for Indigenous groups came from its links to spiritual sunlight and the key role it played in shamanism. Gold was valued for its redness – a redness that was achieved by combining the gold with copper making the resultant colour even more like the sun. Redness, for the Indigenous people was one of gold's key properties. It is not that one of these interpretations is 'scientifically true', or that the properties of gold can only be the ones of the Spanish or the ones of the Indigenous peoples, rather the capacities and properties of gold are relational and true in both cases.

New materialism, in part at least, responds to the linguistic turn in the social sciences. The linguistic turn finds its easiest comparison in archaeology, within some strands of post-processualism. These focused upon structuralism and semiotics as ways to explore the symbolism and meaning of material culture. By contrast, new materialist approaches focus upon the material itself. It is not the case, however, that new materialists necessarily deny the importance of symbolism and meaning, or the linguistic turn. Rather, they seek to avoid drawing a binary between mind and matter and see the two as inseparable. Their work can combine both the analysis of the role of materials with analysis of the meanings that come to reside in them. Jones's (2012) work is a good example of the combination of the two: he considers how materials, and their properties contribute to the development of meaning in the past. For example, Jones (2012: 136–143) considers Migdale-period (c. 2100–1900BC) axe hoards, which sometimes contain a mix of objects but more commonly contain just multiple axes. Axe production required the use of a mould in which to cast the molten bronze. The use of a mould allows the production of simulacra. In hoards, Jones (2012: 139) argues, what we often see is a play on similarity and difference as assemblages of both similar and different axes are brought together (see also Crellin, 2018 for a discussion of difference in hoards). Jones's argument draws upon the material properties of bronze (as a molten liquid that can be cast in a mould) and the specific gathering of axes for hoards in order to consider meaning.

In 2014 Witmore published a paper titled 'Archaeology and the new materialisms' in which he appears to advocate for a turn away from symmetrical archaeology (see Chapter 6) towards new materialism. One of the key issues in the differing interpretation and application of new materialism is the vision that different authors have for what a new materialist archaeology should be. For Conneller (2011) and Jones

(2012), the archaeology that emerges from their engagement with new materialist thinking is wholly recognisable as a study of the material past, but one with a different ontology, where humans alone are not the sole focus nor the locus of change or agency. For Witmore (2014), his new materialist archaeology appears far less concerned with the study of humans as part of the material past and far more concerned with the study of objects alone: as discussed in Chapter 6, I follow Harris and Cipolla (2017: 138) in seeing this move as part of 'second-wave symmetrical archaeology'. Witmore's stance is certainly non-anthropocentric, but I am not sure I would define it as posthumanist: it could be seen as antihuman.[3] His definition of new materialism is not one that I adopt or share.

New materialism opens the door to new understandings of change – it creates a place for us to consider the role of materials in the production of history. It moves us away from an emphasis on a timeless understanding of materials as having inherent (or essential) properties and instead argues that materials have properties that emerge historically and relationally – they are not the same always and everywhere. This moves us away from unilinear explanations and towards a more complex understanding of causality (discussed below). It asks us not to centre upon humans alone as the source of all agency and change in the world, but, once more, to broaden our viewpoint and consider non-human materials too. New materialists are committed to the political, for they are looking to understand the change we see in the world around us and to think about how best we can act to bring about positive changes, especially regarding the climate crisis.

The work of Deleuze and Guattari (2014) is highly influential on new materialists. Their emphasis on flow, flux, and becoming is at the heart of the understanding of materials as unfixed, never defined, and always emergent. In such an approach our current world is never seen as the pinnacle of human achievement but just something in the process of flow. The world emerges as temporary and always on the move, never finished, nor complete, and it is clearly not the project of humans alone; rather, it is a flow and flux that emerges from the relations between materials, animals, plants, things, people, and ideas. They understand the world as an assemblage.

Assemblages

The concept of 'assemblage' is arguably the aspect of the new materialism that is having the most impact within archaeology at present. Assemblage, as a term, is already very familiar to archaeologists. As Gavin Lucas (2012: 193–198) discusses, in the traditional archaeological usage of the term, assemblage has two meanings, referring to a group of objects that are united in some way either by their typological similarity or by their shared depositional history. We might think of a faunal assemblage or a metalwork assemblage as a collection of objects united by their shared material, or we might think of a finds assemblage or burial assemblage as a collection of objects united by being deposited on the same site or in the same content.

The concept of assemblage that the new materialism draws upon is derived from the work of Deleuze and Guattari (2014) and is about the gathering of *explicitly diverse* things rather than the grouping of items based on similarity as common in archaeological parlance. The Deleuzo-Guattarian concept of assemblage has been interpreted and developed most notably by Manuel DeLanda (2006; 2016). I draw upon both the original concept from Deleuze and Guattari, as well as the development of the concept by both Bennett (2010) and DeLanda (2006; 2016). Bennett (2010: 23) describes assemblages as "ad hoc groupings of diverse elements, of vibrant materials of all sorts. Assemblages are living, throbbing confederations" (Bennett, 2010: 23).

The concept of assemblage deployed here is ontological – it is about an understanding of the world as being made up of temporary gatherings of diverse, heterogeneous parts. Assemblages are relational in that all the different parts of an assemblage are enmeshed in multiple and varied relations with other parts and these relations define the properties and potentials of both the parts that make up the assemblage and the whole itself. Elsewhere I have discussed a bus travelling between towns as an example of an assemblage made up of diverse parts such as a driver, an engine, seats, wheels, passengers, and engine oil (Crellin, 2017). Here, I illustrate the concept by thinking about a vegetable patch as an assemblage that consists of plants, soil, manure, weeds, worms, birds, bees, people, water, rain, and many other components besides.

An assemblage approach is non-anthropocentric as it removes humans from the "ontological apex" (Bennett, 2010: ix) and makes them just one of many parts within an assemblage. DeLanda (2006: 10) refers to these different parts as components. A component could be anything: a cow, a teapot, clay, a human, a cloud, or even a concept or belief. There is an easy parallel to draw here between DeLanda's (2006: 10) term 'component' and Latour's (1999: 180) term 'actant'. The relations between these components form assemblages that are capable of action in the world. This explicit gathering of diverse parts means change can never be the product of human action or agency alone, but always emerges from the relations within assemblages. This creates space for cats, trees, axes, gold, gods, and policewomen to all have a role in the emergence of change and history. Returning to our vegetable patch, as anyone who tries to grow plants knows, a vegetable patch is never 'controlled' by human agency but emerges from the relations between diverse components.

Assemblages exist at multiple scales: DeLanda (2006: 17) argues that larger assemblages emerge from the component parts of smaller assemblages as the relations between the component parts of the smaller assemblages become stabilised. On our vegetable patch there is an assemblage that is a courgette plant: it is made up of leaves, stems, capillary systems, flowers, seeds, and other parts. These come together to form a courgette plant, which is but one component of the vegetable patch. The approach to scale that emerges from the concept of assemblage means that there is both space for small-scale and large-scale processes to have a role in the production of our world and in the emergence of change. It is not the case that any one scale is the 'correct' scale at which to work, or indeed that any particular scale is 'driving' change (in contrast to say the *Annales* approach discussed in Chapter 4). Assemblages also exist at scales that do not just stack like Russian dolls – this is not about shuttling between larger and smaller scales of analysis but about folding together different scales of analysis all at once (Harris, 2017). Returning to the vegetable patch, understanding why any given plant might flower and grow is not just about sunlight and climate (things we might classify as large scale), but also about the local pH of soils, localised water flow, and the efforts of the gardener (things we might classify as smaller in scale), and it is about the development of seeds through 'genetic engineering' that stretches across continents and millennia (things existing at complex and multiple scales). To understand the history of the vegetable patch, or the success or failure of the vegetable patch in a particular year, we have to fold together different scales of analysis.

DeLanda (2006: 10; see also 2016) describes the relations within assemblages as 'relations of exteriority'. This means that the same component can exist within multiple assemblages at the same time (and/or over time). Crucially, the component will not have the same effect in each assemblage it is part of. This is because these are not components with essences but components that are defined by their relations. Once enmeshed within a different set of relations, a component can have different properties and effects (Conneller, 2011: 22). I can take a cutting from my vegetable patch and give it to a friend and it will not grow in the same way, nor have the same properties, when they plant it in their own garden. Equally, I can take waste from my kitchen that will have one effect in my rubbish bin and a very different effect were I to compost it and use it to plant tomatoes. The advantage of such an approach, especially when considering the study of change, is that it does not expect components to have the same effect in differing assemblages. It asks us to understand the specificity of a given assemblage and thereby avoid *always* and *everywhere* explanations (see Chapter 6). At the same time, it is also a deeply historical approach that asks one to understand the history that produces the specificity of an assemblage. In an assemblage approach, a Beaker does not have the same effect, and is not understood in the same way, in the south of France as in the north of Scotland, nor does it have the same effect at 2000BC as it does at 2100BC or 2020AD.

Assemblages are "always on the move, disruptive, incessantly active" (Dewsbury, 2011: 150), they are only ever temporary and are always changing. The plants on the vegetable patch shift their orientation to face the sun, or shelter from the cold; they gain and loose leaves, shoots, and flowers as they grow or wilt; they produce vegetables that might be eaten by caterpillars or taken away by humans. Equally, the humans involved in the vegetable patch might go on holiday, or lose interest, and the vegetable patch continues to change without them. For Deleuze and Guattari (2014) the emphasis is not on the production of final form but on how the world is in constant motion, always changing, always becoming. There is no moment we can see the vegetable patch as complete.

Assemblages are tetravalent (Deleuze and Guattari, 2014: 587; Dewsbury, 2011). As Dewsbury (2011: 149) explains, valency is a term taken from biology and chemistry to mean the combining power of elements (or molecules). The tetravalency of assemblages refers to the four dimensions in which they combine. DeLanda (2006: 12) discusses territorialization and deterritorialization as two processes that affect how assemblages combine and change. Components within a given assemblage may act to 'territorialize' it, whereby they make its boundaries more defined and the components within it more homogeneous – this is akin to a form of stabilisation. Equally, components may act to 'deterritorialize' an assemblage, blurring its boundaries and making the identity of the assemblage less clear. Assemblages will have components that are acting to territorialize and those that are acting to deterritorialize; moreover, one component may do both at any given time (DeLanda, 2006: 12). As Dewsbury (2011: 150) argues, there are aspects of assemblages that act to stabilise and cement relations, while there are "lines of flight" that pull it apart. The wooden sleepers around the edge of the patch territorialize it, they hold it together as an assemblage, and define it from the rest of the garden. At the same time the roots of plants might escape beyond the patch and grow outside of the defined bounds, 'ripe' vegetables might be taken away, birds might collect seeds or plants, and the rotting wood inside the sleepers might act to force them apart – all these components are acting to deterritorialize the assemblage, to tear it apart, and blur its boundaries. Without the efforts of the gardener and the sleepers, the garden and the vegetable patch might, over time, become completely indistinguishable: the vegetable patch could completely deterritorialize or, looked at another way, the garden becomes vegetable patch. Such an approach has change at its very heart, change that can come from within the assemblage itself or change that can come from the addition of new components joining, or the loss of components departing.

The other two dimensions of tetravalency are the material and the expressive aspects of assemblages. As Harris (2018: 89–90) explains, these two dimensions are less frequently discussed by archaeologists, but capture how an assemblage approach avoids opposing the study of the real and physical with the study of expression and symbolism (see also Hamilakis, 2017: 172–173). Assemblages have both material aspects and expressive or representational ones: our vegetable patch is made up of physical soil, plants, water molecules, and worms, but it also has symbolically associated meanings. In Britain a hundred years ago those associated meanings might have been related to feeding a family; today they include expressive enunciations relating to the concept of self-sufficiency, a return to producing our own food, and an association with the concept of the 'good life'. For archaeologists an assemblage approach allows space to consider both what we might term post-processual themes such as symbolism, identity, and meaning, and to consider the physical things that make up the world from animal bones, to pollen, to flint scrapers (Harris, 2018).

Within archaeology, assemblage approaches appear to be gaining increasing traction (see, for example, Brittain 2014; Cipolla, 2018; Cobb and Croucher, 2014;

2020; Fowler 2013a,b; Fowler and Harris, 2015; Harris 2013; 2014a,b; 2016; 2017; 2018; Harris and Crellin, 2018; Jervis, 2016; 2018; A. Jones, 2012; 2017; Jones and Sibesson, 2013; Lucas, 2012; Normark, 2009). Yannis Hamilakis and Andrew Jones (2017) published a special issue of *Cambridge Archaeological Journal* that focused on the utility of the concept; this included papers considering the applications of assemblages to the study of art (A. Jones, 2017), the concept of value (Robinson, 2017), the issue of scale (Harris, 2017), the study of typology (Fowler, 2017; see also Beck, 2018 and replies), the study of belief and religion (J. Jones, 2017), and the study of the senses and memory (Hamilakis, 2017; see also Harris, 2016). I characterise the appeal of an assemblage approach to archaeology as having three key aspects. First, it offers an effective way of moving beyond dualistic thinking. Second, the emphasis upon change and becoming within assemblages marries well with a discipline studying millennia of history: it is not the case that considering how the theory works through time is a bolt-on or afterthought. Finally, assemblages specifically combine diverse components and multiple scales – this reflects our archaeological data and our discipline. The concept of assemblage means that pollen data, animal bones, an analysis of symbolic aspects of art, the composition and production processes of pottery, or the chemical composition of an alloy can all have a place in the narratives we produce. No one scale of analysis nor form of data is privileged; rather the best narratives will emerge from combination.

The consequences of assemblages and vibrant matter for agency and causation

I combine the Deleuzian concept of assemblage with the new materialist approach to matter discussed above. In particular, I draw upon the work of Bennett (2010), who in her influential book *Vibrant Matter* (2010) outlines a new materialist approach where matter is always in flux at every scale – from the movement of atoms within a molecule to the shifting nature of clay or stone. At every scale all matter is in process. Even things that appear static, such as a road, are always on the move. Matter shifts, the gravels and tars that make up the assemblage that is the road move, they erode, they are heated by the sun, and they are cooled by the frost – they change.

Bennett's position on the relationship between matter, agency, and humans develops through her concept of 'thing-power'. Thing-power is a term she uses to capture how things are able to act and produce effect, to appear alive, and "exceed their status as objects". Thing-power is effectively opposed to the notion of agency. Bennett seeks to highlight how it is not just humans who are capable of effecting change, nor is it just humans that change. Her goal is political: she is seeking to address the climate crisis and other injustices. Emphasising the vibrant nature of *all* material is about considering the complex array of changes that need to happen in response to the climate crisis, as well as the diverse range of creatures that are affected by these processes. Bennett (2010) utilises the concept of 'thing-power' in order to unseat the human from the "ontological apex" (Bennett, 2010:

ix); for her, human agency is just another example of thing-power (2010: 10), not something greater or more important than it. Read as a whole, agency remains a product of relationships in Bennett's work (as in Latour's) and her concept of thing-power is a rhetorical device. It highlights the ability of non-humans to bring about change, removes agency from being associated with humans alone, and then effectively resituates humans as one form of material among many. Humans, just like plants, animals, rivers, and teacups are made of vibrant matter.

The concept of vibrant matter gives us a sense of constant flux and change that is not only the result of what could be termed human agency. It is a model of change that flows from the smallest atoms through to the largest institutions. By repositioning the human, as another example of vibrant matter, she is able to show that change does not come from human action alone, but equally she does not deny the incredible capacity of humans to affect change in our world. Change comes from vibrant matter that is never stable, nor complete, and is always on the move. This also effectively decouples change from intention.

New materialist thinking has a series of consequences for how we think about causation. Bennett (2010) draws upon the Deleuzian concept of assemblage but uses the Latourian (1999: 180) term 'actant' to label the different constituent parts of assemblages (or what DeLanda (2006) would term components). She focuses on how diverse actants/components are enmeshed within complex relations, and, as a result, she argues that singular causation, of the kind discussed in Chapter 1, cannot be sustained. No part of an assemblage ever acts alone; it always relies upon others, whether that is two parts of a flower or the relationship between a driver, their car, the road, and the oil industry. As no part of an assemblage acts alone it is not possible to trace singular causes of change. Bennett (2010: 36) draws on a quote from Noortje Marres (2005: 216): "it is often hard to grasp just what the sources of agency are that make a particular event happen", suggesting that our inability to grasp a single source of the agency that makes events occur (or change happen) is actually a key feature of change. We cannot identify the source of a given change or event because there is no single source; it is distributed across the relations between diverse parts of a "confederacy" (Bennett, 2010: 36). This is complicated even further when we consider that every component in an assemblage is actually an assemblage itself. The thing that we have come to call agency is always the result of diverse assemblages of vibrant materials.

As a result of this position, Bennett (2010: 32–34) argues for a very different model of causality. She states:

> If one extends the time frame of the action beyond that of even an instant, billiard-ball causality falters. Alongside and inside singular human-agents there exists a heterogeneous series of actants with partial, overlapping, and conflicting degrees of power and effectivity.
>
> Here causality is more emergent than efficient, more fractal than linear. Instead of an effect obedient to a determinant, one finds circuits in which effect and cause alternate position and rebound on each other. If efficient

causality seeks to rank the actants involved, treating some as external causes and others as dependent effects, emergent causality places the focus on the process.

(Bennett, 2010: 33)

Bennett argues that 'efficient causality' is not the way to understand an ontologically relational world. Efficacy here refers to the willed intention of a subject to have an effect (Bennett, 2010: 31) and a cause is understood as a "singular, stable and masterful initiation of events" (Bennett, 2010: 33). Efficient causality is the idea that any simple body might be the sole cause of an effect, or what I refer to in Chapter 1 as singular causation. Bennett suggests that seeing George W. Bush as the cause of the American invasion of Iraq in 2003 is an example of such efficient causality. The reality is that single components are themselves made up of many other components and therefore we cannot identify a single cause. She argues instead for emergent causality where the effect of any given cause cannot be known prior to its emergence (Bennett, 2010: 33). In emergent causality multiple actants are always present, and any one effect becomes infused into other causes until cause and effect cannot be separated. Bennett argues change is not linear, the result of adding two things together and getting merely their sum (where effect is proportional to cause); rather, small changes can have big effects on assemblages (there are parallels between Bennett's position and that advocated for by McGlade (1999) when he was discussing nonlinear concepts of time and causality (see Chapter 3)). She suggests that causality may be better understood in a more fractal manner, where the same pattern is evident at many different scales within a given phenomenon. In such cases we are best to trace the process of change rather than look for a simple cause and effect.

Bennett's position is deeply relational, it is non-anthropocentric, and it is new materialist. This is an understanding of the world where humans are one among many, where change is the product of the vibrancy of all materials, and where simple cause and effect are denied. There is shared ground with Latour in her advocating for the importance of non-humans, but her emphasis on change and flux, coming from her engagement with Deleuze, means she avoids the problems inherent in Latour's approach to change and vanishing networks. The complex, multiple, nonlinear emergent causality that she evokes, and her rejection of singular causality, mean that hers is an approach that avoids determinism and category labels. The vibrant nature of all material not only eschews anthropocentric thinking but also rejects block-time approaches to change, as when we consider change to be constant we can no longer have periods that are static.

Assembling time and change

Time in assemblage thinking is no longer an external container for action, nor is it a measure. Time is not singular and universal. Rather, time is an emergent property of assemblages. It emerges from the vibrancy of matter and the constant shifting and changing that is inherent within assemblages. Our own clock-time emerges from clocks themselves, assemblages formed of mechanisms, gears, cogs, moving fingers, and European concepts of what time is. Equally, time emerges from how our ecosystem assemblages change with the passing of the seasons and it emerges from the way our bodies grow old. As assemblages change, multiple kinds of time emerge. This is not a singular universal time, true everywhere and always, but a multiplicity of times that emerge from different assemblages changing at different scales. In this way we can think about both the type of time that emerges from the measuring of radiocarbon decay and the kind of time that emerges from the relationship between the stones of Stonehenge and the movement of the sun. This allows us to move beyond the debates about time discussed in Chapter 3 about which kind of time (clock, experiential etc.) is more real or more important: neither type is more real, or more correct; rather, in an assemblage approach time is multiple, emergent, and always on the move.

What is it then that is changing in an assemblage approach? Relations are central in assemblages; it is relations that produce the different properties and potentials of the various components within an assemblage and thereby the components and the assemblage itself. It is the relations between the different parts of assemblages that change. Changes to relations produce changes within components and thereby changes within assemblages. As changes to relations occur, the properties and potentials of components and assemblages shift. If we return to our vegetable patch, when bees visit the flowers they change the relations: they remove pollen from the assemblage of one flower (effectively deterritorializing it) and as they fly around they move it to another flower assemblage (reterritorializing it), where it has a different effect. The relations between pollen and flower, and pollen and bee, are shifting, and as a result the flowers, and their plants, gain different properties and capacities and change emerges. As Robb and Harris state,

> there is never a clean transition of the kind where 'first people thought A, then X happened and afterwards, they thought B'. Instead, the pattern tends to be one of rendition through continuity. Both A and B are almost always present both before and afterwards, but the relations between them have changed.
>
> *(Robb and Harris, 2013: 225)*

Our bee, pollen, flower, plant and soil are all still part of the assemblage after pollination has occurred, it is just that the relations between them have changed.

Robb and Harris (2013) developed their thinking on this issue by considering the history of the body across thousands of years (see Chapter 4). Despite the enormity of their scale of analysis, and the vast amount of change that they studied, they do not suggest that the history of the body is a history of clean transitions but rather argue it is a history of messy blurrings (see Figure 7.2). These messy blurrings are what Deleuze and Guattari would term becomings. When we look at the past in a disconnected block-time approach, we can contrast Britain at 2000BC and Britain at 1300BC and talk about the difference between a world where people

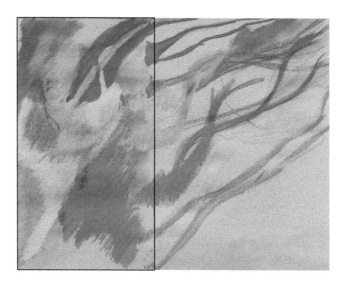

FIGURE 7.2 Change in process. To the right of the image we see a slice through time
trailing off behind, and to the left the processes of ongoing change
Source: R.J. Crellin.

were buried in single inhumations and lived relatively mobile lives with a world
where they lived in roundhouses, constructed field systems, and cremated the dead.
The trick here is that we have disconnected these two scenes, cutting asunder the
trails of connection (or lines of flight) that connect them. We have ignored the
continuous and multiple small changes that, through rendition and continuity,
produce two radically different worlds. It is only when we disconnect these two
images that we produce a history structured by revolutions.

New innovations do not wipe out the worlds that prefigured them. Rather they
are added on to existing assemblages; their presence goes on to cause shifts in
relations that, over time, change the properties of different components and the
assemblage as a whole. Chris Fowler (2013a: 29; 53) highlights how the properties
of any given assemblage are historical: they are the result of past relations. The
form of a given assemblage, at any specific moment in time, is the result of the
history of its relations. Some of those relations might remain relatively steady over
time, whereas others change at different rates. Successful new innovations have to
'fit' within existing assemblages; they have to be understood in the light of the
worlds they enter into (cf. Hodder, 2012: Chapter 6). Once within that assemblage
they do, of course, then go on to produce all kinds of emergent and unpredictable
changes and to reconfigure and shift the relations between components.

New materialist approaches argue for the vibrancy of all matter – this is a world
that is always on the move, always shifting and changing. It is crucial, however,
that we understand that the rate of change is not always the same. Not all matter is
equally vibrant, or vibrant in the same ways. Not all assemblages are changing at

the same rate – within some assemblages a density of relations can work to keep things stable and to mask change, while within other assemblages, components can act as catalysts increasing the vibrancy of the matter within. DeLanda (2006: 20–21) discusses catalytic causality as a key aspect of change in assemblages and form of nonlinear causality. In catalytic reactions, small causes can have large effects, and a series of causes below a certain threshold can have no effect. Assemblages may have components acting both catalytically and to stabilise at the same time. We often fail to see things that are actually changing and instead view them as stable: in assemblage terms, the human components of some assemblages choose to treat relations and components as if they are not changing. Components within assemblage have to 'work' to keep things stable. On our vegetable patch the attentive gardener sees changes every day: she works to keep the weeds away, she replaces the sleepers as they rot, she plants new seeds each season, all to try and hold her vegetable plot stable while all the while actually changing it in order to do so.

We can consider annualised rituals as a good example of this. The majority of the Christmases of my childhood took a very similar form: we did the same kinds of things at the same time each year, we ate a similar meal, and similar people were involved. We used the same tablecloths, decorations, and crockery each year – these things changed in very small gradual ways. We would buy similar foods, buy a tree from the same nursery, use similar candles, and keep to the same recipes and traditions each year. Tree decorations and tablecloths are relatively stable; they change less than candles and turkeys. The assemblage of Crellin-family-Christmas sought to deny the vibrancy of turkeys and trees (which would certainly have very different properties if left alone for 12 months!) by bringing similar components to the assemblage each year. The density of relations in the Christmas assemblage act to keep things the same. At the same time the people involved were constantly on the move, aging, dying, and being born with changing relations between them. At Christmas, change is both at once laid bare – we are not who we were a year ago, nor are we who we were aged 5 years old. – but at the same time, change is denied, we act to keep things similar. Nowadays, I celebrate Crellin-Horan-Christmas; I've made space for new components, both human and non-human, and the result is different from before, but it has been a gradual set of changes, and aspects of Crellin-family-Christmas are retained (as are Horan-family-Christmas). Each year my Christmas emerges in new ways as a heady mix of components as memories, trees, turkeys, and candles are brought together and new components join the assemblage.

Phase transitions

The world that emerges from this theoretical stance is one that is in constant motion, a world where materials are on the move and, as a result, assemblages at every scale are always changing. This is a world where we can leave behind what Tim Pauketat (2013: 35) terms the change–continuity dualism. It is crucial, therefore, that we consider the tempo of change. Not all change occurs at an equal tempo or speed.

The tectonic plates that make up the earth's surface are always moving, but slowly. Stone buildings and monuments are always changing, but slowly. The table I write at and the chair I sit on are made up of materials within which the molecules are always vibrating, but the result is a relatively static table and chair. This slow or fast speed is of course relational, and it is also rooted in my own human vantage point. What is slow to me might well appear fast to a giant sloth.

It is important that we seek to recognise and describe how assemblages change at different rates. Some changes may be imperceptibly slow, but we also have to recognise the more rapid changes that occur. We must avoid a situation where we present change in a homogeneous way. DeLanda's (2011; 2006) concept of a phase transition helps us to do this. Phase transitions are the term DeLanda uses to describe notably marked changes. They are, however, not the result of some radical shift, but instead phase transitions occur through the build-up of numerous smaller interrelated processes. DeLanda (2011: 15) talks about the different forms water can take as being different phases. As we heat water from 1°C to 100°C it is a gradual process, but the change at 100°C is more marked and we should recognise that. The concept of the phase transition allows us to do so.

DeLanda (2011) argues for a nonlinear approach to history where we do not impose progressive, developmental, or teleological models of change onto the past. While DeLanda does not discuss the various models that exist within archaeology, concepts such as Marshall Sahlins and Elman Service's (1960) evolutionary model of bands, tribes, chiefdoms, and states, discussed in Chapter 1, are examples of the kind of history that DeLanda seeks to avoid. Instead he argues that we should consider different ways of being and organising societies as different phases. He draws a parallel with water, which can take the form of snowflakes, ice, liquid, or steam. No one of these forms is superior to the other or should be viewed as part of a directional evolutionary sequence; rather they are just different. DeLanda (2011: 15–16) is clear that each new phase of human history is not a sequential improvement on what went before:

> much as water's solid, liquid and gas phases may coexist, so each new human phase simply added itself to the other ones, coexisting and interacting with them without leaving them in the past. Moreover, much as a given material may solidify in alternative ways (as ice or snowflake, as crystal of glass), so humanity liquefied and later solidified in different forms.
>
> *(DeLanda, 2011: 16)*

The phase transition model allows us to acknowledge that there are marked transitions in the past, but it does so in a way that avoids seeing these changes as crucial thresholds through which we must pass in order to reach modernity as the 'apex of human achievement'. Deleuze and Guattari (2014) emphasise how we should start in the middle of a problem not at the 'origin' where we seek a change that 'came from nowhere' or at the 'end' where we work backwards from the present. We are still in the process of becoming, our assemblages are still shifting.

There is a risk that we simply place phase transitions where we once placed period boundaries. One of my key aims in this book was to create a model of change where we avoided a block-time approach with periods of stasis interspersed by moments of transition. The new materialist concept of vibrant matter allows us to show that change is constant and ongoing, but at many different tempos. The concept of a phase transition allows us to recognise that there are moments of more marked change, but that these moments emerge out of a build-up of smaller changes. When we boil a pan of water, different molecules of water reach 100°C at different moments, some sooner than others, some more slowly. When does the phase transition occur? When the first molecule evaporates? When we see large bubbles occur on the surface? When we reach a rolling boil? Or, when all the water has evaporated and the pan is dry? What if some molecules have recondensed as water elsewhere by that point? This is an issue of scale: are we concerned with the assemblage of a single molecule or the assemblage of the pan as a whole? The scale of observation affects when we can observe the phase transition occurring. This allows us to consider different kinds of assemblages on their own terms, as well as considering how they relate to bigger and smaller assemblages. It does not mean that we have to say 'phase transition X' happened everywhere, in the same way, at the same time. Combined with a concept of vibrant matter, it stops us adopting singular causation. Instead, it allows us to identify numerous smaller changes, in numerous different assemblages, which have varied effects on assemblages both smaller and larger than themselves.

Oliver Harris (2014a: 338–340) has applied the concept of the phase transition to the study of one of the most contentious period transitions in Britain, the emergence of the Neolithic (see, for example, the opposing views of Sheridan, 2010, and Thomas, 2004b). He employs the concept as he asks authors to move beyond seeing the Neolithic and Mesolithic as two opposed and separate blocks of time and ways of life. Similarly, the transition, he argues, is not about a teleological sense of progress or an increase in complexity. He argues that the emergence of the Neolithic was the result of the build-up of numerous small changes and that we need to understand that Neolithic assemblages did not wipe out all earlier practices but were combined with them, leading to the development of further processes of change. This approach has potential in other times and places too; reconsidering processes of ongoing change as part of colonialism in this frame could offer another way to move beyond the change–continuity dichotomy identified by Stephen Silliman (2009).

Meeting the critique

Posthumanist, non-anthropocentric, and new materialist approaches are still in their relative infancy in archaeology, and they are controversial. Julian Thomas (2015: 1294), for example, has commented on the challenge these new approaches have for ethics. These subjects are controversial because they offer radical re-imaginings of our world, they disrupt our normal ways of thinking and doing, and they question our understandings not just of ourselves, but also of our role in the world. In my experience, discussing both non-anthropocentrism and posthumanism at conferences is frequently met with critique from a number of directions (there are also those who choose not to engage entirely). Disagreement among academics is a good thing, because receiving critique leads us to a place where we are asked to refine and clarify our thinking.

One of the most common critiques of non-anthropocentric approaches is that they give agency to objects. This comes with an inherent risk that humans are no longer responsible for their actions: the gun should be on trial not the shooter. As I hope should be clear from both Chapter 6 and this chapter, neither Latour's approach, nor that of new materialists, argues for object agency. In both cases agency is something that is not held by individuals but instead is a quality of relationships. It is not possessed, but emerges from relationships between various diverse components. While we can therefore move past the first part of the argument (object agency), in some ways the concerns of the second part of the argument (that we can no longer blame humans for their unethical behaviour) could still be seen to stand: if I say that it is the assemblage that acts, then are humans negating their responsibility? Thomas (2015: 1294) discusses how it may be uncontroversial to talk about the assemblage of effects that bring about a power cut (cf. Bennett, 2010), but suggesting the Holocaust was the result of an "assemblage of disparate entities" is clearly more than problematic if it results in any diminishing of human responsibility (see also Ribeiro, 2016).

My response to this is clear: what posthumanist and non-anthropocentric approaches do is ask us to look more broadly at the wider relations that lead to any given event. They also ask us to consider and include the role of non-humans. Considering wider causality does not stop us from being outraged at injustice or wrong-doing and it does not stop us acting upon that outrage (Bennett, 2010: 38) (contra Van Dyke, 2015). We are not diluting human culpability or suggesting that bad people should not be brought to justice. Moreover, from my perspective, it puts us in a much stronger position to work to overcome wrong-doing and injustice because it asks us to look directly at the wider assemblage, to untangle the bigger net of components that gave rise to a specific situation. As an example, we should be outraged and reacting against misogyny, and this includes highlighting and bringing to justice misogynists. However, if we want to move beyond the toxic effects of gender inequality, we cannot simply *just* lock-up all those who are sexist; we *also* need to deal with the wider assemblage that brings about gender inequality. We have to also consider the role of education, the media, maternity and paternity policies, dolls and toys, ready meals, bodies, breast milk, period blood, the history of thinking to do with the genders, and our ontologies. Gender inequality has no single cause and there is no single solution to it. Taking a non-anthropocentric, posthumanist, assemblage-based approach gives us the tools to consider the wide range of components that have to change. It highlights how the effects of misogyny flow beyond women. It also helps us see that the key to bringing about a better world will be to work on the relations between components not just simply to remove the components themselves.

Another commonly raised critique of these approaches argues that humans should be our primary concern. Archaeology's position in the humanities (as well as the sciences) reflects its interest in humans. Why would an osteologist, for example, want to adopt a non-anthropocentric or posthumanist approach? The kind of post-humanism I adopt does not want us to ignore humans – it is not antihuman.[4] Instead it asks us to reconsider the category 'human', to make space for those who were never granted full membership of the category, and to take seriously the crucial roles played by non-humans in our world and our subjectivity. As Cipolla and Allard (2018: 1101) state, "assemblage theory does not preclude thinking critically about the past, about human histories, or about political and pragmatic action". What it does demand, though, is that we think critically about how we have understood the category 'human'. This means that non-anthropocentric and posthumanist thinking does not exclude anthropologists, for example, who traditionally study humans, rather it asks them to rethink the humans they study.

This is one of the areas where I think the differences between non-anthropocentric approaches and posthumanist ones are important. Some non-anthropocentric approaches, particularly object-orientated ontology and second-wave symmetrical archaeology, are building a new kind of study that is much less concerned with humans and could even be described as antihuman. Other non-anthropocentric approaches are not doing this. Combining posthumanist and non-anthropocentric approaches allows us to first critique both human exceptionalism and humanism and then to build new definitions and understandings of what it means to be human. The humans that emerge from this position are one-among-many, they are entangled in complex relationships with a whole host of diverse non-human others, and they are not the lone seat of agency or cause of change in the world. This is a reworking of humans where there is space for diversity, where a multiplicity of humans emerges, where we can explore the diversity and nuance of multiple historical trajectories and thereby move well beyond a unilinear history. Posthumanism is a call to be more inclusive, more inclusive of the diversity of humanity and less self-centred by taking seriously the role of non-humans. This is why I prefer the term post-anthropocentric (see also Crellin, in press;) rather than non-anthropocentric. I am not suggesting that we stop talking about humans, rather I am asking that we stop presuming they are the most important thing on the planet and instead realise that they are deeply embedded and entangled in relations. The term post-anthropocentric indicates that this is not an antihuman stance but rather a stance that seeks to relocate humans among the many non-human others who share our world. While the difference between non-anthropocentric and post-anthropocentric might appear semantic, I think it is a clear way of addressing some of the critique directed at non-anthropocentric approaches.

There is also a critique in a number of papers from those working on Bayesian analyses of Neolithic Europe (see Chapter 4) that argue that we are taking agency away from humans just as we are gaining the chorological control to begin to talk about human action and decision making in ever more detailed ways (see, for example, Draşovean et al., 2017; Ebersbach et al., 2017), and that relational approaches advocate for slow drifting change (Ebersbach et al., 2017). Responding to this critique, I return first to the point above: I do not argue for object agency (or human agency); rather, my approach argues that agency is a quality of relationships. I think relational, post-anthropocentric, and posthumanist approaches actually serve to strengthen the impact of the kinds of narratives that emerge from Bayesian models. Radiocarbon dating is a process that looks at the constant ongoing change in matter, and it elevates charcoal, seeds, and bones to a position where they become the keys to revealing the past: it is new materialist and post-anthropocentric. Moreover, the very detailed mapping of change that I promote stands to benefit from Bayesian analysis as we reveal the nuance of change in the past in ever more detailed ways. There is nothing about assemblage theory that stops us exploring quick change where components have a catalytic effect; change does not have to be slow and drifting (indeed I speculate that Bayesian analyses will reveal an increasing number of phase transitions in our past). One of the frequent position statements that emerges from archaeologists deploying Bayesian analysis suggests that it is allowing us to abandon the term prehistory and talk instead about history (Draşovean et al., 2017; Whittle, 2018; Whittle et al., 2011). The error here is in thinking that history focuses on human decision making and agency alone – it is a mistaken version of history that believes it is driven only by people and that there is no place (or only a secondary place) in it for analyses that might elevate rivers, metals, cows, or clay.

Moving away from the critiques of non-anthropocentrism and posthumanism and towards my utilisation of assemblage theory to think about change, the model of constant change that comes from a new materialist approach to matter could be accused of creating a homogeneous past. If everything is changing, then how do we know which changes are more significant? How do we texture our narratives? A focus upon tempo, speed, and the careful consideration of phase transitions should allow us to avoid this.

The argument, drawn from Bennett (2010), that simple linear causality cannot be sustained means that the kind of narratives I aim to write will not focus on *simple* causal explanations (see Lucas, 2017: 189) because I do not see them as a particularly helpful or accurate interpretation of the past. Rather, what emerges are detailed and nuanced narratives where I map change in the past. It is indeed true that the kind of narratives I want to write are not ones where simple causal explanations emerge, but this stems from my belief that looking for simple cause and effect explanations is mistaken. A critique that could arise here is that we are only describing change and no longer interpreting it (see, for example, Barrett, 2016). Deleuze and Guattari's (2014: 12–15) thinking is, once again, useful here: they draw a distinction between mapping and tracing.[5] Mapping is an active process that creates connections and has multiple entrance points, whereas tracing is seen as a passive process. Mapping is a process through which the map-maker intervenes in the world and draws new connections between assemblages and in the process creates new knowledge. Mapping is a process that acknowledges the active role of the map-maker (cf. Fowler, 2013a; Lucas, 2012). A new materialist and assemblage approach asks us to map change. Following Deleuze and Guattari (2014) I argue that mapping change in this way is not mere description, but allows me to draw out and create new connections in the past. From this detailed mapping new interpretations and narratives of change emerge.

Finally, I want to shift back to the broader picture: is what I argue for in this chapter a metaontology? Benjamin Alberti (2016a,b) has argued that the recent development of relational ontological approaches has led to the emergence of a new universal over-arching framework (or metaontology). Yes, I am presenting a metaontology. I find dualistic thinking, and the Cartesian-Newtonian view of matter do not align with the world that I live in; moreover, I think they are deeply damaging: the way they frame the category 'human' as opposed and separate from the rest of the world and ontologically superior and exceptional is damaging. It is damaging for the many people excluded from the category human and damaging for our relationships with the rest of the world. For me, relational, post-anthropocentric, posthumanist, new materialist approaches are "better ways of seeing and understanding how the world works" (Cipolla, 2019: 616).

Zoe Todd (2016) has highlighted the failure of relational and ontological theorists, particularly Latour, to acknowledge and cite their relationship to, and adoption of, Indigenous ideas, which devalues and erases Indigenous philosophy. Alberti's (2016a: 171) critical point is related, as he argues that there are alternative ontologies available, particularly those that emerge from Indigenous thinking, and that imposing a universal metaontology, drawn from western theory and philosophy, devalues alternative ontologies by refusing to elevate them to the status of theory. Todd (2016) and Alberti (2016a,b) make key critical points, asking us to question our relationships with alternative, and particularly Indigenous, ontologies. As Cipolla (2019: 623) highlights, though, even if we were to elevate Indigenous thinking to the status of theory in the way Alberti (2016a: 171) suggests, it may not necessarily be possible to step out of our own Eurocentric perspectives entirely. Moreover, Indigenous ontologies are multiple and varied: as someone who studies the European past, adopting one risks misunderstanding, mistranslating, and appropriating those ideas (cf. Harris and Crellin, 2018). There are two crucial points here: this is the metaontology I adopt, and I adopt it as a specific critique of western–Cartesian thinking. This does not mean that there are not other relational ontologies that provide excellent ways of understanding the world that we should explore, celebrate, and most certainly employ where historically appropriate. But as someone who is situated in a European western context, I adopt this relational metaontology as a form of critique of western ways of thinking.

Adopting assemblage theory and a flat ontology are also best thought of as *starting points* in my research (cf. Harris in Harris and Cipolla, 2017: 206). They open my mind up to allowing other kinds of stories to emerge. They allow me to think about my work in a more open and flexible manner, so that I can allow alternative ontologies and pasts to emerge. Those could be pasts where humans are key protagonists and where strict ontological hierarchies exist but there is also space for more radical other pasts. It is a metaontology – but it can also be used as a way into exploring alternative ontologies too.

Conclusion

In this chapter I have explained my theoretical approach to change. It is an approach that aims to write archaeologies of change that describe the diversity of the past in nuanced ways. The approach is post-anthropocentric and posthumanist. Both terms are often elided in archaeology, but there are subtle and important differences. Post-anthropocentric and posthuman approaches both critique human exceptionalism, but posthumanist approaches (following Braidotti, 2013; 2019; Ferrando, 2019) do this while at the same time also redefining what it means to be human. Here the human does not emerge as an essential, ahistorical category associated with white, western, straight men, but instead as a historical, shifting, multiple category with space for all those who were once excluded. Combining these two ways of thinking allows us to consider the important role of non-humans and the re-imagined humans who are one-of-many producing our past, present, and future. These approaches are combined with new materialism to argue that all matter is always changing and in process. Assemblage theory offers a way of thinking about how diverse and ever-shifting matter makes up our world at a multitude of scales, scales that stretch across time and space in complex ways and must be folded together. There is no 'correct scale' that produces history. Time emerges not as a container or measure but as a product of changing relations. Change emerges as constant, but constant across a range of tempos from the imperceptible (be it because of scale or speed) to the very rapid.

At the outset I described the hurdles from Chapter 1, which, I argued, my approach to change needs to move beyond; I now reflect on these in relation to my own theoretical framework. First and foremost, I wanted to avoid a block-time approach to the past where periods of stasis were surrounded by more frenetic moments of transition. Arguing for constant change at every scale from the molecule to the institution avoids a block-time approach. It is easy to see why block-time models of change arise. They make it much easier to describe and comprehend the vast depth and breadth of the past. We can take the past and break it down into opposed periods that deny the constant flow of change. As Elizabeth Grosz (2009: 132) tells us, "the curve, the continuous stroke, the single movement of an arm, is certainly able to be decomposed into as many stops or breaks as one chooses". Drawing on Henri Bergson (2001), she argues that we can take a continuous flow and break it down into smaller and smaller chunks; the smaller the chunk we examine, the nearer to a straight line it appears. Grosz (2009) is arguing that our minds try to divide up that which is in constant flow to create a series of frozen moments of stasis. All matter, both past and present, is in constant flow at a multitude of scales and tempos. When we divide up the past into periods of stasis, we pixilate it, producing snapshots and stopping the flow of change. Rather than pixilating and stopping change I want to map the flow of change considering its different tempos and speeds and the scales at which it operates. Arguing for a new materialist stance on matter avoids a stop-start approach to change and continuity and places us in the middle of a flow.

I aim to avoid progressive or evolutionary models of change and teleological thinking. Deleuze and Guattari's (2014) emphasis on how we are always in process and becoming dislodges our present day from being the pinnacle of human achievement and relocates the present as merely a moment in a flow of becoming. We are always changing, and not in a manner where the present is an improvement on the past, rather it is just different. DeLanda's (2011) concept of the phase transition clarifies this: he describes different phases as no more superior to each other nor directional – they are just different. The kind of difference that Deleuze's thinking (2004) tells us to revel in is not difference from a perfect type but difference in itself. There is no unilinear story of human history to tell; there are, instead, multiple, varied, and diverse narratives of a changing past to map – changing both in the sense that all matter is always in process and in the sense that the pasts that emerge today are always themselves on the move.

I aimed to avoid an emphasis on both origins and revolutions. Here again, Deleuze and Guattari's (2014) position on becoming, flow, and flux are helpful, as is their suggestion that we jump into the middle of things. There are no pure origins; new innovations always come from the build-up of change, and they must always fit within existing assemblages (though this does not deny they then go on to allow more change to emerge). Similarly, searching for moments of revolution severs the flow of change as it relies upon block-time thinking. More problematically, when searching for the origins of a given phenomenon is about looking for the purest and earliest version of something, it reifies a 'type' as ideal and then asks us to hold up others against it and show that they fail to measure up: this is the real Beaker burial, others are deviant, incomplete, or only partial – they do not measure up. This is damaging enough in supressing our understanding and appreciation of diversity and locality, and even more damaging when we place things on a teleological trajectory that says this is the origin of some crucial aspect of the past that is fundamental to who we are today.

I wanted my approach to change to avoid being deterministic. Assemblage thinking eschews deterministic thinking. It rejects the Cartesian dualisms that allow us to categorise things as 'natural' or 'cultural' and thereby it presents a much more complex view of what the 'environment' or 'technology' (the two most common forms of determinism) are. It shows the multiplicity of heterogeneous components that make up any assemblage we might term 'technology' or 'environment', it asks us to look more broadly, to think about the diverse humans and non-humans that bring about any given event. This antideterminist stance is further strengthened by the position on causation: the rejection of simple causation means we should not, and cannot, look for a single determining cause for any given phenomenon. The relations within assemblages are also relations of exteriority (DeLanda, 2006: 10), which means that it is not the case that we should expect a given phenomenon, such as a certain technology, to have the same effect always and everywhere.

The approach I describe is post-anthropocentric and highly relational. It is also, importantly, posthumanist. It is an approach that rejects human exceptionalism and makes space for a whole host of non-human others from materials, to plants, to landscapes, to beliefs, to gods, and things to play a role in the production of change and our past. It is also an approach with space for humans within it, but humans refigured not as the seat of agency, not drawn in the image of Vitruvian man, and not limited to agentic white, western, straight men. Instead the humans in this approach are always relational, deeply entangled with the rest of the world, produced through heterogeneous assemblages of humans and non-humans, always changing, always multiple, and always diversely different. Their difference is not measured against an ideal type, they are not defined ahistorically, and they are all *equally capable* of having an effect in the world through their relations. This flat ontology is the starting point for analysis from where inequality (across both humans and non-humans) can be mapped. Humans are removed from the ontological apex and restored to a position as one-of-many.

Notes

1 I note Sundberg's (2013: 37–8) critique of Bennett's as suggesting that a belief in nonhuman agency can be viewed as primitive. I reject this aspect of Bennett's thinking: it is founded in a progressive narrative that suggests western ways of thinking are more advanced than Indigenous and nonwestern groups.
2 Ingold (2007a,b; 2011; 2012; 2013; 2015) occupies a complex position in relation to new materialist and Deleuzian-inspired assemblage approaches. In *Being Alive* Ingold (2011: 13–4) acknowledges the link between his own work on lines and meshworks and that of Deleuze. His concept of lines predates his engagement with Deleuze, but since the link became obvious, Ingold has adopted some aspects of Deleuzian thought (Ingold, 2012). He argues that all life (whether human or non-human) is open ended and in becoming; however, unlike in assemblage theory, he draws a hard line between living and nonliving things and sees the agency of living creatures as very different to that of inanimate things (Ingold, 2014: 235; see also Barrett, 2014) (but see Ingold, 2007b where this difference seems less important).
3 Olsen and Witmore (2015: 190–1) explicitly reject the critique that they are no longer concerned with humans; however, the absence of humans in much of their current work appears to suggest otherwise.
4 There is a strand of posthumanism, termed ahumanism, that is specifically antihuman emerging from the work of Patricia MacCormack (2014; 2020) but it is not the same as the form of posthumanism I advocate for here.
5 I must state my debt to Ben Jervis here. I used to think about what I was aiming to do as tracing change. In a peer review he directed me to the passage of Deleuze and Guattari (2014: 12–15) on mappings versus tracing: this clarified both my writing and my thinking.

Bibliography

Alberti, B. 2016a. Archaeologies of ontology. *Annual Review of Anthropology* 45: 163–179.
Alberti, B. 2016b. Archaeologies of risk and wonder. *Archaeological Dialogues* 23(2): 138–145.
Banfield, E. 2018. *Tales from the Ontological Tern: An Examination of the Role and Meaning of Faunal Remains in the Neolithic Long Barrows of Wiltshire*. Unpublished PhD thesis, University of Leicester.
Barad, K. 2003. Posthuman performativity: towards an understanding of how matter comes to matter. *Signs: Journal of Women in Culture and Society* 28: 801–831.

Barad, K. 2007. *Meeting the Universe Halfway: Quantum Physics and the Entanglement of Matter and Meaning*. Durham, NC: Duke University Press.

Barrett, J.C. 2014. The material constitution of humanness. *Archaeological Dialogues* 21: 65–74.

Barrett, J. 2016. The new antiquarianism? *Antiquity* 90(354): 1681–1686.

Beck, A. 2018. Revisiting the Trelleborg house: a discussion of house types and assemblages. *Norwegian Archaeological Review* 51(1–2): 142–161.

Bennett, J. 2010. *Vibrant Matter: A Political Ecology of Things*. London: Duke University Press.

Bergson, H. 2001. *Creative Evolution*. London: Electric Book Co.

Bickle, P. 2019. Thinking gender differently: new approaches to identity difference in the Central European Neolithic. *Cambridge Archaeological Journal online first*: doi:10.1017/S0959774319000453

Braidotti, R. 2013. *The Posthuman*. London: Polity.

Braidotti, R. 2019. A theoretical framework for the critical posthumanities. *Theory, Culture and Society*36(6): 31–61.

Brittain, M. 2014. Assembling bodies, making worlds: an archaeological topology of place, in Alberti, B., Jones, A.M. and Pollard, J. (eds), *Archaeology After Interpretation: Returning Materials to Archaeological Theory*. Walnut Creek: Left Coast Press: pp. 257–276.

Cipolla, C. 2018. Earth flows and lively stone: what difference does 'vibrant' matter make? *Archaeological Dialogues* 25(1): 49–70.

Cipolla, C. 2019. Taming the ontological wolves: learning from Iroquoian effigy objects. *American Anthropologist* 121(3): 613–627.

Cipolla, C. and Allard, A. 2018. Recognizing river power: watery views of Ontario's fur trade. *Journal of Archaeological Method and Theory* 26: 1084–1105.

Cobb, H. and Croucher, K. 2014. Assembling archaeological pedagogy. A theoretical framework for valuing pedagogy in archaeological interpretation and practice. *Archaeological Dialogues* 21(2): 197–216.

Cobb, H. and Croucher, K. 2020. *Assembling Archaeology: Teaching, Practice and Research*. Oxford: Oxford University Press.

Conneller, C. 2011. *An Archaeology of Materials: Substantial Transformations in Early Prehistoric Europe*. London: Routledge.

Coole, D. and Frost, S. 2010. Introducing the new materialisms, in Coole, D. and Frost, S. (eds), *New Materialisms: Ontology, Agency and Politics*. Durham, NC: Duke University Press: pp. 1–43.

Crellin, R.J. 2017. Changing assemblages: vibrant matter in burial assemblages. *Cambridge Archaeological Journal* 27(1): 111–125.

Crellin, R.J. 2018. Examining the British and Irish Early Bronze Age flat axes of the Greenwell collection at the British Museum. *Journal of Archaeological Science: Reports* 18: 858–888.

Crellin, R.J. in prep. Posthumanist power, in Crellin, R.J., Cipolla, C., Montgomery, L., Harris, O.J.T. and Moore, S. in prep. *Archaeological Theory in Dialogue: Situating Relationality, Ontology, and Posthumanism*. London: Routledge.

Dawney, L., Harris, O.J.T. and Sørensen, T.F. 2017. Future world: anticipatory archaeology, materially affective capacities and the late human legacy. *Journal of Contemporary Archaeology* 4(1): 107–129.

DeLanda, M. 2002. *Intensive Science and Virtual Philosophy*. London: Continuum.

DeLanda, M. 2006. *A New Philosophy of Society: Assemblage Theory and Social Complexity*. London: Continuum.

DeLanda, M. 2011. *A Thousand Years of Nonlinear History*. New York: Swerve.

DeLanda, M. 2016. *Assemblage Theory*. Edinburgh: Edinburgh University Press.

Deleuze, G. 2004. *Difference and Repetition*. London: Bloomsbury.

Deleuze, G. and Guattari, F. 2014. *A Thousand Plateaus: Capitalism and Schizophrenia*. London: Bloomsbury.

Dewsbury, J-D. 2011. The Deleuze-Guattarian assemblage: plastic habits. *Area* 43:148–153.

Draşovean, F., Schier, W., Bayliss, A., Gaydarska, B. and Whittle, A. 2017. The lives of houses: duration, context and history at Neolithic Uivar, Romania. *European Journal of Archaeology* 20(4): 636–662.

Ebersbach, R., Doppler, T., Hofmann, D. and Whittle, A. 2017. No time out: scaling material diversity and change in the Alpine foreland Neolithic. *Journal of Anthropological Archaeology* 45: 1–14.

Ferrando, F. 2019. *Philosophical Posthumanism*. London: Bloomsbury.

Fowler, C. 2013a. *The Emergent Past: A Relational Realist Archaeology of Early Bronze Age Mortuary Practices*. Oxford: Oxford University Press.

Fowler, C. 2013b. Dynamic assemblages, or the past is what endures: change and the duration of relations, in Alberti, B., Jones, A.M. and Pollard, J. (eds), *Archaeology After Interpretation: Returning Materials to Archaeological Theory*. Walnut Creek: Left Coast Press: pp. 235–256.

Fowler, C. 2017. Relational typologies, assemblage theory and Early Bronze Age burials. *Cambridge Archaeological Journal* 27(1): 95–109.

Fowler, C. and Harris, O.J.T. 2015. Enduring relations: exploring a paradox of new materialism. *Journal of Material Culture* 20: 127–148.

Gosden, C. and Malafouris, L. 2015. Process archaeology (P-Arch). *World Archaeology* 47(5): 701–717.

Grosz, E. 1994. *Volatile Bodies: Towards a Corporeal Feminism*. Bloomington: Indiana University Press.

Grosz, E. 2009. The thing, in Candlin, F. and Guins, R. (eds), *The Object Reader*. London and New York: Routledge: pp. 124–138.

Hamilakis, Y. 2017. Sensorial assemblages: affect, memory and temporality in assemblage thinking. *Cambridge Archaeological Journal* 27(1): 169–182.

Haraway, D. 2003. *The Companion Species Manifesto: Dogs, People, and Significant Otherness*. Chicago: Chicago University Press.

Harris, O.J.T. 2013. Relational communities in Neolithic Britain, in Watts, C. (ed), *Relational Archaeologies: Humans, Animals, Things*. London: Routledge: pp. 173–189.

Harris, O.J.T. 2014a. (Re)Assembling communities. *Journal of Archaeological Method and Theory* 21: 76–97.

Harris, O.J.T. 2014b. Revealing our vibrant past: science, materiality and the Neolithic, in Whittle, A. and Bickle, P. (ed), *Early Farmers: The View from Archaeology and Science*. Oxford: Proceedings of the British Academy: pp. 327–345.

Harris, O.J.T. 2016. Affective architecture in Ardnamurchan: assemblages at three scales, in Bille, M. and Sørensen, T.F. (eds), *Elements of Architecture: Assembling Archaeology, Atmosphere and the Performance of Building Space*. London: Routledge: pp. 195–212.

Harris, O.J.T. 2017. Assemblages and scale in archaeology. *Cambridge Archaeological Journal* 27(1): 127–139.

Harris, O.J.T. 2018. More than representation: multiscalar assemblages and the Deleuzian challenge to archaeology. *History of the Human Sciences* 31(3): 83–104.

Harris, O.J.T. and Cipolla, C. 2017. *Archaeological Theory in the New Millennium: Introducing Current Perspectives*. London: Routledge.

Harris, O.J.T. and Crellin, R.J. 2018. Assembling new ontologies from old materials: towards multiplicity, in Astor-Aguilera, M. and Harvey, G. (eds), *Rethinking Relations and Animism: Personhood and Materiality*. London: Routledge: pp. 55–74.

Hodder, I. 2011. Human–thing entanglement: towards an integrated archaeological perspective. *Journal of the Royal Anthropological Institute* 17: 154–177.

Hodder, I. 2012. *Entangled: An Archaeology of the Relationships Between Humans and Things*. Oxford: Wiley-Blackwell.

Hodder, I. 2014. The entanglements of humans and things: a long-term view. *New Literary History* 45: 19–36.

Hodder, I. 2016. *Studies in Human–Thing Entanglement*. Published online under creative commons.

Hodder, I. 2018. *Where Are We Heading? The Evolution of Humans and Things*. New Haven: Yale University Press.

Ingold, T. 2000. *The Perception of the Environment: Essays in Livelihood, Dwelling and Skill*. London: Routledge.

Ingold, T. 2007a. *Lines: A Brief History*. London: Routledge.

Ingold, T. 2007b. Materials against materiality. *Archaeological Dialogues* 14: 1–16.

Ingold, T. 2011. *Being Alive: Essays in Movement, Knowledge and Description*. London: Routledge.

Ingold, T. 2012. Toward an ecology of materials. *Annual Review of Anthropology* 41: 427–442.

Ingold, T. 2013. *Making: Anthropology, Archaeology, Art and Architecture*. London: Routledge.

Ingold, T. 2014. Is there life amidst the ruins? *Journal of Contemporary Archaeology* 1(2): 29–33.

Ingold, T. 2015. *The Life of Lines*. London: Routledge.

Jervis, B. 2016. Assemblage theory and town foundation in Medieval England. *Cambridge Archaeological Journal* 26(3): 381–395.

Jervis, B. 2018. *Assemblage Thought and Archaeology*. London: Routledge.

Jones, A.M. 2012. *Prehistoric Materialities: Becoming Material in Prehistoric Britain and Ireland*. Oxford: Oxford University Press.

Jones, A.M. 2017. The art of assemblage: styling Neolithic art. *Cambridge Archaeological Journal* 27(1): 85–94.

Hamilakis, Y. and Jones, A.M. 2017. Archaeology and assemblage. *Cambridge Archaeological Journal* 27(1): 77–84.

Jones, A.M. and Sibbesson, E. 2013. Archaeological complexity: materials, multiplicity, and the transitions to agriculture in Britain, in Alberti, B., Jones, A.M. and Pollard, J. (eds), *Archaeology After Interpretation: Returning Materials to Archaeological Theory*. Walnut Creek: Left Coast Press: pp. 151–172.

Jones, J. 2017. Being, belief, comprehension and confusion: an exploration of the assemblages of English Post-Reformation parochial religion. *Cambridge Archaeological Journal* 27(1): 141–154.

Latour, B. 1993. *We Have Never Been Modern*. Cambridge: Harvard University Press.

Latour, B. 1999. *Pandora's Hope: Essays on the Reality of Science Studies*. Cambridge: Harvard University Press.

Latour, B. 2005. *Re-assembling the Social*. Oxford: Oxford University Press.

Lucas, G. 2012. *Understanding the Archaeological Record*. Cambridge: Cambridge University Press.

Lucas, G. 2017. Variations on a theme: assemblage archaeology. *Cambridge Archaeological Journal* 27(1): 187–190.

MacCormack, P. (ed) 2014. *The Animal Catalyst: Toward Ahuman Theory*. New York: Bloomsubry.

MacCormack, P. 2020. *The Ahuman Manifesto*. London: Bloomsbury.

Marres, N. 2005. Issues spark a public into being: a key but often forgotten point of the Lippmann-Dewey debate, in Latour, B. and Weibel, P. (eds), *Making Things Public*. Cambridge: MIT Press: pp. 208–217.

McGlade, J. 1999. The times of history: archaeology, narrative and non-linear causality, in Murray, T. (ed), *Time and Archaeology*. London: Routledge: pp. 139–163.

Normark, J. 2009. The making of a dome: assembling houses at Nohcacab, Mexico. *World Archaeology* 41: 430–444.

Olsen, B. and Witmore, C.L. 2015. Archaeology, symmetry and the ontology of things. A response to critics. *Archaeological Dialogues* 22: 187–197.

Overton, N. and Hamilakis, Y. 2013. A manifesto for a social zooarchaeology. Swans and other beings in the Mesolithic. *Archaeological Dialogues* 20: 111–136.

Pauketat, T. 2013. Bundles of/in/as time, in Robb, J. and Pauketat, T. (eds), *Big Histories, Human Lives*. Santa Fe: SAR Press: pp. 35–56.

Ribeiro, A. 2016. Against object agency. A counterreaction to Sørensen's 'Hammers and nails'. *Archaeological Dialogues* 23(2): 229–235.

Robb, J. and Harris, O.J.T. 2013. *The Body in History: Europe from the Palaeolithic to the Future*. Cambridge: Cambridge University Press.

Robinson, D. 2017. Assemblage theory and the capacity to value: an archaeological approach from Cache Cave, California, USA. *Cambridge Archaeological Journal* 27(1): 155–168.

Sahlins, M. and Service, E. 1960. *Evolution and Culture*. Ann Arbor: University of Michigan Press.

Sheridan, A. 2010. The Neolithization of Britain and Ireland: the 'big picture', inFinlayson, B. and Warren, G. (eds), *Landscapes in Transition*. Oxford: Oxbow: pp. 89–105.

Silliman, S. 2009. Change and continuity, practice and memory: Native American persistence in colonial New England. *American Antiquity* 74(2): 211–230.

Sundberg, J. 2013. Decolonizing posthumanist geographies. *Cultural Geographies* 21(1): 33–47.

Thomas, J. 2004a. *Archaeology and Modernity*. London: Routledge.

Thomas, J. 2004b. Current debates on the Mesolithic-Neolithic transition in Britain and Ireland. *Documenta Praehistorica* 31:113–130.

Thomas, J. 2015. The future of archaeological theory. *Antiquity* 89: 1287–1296.

Todd, Z. 2016. An Indigenous feminist's take on the ontological turn: 'ontology' is just another word for colonialism. *Journal of Historical Sociology* 29(1): 4–22.

Tsing, A. 2015. *The Mushroom at the End of the World: On the Possibility of Life in Capitalist Ruins*. Princeton: Princeton University Press.

Van der Veen, M. 2014. The materiality of plants: plant-people entanglements. *World Archaeology* 46: 799–812.

Van Dyke, R. 2015. Materiality in practice: an introduction, in Van Dyke, R. (ed), *Practicing Materiality*. Tucson: University of Arizona Press: pp. 3–32.

Whittle, A. 2018. *Times of their Lives*. Oxford: Oxbow.

Whittle, A., Healy F. and Bayliss, A. 2011. *Gathering Time: Dating the Early Neolithic Enclosures of Southern Britain and Ireland*. Oxford: Oxbow Books.

Witmore, C.L. 2006. Vision, media, noise and the percolation of time: symmetrical approaches to the mediation of the material world. *Journal of Material Culture* 11: 267–292.

Witmore, C.L. 2007a. Symmetrical archaeology: excerpts of a manifesto. *World Archaeology* 39: 546–562.

Witmore, C.L. 2007b. Landscape, time, topology: an archaeological account of the Southern Argolid, Greece, in Hicks, D., McAtackney, E. and Fairclough, G. (eds), *Envisioning Landscape: Situations and Standpoints in Archaeology and Heritage*. Walnut Creek: Left Coast Press.

Witmore, C.L. 2014. Archaeology and the new materialisms. *Journal of Contemporary Archaeology* 1: 203–246.

8

BECOMING METALLIC

In Chapter 7 I outlined my approach to change: a posthumanist and new materialist approach, drawing on assemblage theory, which emphasises that change is constantly ongoing. The theoretical stance outlined in Chapter 7 aims to overcome the hurdles identified in Chapter 1. In this chapter I apply my theoretical approach to an extended case study. The chapter begins by outlining the key debate about the start of the Bronze Age in Britain and Ireland: what was the role of migration? The presentation of this debate is not comprehensive but sets the scene for what follows.[1] I contrast the large-scale debates about the role (or otherwise) of migration in the emergence of the Bronze Age with a detailed, often small-scale, study of metalwork. The narrative offered of material change at the start of the Early Bronze Age focuses on a single typological form: the flat axe. I explore how flat axes were used and understood over the period 2500–1700 cal BC in order to tell a material history. I consider how copper and bronze changed during this period and how this connects to other materials, assemblages, and practices. I conclude by resituating my story of material change in the larger debates about the start of the Bronze Age in Britain and Ireland to offer an alternative narrative. The chapter is written for scholars of the British and Irish Late Neolithic and Bronze Age, but also for those who have read this book with an interest in theory. I provide a detailed case study, drawing on my own specialism to demonstrate my approach. I hope readers from both camps will forgive the times when there is too much or too little detail for their liking.

Changes come from across the seas?

Migration plays a key role in narratives about the start of the Early Bronze Age in Britain and Ireland. There has been a pendulum swing in interpretation, from early accounts where migration and invasion were the driving force for change, over to debates that emphasised the adoption of practices without the necessary movement of people, back to stories of small-scale migration, and recently a continued swing towards arguments for large-scale migration (Figure 8.1). That this debate focuses on migration is indicative of the singular model of causation that is being evoked.

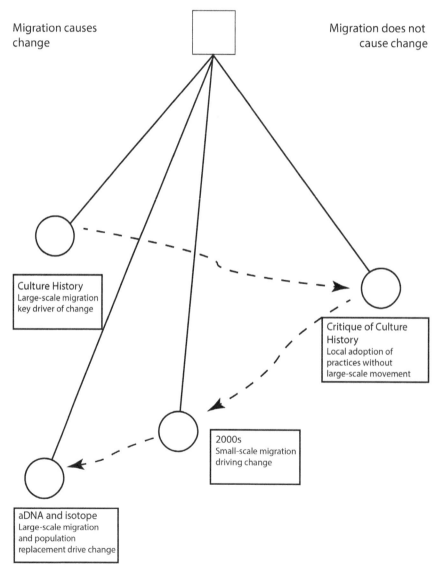

Migration causes change

Migration does not cause change

Culture History
Large-scale migration
key driver of change

Critique of Culture History
Local adoption of practices without large-scale movement

2000s
Small-scale migration driving change

aDNA and isotope
Large-scale migration
and population
replacement drive change

FIGURE 8.1 The pendulum swing of interpretation for the emergence of Beaker burial in Britain

Source: R.J. Crellin.

The beginning of the Bronze Age in Britain and Ireland is usually considered to be indicated by either the appearance of metalwork (a technologically determinist model) or Beaker burials. In a block-time model the arrival of either indicates we are in a new period (see Figure 8.2). Classically, a Beaker burial consists of a single crouched inhumation accompanied by a Beaker pottery vessel and a range of grave goods that, depending on the date of the burial and where it was found, could include flint tools, arrowheads, bracers, knives, daggers, and in some cases sheet-gold objects.[2] These burials marked a shift from Late Neolithic burial practices when burial evidence is sparse. Where evidence does exist it indicates cremation was utilised; for example, at Stonehenge there is evidence for the deposition of cremated remains between c.3015–2500 cal BC (Parker Pearson et al., 2009; 2013; see also the dating of cremation at Forteviot (Noble and Brophy, 2017)). Depending on how we model the radiocarbon dates for Late Neolithic cremations, we can either argue that cremation continued until the appearance of the first Beakers or that it marked a relatively short-lived trend between c.3000 and 2800 cal BC – in the latter model we are left knowing very little about what people in Britain were doing with their dead in the c.300 years before the appearance of the very first Beaker burials (Noble and Brophy, 2017: 224–232).

The appearance of Beaker burials, alongside metalwork, has often been explained by the arrival of new people from continental Europe where Beaker pottery and metalwork originated. Abercromby (1912: 9) infamously associated the arrival of Beakers with the arrival of a "new race" who he asserted had a different appearance. British Beaker ceramics are part of a much wider European repertoire and were tied into Childe's (1925; 1930; 1940) models of the spread of the Bronze Age through the movement of both prospectors and itinerant smiths. Parker Pearson et al. (2019: 2–4) term these models the "migrationist/invasion paradigm" because they argue that the Bronze Age began as the result of the arrival, or invasion, of migrants.

Critiques of culture history shifted the argument as they disputed the mantra that 'pots equal people' and suggested that the distributions of pottery vessels did not necessarily indicate the distributions of past 'cultures'. In the British Bronze Age context this resulted in more complex modelling of the spread of Beakers and a

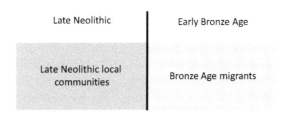

FIGURE 8.2 Block-time approach to early explanations of the arrival of the Early Bronze Age with migrants

Source: R.J. Crellin.

move towards models that considered the movement and circulation of objects. Burgess and Shennan (1976) paralleled the spread of the 'Beaker package' with the Peyote cult in Mexico and North America, arguing that Beakers were evidence of a male cult package, probably centred on alcohol, which transcended cultural borders spreading across Europe without large-scale movement of people. This marks a shift towards a more open model of culture where both people and objects were able to circulate within and beyond cultural boundaries. In such models the rapid adoption of exotic material culture (i.e. Beakers and metal) and associated practices by local elites was the result of the prestigious and valuable nature of the goods: elites adopted them to further enhance their social position (Harrison, 1980; Thorpe and Richards, 1984). In these interpretations, metal and Beakers are viewed as inherently and obviously valuable, and things that had come from the continent were, as a result of their foreignness, exotic and desirable.

The swing towards models that downplayed the role of migration was part of the critical response to culture history. Throughout the 2000s the pendulum swung back towards the centre as archaeologists began to reconsider a role for migration. Stuart Needham's (see, for example, 2005; 2007; 2012) extensive typo-chronological work in the Early Bronze Age is predicated on the period being marked by the interaction of migrants and indigenous groups. Considering Beaker use he suggests the Early Bronze Age can be divided into three key phases. The first was marked by the arrival of small groups of Beaker-using migrants, from a diversity of continental sources, who brought with them Beaker 'culture' from the continent (see also Sheridan, 2008). Needham (2007) argues that these 'isotopic aliens' interacted with indigenous groups, leading to some intermarriage. These first Beaker users were part of an exclusive cultural group. This 'pioneering phase' lasted for 10–12 generations from c.2450 cal BC. Over time 'Grooved Ware-using women' (i.e. Late Neolithic women) married 'Beaker-using males', resulting in the gradual decline of Grooved Ware leading to a 'fission horizon' from 2250 to 1950 cal BC (Needham, 2005: 43). Needham (2005: 205–207) describes this as a fission–fusion horizon. The 'fusion' emerged from interaction between the two different and distinct cultural groups, which resulted in a fission where there was a diversification of practices and thereby an increase in regionality. It is clear that for Needham (2005: 209) the Beaker group was to be the 'winner' in this cultural interaction; he describes how Beaker "cultural values, both material and conceptual, insidiously overcome pre-existing values". Copper and gold, brought to Britain and Ireland by the earliest migrants, was deeply attractive to local groups and this caused local groups to first interact with, and then later adopt, Beaker practices and material culture (Needham, 2007: 42). Beaker use continued in Britain for longer than it did in the rest of Europe: between 1950 and 1700/1600 cal BC Beakers were being used in a nostalgic way by a subset of the population (Needham, 2005: 210).

The idea of metal as desirable is part of the progressive and technologically deterministic Bronze Age grand narrative. Bronze is presented as an early form of wealth capital for which chiefs (always presented as male) would compete to accumulate. Bronze tools and weapons are linked to ideas of improved productivity and efficiency (Brück, 2019: 6): bronze equals progress and improvement. The Bronze Age is effectively presented as the foundation of a modern capitalist society: people wanted and desired bronze, it was traded in order to acquire wealth, and this allowed the development of the competitive, rational, entrepreneurial, 'individual' – this narrative is capitalist, modernist, and teleological. It is also anthropocentric: it is the actions of humans making, trading, and killing with bronze that drove social change. This anthropocentrism is also deeply humanist: our Bronze Age has been populated with male chiefs (as well as warriors; see Crellin, in press) who owned property, were fit and able, heterosexual, and, of course, European and white; everyone else is presented as less-than the Bronze Age chief, they are othered, and shown to have been less rational, less successful, and closer to nature. This model of the Bronze Age has been extensively critiqued (see, for example, Brück, 2019; Brück and Fontijn, 2013; Carlin, 2018: 34–37; Díaz-Guardamino, 2014; Fowler, 2013: 87–88), yet it remains hidden at the heart of explanations of the emergence of the Bronze Age: the arriving migrants were technologically superior, and people naturally wanted to be like them.

Needham's (2005; 2007; 2012) narrative for the emergence of the Early Bronze Age is predicated on two clearly defined and very different cultures meeting. The narrative has a culture historical undertone; while Needham often refers to 'Beaker-using' people, rather than the more clearly culture historical 'Beaker folk', the result is not all that different. Pottery types are indicators of clearly defined cultural difference. Beaker culture is presented as impressive and superior to local indigenous culture. While the fission–fusion phase in the model allows for indigenous influence on changing cultural practices, the overall sense is that local people abandoned their pre-existing ways in awe of those of the migrants. This is compounded by how these arguments are linked to concepts of 'marriage exchange'. Brodie (1997; 2001) argued that the spread of Beaker pottery was the result of marriage exchanges where women with potting skills moved across Europe. Needham (2005: 207) developed these ideas, suggesting that indigenous populations would have offered their women as wives to Beaker males in order to access metals and Beaker culture. In these interpretations, women are traded like commodities, rather than presented as equal humans (see also Kristiansen and Larsson, 2005: 234; Fig 107).

Needham's careful style of typo-chronological analysis builds multiple strands of evidence together and the result has been highly influential in British Bronze Age studies. We have seen the pendulum swing back towards migration models, "not a return to sweeping pan-European uniform migration processes, but a series of more nuanced approaches which take account of local cultural contexts" (Needham, 2007: 41). On the one hand, Needham's (2005; 2007; 2012) models produce a vision of change where we can see the actions and decisions of individuals: this is not the spread of faceless arrows on a map (as in culture history) but something more nuanced. On the other hand, this is still a technologically deterministic and progressive model – Beaker culture was superior and its eventual domination was inevitable, and, it would seem, necessary for the emergence of the Bronze Age.

Migration returns: genetics and isotopes

A wave of new scientific research has emerged from the analysis of ancient DNA (hereafter aDNA) sequences extracted from inhumation burials across Europe, all of which argue for migration as a key driver of change (for example, Allentoft et al., 2015; Brace et al., 2019; Haak et al., 2015; Lipson et al., 2017; Olalde et al. 2018). The thing that the geneticists are interested in tracking, the movement of genetic signatures across time and space, is their explanation for change. These papers focus on 'transition' moments, e.g. the start of the Neolithic and Bronze Ages, despite pulling data from a far wider chronological scope of burials.

In the current global political context, we need to talk about migration in a very careful and nuanced manner (cf. Brophy, 2018; Frieman and Hofmann, 2019; Hakenbeck, 2019). aDNA research has proven to be popular with the press. We therefore need to be careful about the presentation of narratives about migration to the general public and we should expect these stories to be picked up, and manipulated, by people whose politics we might not share. Terms like 'population replacement' (Olalde et al., 2018: 193) need very careful and clear unpacking for the public, no matter how 'scientifically accurate' they might be.[3] As Latour (1987) has demonstrated, there is no science carried out in a perfectly objective laboratory; we need to be aware of both the influence of our context on our science and vice versa. For many archaeologists (see, for example, Carlin, 2018; Frieman and Hofmann, 2019; Furholt, 2018; Hakenbeck, 2019; Heyd, 2017; Vander Linden, 2016) one of the things that is uncomfortable about aDNA papers is how they seem to mirror culture historical explanations of change, as they appear to be predicated upon clearly defined and bounded cultures and the spread of superior technological practices through migration (but see Booth, 2019: 5–6). The much-discussed use of Gustav Kossina's culture historical ideas by the Third Reich acts as an 'elephant in the room' as archaeologists fear the use of their data to support damaging narratives (Frieman and Hofmann, 2019; Heyd, 2017). It is frustrating for archaeologists, who have spent decades understanding the complex, multiple, and intersectional nature of past and present identity, and the complex, multiple, and nuanced world of cultural interaction and postcolonial theory, to see very simplistic models of identity, culture, and interaction presented in both academic publications and the press (Crellin and Harris, in press).[4] More worrying yet, archaeologists know the power of genetic evidence in the imagination of the public as scientific 'fact' and 'truth', and therefore fear that these narratives will be presented as irrefutable by those who manipulate them for political reasons (Hakenbeck, 2019). There has been, and will continue to be, much archaeological angst about the rise of aDNA analysis.

Returning to the specifics of the evidence from the start of the Bronze Age, Iñigo Olalde et al.'s (2018) analysis of the genomes of 226 people from within Beaker-associated graves has been used to argue for a large-scale movement of people westwards across Europe from the central steppe in tandem with the spread of Beaker pottery. The arrival of new genetic signatures is particularly evident in Britain where Olalde et al. (2018) revealed significant differences between the

DNA of the Neolithic inhabitants of Britain and those who came afterwards. Those coming into Britain came from places such as the Netherlands, central Europe, and Iberia, and the genetic evidence suggests not only the movement of people but that there was a 90 ±2% genetic 'turnover' by 1500 BC (Olalde et al., 2018). This has been used to argue that those who migrated to Britain at the start of the Bronze Age effectively replaced the local population. There is some indication that these migrants may well have looked different with lighter skin and eye pigmentation (Olalde et al., 2018: 194). This change in genetic signature is presented as having happened in tandem with the arrival of Beaker material culture and practices. Even in the left-leaning popular press this evidence has been associated with headlines such as "Did Dutch hordes kill off the early Britons who started Stonehenge?" (McKie, 2017). While this is clearly a sensationalist reading of the evidence presented for a popular audience, the implications of this new research have been a move to reconsider the role of migration.

We are beginning to see the gradual emergence of a series of more complex re-interpretations of the evidence by archaeologists (see, for example, Carlin, 2018: 198–200; Parker Pearson et al., 2019: 435–436). Both Carlin (2018: 198) and Parker Pearson et al. (2019: 14) highlight that there are things the aDNA evidence is not able to grasp: it cannot give us information on the scale of mobility or the pace of change during this period. aDNA can, however, be used to answer some older questions. For example, Carlin (2018: 198) highlights that the genetic evidence (Olalde et al., 2018: 193) shows both men and women were moving and therefore the models predicated on the movement of either wives across Europe or 'Neolithic women' into marriages with 'Beaker men' can be clearly refuted (see also Parker Pearson et al., 2019: 436).

Accepting that migration occurred, the key issue for archaeologists to consider is the nature of that migration and what happened following it. Olalde et al. (2018) argue for population 'replacement' but Parker Pearson et al. argue that

> the local Late Neolithic population was not exterminated by these immigrants ... the genetic data show mixing with that population to widely varying degrees, from the period c.2450–2000 BC, followed by greater homogeneity and a modest increase in Neolithic-related ancestry within the post-2000 BC population.
>
> *Parker Pearson et al. (2019: 13)*

Carlin (2018: 198) highlights the overall genetic diversity of those who used Beakers across Europe to argue that what we are seeing is not closed cultures but local, regional cultures responding differently to new peoples and technologies.

Parker Pearson et al. (2019: 15) argue that the aDNA evidence actually aligns with Needham's (2005; 2007; 2012) models (discussed earlier) and new isotopic evidence. The discovery of the potential continental origins of the so-called Amesbury Archer (Evans et al., 2006; see also Fitzpatrick, 2011) provided the impetus for the Beaker People Project (Parker Pearson et al., 2019), which has carried out the largest and most comprehensive isotopic analysis of a prehistoric population to date (Parker Pearson et al., 2019: 425). The results of their project present a complex and nuanced narrative that argues for "some degree" (Parker Pearson et al. 2019: 435) of migration from the continent, but that this was likely on a small scale, in the "hundreds rather than thousands" (Parker Pearson et al., 2019: 427). The clearest evidence for this small-scale migration is between c.2450 and 2300 cal BC (Parker Pearson et al., 2019: 445–447), but it came to have a long-term impact as those from the continent mixed with those already living in Britain and Ireland. Parker Pearson et al. (2019) argue for multiple migrations, to multiple parts of Britain, from multiple parts of continental Europe (for example, the northern Netherlands, the Rhine, northwest France, and Iberia). This is not the single arrival of a boat of 'invading migrants', nor is it a 'master plan' put in place by an expansionist culture, but rather, multiple small migrations over generations, some of which were probably not even aware of each other. Adopting Needham's (2007) terminology, they argue that the fission phase, where we see numerous regional adaptations of Beaker practices, was driven by the desire of the local population to gain access to metal, leading to interaction (Parker Pearson et al., 2019: 428). Isotopic evidence fails to confidently identify migration from continental Europe after 2300 cal BC,[5] but is able to identify a high degree of lifetime mobility within Britain that continues in their data through to 1500 cal BC (Parker Pearson et al., 2019: 447–451).

Olalde et al. (2018: 194) are advocating for substantial migration into Britain at the start of the Early Bronze Age and their work can be interpreted as suggesting that changes at this time were caused by migration. For archaeologists this interpretation is hard to marry with the archaeological evidence where there are both significant changes but also key continuities that we would not expect with a complete population replacement (for discussions of these continuities see Carlin and Brück, 2012; Cleal and Pollard, 2012). Parker Pearson et al's (2019: 435–436) interpretation better considers the archaeological evidence and focuses on the telling of a more nuanced and careful narrative, arguing for migration from the continent in small(ish) numbers followed by interaction between locals and newcomers leading to changes in practice. High levels of mobility within Britain and Ireland played a key role in both the spread of practice and in driving change.

Much ink has been (and will continue to be) spilt over the Beaker phenomenon and the beginnings of the Early Bronze Age. On the one hand, some of this is driven by new evidence: new dates, discoveries, and interpretations are constantly emerging and provoke reassessments of older evidence. This is as it should be. On the other hand, much of what we see in these debates is driven by the problem of change itself. How do we describe, explain, and interpret change? Our disciplinary history has seen culture historical narratives critiqued by many (but not all) archaeologists and, as a result, the role of migration questioned, leading to pendulum swings in interpretation. In many of these models authors seek to explain causation: how was it that the world came to change? They seek single explanations: migration, trade, marriage, desire for metals. Ultimately, the narratives

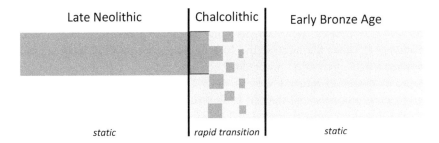

Late Neolithic	Chalcolithic	Early Bronze Age

| static | *rapid transition* | static |

FIGURE 8.3 Current models of the emergence of the Early Bronze Age. The addition of a rapid transition period between the Late Neolithic and Early Bronze Age reinforces the block-time model of change

Source: R.J. Crellin.

emerging from aDNA and isotope analysis, as well as Needham's model, are all predicated on the same explanation of change. Change is driven by migration; it comes from outside. Both the local and migrant cultures are presented as effectively closed, separate, and static groups initially; they then briefly mix, but the migrant culture ultimately triumphs (see Figure 8.3). While Olalde et al. (2018) do not comment on what causes this, Needham (2005; 2007; 2012) and Parker Pearson et al. (2019) both fall back on the appeal of metalwork to locals. The recent adoption of the term Chalcolithic by some archaeologists to capture the period of change between the Neolithic and the Bronze Age in Britain and Ireland serves to reinforce the block-time model by relegating change to a transition between two static blocks (see Allen et al., 2012 and debates therein). These narratives suggest there was a single route into the Bronze Age: via Beakers. They rely on a singular explanation of change: migration. The singular nature of these narratives denies the complexity of the evidence and the amount of time flow involved, and it quashes regional diversity and difference in favour of a master narrative.

Metallic assemblages

Setting the scene

In order to tell my narratives of the British and Irish Early Bronze Age I avoid focusing on aDNA, isotopes, and migrants, and instead focus on the histories of materials, placing copper and bronze at the centre of my assemblage. I choose to do so because I am a metalwork specialist. I know, however, that I leave myself open to the criticism that focusing on metal risks upholding a technologically determinist narrative. Cleal and Pollard (2012: 317; 330) and Roberts and Frieman (2012: 32) have written specifically about the risk of privileging metal over all the other evidence when considering the start of the Bronze Age. Focusing on metal is part of my attempt to strike at the heart of the problem, to show how metallurgy was connected to other technologies, how it was made to fit within pre-existing assemblages, and that it was not a singular cause of change. As Roberts and Frieman (2012: 32) state: "archaeologists studying this period tend to treat metal in isolation – as either the most or the least important material". Taking an assemblage approach means that metal does not sit apart from the rest of our Early Bronze Age worlds; rather I seek to show how it connects to other materials, components, processes, and threads. I think of metal as one strand within a messy 3D knot that flows through time. I pull on the metal thread and thereby shake and shift other threads and knots. I map the metal thread and it leads me to other parts of the assemblage.

What follows draws extensively on research funded by the Leverhulme Trust as part of an Early Career Fellowship at the University of Leicester. The project involved the study of 259 copper and bronze flat axes from across Britain and Ireland and focused on using axes to understand change at the beginning of the Bronze Age (a small subset of the data has been published: Crellin, 2018). Early Bronze Age flat axes and blades, first made of copper and later bronze, were probably the forms in which most communities first encountered metal. The emphasis on axes in my own work is because their thicker form and deposition away from grave contexts[6] means they are often much better preserved than metal blades, like knives or daggers, making them more suitable for analysis.[7] My understanding of these objects draws extensively on metalwork wear-analysis (Dolfini and Crellin, 2016), which allows me a window into understanding how metal objects were produced and used. I use the term 'use' in the broadest possible sense to include not only practical uses but also depositional practices and symbolic aspects reflecting the tetravalent nature of assemblages (see Chapter 7).

What does my theoretical framework mean for my starting point? First, I treat my data as a series of relational assemblages. This means knowing that they are made up of heterogeneous components, including both humans and non-humans and knowing that they are constantly in motion. In the case of copper and bronze, my new materialist approach means I consider them not as the fixed materials with clearly defined properties that we know today from material science, but instead I seek to uncover what properties, potentials, and uses they had during the Bronze Age and how these changed. I work from the starting point that copper, and later bronze, entered into pre-existing assemblages. These assemblages were already complex, with multiple relations, and were not static or fixed when copper (and later bronze) emerged. That said, copper and bronze as materials, and more specifically copper and bronze axes, did alter the assemblages they entered and the components within in unpredictable ways.

The Early Bronze Age flat axe as a form dates to between c.2500 and 1700 cal BC (Harbison, 1969; Needham, 1996; 2017; Schmidt and Burgess, 1981): typologically, over this period there were a number of changes in form from thick, square, broad-butted copper flat axes through to thinner, narrower-butted bronze axes with more flaring blades (see Figure 8.4). These axes have been typologised by Peter Harbison (1969) in Ireland, Stuart Needham (2017) in Southern Britain, and Peter Schmidt and Colin Burgess (1981) in Northern Britain and Scotland. For the sake of chronological comparison, I adopt Needham's (1996) metalwork assemblages (hereafter MA) as an overall chronological scheme into which the changes in axe typology can be fitted (Table 8.1).[8] These assemblages are based on associations between groups of metal objects found together in hoards and as such are suggested to be the product of not only temporal change but also changes in production and depositional practices (Needham, 1996: 123). In Needham's (1996: Fig 2) own illustration of this, the different assemblages overlap at the start and end, blurring into each other. Two key points arise: first, the changing typology is already indicating constant change through the period. Second, copper at 2500 cal BC and bronze at 2200 cal BC were not the same materials as they were by 1700 cal BC; the properties, qualities, and potentials of these materials changed significantly over this period. While we call everything in this sequence a flat axe, what a flat axe did, how it was understood, and what it meant, changed between 2500 and 1700 cal BC.

Peter Bray (2012: 57) has explored the concept of metalleity as the "collective properties and potentials that come with metal". These ideas are effectively new materialist: the specific properties and potentials that a metal has are not universal but a product of context, or in new materialist terms, the relations through which materials emerge. Different communities have different understandings of the properties and qualities of metals. Today we might suggest the properties of metals

FIGURE 8.4 A selection of Early Bronze Age flat axes. Left: MA1/2, type Ballybeg/Roseisle; Yorkshire Museum 1948–1108; Middle: MA3, type Migdale; Yorkshire Museum 1948–1181; Schmidt and Burgess, 1981: #171; Right: MA4, type Falkland; Yorkshire Museum 1948–1101; Schmidt and Burgess, 1981: #331
Source: Yorkshire Museum, licensed under creative commons.

TABLE 8.1 Approximate date range of the Needham's Metalwork Assemblages

Metalwork assemblage	Dating range (cal BC)	Material
MA 1/2	c.2500–2200	Copper (and gold)
MA 3	c.2200–2000	Bronze
MA 4/5	c.2000–1700	Bronze

are universally scientifically true, but that is not the case. Different communities think about metals differently. Chantal Conneller's (2011: 4–7; discussed in Chapter 7) excellent example of the differing attitudes of the Incas and the Spanish conquistadors to metals serves as a case in point. Bringing Bray (2012) into conversation with new materialism I aim to map how the properties and potentials of metal changed from 2500 to 1700 cal BC.

The largest distribution of early copper flat axes comes from Ireland; they have broad, square butts and relatively straight sides. The discovery of the Ross Island mines in the south-west of Ireland by William O'Brien (2004; see also 2012) is key to our understanding of early metalwork and metalworking in Ireland and Britain. At the site of Ross Island, O'Brien (2004) has found evidence of copper extraction and working associated with Beaker pottery and potential hut structures.[9] The discovery that the ores that were extracted from Ross Island shared the same chemical signature as the earliest copper and bronze objects known in Ireland and in much of Britain (over 70 per cent of the earliest material (Bray and Pollard, 2012: 858)) tied this mining site into the narrative of the emergence of the period (Bray, 2012; Bray and Pollard, 2012; O'Brien, 2004). O'Brien (2004: 3–4; 558–569; see also Bray, 2012: 61) has convincingly argued that mining and metallurgy were not independent inventions in Ireland, but that the technology to carry out both activities emerged from the migration of skilled miners and metallurgists from Europe, and most likely from Atlantic France and Iberia.

While the technology appears to have continental origins, interestingly the adoption of copper (and later bronze) metalwork in Ireland takes a clearly insular form (O'Brien, 2004: 2–3). William Schaniel (1988: 493) points out that adopting a 'foreign technology' does not mean adopting the 'logic' associated with the technology in its original setting. Introduced technologies are not merely adopted, they are also adapted and made to fit existing value systems and relations (Schaniel, 1988: 497); in assemblage terms they are territorialized into existing assemblages of relations. The effect of a component in one assemblage (say in Ireland) is not the same as the effect in another (say in Iberia). Neither is it the case that metal forms a new separate assemblage that is added into the mix of assemblages from 2500 cal BC onwards in Britain and Ireland, or that it simply replaces earlier assemblages; rather, it has to fit within pre-existing assemblages. During this process both the new component (metal) and the existing assemblages are changed. Joanna Sofaer Derevenski and Marie-Louise Stig-Sørensen (2002: 117) highlight how new objects and technologies involve the renegotiation of, and changes to, existing social relations, rights, and responsibilities. Metal as a new component both had to fit within an existing assemblage but was also disruptive. Taking this kind of assemblage approach to technological change stops us positing breaks and ruptures in technology that produce block-time narratives and instead encourages us to map the gradual changes in both what we might term technology and the wider assemblages in which technologies exist and act. This position also stops us from making 'always and everywhere' explanations because adopted technologies are adapted and understood within specific local contexts: metals were adopted and adapted differently across Europe and the types of changes that came from their emergence were not standardised.

Continuing with an assemblage approach, how might we think through the introduction of metal more broadly? David Kingery (1993: 225) argues that Khunian models of revolutionary change, where new (therefore better) technologies completely replace older ones causing a paradigm shift (Kuhn, 1962), often exist surrounding the adoption of new technology. In the case of metalwork this has certainly been the model: the start of the Bronze Age is presumed to mark a significant shift where stone technology is presumed to fall out of favour. Axes, as tools and as a form, were not novel. Polished stone axes and flint axes have a wide distribution across Britain and Ireland throughout the Neolithic, and were clearly both functionally and symbolically important. It is not an accident that the form in which we first see metal truly proliferate in Britain and Ireland is that of the axe. Ben Roberts and Catherine Frieman (2012: 33) argue that metal was not adopted in Britain and Ireland because stone was "broken" but because it could play a suitable role. O'Brien (2004: 515) argues that there is a basic "conservatism" in the earliest Irish metallurgy as it focuses on both axe heads and blades rather than some radically new form of material culture. I disagree with O'Brien: this is not conservatism; it is about new technologies emerging within pre-existing assemblages. In order to understand the new technology of metalworking in relation to axes, we have to consider stone and metal together. We need to consider the pre-existing assemblages surrounding stone axes and think about how metal axes fitted into this.

Stone and metal in the same frame

Carlin (2018: 208) argues that the development of metallurgy in Ireland was "strongly influenced by Neolithic traditions, particularly those associated with the production and exchange of polished stone axes". Comparing the processes of making stone and metal axes is a good starting point as it shows us the existing knowledge people had about what an axe was, how it should be made, and what it did. Rather than treating axes (of either stone or metal) as a closed category, I seek to open up their assemblages to reveal the components and processes within. Before we begin, some chronological clarifications are necessary. The dating of Neolithic stone axes is notoriously difficult as the axes themselves cannot be dated. In Britain they appear to have played a key role in the development of Neolithic lifeways, though their long-distance exchange appears to begin c.3650 cal BC

(Whittle et al., 2011: 794) and they are found across a range of Neolithic contexts, dating throughout the period, from causewayed enclosures, to long barrows, to henges. Recent work has tried to date mining and extraction sites (for example, Schauer et al., 2019), but this too creates problems as there may be multiple quarry sites on any one rock source, more recent workings may erase or bury older ones, and finding closed contexts to date can be difficult. This work suggests that in Britain mining and quarrying activity began synchronously with the start of farming, increased rapidly, before declining around 3600 cal BC, and then perhaps having a short-lived peak around 3000 cal BC before further decline and eventual disappearance around 2000 cal BC (Schauer et al., 2019: 155–156). In terms of the interpretation offered here this means that mining and extraction of stone and the production of polished stone axes was probably waning as the earliest exploitation of metals occurred. Despite this, I still argue that stone axes played a significant role in the adoption of the earliest metals in Britain and Ireland. The coming years are likely to see more debate over the dating of mining and extraction sites in Britain, and what will emerge will inevitably affect our understanding of how the production, circulation, and meaning of stone axes changed through the Neolithic. From my perspective this is positive: our understanding of Neolithic stone axes is relatively homogeneous, as it is hard to trace change over the period. Increased chronological resolution will allow us to show that this was not a static category but an assemblage that changed over time; just as I argue bronze axes were not the same at 2200 and 1700 cal BC, so too stone axes changed from 4000 to 2500 cal BC. This might mean some of my argument becomes debatable as we learn that various sources of rock, or specific extraction or making techniques, were not being used between 3600 and 2000 cal BC. Nevertheless, there is real merit in contextualising metal within stone assemblages; moreover, we know that the production of new forms of stone tools – battle axes, perforated mace heads, axe hammers, and bracers – began in the Early Bronze Age, demonstrating the clear and continued connection between these technologies.

Figure 8.5 shows a generalised and simplified comparison of the *chaînes opératoire* for the production of stone and metal axes in the British and Irish Neolithic and Bronze Age. There is much overlap at many stages between the two technologies. Both begin with material being extracted from the earth through mining and quarrying, which must then be processed and sorted. We then see the key divergence, as smelting is the next step in the making of a metal axe. However, they later reconverge as grinding and polishing are shared finishing processes, with similar aims (the creation of shape and shine).

Focusing in more detail on the process of mining and quarrying, we can consider how pre-existing assemblages for the extraction of both stone and flint provided the context for, and shaped how, metal ore extraction was understood. Peter Topping's (2017) extensive comparative analysis of Neolithic mining and extraction sites in Britain (79 flint mines and 51 axe quarries) demonstrates the complex and often ritualised nature of Neolithic extraction. Topping (2017: 279) argues that extraction sites were 'special places' in the Neolithic; frequently materials were

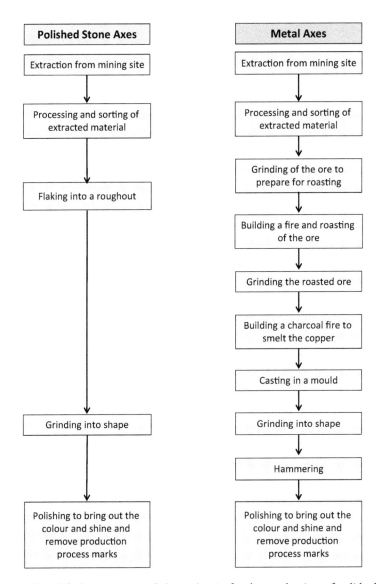

FIGURE 8.5 Simplified comparative *chaînes opératoire* for the production of polished stone
(left) and metal (right) axes
Source: R.J. Crellin.

extracted from dangerous and difficult sources (when more easily accessible sources
were available), and that many mines contain nonfunctional deposits that indicate
mining was ritualised (see also Cooney, 2015). Neolithic lithic mines and quarries
were usually isolated and located away from both evidence of domestic activity and
monumental sites, which may be interpreted as evidence of their special and separate nature (Topping, 2017: 284–285). Key sources of stone in the Neolithic (e.g.

Group VI rocks from Langdale) are often discussed in relation to their specific colour (in the case of Langdale a greenish hue); prospecting for metal ores, like stone sources, was about the recognition of specific coloured rocks (Roberts, 2008: 357). Common tools for Neolithic mining include antler and stone picks, mauls, and hammerstones. There is also good evidence, in the form of hearths found on shaft floors, for the use of fires within the flint mining process, which is less common at axe quarrying sites (Topping, 2017: 227–229; 281). While such fires may have served a practical function, Topping (2017: 282) suggests the fires were used to create smoke for the ritual purification of the miners. Excavation at lithic extraction sites in Britain often points to the seasonal or episodic nature of extraction (Topping, 2017: 223–225). Combining this evidence, the dangerous nature of many extraction sites, their seasonal usage, and isolated locations, Topping (2011) argues that mining was a specialised pursuit.

Topping (2017) argues that the materials extracted from special and often dangerous mining and extraction sites were most frequently used to produce axes.[10] Drawing on the work of Mark Edmonds (1993: 72), which argues that the proliferation of axes at the start of the Neolithic was not purely functional (i.e. to clear woodland and for agricultural purposes), Topping (2017: 280) argues that axes became a "leitmotif" during the Early Neolithic in Britain and retained their significance through the period (though I would add that their significance would have changed over time). The axe was not merely a functional tool: it also played a symbolic role, made of special material, extracted from specific dangerous and special places, distributed widely across Britain and Ireland, and often deposited in nondomestic contexts separate from more quotidian and easily available materials (e.g. surface flint and pottery). Assemblages of Neolithic flint and polished stone axes were tetravalent with both clear material elements (it is evident that specific types of stone had specific kinds of properties and functions and were therefore valued differently) and more symbolic elements. Axes were not only tools, they were a central part of the lives of Neolithic people.

Drawing this evidence together, we can see that mining for specific materials to produce axes was already a key part of Neolithic assemblages before mining for metalliferous ores began. There was a well-developed technology of extraction, as well as understandings of the special nature of material removed from the earth. Moreover, the association of mining with axes and blades was already clear. The processes of ore extraction clearly articulated easily with pre-existing assemblages surrounding mining and quarrying. It is not coincidental that the evidence from Ross Island indicates seasonal extraction of ores, potentially related to episodic flooding, and an extraction tool kit including hammerstones and fire setting (O'Brien, 2004). One of the two main sources of ore at Ross Island is termed the 'Blue Hole' because the hair and nails of the eighteenth-century miners were stained blue through mining (Heath, 2012: 35). Neolithic mining may already have been associated with small groups of seasonal specialists who left the wider social context and returned with a harvest of stone for their toil (Topping, 2011). The miners at Ross Island, at least initially, though perhaps more long term, included new people, probably from Iberia or Atlantic France, who spoke differently and were different from surrounding communities; they perhaps even looked different, with blue nails and hair. These ore miners were just the latest group of slightly unusual specialists to carry out a dangerous and transformative job, extracting materials from the earth with magical and unusual properties that would be turned into axes.

The links between the mining of lithics and ores are not accidental; while it would be incredibly difficult to prove, I suggest that the earliest copper and bronze axes may well have been thought about in similar terms to Neolithic ones – as "pieces of places" (Bradley, 2000: 88), where the earth produced special materials, with specific properties and meanings. The assemblages that surrounded the production of lithic axes and blades provided the context into which metal axes emerged and fitted. In order to consider how the earliest metal axes were understood, I turn to a small subset of the metal data. Harbison (1969: 22) and Schmidt and Burgess (1981: 30) both identify a category of ovoid or trapezoidal object they refer to as 'ingots' (see Figure 8.6). Analysis of 11 examples reveals they are all under 10cm in length, very flat, were probably cast in one-part moulds, none have a prepared blade, and I cannot confidently identify wear traces on any of them.

cm
0   5

FIGURE 8.6 'Ingots' Left: Manx Museum 2008:250. Middle: Manx Museum 2009–0035.
        Right: Yorkshire Museum 1993–317
Source: Left and middle: with permission of Manx National Heritage; right: Yorkshire Museum, licensed under creative commons.

Compositional analysis by Peter Northover (2008) of one example of an 'ingot' from the Isle of Man (MM 2009–0035) revealed it to be made of bronze produced from primary (i.e. first cast) Ross Island copper using the very earliest alloying techniques. Calling these 'ingots' is misleading as they contain small amounts of metal that would not have been enough to cast a flat axe from. Needham (2017: 39) speculates that they could have been blanks for knives or daggers. I suggest that the shape of these objects is key: it is most similar to that of a polished stone axe rather than a copper or bronze flat axe. These objects may have been part of the processes of the adaption for early metalworking: their shape was that of a traditional polished stone but their material was new. Did these objects form part of the earliest bridging of these technologies as people accepted the new material in a miniature version of a form they already understood?

The magic of smelting

Shifting from the processes of extraction to the processes of smelting, we begin to see the clear points of difference between metal and stone technologies. To smelt and alloy metal is a complex and dangerous process: specific temperatures need to be sustained for specific periods of time and the ratio of metals needs to be correct. The process of producing copper and/or bronze has multiple complex steps and was inevitably connected to ontological ideas about the nature of materials and likely had a magical element (Budd and Taylor, 1995). Ben Roberts (2008: 364) has argued that the complexity of metalworking expertise means that it was transferred from person to person, probably through an apprenticeship type process. The skills and knowledge necessary do not just involve technical know-how but are also deeply embodied. We can make connections between the control of fire necessary to produce ceramics and that needed to smelt metal; however, as Roberts (2008: 359) points out, one has to both reach and sustain a much higher temperature to smelt. While archaeological evidence for the earliest smelting in Ireland and Britain is sparse, we need to presume that some form of bellow was necessary and charcoal; charcoal would not have been needed to fire ceramics, but to maintain high temperatures and, crucially, produce a reducing atmosphere, charcoal was necessary for metallurgy (Roberts, 2008: 359). Considering the wider assemblage, we can draw in other materials and processes such as ceramic firing and cooking to help us understand early metallurgy; however, there are also key differences in processes that required new expertise. These new processes and expertise were territorialized into existing assemblages. Existing components in various assemblages laid the ground for metallurgy while new components became territorialized.

Producing metal was a peculiar (and magical) process: taking solid material extracted from the earth, grinding it up, then placing it within a fire to produce a molten liquid that, as it cooled, formed a solid. To create the molten metal, one has to maintain specific temperatures for the correct amount of time; to do that the crucible needs to be hidden within the fire, meaning one cannot see whether or not it has worked. We can imagine witnessing this process for the first time and being astounded, and probably, when trying it alone without your teacher, failing multiple times. Traditional ideas surrounding the high value of metal are related to the concept of the metalworker being a specialist who guarded *his* knowledge. From a posthumanist perspective, alternative narratives regarding metalworkers are not just possible but necessary. There is no archaeological evidence to suggest that metalworkers were men rather than women in this period. Sustaining a model of male metalworkers continues to elevate the status of men as knowledge holders and specialists. We can also disrupt the idea that metalworkers were particularly protective of their knowledge. The knowledge of how to produce metalwork (or for that matter lithics) takes a great deal of embodied skill, and this knowledge might well have remained restricted initially, not because it was being guarded, but because it took time for people to gain the necessary embodied skills to produce metal (see Kuijpers, 2017). Considering the relatively rapid spread of metal axes and the swift appearance of regional diverse forms, it appears that people were recasting objects into local forms to fit within their localised assemblages. It does not appear, therefore, that knowledge remained restricted for long, and that the initial restriction was perhaps more to do with skill than secretiveness.

Molten metal was poured into moulds. Traditionally, one-part moulds are seen as a simpler technology, used to produce the earliest axes. The later development of two-part (and later three-part) moulds is seen as evidence of the progressive nature of metalwork technologies. The use of a mould is novel: creating the negative space you want the final product to be is not something that we think can be paralleled in the period. The production of moulds, however, drew upon pre-existing assemblages of technologies. Unsurprisingly, the few surviving moulds we have from this period are made of stone (Schmidt and Burgess, 1981: 52–54); they would have been produced using similar techniques of grinding and pecking that were already in use producing stone axes, tools, and rock art. It is likely, however, that these stone moulds were not the norm and that other materials were more frequently used (Needham, 2004: 224). Maikel Kuijpers (2008: 87–89), discussing Bronze Age metallurgy in the Netherlands, argues that the most frequently used material for moulds was probably clay because an existing axe, or a model of one, could be pressed into the clay to create the mould. While mould finds are rare, the use of a mould has an aesthetic consequence for the surface of axes, allowing us to infer some information about the form of moulds used in the past even if we cannot be certain of the material.

Moulds indicate one of the ways in which the new materials copper and bronze radically transformed assemblages. Moulds allow the production of copies that replicate each other; Andrew Jones (2012: 138) refers to axes as a form of simulacra as a result. Replicating the form of stone axes, flint tools, and ceramics took a great deal of personal skill. Jones (2012: 103–105) explores how categories of objects emerge from the making processes. Combining a performance approach with new materialism, Jones (2012: 103–105) argues that categories of object are not fixed but in process: when we produce an object we take part in an embodied process of improvisation where we might 'cite' an original we are trying to copy, but our copy will always differ from that original. As such, objects within a category, for example Beakers, both hold things in common and have key differences. Moulds are a disruptive technology giving the ability to create more similar copies of the same form multiple times, yet each axe is not identical, because the mould is but part of a broader assemblage of processes necessary to make an axe. In addition, the vibrancy of metals, as materials, means that even with the same mould the material will behave differently each time. This ability to create multiple similar objects had consequences for how metal axes were understood, a point I return to below.

Finishing axes

Once an axe has been cast it takes further work to give the axe a shiny, symmetrical form. Newly cast axes are covered in sprue, darkly coloured, and unlikely to have a perfect or symmetrical form. To produce the final shape, grinding is necessary. Grinding was a process shared with stone axe production and probably utilised similar toolkits. The axe also needs to have a blade prepared and sharpened. Initially this appears to have just involved sharpening the blade of the axe; however, from c.2200 cal BC clearly defined blade areas were produced through hammering. Sharpening axes drew upon existing assemblages of toolkits and techniques. Hammering is a process we consider later.

Polishing and planishing are also finishing processes that overlap with the production of polished stone axe assemblages. Gabriel Cooney (2005: 24–25) argues that the grinding and polishing of porphyry from Lambay Island to produce polished stone axes brought out the whiteness of the rock and the crystals within it. Polishing flint makes it more lustrous (Frieman, 2012: 80). The process of polishing stone axes appears to have been key in bringing out the qualities of the rock or flint, its particular colour, and making it shine. These processes were already part of axe assemblages; it is not surprising, therefore, that even the earliest copper and bronze flat axes were well polished.

Smelting was undeniably a radically different and innovative process. There are, however, also clear points of connection between the extraction, production, and finishing processes of stone and metal axes. The overlapping nature of the assemblages of metal and stone axes were key to the process of metal adoption and adaptation: this was why, and how, metal, in the form of the axe, came to make sense in Britain and Ireland (see Figure 8.7). Communities in the south-west of Ireland came to understand the smelting process with some degree of overlap with their European counterparts, as well as some clear differences, which gave rise to uniquely Irish (and later British) shapes and forms: the knowledge and skill might have come from elsewhere initially, but how it was implemented and produced were clearly local. Those who received cast axes, in geographically distant parts of Britain and Ireland, may not, initially at least, have understood the magical new production processes that made these axes and the connection between ores and heat at all (Bray, 2012). They may well have presumed they were made in similar

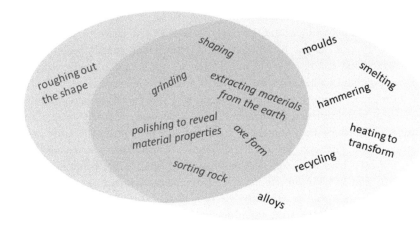

FIGURE 8.7 Overlapping assemblages of production processes for metal and stone axes. Darker circle on the left contains assemblage of stone axe production processes. Lighter circle on the right contains assemblage of metal axe production processes. Overlapping area shows shared processes
Source: R.J. Crellin.

ways to the stone axes they already knew, then later (perhaps months, or years), as metalworking techniques arrived in these communities, they were effectively already pre-exposed to the material itself when the production processes were revealed to them.

The properties of early metals in Britain and Ireland

As discussed above and in Chapter 7, the properties of a given material are not intrinsic to them but a result of the relational assemblages they exist within. Different metals have differing properties, and different properties emerge from the same material as a result of the assemblages they exist within. Today copper conducts electricity in assemblages with wires, power stations, and electricity; such assemblages did not exist in the Early Bronze Age.

We know that Early Bronze Age metallurgy in Britain and Ireland relied on smelting (rather than, as in the Old Copper Culture of the Americas, cold-working copper ore (Binford, 1962)). It is clear, therefore, that one of the earliest properties associated with copper, at least for those who worked it, was that it could be made into a molten liquid. Metalwork wear-analysis reveals that even the earliest copper flat axes show signs of polishing and grinding. This indicates that copper, and later bronze, objects should have smooth edges and a clear (and often symmetrical) form. The evidence for grinding and polishing is also indicative of a desire to bring out the colours and shine of the material.

Bray (2012) argues that a number of the properties of copper were unknown during the period 2500–2200 cal BC. In particular, he argues that copper's ability to respond to heat and hammering, as part of the finishing processes for making an axe, were only slowly understood. Hammering is a key process in the hardening of copper and bronze. When hammered the crystals within metals become more clearly aligned and as a result the material becomes harder and stronger; however, when we continue to hammer, we begin to make the material brittle and more likely to fracture. Heating a hammered metal (the process of annealing) allows a reduction in this brittleness. Hammering was a peculiar technique in an Early Bronze Age British or Irish context – there were no other materials made harder by hitting them. That said, the bodily techniques of hammering (knowing when, where, and how hard to strike) may well have had links to the percussive use of hammers in flint knapping for reduction. Heating materials to make them harder was, however, well known, from the firing techniques of clay to fire-hardening wooden posts and tools to make them durable.

The earliest Irish copper flat axes (MA1)[11] show no evidence of hammering; however, in Irish copper flat axes from MA2 onwards there is evidence of "a relatively regular approach to" both hammering and heating (Bray, 2012: 64). This is further supported by my own work; effective hammering can be very hard to recognise through metalwork wear-analysis, but there are early examples where unskilled hammering is evident (see Figure 8.8); however, from MA3 onwards hammering becomes quite hard to identify unless it is being used as a decorative technique. Bray (2012) suggests this shift in processes indicates a shift in how the material was understood. In MA1 in Ireland the specifically 'metallic' properties of copper were not understood, and it was probably thought of more like a rock, whereas in MA2 new properties emerged. The situation was different in Britain where, Bray (2012: 65–67) argues, communities did not begin to understand the properties and potentials of metal to be hardened through hammering and annealing until post 2200 cal BC. Exploring hammering as a property shows that what metal was, as a material, was changing. This change was also regional and patchy as a result of the localised assemblages that metals existed within.

The addition of tin to bronze acts to produce a harder material and as a result bronze tools can be used for longer periods before they need to be resharpened or reworked in comparison to copper tools (Kienlin and Ottaway, 1998). Comparative work with bronze and stone axes suggests bronze axes were more efficient, though this may have been a product of shape (metal axes are thinner) as much as hardness (Mathieu and Meyer, 1997; Saraydar and Shimada, 1971). In the Bronze Age, where scientific hardness testing was not an option, communities learned that tin-bronze axes not only had a different colour but also a different temporality: bronze was a material that lasted longer and needed reworking less. The literature currently suggests a relatively rapid shift from copper use in MA1/2 to the use of tin-bronze in MA3. This rapid shift seems unusual when we consider the gradual development of processes like hammering. Bray (2012: 67) has argued that there may actually have been a more gradual lead-in to the transition to bronze via the production of early tin-bronzes in Cornwall that were later preferentially recycled, effectively obscuring them from archaeological view.

FIGURE 8.8 Hammering on an early type Lough Revel Axe from Ireland (MA1/2). Image on the left gives an overview of the axe and the two images on the right are micrographs of the surface showing the unusual hammering. British Museum 1854–0714.184; Harbison, 1969: #306

Source: R.J. Crellin with permission of the British Museum.

One of the key properties of metal today is that we can recycle it. Recycled metal is often cited as a specifically Bronze Age innovation (for example Bradley, 1998: 82; Edmonds, 1995: 156; Roberts, 2008: 365). The melting down of existing, older, or broken metal objects to make more molten copper or copper alloy for new objects does have links to pre-existing assemblages. The sharpening and resharpening of lithics was common in the Neolithic and was effectively a form of re-enlivening a blunt tool to make it new again. Frieman (2012: 79–80) argues that objects such as flint daggers may well have been recycled and reused as spearheads or strike-a-lights. Similarly, we know that older pots and burnt flint were sometimes used as a form of temper in new vessels (Brück, 2006: 85–86). Reusing an object by resharpening or repurposing the form was not new. Returning an object to a molten form and thereby completely erasing its earlier shape was innovative.

We think of recycling as a relatively anonymous process where we do not know what our can or plastic bottle will become; there is no reason to assume this was the case in the Early Bronze Age, where specific objects could have been brought together to create new objects. Considering burial assemblages, Brück (2019: 74) has argued that these were specifically gathered collections of objects brought together by mourners, indicating the relations the dead existed within. She goes on to argue that this was indicative of a relational and composite model of personhood in the Bronze Age (Brück, 2019: 112). In the specific case of necklaces and beads found within Early Bronze Age burials (roughly contemporary with the development and increase in recycling), Anne Woodward (2002; see also Woodward and Hunter, 2015: chapters 7 and 8) has argued that these were collections of beads from different sources with different histories that were being brought together to create a composite whole, and then perhaps redistributed at the grave side. As recycling developed it was perhaps thought of in the same way, a bringing together of a composite of objects with different histories, to make something new. One could imagine communities building connections in this way as they combined their axes and blades to make new ones, perhaps at specific stages in the lifecycle.

Recycling is not just about reusing what is perhaps broken or tired but can also be about reshaping things into new forms:

> Recycling was not dictated only by necessity, but was equally directed towards modifying the shape of an axe to make it more acceptable as it was passed from hand-to-hand by infusing local ownership and values into the metal.
>
> *(Pollard et al., 2014: 630)*

Early recycling in Britain and Ireland was, given the flow of copper, probably often about the reshaping of axes and blades into locally appropriate forms: axes were being territorialized through recycling processes to make them fit within local assemblages. Their previous form was effectively erased (though perhaps not forgotten) and a new local form emerged. The lack of 'proper ingots' in the British and Irish Bronze Age is not because we have not found them, rather it is because one community's axe, when traded with a neighbour, effectively acted as an ingot (Pollard et al., 2014: 630).

As we move through the Early Bronze Age, recycling increases; by around 2200 cal BC people had begun to appreciate the potential for recycling (Bray, 2012: 66). Analysis suggests about 10 per cent of MA3 axes were recycled, 30 per cent of MA4/5, and 40 per cent of MA6 (Bray, 2012: Fig 4.5). By c.1800–1600 cal BC there were metal objects in circulation that were made of Ross Island metal that was first smelted around 500 years earlier and had been remelted and recycled multiple times (Bray and Pollard, 2012: 862). Like the necklaces discussed above, these objects were composite heirlooms. Bray (2012: 66–67: Fig 4.6) also suggests that early recycling might have been used as a way to increase the amount of tin within an alloy; recycling could therefore have been associated with changing the specific properties of metal, taking a softer metal and making it harder, for example. For Bray (2012: 66), recycling is key to understanding the circulation of material and, more importantly, the changing mindset of Bronze Age people: full recycling of metal represents a different mindset from the Neolithic, and a wider understanding of the properties of metal. I interpret the shift towards recycling as a phase transition in this period. It is the build-up of a series of changes, across a range of assemblages and technologies, bringing together processes of reuse, recombination, fragmentation, and the practice of including older and different materials within composite collections. Bray (2012: 66) is right that it marks a significant shift in understanding of materials, but this is gradual, something that happens over centuries and brings with it pre-existing understandings of materials. It is not a key difference between Neolithic and Bronze Age mindsets, rather it is one of many changes that emerged over time.

At the same time as these changes in recycling practices occurred, there were also changes in the treatment of the dead. There was a broad trend over the course of the Early Bronze Age for a shift from inhumation to cremation, though this was not a unilinear progress; instead, clear choices about the preference for inhumation or cremation were being made by mourners (Appleby, 2013; Brück, 2019: 36). This was also a highly regionalised process where different communities made different decisions (Appleby, 2013: 83), reflecting local choices and assemblages of practices (parallel to the adaptation of metalwork). Brück (2006) has highlighted the connections between cremation and metalworking. Cremation involves fire as the catalyst for a transformative and spectacular process that is both controllable and uncontrollable (Downes, 1999). Similarly, the processes of smelting involve fire as the catalyst for transformation. Combining multiple strands of evidence we can suggest that communities were recasting bronze into locally appropriate forms, which indicates a spread of metalworking knowledge throughout Britain and Ireland. Bray's (2012) work illustrates an increased understanding of the ability to remelt metal from 2200 cal BC and higher levels of recycling from then onwards; these shifts coincide with the changes in burial practice as communities came to adopt cremation (see also Brück, 2006: 86). The assemblages of metalworking and cremation overlap: they share components and processes in common. Evidence for both smelting sites (Timberlake, 2014) and pyre sites (McKinley, 1997) is rare in Britain and Ireland, which may be a product of their ephemeral nature and poor archaeological recognition, but it may also be indicating how material related to fiery transformations was understood and treated. Following cremation, the bones of the deceased were picked out from the charred remains of the pyre, and there may be a link here to how the remains of the smelt would have been picked through to discover the prills of copper within. I am not arguing that cremation is the cause of recycling (or vice versa), but that these two processes were entangled and connected, affecting the development of each other.

Moving materials, connecting communities

Petrographic analysis of polished stone axes has enabled the many sources of rock used to produce Neolithic stone axes to be identified, and as a result, we know that polished stone axes were circulating widely through Britain and Ireland and away from their sources during the Neolithic (Clough and Cummins, 1988; Cooney and Mandal, 1998; Cooney et al., 2011; Davis, 1997; Davis and Edmonds, 2011). Rock and flint sources are widely geographically distributed across Britain and Ireland and as a result it is likely that rocks of different types were moving in numerous directions, connecting different communities during the Neolithic.

It has been suggested that pre-existing exchange routes for the movement of Antrim porcellanite out of Ireland and across the Irish sea were used for the movement of early copper from Ross Island (Carlin, 2018: 203; Cooney, 2000: 204; Needham, 2004: 241; Sheridan, 1986). What is different about the exchange and movement of copper is how, we presume, it re-oriented the movement of materials. In the Neolithic, stone came from multiple sources distributed across Britain and Ireland. By contrast, copper for axes was, in the main, coming only from Ross Island.[12] While other materials, animals, people, and things, probably even including polished stone axes (Carlin (2018: 203) notes that many polished stone axes have been found in Beaker contexts in Ireland), were moving along pre-existing exchange routes in multiple directions, we know that the vast majority of copper for axes at the start of the Early Bronze Age was coming from a single source. Copper, as a new material, exploited existing exchange networks, but this new component inevitably disrupted the overall regional flow of materials to be more squarely related to one main source.

Bray and Pollard (2012: 860–861) have shown that between c.2200 and 2000 BC we can track the flow of metal away from Ross Island; as we move geographically further away from the source there is evidence that the metal has been remelted more frequently. The data suggest metal in Ireland was remelted the least, then metal in Scotland, then south-west England, then central England, and in Eastern England the metal has been remelted the most times. Metal appears to be flowing out of Ireland into Scotland and Northern England and also, arguably, into south-west England (the likely source of tin) and then probably onward to central and eastern England. Bray (2012: 60–61) notes that there is excellent evidence for extraction of arsenical copper from Cornwall making up a small proportion of the copper that had not come from Ross Island at this time.

From 2200 cal BC, as bronze enters into assemblages, we also have to consider the movement of tin. Clear evidence for the source(s) of Bronze Age tin are not unequivocal; however, "circumstantial evidence and a strong narrative tradition" (Timberlake, 2017: 716) indicate that Cornwall and Devon were probably the source of alluvial tin (see also Rohl and Needham, 1998). The addition of tin to copper to make bronze means that we now have multiple exchange networks flowing through Britain and Ireland. We have both the movement of primary copper and tin to be alloyed together as well as the movement of already alloyed bronze that could be remelted and cast into new more locally appropriate forms.

The excavations at Ross island indicate that mining was abandoned at the site due to flooding (O'Brien, 2004: 572). Mining in the Blue Hole is thought to have ceased around 2100 cal BC while mining at the Western Mine may have continued for another 200 years. This archaeological evidence is supported by that drawn from chemical composition analysis that shows a significant drop-off in the amount of Ross Island copper in circulation from around 2000 cal BC (Bray and Pollard, 2012: Table 1).

Following the flooding of Ross Island there was a switch in copper sources: Irish sources at Mount Gabriel were utilised (O'Brien, 1994) as well as British sources of copper, particularly around the Welsh Irish Sea basin.[13] A range of small-scale prospecting sites have been identified across mid-Wales (Timberlake, 2014; 2017), as well as clear evidence of mining at sites such as Copa Hill (Timberlake, 2003), Parys Mountain (Jenkins, 1995), the Great Orme (Williams, 2017; Williams and Le Carlier de Veslud, 2019), Alderly Edge (Timberlake and Prag, 2005) and Ecton Hill (Timberlake, 2014). Bayesian modelling of the radiocarbon dates associated with these sites suggests a gradual, overlapping chronological development through the Early Bronze Age from mid-Wales, to north Wales, and then north-west central England (Timberlake, 2017: 714). Timberlake (2014; 2017: 714) argues that there were key similarities in mining methods, tool use, and technical expertise in the three regions. He also suggests the connections in methods and tools stretch back to Ross Island. No evidence for settlement has been found at any of these Early Bronze Age mining sites (Timberlake, 2014). In the Early Bronze Age there was a shift away from Irish sources towards Welsh ones for copper and the probable continuing exploitation of Cornish tin.

The increasing rise of recycling probably played a role in shifting exchange networks once more. As more metal became available, both as newly smelted copper from Wales was utilised and as increasing amounts of already smelted and cast metal objects circulated, we might expect to see more distributed networks of exchange from c.2000 cal BC onwards where multiple local sources were feeding in new materials and objects creating a more distributed network.

Changing axes

Turning to the axes themselves, I map how what a flat axe was and what it did changed between c.2500 and 1700 cal BC. The earliest flat axes, dating to MA1/2, are often the most badly corroded because they are made of copper rather than bronze, meaning they are often harder to interpret through metalwork wear-analysis. Despite these corrosion issues, MA1/2 axes show clear signs of use. There are four key strands of evidence to interpret here: axe blades are often very worn and blunted, sometimes showing signs of fracture from use; they are also frequently very asymmetrically worn; there are frequent signs of striations indicative of use in woodworking; and there are also some marks on MA1 axes that are hard to parallel experimentally. This evidence is complex to interpret as copper is softer than bronze and therefore wears more easily, and this is further compounded by the limited use of hammering to harden copper in MA1/2, so we have to weigh up whether what we are seeing between c.2500 and 2200 cal BC is very heavy use or a product of the (relative) softness of copper axes.

Bringing the four lines of evidence together gives us the strongest interpretation: the data indicate that these axes were being used for woodworking. The unparalleled wear marks also suggest that some of these axes were being used in ways we might not expect and have not recreated experimentally. I interpret this as indicating very flexible use of MA1/2 copper flat axes. Communities were using axes in innovative and varied ways as the 'rules and traditions' that defined what this kind of axe was for were being shaped. I suggest that communities first tried to use them in similar ways to stone axes and then, as they learned of their properties, began to experiment with other uses. The proportion of blunt and asymmetrical axes is indicative of heavy use, but also of the understandings communities had of these materials. It is possible to take an asymmetrically worn axe and re-orient it in the haft to make it wear more symmetrically: this does not seem to have happened often (see Figure 8.9). It is also possible to rework such an axe to give it a fresher and more symmetrical blade: again, this does not seem to have happened. Read alongside Bray's (2012) chemical analyses this confirms that the understanding of how metal blades could be worked, reworked, and recycled was developing rather than established at this time.

Axes from MA1/2 are most frequently recovered as single finds; deposition in hoards was less common and metal axes were not deposited in either burials or on settlement sites. Many of the axes that were deposited were highly worn; they could have been reworked and recycled, but they were not. Instead they were deposited in a worn state, returning an axe that may have been interpreted as 'no longer usable' to the ground.

From c.2200 cal BC there were changes in what an axe was and what an axe did. As discussed above, the most significant aspect was the shift from the use of copper to bronze. In concert with this there were changes in the working process: hammering to harden and work bronze became the norm; blunt blades were being reworked and resharpened; and a wider range of regional forms of axe developed, indicating recycling into locally appropriate forms. Taken together we can see that the properties of metal shifted: it was becoming associated with an ability to transform and rework and was treated less like stone. This was a material that could be shaped and reworked multiple times, where the application of heat was a key transformative process. These changes happened alongside the emergence of a range of regional pottery forms and cremation as a key funerary practice.

The regionalisation of practices at this time is clearly evident in the Migdale-Marnoch metalworking tradition of north-east Scotland dating to MA3. The most common flat axe form in Ireland at this date was the Killaha axe; however, in Scotland and Northern Britain it was the Migdale axe (Schmidt and Burgess, 1981: 34). Migdale axes were produced using copper from Ross Island, presumed to have been combined with tin from south-west England (Needham, 2004). Most of the materials probably made their way to Scotland in the form of Killaha axes. This specifically Scottish form of axe is indicative of a specifically Scottish form of metalworking. Migdale-Marnoch metalworking was the re-territorialization of Irish metalworking practices into Scottish assemblages, where they were altered and adjusted, causing different properties to materialise and, as a result, what emerged was a specifically local assemblage.

Migdale axes are thought to have been cast in one-part moulds, primarily made from hard rocks such as sandstone and probably capped with a flat stone during

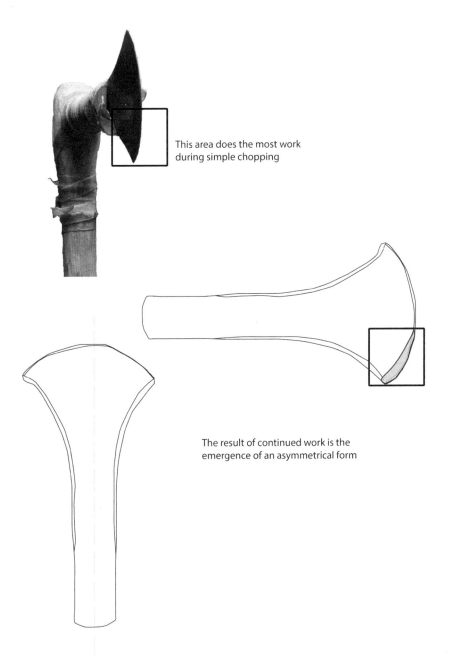

This area does the most work during simple chopping

The result of continued work is the emergence of an asymmetrical form

FIGURE 8.9 How wear produced asymmetrical axe blades
Source: R.J. Crellin.

casting (Needham, 2004: 223). This provides somewhat of a conundrum in analysis. Around half of earlier flat axes from MA1/2 from my sample (28 of the 54 axes) appear to have been cast in a one-part mould, but the rest show evidence of either surface symmetry or casting seams indicative of casting in a two-part mould. On that basis I suggest that use of two-part moulds was developing during MA1/2, probably in Ireland. In MA3 (when Migdale axes emerged) there are only five axes in the sample showing unequivocal evidence of casting in a one-part mould, though there are eight additional Migdale axes where I cannot identify the type of mould they were cast in. The evidence from the moulds themselves seems to indicate one-part mould casting was the norm in the Migdale-Marnoch tradition (Needham, 2004: 224), demonstrating a probable difference in metalworking practices between Ireland and Scotland. However, the surface of the axes themselves somewhat confuses this story. There are some that have been cast in one-part moulds, but there are also some where either their surfaces were post-cast-worked to such a degree as to disguise their casting in a one-part mould or they were cast in two-part moulds. What appears here as a problem in the data is probably indicative of shifting and changing assemblages of practices over time and potentially also of the continued relations between Scottish and Irish metalworkers. Rather than expecting all the data to agree, it seems that some axes were being cast in one-part moulds, some were perhaps cast in one-part moulds and then worked to make them appear symmetrical, and others were being cast in two-part moulds, showing that the Migdale tradition was not homogeneous nor static.

Another particular 'peculiarity' of the Migdale tradition is the practice of tin-coating (Needham, 2004: 235; Needham and Kinnes, 1981). Some Migdale axes have a surface coating of tin and a bronze interior. Needham (2004: 235) associates this practice with some of the earliest tin-bronze axes produced in Scotland and interprets the use of tin as a conspicuous practice. Tin-coated axes look different, with a greyer colour. Needham (2004: 235) argues that access to tin might have been limited, making it a 'precious' material; when metalworkers chose to coat their axes in tin they were thereby demonstrating their access to the metal. Needham's (2004) interpretation of the Migdale-Marnoch tradition sees it as a local form of metalworking, which I agree with, but argues that the aim of metalworkers was to maximise prestige, which I dispute because I do not interpret axes as a form of early capital or prestige good. There are other ways to interpret this practice; focusing on the metals themselves allows us to tell a different story. Bronze and copper have different properties because of the addition of tin, one of which is that bronze is harder. As communities came to understand that this new material, bronze, had been made stronger through combining copper with another material, perhaps this understanding led to the decision to coat some axes in tin to exploit the association between tin and hardness.

The Migdale-Marnoch tradition demonstrates that metalworking did not develop in a unilinear way in Britain and Ireland. The use of what in technological terms would be described as 'simpler' moulds indicates change was not linear or progressive. Furthermore, the development not only of the local form of the

Migdale axe but also the tin-coating techniques shows how metals were adapted locally to fit within pre-existing assemblages, but also how a new component can cause unpredictable changes and does not have the same effects everywhere.

MA3 axes from across Britain and Ireland show clear evidence of having been used for woodworking. Drawing a broad comparison with MA1/2 copper axes, many of the MA3 axes appear less worn, less asymmetrical, and there are fewer marks that are hard to parallel. I interpret this data to show that not only was bronze a more hard-wearing material but also communities were becoming better at working, maintaining, and reworking their axes, and also manipulating them within their hafts in order to extend their use-life. This was also likely connected to more controlled, less flexible, use of bronze axes.

Whereas earlier axes were often deposited very worn (though they had the potential to be reworked or recycled), axes deposited in MA3 were often still functional. This is indicative of a shift in understanding: communities both knew that axes could be recycled and were choosing to deposit axes when still usable. During this period practices of breaking and damaging axes before deposition developed. This might involve breaking an axe into pieces or specifically damaging the butt, blade, or margins. One way to interpret this practice is as a form of anticipatory action. In Chapter 3 I discussed how we often wrongly presume that things that are buried are static because they are away from humans. Hoarding, as a form of anticipatory action (cf. McFadyen, 2007; 2010 on lithic scatters as future oriented), suggests Bronze Age communities thought that the axes they deposited continued to have future potential: their life and usefulness was not over. In some cases, this resulted in depositing tools ready for use and in others it resulted in practices aimed at reducing the future potential of the axes through damage. While ideas abound about hoarding practices (see, Bradley, 2017), what I think can be agreed upon is that axes that were being buried by communities had the potential to continue to work, whether that was in the hands of gods, in thanks to the earth, or for future generations.

Earlier in this chapter I discussed how the use of moulds allowed the production of axes that were more similar to each other than was previously possible (see also Jones, 2012: 138). My discussion above suggests that in the Early Bronze Age metal's transformability was something that emerged gradually. Hoards offer us an interesting lens onto this problem. It would be possible to produce an Early Bronze Age hoard consisting of axes with very similar forms. As Jones (2012: 136–137) highlights, in Scotland and northern Britain at this time most hoards consisted of multiple axes. Yet, as hoarding practices develop during this period, my analysis shows that axes with explicitly diverse forms and histories were being brought together for deposition (Crellin, 2018: 871–872). Just as metalwork wear-analysts can look at the surface and begin to elucidate some of the history of an axe, past communities would have been able to observe the history of specific axes, effectively scratched on their surface, and known through oral histories. Metal was increasingly understood as a transformable material in this period, but at the same time, hoarding practices indicate that the histories of objects selected for deposition in hoards mattered. Hoards gathered axes with diverse histories.

The Hill of Finglenny hoard from Scotland is an excellent example to illustrate this tension between similarity and difference and the gathering of diverse histories. The hoard consists of seven tinned axes, four of which were deposited intact and three that were deposited broken (Jones, 2001: 347; Schmidt and Burgess, 1981: #67; #85; #87; #95; #96; #97; #137) (see Figure 8.10). The axes were placed underneath a stone overlooking the Wormy Hillock henge (Cowie, 2004: 258). Needham (2004: 222) has argued that the hoard was probably gathered over several generations and Shaun Moyler (2008: 84) has argued the dissimilar wear across two of the breaks (NMS DQ309, DQ310; the butt-end breaks are more worn than the blade-end breaks) supports the idea that they had different circulation histories prior to deposition. Metalwork wear-analysis further highlights the different histories of the axes gathered into this assemblage. Two of the axes in the assemblage have a really marked asymmetry to their blades (NMS DQ307, DQ 312), which usually indicates heavy use. However, the story may be more complex: both axe blades have their opposite blade corners in good

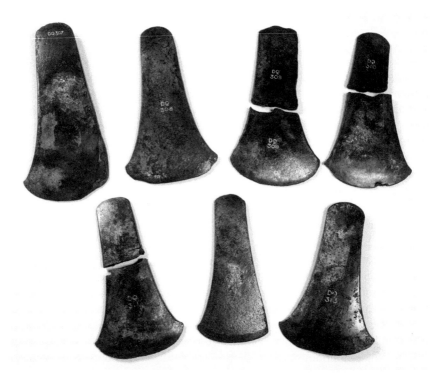

FIGURE 8.10 Hill of Finglenny hoard from Scotland. Top row, left to right: National Museum of Scotland DQ-307; DQ-308; DQ-309; DQ-310; Schmidt and Burgess, 1981: #137; #97; #95; #96; Bottom row, left to right: National Museum of Scotland DQ-311; DQ-312; DQ313; Schmidt and Burgess, 1981: #87; #67; #85

Source: © National Museums Scotland.

condition, suggesting that these axes were not rehafted to wear evenly; these were axes that were being given an asymmetrical form through uneven wear. Moreover, I suggest that in addition to heavy use, there may have been some deliberate reshaping of these blades as DQ307 shows signs of heavy grinding over the top of wear marks. In contrast, DQ308 shows signs of wear across the blade that suggest it was rehafted during use to produce a more symmetrical blade. The three broken axes were intentionally fragmented (contra Moyler (2008: 85)); Matt Knight's (2018; 2019) work shows that to achieve this the axe was probably heated. DQ310 has a wide, deep incision on the blade fragment near the break, and DQ311 has an incision to the surface on the butt piece – in both cases I suggest these marks indicate failed attempts to fragment the axes. One side of the body of DQ313 shows signs of numerous small incisions to the surface with a shape indicating these incisions were deliberately produced by a thinly bladed object. Interpreted as a whole, this is an assemblage of relatively similar looking axes, tied together by their shared tinning giving them a similar colour, yet each had a different history associated with it.

MA4/5 axes show similar signs of hammering, working, sharpening, and resharpening as MA3 axes. However, they are more likely to be decorated than earlier axes. This decoration is itself an interesting transformation. Decoration on these axes takes the form of incised designs on the surface and the use of decorative hammering techniques (see Figure 8.11). Both the method of design by incising and the patterns that were utilised have clear parallels with Beaker and Food Vessel pottery. Just as pottery vessels were incised with complex designs, so too was metal. Stone axes were apparently not decorated, and I suggest it was the weight of pre-existing relations that meant this too was the case for earlier metal axes.

Evidence of use remains similar to that discussed above for MA3 axes and it also appears that hoards continued to be about the gathering of similar but different axes, with clearly different histories. The probable axe hoard of Ballyvalley-type axes from Connor in County Antrim (British Museum WG.1542, WG.1543, WG.1544; Harbison, 1969: #883, #884, #885) is a good example of this (see Crellin, 2018: 871–872: Figure 5). The three axes each have very different histories. As is common in hoard deposits, one axe is more corroded than the others, making it harder to interpret; however, the most corroded axe, WG.1542, is highly symmetrical with no damage to the butt; it was either very lightly used, or perhaps even unused when it was deposited. WG.1544 is a decorated axe with clear signs of use on the blade and what appears to be intentional damage: there are two large, gently curved fractures to the blade that are unlikely to have formed through use. WG.1543 is a very unusual axe as the entire blade has been carefully removed. What makes this removal even more impressive is that it has been done to complement the decorated surface of the axe. These three axes had distinctly different histories written on their surfaces despite having the same overall form. The removed blade of WG.1543 is not only indicative of a complex history but also of the understanding of metal properties and processes; the way in which this axe has had its blade removed, to mirror its decoration, is indicative of the expertise in manipulating this material that was developing at this time:

FIGURE 8.11 Decorated axe surfaces showing the use of incised and hammered decorative techniques, which overlap with the patterns seen on pottery vessels from the same period. Top left and right: Bandon axe, County Cork, Ireland, from a hoard; British Museum 1854–1227.26; Harbison, 1969: #846. Bottom left: Axe from "Yorkshire", England; British Museum 1853–1115.9; Schmidt and Burgess, 1981: #336. Bottom right: near Fivemiletown, County Tyrone, Ireland, from a hoard; British Museum 1843–1226.2; Harbison, 1969: #926

Source: R.J. Crellin with permission of the British Museum.

this axe was not just fragmented in two but broken along a curve to remove the blade in concert with the decoration.

I have demonstrated how one type of axe, the Early Bronze Age flat axe, changed constantly through its history. This is not a radical and rapid transformation provoked by the arrival of metal, but is a series of gradual and locally situated changes where pre-existing ideas and processes surrounding axe assemblages greatly affected how metal axes would be understood and used. We see a transition from axes understood to have similar properties to stone axes, through to axes that were locally appropriate and reveal an understanding of metal as a material that can be transformed through work and heat, to metal as something that needed to be deposited in specific ways. Copper and bronze axes were excluded from graves and settlement sites. Read together with the interpretation of hoarding as anticipatory action, I argue that axes were seen as active away from humans. Metal came to be a powerful and vibrant material with future potential beyond the control of communities, causing its exclusion from settlement and burial sites. Two other emergent properties of metals, the potential to be transformed from solid to liquid to solid and the ability to create copies, affected the development of hoarding practices. Through MA3 and MA4/5, hoarding played on concepts of similarity and differences, as axes with different histories were brought together. Metal was not at this time a material that could be fully controlled or understood by humans; it was vibrant, capable of transformation, and unpredictable.

Emerging narratives

At the outset I said that I was choosing to focus on metal, knowing the risks inherent and the possible criticisms. What I hope to have shown is that metal was related to, and became deeply embedded in, heterogeneous assemblages; metal did not stand alone but connected to other technologies, materials, and processes. When metal emerged in Britain and Ireland it emerged alongside people who could prospect, smelt, and work metal. It is most likely that the migrants came from Atlantic France or Iberia. Yet what happened when they arrived and began metalworking was deeply local. Axes were cast in local 'Irish' forms. While these new people certainly knew how to make metal, the evidence suggests that local communities (and I would add the metalworkers themselves) came to develop and transform their understanding of this new material over generations and centuries in conversation with each other. The arrival of these new people did not wipe out earlier assemblages, rather it was made to fit within them. Metal axes came to be understood, initially at least, on stone terms. There was not a radical shift the moment metal arrived or became widespread; rather, what metal was and what metal did changes constantly throughout the period of flat axe use (and beyond).

What of our grand narrative of metal as an early form of wealth finance and the driver of inequality? Large numbers of flat axes were deposited across Britain and Ireland, they were produced in regional forms, and used in differing ways. Over time, large numbers of flat axes were also recycled. The evidence does not suggest that access to metal was limited, nor does it suggest that access to metalworking knowledge was particularly restricted. When we look to the Irish evidence it does not seem that access to copper or bronze was what drove interaction with those from elsewhere; rather, it seems that from the outset they were working together, combining skills and resources and producing something new. I interpret the evidence of inequality in the Early Bronze Age to be limited. What I do think emerges with metal is an increase in movement, movement of materials, things, and people around Britain and Ireland producing both shared commonality and regional identities.

How does this fit into the bigger debate about the start of the Early Bronze Age in Britain and Ireland? I want to briefly engage with the two materials that have dominated the recent debate: pottery and human bone. As discussed earlier, the start of the Bronze Age is often identified on the basis of the appearance of Beaker pottery. The detailed typologies of changes in Beaker form are possible because this was not a static or homogeneous category: Beaker forms shifted chronologically and regionally. Beaker pottery encompasses both "flexibility and convention" (Jones, 2012: 120). Beakers do not, however, come to proliferate everywhere: for example, in Ireland, Beakers are more commonly found fragmented on settlement sites and are rarely associated with burials, and it is not until c.2200 cal BC that Ireland develops its own ceramic vessel that was deposited in burials: the Food Vessel (Brindley, 2006; Carlin, 2018). Later in the period, from c.1800 cal BC, Collared, Cordoned, and Encrusted Urns developed across Britain and Ireland. These were much bigger vessels, which were often used to contain cremations within burial contexts, quite different from the earlier Beaker. The burial urn increasingly came to take the place of earlier cists and coffins as a container for the deceased when cremated. Early Bronze Age ceramics teach us four key lessons about change. First, that change is continuous and ongoing throughout the period, not clustered at the start and end. Second, the multitude of changes in ceramic form through the Early Bronze Age are not simply sequential, they overlap in messy and complex ways; they represent not a chronological development, but choices made by local communities when burying the dead. These choices produced a gradient of change over the period but not in a unilinear or progressive way, by which I mean that even though one might be more likely to use a Food Vessel at 2000 cal BC and a Collared Urn at 1800 cal BC, these vessels have such overlapping currencies that mourners were making choices about what to use. Third, that responses to the arrival of new components, whether in the form of people, ceramics, or burial practices, were always local and had to fit with pre-existing assemblages. Fourth, new components (whether human or non-human) do not just fit within assemblages, they also come to change them, and in this way change can be seen to produce yet more change.

Turning to human bone, Late Neolithic burial practices are poorly understood. From c.2500 cal BC inhumation emerged, but it was not used for everyone or everywhere. Inhumation burials indicate a shift in approach to the human body – bodies were kept whole and buried in the ground. Isotopic research indicates that the very earliest inhumation burials were often those of migrants (Parker Pearson et al., 2019: 445–447); we can perhaps infer that local populations continued to treat their dead in archaeologically less visible ways. As above, not only were Beakers not adopted everywhere, but inhumation burial was not either; Ireland and the Isle of Man provide key examples of places where these burial practices never appeared to fully articulate with local assemblages. Ireland and the Isle of Man make it clear that there are multiple ways to become Bronze Age, and that this is not a singular process brought about by the emergence of Beaker burial. Furthermore, there is no completely standard Beaker burial; rather, over time different combinations of practices formed new assemblages. We can also tell this story a little differently, thinking about how migrating communities chose to change many of their practices as they moved into new landscapes. Influenced by what they saw and their interaction with local people, they became something new, 'not Beaker migrants' and 'Late Neolithic indigenous groups', but a hybrid community formed of the two where new practices developed that enfolded aspects of past practice.

It is not the case that practice stabilises a few generations after the start of the Bronze Age and the arrival of new people. Cremation burials emerged around the same time as the first uses of bronze and the increasing understanding of the use of fire as a catalyst to transform materials. With cremation a transformation in the materiality of the deceased from a fleshy soft body to hard, white fragments of burnt bone became appropriate before deposition. As with pottery, there were long-term trends in burial practices over the period, most notably the shift from inhumation to cremation; however, once again, this trend is not simple or linear. Between c.2100 and 1700 cal BC the two practices overlapped, and community choices played a key role (Brück, 2019); at many sites the two practices were deployed together and there is no reason to assume inhumations predate cremations (see for example Over (Garrow et al., 2014)). As Jo Appleby (2013) highlights, the two different processes actually shared much in common and are best considered in relation.

As with metal, I argue that the ceramic and burial evidence does not indicate a complete wiping out of what went before, nor a population replacement, nor that there was no movement of people, but something more complex. The existing dominant models for the transition to the Bronze Age in Britain and Ireland are all driven by migration. They are based on the existence of a closed migrating community and a closed local community. They all implicitly work on the basis that the migrating community was in some way superior, whether in terms of genetic replacement (cf. Olalde et al., 2018), or suggesting that Beaker "cultural values … insidiously overcome pre-existing values" (Needham, 2005: 209), or the technical superiority or appeal of metalwork. This progressive undertone is usually implicit rather than explicit, but ultimately it leads to the abandonment of pre-existing practices. The form of this description feeds into right-wing migration tropes where outsiders replace and overwhelm local communities (cf. Frieman and Hoffmann, 2019). We need to tell the story differently. That does not mean denying the evidence from aDNA or isotopes, but instead placing it in a different theoretical framework. It is clear that there were new arrivals in the period 2500–2300 cal BC from continental Europe who brought new materials and traditions with them. These new people came to live alongside and with pre-existing communities of non-humans and humans (even if you do not want to believe they mixed with 'local' humans they certainly mixed with 'local' non-humans). In assemblage terms, these communities were confederations of people, pottery, axes, animals, and traditions with permeable borders open to the territorialization of new components of various kinds. Focusing on my material history, the earliest migrating communities did not bring the copper and bronze we know from material science with them. They brought a stoney kind of a metal, one that was not necessarily an alloy, not all that hard, and not recyclable. Over time, communities that were mixtures of humans and non-humans (some with continental and some with local histories) allowed new material properties to emerge, so that by 2000 cal BC a different, metallic, metal was in use, one that would go on to continue changing. This is not a story of a migrating community with a superior 'Bronze Age lifestyle' arriving and changing a local 'Neolithic' community. It is a story about open assemblages of communities that mixed and from them new humans, non-humans, and practices emerged.

We need to stop talking about 'Beaker' and 'Late Neolithic' groups as if they were closed, separate, and static categories. Different migrating communities came from different places, arriving at different times, into different parts of Britain and Ireland (cf. Parker Pearson et al., 2019), contributing to continued dynamic, historical, local processes of change. The variety of regional practices we see across Britain and Ireland in the Early Bronze Age are the result of the complexity of this process. Different regions responded differently to the emergence of new human and non-human components. Equally, as Brück (2019: 3) highlights, the period of arrival is one marked by the expansion of building at Stonehenge, a site that had already been a focus for centuries and had already been modelled and remodelled multiple times. Not all the old ways were now irrelevant (cf. Carlin and Brück, 2012; Cleal and Pollard, 2012). This is a story of relations and interaction. We cannot tell whether it mattered by c.2200 cal BC if your ancestors came from the continent or over the hill or both, or how stories mixed these differing scenarios together.

One of the things that emerges clearly from the isotopic data is that there was a high level of movement within Britain and Ireland between childhood and death (Parker Pearson et al., 2019: 447–449). This degree of mobility was key in the spread of ideas and it is part of why we continue to see constant changes in materials and practices through this period. It is also part of what drives both similarity and difference: contact with others both highlights regionality and the locality of practices as well as similarities shared between communities. We can zoom out our scale of analysis and talk about the British and Irish Bronze Age at a larger scale. We make a mistake though when we fall back on the culture historical method and presume that shared practice means shared culture, or that culture is singular or fixed. The archaeological evidence suggests that what axes were, and what they did, differed through time and space, similarly what Beakers, and later Food Vessels were, was not singular or fixed either.

There was not one way to become-metallic or become-Bronze Age. Rather, there were multiple routes into the Bronze Age. We should not seek to squash or suppress regional differences but rather to appreciate them. Change is messy, complex, and multiple. There are no single origins or explanations for the emergence of the Bronze Age in Britain and Ireland; rather, there are many different stories where cause and effect blur together and what we need to do is to try and map flows of materials, both human and non-human, and use them to tell interesting, thoughtful, and politically engaged stories.

Notes

1 For a comprehensive discussion, see Carlin, 2018: Chapter 2.
2 But see, Gibson, 2007.
3 Although Tom Booth (2019: 8) has argued we should work to reclaim the term for its 'accurate' scientific meaning.
4 But see Booth, 2019: 7 on the relationship between palaeogenetics and simplistic modelling.
5 The authors take the most conservative reading of their data, working on the basis that individuals are likely to have come from the "nearest scientifically possible place of origin" (Parker Pearson et al., 2019: 436). This means that where multiple explanations for the 'home' of a migrant are possible, they favour mobility within Britain and Ireland. This interpretive decision, combined with the nature of isotope analysis, means that there was probably more migration taking place than they are able to identify from their evidence.
6 Graves are chemically and biologically active environments and therefore can be highly corrosive.
7 That said, Beyond the Three Age System, a Leverhulme funded project at the University of Leicester, will seek to specifically compare metal and stone blades from the start of the Early Bronze Age and attempt comparative wear analysis (https://www2.le.ac.uk/departments/archaeology/news-and-events/november/beyond-the-three-age-system-mapping-a-history-of-materials-3000-2013-600-bc).
8 This also follows Bray (2012), whose work complements and informs my own.
9 But see Carlin 2018: 56–59; 75–76.
10 But see Grime's Graves, where knives were probably the main product (Healy et al., 2018).
11 In the British material the divide between MA1 and MA2 makes little difference; however, in Ireland, where there are many more objects, this divide is of consequence (Needham, 1996: 126).
12 The copper in early daggers and knives has a different chemical signature and appears to be coming from the continent (Bray, pers. comm.).
13 There was, of course, also continental European copper entering Britain and Ireland (Rohl and Needham, 1998).

Bibliography

Abercromby, J. 1912. *A Study of the Bronze Age Pottery of Great Britain and Ireland and its Associated Grave Goods.* Oxford: Clarendon Press.

Allen, M., Gardiner, J. and Sheridan, A. (eds) 2012. *Is there a British Chalcolithic?* Oxford: Prehistoric Society and Oxbow Books.

Allentoft, M.E. et al. 2015. Population genomics of Bronze Age Eurasia. *Nature* 522: 167.

Appleby, J. 2013. Temporality and the transition to cremation in the late third Millennium to mid second millennium BC in Britain. *Cambridge Archaeological Journal* 23(1): 83–97.

Binford, L. 1962. Archaeology as anthropology. *American Antiquity* 28(2): 217–225.

Booth, T. 2019. A stranger in a strange land: a perspective on archaeological response to the palaeogenetic revolution from an archaeologist working amongst palaeogeneticists. *World Archaeology.* doi:10.1080/00438243.2019.1627240.

Bradley, R. 1998. *The Passage of Arms: An Archaeological Analysis of Prehistoric Hoard and Votive Deposits,* 2nd Edition. Oxford: Oxbow Books.

Bradley, R. 2000. *An Archaeology of Natural Places.* London: Routledge.

Bradley, R. 2017. *A Geography of Offerings.* Oxford: Oxbow.

Brace, S., Diekmann, Y., Booth, T., van Dorp, L., Faltyskova, Z., Rohland, N., Mallick, S., Olalde, I., Ferry, M., Michel, M., Oppenheimer, J., Broomandkhoshbacht, N.,

Stewardson, K., Matiniano, R., Walsh, S., Kayser, M., Charlton, S., Hellenthal, G., Armit, I., Schulting, R., Craig, O., Sheridan, A., Parker Pearson, M., Stringer, C., Reich, D., Thomas M. and Barnes, I. 2019. Ancient genomes indicate population replacement in Early Neolithic Britain. *Nature Ecology and Evolution 3*: 765–771.

Bray, P. 2012. Before $_{29}$Cu became copper: tracing the recognition and invention of metalleity in Britain and Ireland during the 3rd millennium BC, in Allen, M., Gardiner, J. and Sheridan, A. (eds), *Is There a British Chalcolithic?* Oxford: Prehistoric Society and Oxbow Books: pp. 56–70.

Bray, P. and Pollard, A. 2012. A new interpretative approach to the chemistry of copper-alloy objects: source, recycling and technology. *Antiquity* 86: 853–867.

Brindley, A.L. 2006. *The Dating of Food Vessels and Urns in Ireland*. Bronze Age Studies 7. Galway: National University of Ireland, Galway.

Brodie, N. 1997. New perspectives on the Bell Beaker culture. *Oxford Journal of Archaeology* 16: 297–314.

Brodie, N. 2001. Technological frontiers and the emergence of the Beaker Culture, in Nicholis, F. (ed), *Bell Beakers Today: Pottery, People, Culture, Symbols in Prehistoric Europe 2500–500 BC*. Trento: Offico Beni Archeologici: pp. 487–496.

Brophy, K. 2018. The Brexit hypothesis and prehistory. *Antiquity* 92: 1650–1658.

Brück, J. 2006. Death, exchange and reproduction in the British Bronze Age. *European Journal of Archaeology* 9(1): 73–101.

Brück, J. 2019. *Personifying Prehistory: Relational Ontologies in Bronze Age Britain*. Oxford: Oxford University Press.

Brück, J. and Fontijn, D. 2013. The myth of the chief: prestige goods, power and person-hood in the European Bronze Age, in Fokkens, H. and Harding, A. (eds), *The Oxford Handbook of the European Bronze Age*. Oxford: Oxford University Press: pp. 197–215.

Budd, P. and Taylor, T. 1995. The faerie smith meets the bronze industry: magic versus science in the interpretation of prehistoric metal-making. *World Archaeology* 27(1): 133–143.

Burgess, C. and Shennan, S. 1976. The Beaker phenomenon: some suggestions, in Burgess, C. and Miket, R. (eds), *Settlement and Economy in the Third and Second Millennium BC*. Oxford: BAR British Series 33: pp. 309–331.

Carlin, N. 2018. *The Beaker Phenomenon? Understanding the Character and Context of Social Practices in Ireland 2500–2000 BC*. Leiden: Sidestone Press.

Carlin, N. and Brück, J. 2012. Searching for the Chalcolithic: continuity and change in the Irish Final Neolithic/Early Bronze Age, inAllen, M., Gardiner, J. and Sheridan, A. (eds), *Is There a British Chalcolithic?* Oxford: Prehistoric Society and Oxbow Books: pp. 193–210.

Childe, V.G. 1925. *The Dawn of European Civilisation*. London: Kegan Paul.

Childe, V.G. 1930. *The Bronze Age*. Cambridge: Cambridge University Press.

Childe, V.G. 1940. *Prehistoric Communities of the British Isles*. London: Kegan Paul.

Cleal, R. and Pollard, J. 2012. The revenge of the native: monuments, material culture, burial and other practices in the third quarter of the 3rd millennium BC in Wessex, in Allen, M., Gardiner, J. and Sheridan, A. (eds), *Is There a British Chalcolithic?* Oxford: Prehistoric Society and Oxbow Books: pp. 317–332.

Clough, T. and Cummins, W. (eds) 1988. *Stone Axe Studies, volume 2*. London: Council for British Archaeology Research Report No. 67.

Conneller, C. 2011. *An Archaeology of Materials: Substantial Transformations in Early Prehistoric Europe*. London: Routledge.

Cooney, G 2000. *Landscapes of Neolithic Ireland*. London: Routledge.

Cooney, G. 2005. Stereo porphyry: quarrying and deposition on Lambay Island, Ireland, in Topping, P. and Lynott, M. (eds), *The Cultural Landscape of Prehistoric Mines*. Oxford: Oxbow Books: pp. 14–29.

Cooney, G. 2015. Stone and flint axes in Neolithic Europe, in Fowler, C., Harding, J. and Hofmann, D. (eds), *The Oxford Handbook of Neolithic Europe*. Oxford: Oxford University Press: pp. 515–534.

Cooney, G. and Mandal, S. 1998. *Irish Stone Axe Project Monograph I*. Dublin: Wordwell.

Cooney, G., Mandal, S. and O'Keeffe, E. 2011. The Irish stone axe project: reviewing progress, future prospects, in Davis, R. and Edmonds, M. (eds), *Stone Axe Studies III*. Oxford: Oxbow: pp. 427–441.

Cowie, T. 2004. Special places for special axes? Early Bronze Age metalwork from Scotland in its landscape setting, in Shepherd, I. and Barclay, G. (eds), *Scotland in Ancient Europe: The Neolithic and Early Bronze Age of Scotland in their European Context*. Edinburgh: Society of Antiquaries of Scotland: pp. 247–261.

Crellin, R.J. 2018. Examining the British and Irish Early Bronze Age flat axes of the Greenwell collection at the British Museum. *Journal of Archaeological Science: Reports* 18: 858–888.

Crellin, R.J. and Harris, O.J.T. in press. Beyond binaries: interrogating ancient DNA. *Archaeological Dialogues*.

Davis, R. 1997. Implement petrology: 60 years of service to the archaeological sciences, in Sinclair, A., Slater, E. and Gowlett, J. (eds), *Archaeological Sciences 1995*. Oxford: Oxbow: pp. 1–4.

Davis, R. and Edmonds, M. (eds) 2011. *Stone Axe Studies III*. Oxford: Oxbow.

Díaz-Guardamino, M. 2014. Shaping social identities in Bronze Age and Early Iron Age western Iberia: the role of funerary practices, stelae, and statue-menhirs. *European Journal of Archaeology* 17(2): 329–349.

Dolfini, A. and Crellin, R.J. 2016. Metalwork wear analysis: the loss of innocence. *Journal of Archaeological Science* 66: 78–87.

Downes, J. 1999. Cremation: a spectacle and a journey, in Downes, J. and Pollard, T. (eds), *The Loved Body's Corruption: Archaeological Contributions to the Study of Human Mortality*. Scottish Archaeological Forum: Cruithne Press: pp. 19–29.

Edmonds, M. 1993. Towards a context for production and exchange: the polished stone axe in earlier Neolithic Britain, in Scarre, S. and Healy, F. (eds), *Trade and Exchange in Prehistoric Europe*. Oxford: Oxbow Books: pp. 69–86.

Edmonds, M. 1995. *Stone Tools and Society: Working Stone in Neolithic Britain*. London: Batsford.

Evans, J.A., Chenery, C.A. and Fitzpatrick, A.P. 2006. Bronze Age childhood migration of individuals near Stonehenge, revealed by strontium and oxygen isotope tooth enamel analysis. *Archaeometry* 48(2): 309–321.

Fitzpatrick, A.P. 2011. *The Amesbury Archer and the Boscombe Bowmen: Bell Beaker Burials at Boscombe Down, Amesbury, Wiltshire*. Wessex Archaeology 27. Salisbury: Wessex Archaeology.

Fowler, C. 2013. *The Emergent Past: A Relational Realist Archaeology of Early Bronze Age Mortuary Practices*. Oxford: Oxford University Press.

Frieman, C. 2012. *Innovation and Imitation: Stone Skeuomorphs of Metal from 4th–2nd Millennia BC Northwest Europe*. Oxford: BAR International Series 2365.

Frieman, C. and Hofmann, D. 2019. Present pasts in the archaeology of genetics, identity, and migration in Europe: a critical essay. *World Archaeology* doi:10.1080/00438243.2019.1627907.

Furholt, M. 2018. Massive migrations? The impact of recent aDNA studies on our view of third millennium Europe. *European Journal of Archaeology* 21(2): 159–178.

Garrow, D., Meadows, J., Evans, C. and Tabor, J. 2014. Dating the dead: a high resolution radiocarbon chronology of burial within an Early Bronze Age barrow cemetery at Over, Cambridgeshire. *Proceedings of the Prehistoric Society* 80: 1–30.

Gibson, A. 2007. A Beaker veneer? Some evidence from the burial record, in Larsson, M. and Parker Pearson, M. (eds), *From Stonehenge to the Baltic: Living with Diversity in the Third Millennium BC*. Oxford: BAR International Series 1692: pp. 47–64.

Haak, W. et al. 2015. Massive migration from the steppe was a source for Indo-European languages in Europe. *Nature* 522: 207.

Hakenbeck, S. 2019. Genetics, archaeology and the far right: an unholy trinity. *World Archaeology* doi:10.1080/00438243.2019.1617189.

Harbison, P. 1969. The axes of the Early Bronze Age in Ireland. *Prähistorische Bronzefunde* IX(1).

Harrison, R. 1980. *The Beaker Folk: Copper Age Archaeology in Western Europe*. London: Thames and Hudson.

Healy, F., Marshall, P., Bayliss, A., Cook, G., Brink Ramsey, C., van der Plicht, J. and Dunbar, E. 2018. When and why? The chronology and context of flint mining at Grime's Graves, Norfolk, England. *Proceedings of the Prehistoric Society* 84: 277–301.

Heath, J. 2012. *Life in Copper Age Britain*. Stroud: Amberley.

Heyd, V. 2017. Kossinna's smile. *Antiquity* 91(356): 348.

Jenkins, D.A. 1995. Mynydd Parys copper mines. *Archaeology in Wales* 35: 35–37.

Jones, A. 2001. Drawn from memory: the archaeology of aesthetics and the aesthetics of archaeology in Earlier Bronze Age Britain and the present. *World Archaeology* 33(2): 334–356.

Jones, A.M. 2012. *Prehistoric Materialities: Becoming Material in Prehistoric Britain and Ireland*. Oxford: Oxford University Press.

Kienlin, T.L. and Ottaway, B.S. 1998. Flanged axes of the north-alpine region: an assessment of the possibilities of use-wear analysis on metal artefacts, in Mordant, C., Perno, M., Rychner, V. (eds), *L'Atelier du bronzier en Europe du XX au VIII siècle avant notre ère, vol. II*. Paris: Comité des travaux historiques et scientifique: pp. 271–286.

Kingery, W.D. 1993. Technological systems and some implications with regard to continuity and change, in Lubar, S. and Kingery, W.D. (eds), *History from Things: Essays on Material Culture*. Washington DC: Smithsonian Institute: pp. 215–230.

Knight, M. 2018. *The Intentional Destruction and Deposition of Bronze Age Metalwork in South West England*. Unpublished PhD thesis: University of Exeter.

Knight, M. 2019. The deliberate destruction of Late Bronze Age socketed axeheads in Cornwall. *Cornish Archaeology* 56: 203–224.

Kristiansen, K. and Larsson, T. 2005. *The Rise of Bronze Age Society: Travels, Transmissions and Transformations*. Cambridge: Cambridge University Press.

Kuhn, T. 1962. *The Structure of Scientific Revolutions*. Chicago: Chicago University Press.

Kuijpers, M. 2008. *Bronze Age Metalworking in the Netherlands (c.2000–800 BC)*. Leiden: Sidestone.

Kuijpers, M. 2017. *An Archaeology of Skill: Metalworking Skill and Material Specialization in Early Bronze Age Central Europe*. London: Routledge.

Latour, B. 1987. *Science in Action: How to Follow Scientists and Engineers through Society*. Cambridge: Harvard University Press.

Lipson, M. et al. 2017. Parallel palaeogenomic transects reveal complex genetic history of early European farmers. *Nature* 551: 368.

McKie, K. 2017. Did Dutch hordes kill off the early Britons who started Stonehenge. *Guardian*20 May2017: https://www.theguardian.com/uk-news/2017/may/20/dutch-invaders-stonehenge-ancient-britons

Mathieu, J. and Meyer, D. 1997. Comparing axe heads of stone, bronze and steels: studies in experimental archaeology. *Journal of Field Archaeology* 24(3): 333–351.

McFadyen, L. 2007. Mobile space in the Late Mesolithic of Britain: connected space. *Home Cultures* 4(2): 117–128.

McFadyen, L. 2010. Spaces that were not densely occupied – questioning 'ephemeral' evidence, in Garrow, D. and Yarrow, T. (eds), *Archaeology and Anthropology: Understanding Similarity, Exploring Differences*. Oxford: Oxbow Books: pp. 40–52.

McKinley, J. 1997. Bronze Age 'barrows' and funerary rights and rituals of cremation. *Proceedings of the Prehistoric Society* 63: 129–145.

Moyler, S. 2008. Doing away with dichotomies? Comparative use-wear analysis of Early Bronze Age axes from Scotland, in Hamon, C. and Quilliec, B. (eds), *Hoards from the Neolithic to the Metal Ages: Technical and Codified Practices*. Oxford: BAR International Series S1758: pp. 79–90.

Needham, S. 1996. Chronology and periodisation in the British Bronze Age. *Acta Archaeologia* 67: 121–140

Needham, S. 2004. Migdale-Marnoch: sunburst of Scottish metallurgy, in Shepherd, I. and Barclay, G. (eds), *Scotland in Ancient Europe: The Neolithic and Early Bronze Age of Scotland in their European Context*. Edinburgh: Society of Antiquaries of Scotland: pp. 217–245.

Needham, S. 2005. Transforming Beaker culture in north-west Europe: processes of fusion and fission. *Proceedings of the Prehistoric Society* 71: 171–218.

Needham, S. 2007. Isotopic aliens: Beaker movement and cultural transmissions, in Larsson, M. and Parker Pearson, M. (eds), *From Stonehenge to the Baltic: Living with Diversity in the Third Millennium BC*. Oxford: BAR International Series 1692: pp. 47–64.

Needham, S. 2012. Case and place for a British Chalcolithic, in Allen, M., Gardiner, J. and Sheridan, A. (eds), *Is There a British Chalcolithic?* Oxford: Prehistoric Society and Oxbow Books: pp. 1–26.

Needham, S. 2017. *The Classification of Chalcolithic and Early Bronze Age Copper and Bronze Axe-heads from Southern Britain*. Oxford: Archaeopress, Access Archaeology.

Needham, S. and Kinnes, I. 1981. Tinned axes again. *Antiquity* 55: 133–134.

Noble, G. and Brophy, K. with Hamilton, D., Leach, S. and Sheridan, A. 2017. Cremation practices and the creation of monument complexes: The Neolithic cremation cemetery at Forteviot, Strathearn, Perth and Kinross, Scotland, and its comparanda. *Proceedings of the Prehistoric Society* 83: 213–245.

Northover, P. 2008. *Analysis of Chalcolithic and Early Bronze Age Metalwork from the Isle of Man*. Unpublished Report held at the Manx Museum.

O'Brien, W. 1994. *Mount Gabriel. Bronze Age Mining in Ireland*. Galway: Galway University Press.

O'Brien, W. 2004. *Ross Island: Mining, Metal and Society in Early Ireland*. Galway, Ireland: Department of Archaeology, National University of Ireland, Galway.

O'Brien, W. 2012. The Chalcolithic in Ireland: a chronological and cultural framework, in Allen, M., Gardiner, J. and Sheridan, A. (eds), *Is There a British Chalcolithic?* Oxford: Prehistoric Society and Oxbow Books: pp. 211-225.

Olalde, I., et al. 2018. The Beaker phenomenon and the genomic transformation of north-west Europe. *Nature* 555: 190.

Parker Pearson, M., Chamberlain, A., Jay, M., Marshall, P., Pollard, J., Richards, C., Thomas, J., Tilley, C. and Welham, K. 2009. Who was buried at Stonehenge? *Antiquity* 83: 23–39.

Parker Pearson, M., Marshall, P., Pollard, J., Richards, C., Thomas, J. and Welham, K. 2013. Stonehenge, in Fokken, H. and Harding, A. (eds), *The Oxford Handbook of the European Bronze Age*. Oxford: Oxford University Press: pp. 159–178.

Parker Pearson, M., Sheridan, A., Jay, M., Chamberlain, A., Richards, M. and Evans, J. (eds) 2019. *The Beaker People: Isotopes, Mobility and Diet in Prehistoric Britain*. Oxford: Prehistoric Society and Oxbow Books.

Pollard, A., Bray, P. and Gosden, C. 2014. Is there something missing in scientific prove-nance studies of prehistoric artefacts? *Antiquity* 88(340): 625–663.

Roberts, B. 2008. Creating traditions and shaping technologies: understanding the ear-liest metal objects and metal production in Western Europe. *World Archaeology* 40(3): 354–372.

Roberts, B. and Frieman, C. 2012. Drawing boundaries and building models: investigating the concept of the 'Chalcolithic frontier' in north-west Europe, in Allen, M., Gardiner, J. and Sheridan, A. (eds), *Is There a British Chalcolithic?* Oxford: Prehistoric Society and Oxbow Books: pp 27–39.

Rohl, B. and Needham, S. 1998. *The Circulation of Metal in the British Bronze Age: The Application of Lead Isotope Analysis.* London: British Museum Occasional Paper 102.

Saraydar, S. and Shimada, I. 1971. A quantitative comparison of efficiency between a stone axe and a steel axe. *American Antiquity* 36(2): 216–217.

Schaniel, W.C. 1988. New technology and culture change in traditional societies. *Journal of Economic Issues* 22(2): 493–498.

Schauer, P., Shennan, S., Bevan, A., Cook, G., Edinborough, K., Fyfe, R., Kerig, T. and Parker Pearson, M. 2019. Supply and demand in prehistory? Economics of Neolithic mining in northwest Europe. *Journal of Anthropological Archaeology* 54: 149–160.

Schmidt, P. and Burgess, C. 1981. *The Axes of Scotland and Northern England. Prähistorische Bronzefunde* IX(7).

Sheridan, A. 1986. Porcellanite artefacts: a new survey. *Ulster Journal of Archaeology* 49: 19–32.

Sheridan, A. 2008. Upper Largie and Dutch-Scottish connections during the Beaker period, in Fokkens, H., Coles, B., van Gijn, A., Kleijne, J., Ponjee H. and Slappendel, C. (eds) *Between Foraging and Farming: An Extended Broad Spectrum of Papers Presented to Leendert Louwe Kooijmans.* Analecta Praehistorica Leidensia 40. Leiden: University of Leiden: pp. 247–260.

Sofaer Derevenski, J. and Stig-Sørensen, M.L. 2002. Becoming cultural: society and the incorporation of Bronze, in Ottaway, B. and Wager, E. (eds), *Metal and Society.* Oxford: BAR International Series 1061: pp. 117–121.

Thorpe, I. and Richards, C. 1984. The decline of ritual authority and the introduction of beakers into Britain, in Bradley, R. and Gardiner, J. (eds), *Neolithic Studies: A Review of Some Current Research.* Oxford: BAR British Series 133: pp. 67–84.

Timberlake, S. 2003. *Excavations on Copa Hill, Cwmystwyth (1986–1999): An Early Bronze Age Copper Mine Within the Uplands of Central Wales.* Oxford: BAR: 348.

Timberlake, S. 2014. Prehistoric copper extraction in Britain: Ecton Hill, Staffordshire. *Proceedings of the Prehistoric Society* 80: 159–206.

Timberlake, S. 2017. New ideas on the exploitation of copper, tin, gold, and lead ores in Bronze Age Britain: the mining, smelting, and movement of metal. *Materials and Manufacturing Processes* 32: 709–727.

Timberlake, S. and Prag, A. 2005. *The Archaeology of Alderley Edge –Survey, Excavation and Experiment in an Ancient Mining Landscape.* Oxford: BAR: 396.

Topping, P. 2011. The evidence for the seasonal use of the English flint mines, in Capote, M., Consuegra, S., Diaz-del-Rio, P. and Terradas, X. (eds), *Proceedings of the 2nd International Conference of the UISPP Commission on Flint Mining in Pre- and Protohistoric Times.* Oxford: BARInternational Series 2260: pp. 35–43.

Topping, P. 2017. *The Social Context of Prehistoric Extraction Sites in the UK.* Unpublished PhD thesis, University of Newcastle.

Vander Linden, M. 2016. Population history in third-millennium-BC Europe: assessing the contribution of genetics. *World Archaeology* 48(5): 714–728.

Williams, A. 2017. *Characterising Bronze Age Copper from the Great Orme Mine in North Wales to Determine and Interpret its Distribution*. Unpublished PhD thesis, University of Liverpool.

Williams, A. and Le Carlier de Veslud, C. 2019. Boom and bust in Bronze Age Britain: Major copper production from the Great Orme mine and European trade, c. 1600–1400 BC. *Antiquity* 93(371): 1178–1196.

Whittle, A., Healy F. and Bayliss, A. 2011. *Gathering Time: Dating the Early Neolithic Enclosures of Southern Britain and Ireland*. Oxford: Oxbow Books.

Woodward, A. 2002. Beads and Beakers: heirlooms and relics in the British Early Bronze Age. *Antiquity* 76: 1040–1047.

Woodward, A. and Hunter, J. 2015. *Ritual in Early Bronze Age Grave Goods*. Oxford: Oxbow.

9

A WORLD IN MOTION

All archaeologists study change. We study changing sites, changing regions, changing communities, changing ways of life, changing ontologies, changing environments, changing relations – the list goes on. We do this at both microscopic scales and vast time scales as we try to map change across millennia and continents. Yet talking about change is far from simple, because change is far from simple. This book has argued that studying change is central to what we do as archaeologists, and that exploring change over the long term is one of the defining strengths of our discipline, yet we have under-theorised how we describe, interpret, and explain it.

In this book I have outlined the strengths and weaknesses of our existing approaches to change (summarised below). I have argued that relational approaches offer archaeology scope for exploring change in exciting new ways that more effectively capture the complexity of our world. I have developed a relational approach rooted in posthumanism and new materialism. It is an approach where change is central to our understanding of the world. Materials, of all kinds and all types, are constantly changing, from human bodies to plant life, from bronze to stone, from telephones to parrots. Our world is constantly in the process of becoming, it is never finished or complete and the changes that emerge are not progressive. Today is not the zenith of human achievement, it is just another moment in a flow of change.

In this chapter I reflect on the argument developed in this book considering both its strengths and weaknesses. While there are a multiplicity of theoretical frameworks that we can adopt, I argue that not only is the approach I have developed particularly well suited to the study of change by archaeologists, but that it is also a politically and ethically positive approach to adopt in the current context that I, and many others, live within.

Politics and change

Change is a deeply political subject. Our current context is testament to that: we live in a world in climate crisis, where some communities already pay the price for the effects of complex assemblages of humans and non-humans that are beyond their control. The rise of populism and the far right is presented as a reaction to the changes of late capitalism: politicians present minority groups as the cause of problems within their own nations. Our world is changing and many people do not like it. The solution to both problems is more change; change that is hopeful, ethical, and positive and brings us to alternative futures. Because our world is complex and because change is complex there is no simple solution to our problems; rather, we need to work to alter the multitude of relationships with non-humans that we are all enmeshed within.

The narratives that archaeology produces can help: we can talk about change. We can describe concrete examples of complex change in the past. We have examples of times where changes emerged that were positive and times where changes were negative. We also have many more examples of the much more common situation, that change brings both positive and negative consequences, and those consequences are a matter of perspective. We have examples of how people have caused unintended changes in environments and the myriad consequences that emerge; of how societies can be refigured and reorganised in alternative ways; of how people, animals, plants, and materials have responded to changing environments; and of how new technologies emerge and the change that comes in their wake.

Archaeologists know that the past has always been political – a resource for leaders to utilise to legitimate themselves, or to find fresh bogeymen to scare us with. Archaeology produces many of the stories we have come to tell ourselves about our past, about who we are and where we have been. The stories archaeologists write about change are necessarily political because we are able to construct the stories that define what it is to be human in the long term. We have to deal with the grand narrative of human history, because if we do not others will (Robb and Pauketat, 2013). We need to accept the responsibility that comes with being archaeologists and use our detailed, nuanced, complex archaeological data to tell stories about the past *and* to actively critique stories that we see as problematic and damaging. This requires a shift from grand narrative to grand narrative*s*. We need to tell stories about the past that demonstrate the multiplicity of different ways to be in our world that have existed. We need to show that history is multiple and complex, and that alternative ways of being and doing are possible. We need to find ways of telling complex and nuanced stories that are easily comprehensible but do not simplify the complexity within. We need to tell not just a single grand narrative but multiple interwoven and complex narratives, not told from the position of 'winners', or underwritten by concepts of 'progress', but ones that show the awful things that humans do to each other, and that things are not always 'getting better'. Crucially these stories must also explore alterity and show that different hopeful futures are possible.

What humans are, what they have been, and what they can become is multiple. History is not just a single story; it is one that revels in multiplicity, one where what it means to be human has changed multiple times.

Challenges to change

It is challenging to describe and interpret change and very difficult to explain change because it is constant, messy, and complex. It is hard to describe and interpret because it always necessarily involves complex relational confederations of humans and non-humans that stretch and fold together multiple scales of analysis.

In Part I of the book I discussed stasis and how hard it is to explain (particularly over the long term). My position necessarily means that I see stasis as taking work and requiring constant change to achieve. Consider your home (whatever that means to you), a place where you might want stasis. That stasis takes work: it takes cleaning, mending, and maintaining (cf. Harris, 2018). The materials of our world are in constant motion: to hold them steady, to create stasis, takes work.

The messy, complex, relational nature of change is compounded when we turn to the archaeological record. How do we describe and interpret change in the past? In Chapter 1 I introduced a series of hurdles to the study of change – these hurdles exist precisely because change is messy and complex. Block-time approaches to change produce models where we have periods of stasis interspersed with rapid transitions at the end of periods. While they might effectively capture a sense of dynamic change at the borders of periods, they fail to capture the constant and ongoing nature of change in our world. The result is a caricature picture where change within periods is reduced and eclipsed, and change at the start and end of periods is emphasised.

This model becomes all the more problematic when it is comes into contact with models of change where transitions are driven by the arrival of new people. As we saw in Chapter 8, in Europe the growing aDNA literature appears to be creating hard boundaries between periods and presenting a model where rapid transition and 'progress' arrive with migrants and cause population replacement, wiping out what went before. The narratives that are emerging appear to be predicated on the idea of closed and very different cultural groups. The model fails to appreciate how migrants themselves were changed by the experience of moving, by living in new places, and interacting with new people, plants, animals, places, things, and materials. In colonial situations, the problems are compounded further as the lives of Indigenous people are presented as static while colonists are presented as bringing a more developed way of life causing change. The imposition of the block-time model serves to make earlier things 'Indigenous' and everything afterwards 'colonist', erasing the ways in which some practices persisted and how colonist practices changed as a result of their new context and their interactions with Indigenous groups. Block-time models might be a starting place in our research, but we should look, especially with the emergence of Bayesian chronologies, to move beyond them and to tell new, more detailed, and nuanced stories of change.

Progressive models of change are based on ideas of improvement, they are rooted in ideas where change progresses from simple to complex. They present the western world as the apex of our current achievements and all other histories and ways of being are presented as primitive or simpler. They have two particularly pernicious consequences: first, they have allowed us to believe that we are necessarily always making our world better. Second, they provided the theoretical justification for the exploitation, denigration, and, in some cases, destruction of other ways of life. It is our responsibility to show that history is not a story of progress from simple to complex, from primitive to developed. Progressive narratives can be linked to teleological explanations of change, another of my hurdles from Chapter 1. Teleological explanations make today the explanation for change in the past and uphold the present as the zenith of human achievement.

Many communities, both past and present, are interested in their origin stories. Archaeology is very often part of our search for origins. In Chapter 1 I argued against origins-oriented research, not because I object to us wanting to understand our past but because of the specific form that much origins research takes. Origins research is often directed at finding the first and original version of a given phenomenon – as a result it frequently focuses on providing a singular point of origin. The problem with this kind of research is that it suggests a given phenomenon has a singular origin and original form. This serves to ignore the complex nature of causality and fails to acknowledge how some phenomena emerge multiple times in multiple different forms (agriculture is a good example of this). The problem is compounded when that original form is then held up as a pure origin that can be used to define the essence of a phenomenon. This pure definition can then be used to judge other instances of the phenomenon negatively and to suggest that it is unchanging and static. Revolutions thinking is linked into this same framework because it too suggests that significant changes have their origins in singular moments (and often singular causes). Rather than focusing upon origins-oriented research or writing histories of revolution, we should instead focus on mapping the emergence of phenomena. We should reframe our work to consider how phenomena change over time and how they emerge from multiple different factors in differing ways in different places.

The messy and complex nature of change means that deterministic explanations and explanations that rely on singular linear causation cannot be sustained. The two most common forms of deterministic explanations are environmental and technological. Explanations that rely on either determinism fail to appreciate the complex relational nature of our world, where humans and non-humans are always thoroughly entangled in such a way as to make separating out an environmental cause from a technological one impossible. Moreover, the use of either form of explanation is based on the deeply problematic and damaging nature–culture dualism, which suggests humans are both separate from and ontologically elevated above nature and the environment. These kinds of explanations fail because they are singular, simplistic, and therefore inaccurate. As a result, I also argued that singular causation, more broadly, is a hurdle to effectively describing and interpreting change in the past.

The final of my hurdles to understanding change is probably the most controversial: anthropocentrism. Our anthropocentrism is both mistaken and damaging. Believing that humans are exceptional creatures on earth and that they are endowed with more rational intelligence than everything else has led to a position where we have placed ourselves at the "ontological apex" (Bennett, 2010: ix) and relegated everything else that makes up the world, including animals, plants, landscapes, and things, to a secondary, and less-than status. Our anthropocentrism has allowed us to believe that we are separate from the rest of the world. I argue that humans are always enmeshed in relations with a wide range of non-human others and that they never act alone. Rather than being the most important species in the universe we are just one-of-many. Moving beyond anthropocentrism allows us to more accurately understand our world, but also allows us to rethink our relationships with the non-humans with whom we share the earth.

The shape of the argument

Part II of the book considered the strengths and weaknesses of various approaches to change. Chapter 2 offered a history of archaeological theory from the perspective of change. The chapter explored the differing approaches to change, focusing particularly on culture history, processual, Marxist, post-processual, and postcolonial approaches. It considered how the different approaches intersected with the hurdles identified in Chapter 1. The chapter also stands as an extended case study of why the block-time approach might be a good foundation for describing and interpreting change, but that it always ends up simplifying and caricaturing it. It erases the connections between different ways of thinking and overemphasises the differences, pushing change into moments of transition and creating periods of stasis.

Chapters 3, 4, and 5 offered more in-depth explorations of archaeological approaches to change, focusing on three key themes: time, scale, and biography. Chapter 3 explored how universal, unilinear, uniform, and progressive models of time produce models of change with the same shape. Traditional models of clock-time take an epistemological approach to the measurement of time and turn it into a singular ontological approach to understanding what time is. These models suggest that change can be fixed into singular moments and in turn this continues to support singular causation models and results in our emphasis on singular static origins and revolutions. Cleaving apart past and present, and thereby making them appear disconnected, creates problems for our narratives of change. In particular, the idea that once things are buried in the archaeological record they are static and no longer changing, and simply awaiting re-enlivening by an archaeologist, is problematic. This model is anthropocentric, suggesting things that are separated from human action no longer change. At the close of the chapter I argued that time emerges from change and that multiple ontologies of time exist because there is a difference between how we measure time and what time actually is.

Chapter 4 explored the relationship between scale and time. Many of the different approaches to scale in archaeology have focused on identifying the correct scale at which to work, and these approaches are usually shaped by a nature–culture dualism. Arguments about working at the large or the small scale are often structured by a view that either the natural world and climate shapes change or that our actions and agency shape change. Both environmentally and technologically determinist explanations of change are caught in this trap, privileging either the non-human (read environmental) or human (read technological and cultural) components of the world. These arguments are caught between believing that human action has a negligible effect on history or that it is the driver of history. The nature–culture dualism that shapes these arguments once again fails to understand the complexity of our world. It misunderstands how nature and culture are deeply entangled together and inseparable. There is no pure 'nature' or 'culture': hybrids proliferate. Abandoning this dualism, I argued that we are best to think about scale not as small and large, or even small, medium, and large, but instead to think about scales as folding together in complex ways.

Chapter 5 explored biography as a way of constructing narratives of change about both humans and non-humans. The biographical metaphor provides an effective means of storytelling, but forces us to understand different types of change within an anthropocentric framework. Animals, plants, and things change in different ways and at different tempos from people. The chapter bridges Parts II and III of the book, as not only does it explore existing approaches to change, it also illustrates one of my key arguments in Part III: that change is constantly ongoing in our world. The chapter demonstrates that both bodies and things are constantly in motion. The change to non-human things is not just about the layering on of changing meaning to static things (as in early object biographies); rather, the materials that make up the world are in constant motion.

Part III outlines the power of relational approaches to offer us a new way to consider change. Chapter 6 began by considering the work of Bruno Latour and the symmetrical archaeology that he has inspired. In Latour's actor network theory, a new image of the world emerges as humans and non-humans are entangled in complex networks of relations that effectively break down simple categories such as nature–culture to reveal the complexity of our world. The relational aspect of Latour's work offered a way to overcome many of the hurdles from Chapter 1; however, his emphasis on being over becoming means that change through time is difficult to consider within his framework. Latour argues that any change in an actant effectively results in the formation of a brand new network; as a result, his networks effectively capture a moment in time, but do not help us understand their own emergence or how networks go on to change. This makes exploring how actants change and persist through time, a central and defining aspect of what archaeologists do, very difficult. Symmetrical archaeologists initially adopted Latour's ideas, but more recently, in what has been termed second-wave symmetrical archaeology (Harris and Cipolla, 2017: 130–131), they chose to resolve the problem of change through time by turning to the concept of essence, drawing on the world of Graham Harman. This argues that there is some 'essence' that defines a thing and remains stable through time despite the changing relations the thing might be enmeshed within. I rejected this appeal to essences because I do not believe there are any truly static parts of our world, but also because I think that this kind of argument leads to a dangerous place where we decide that the essence of a 'cup', or a 'chair', or a 'human' is 'this' or 'that', which then allows us to create exclusionary definitions where difference from the 'essence' (effectively a norm) is seen negatively.

At the close of Chapter 6 I explored Ian Hodder's relational approach: entanglement. His argument is that human history is directed but not progressive. He argues that human history is the story of the increasing entanglement of humans and things. He offers a political grand narrative that tells an alternative story about how we have become enmeshed in increasingly demanding (and often damaging) relationships with things. Despite the potential strength of his approach and some shared ground, I ultimately find the singular nature of his narrative unsatisfactory. Moreover, he upholds a problematic human–thing dualism (albeit mediated by a dialectical of dependency).

A post-anthropocentric, posthumanist position

In Chapter 7 I outlined my own, alternative relational approach to change. In line with my critique of anthropocentrism as a hurdle to writing good narratives of change in Chapter 1, I adopt a post-anthropocentric approach. Humans are not isolated or separate from this world, they act in confederations with non-humans. There are no humans born outside relations, nor are there any humans who have ever lived who have not been entangled in complex webs of relations with non-humans. I choose to use the term post-anthropocentric (following Braidotti, 2013; 2019) to describe my position rather than non-anthropocentric. This move directly addresses the critiques of non-anthropocentric approaches that see them as ignoring humans or being incompatible with the study of humans. The term post-anthropocentric recognises that anthropocentrism is problematic while also highlighting that my way of thinking does not exclude humans but instead asks us to re-imagine them.

For me, post-anthropocentrism is always necessarily entangled with a commitment to posthumanism. Posthumanism critiques human exceptionalism and removes humans from the "ontological apex" (Bennett, 2010: ix). Drawing heavily on the work of Rosi Braidotti, and embedded in feminist critique, my posthumanist position argues that humanism has served to uphold a static, ahistorical model of what it means to be human that is exclusionary. By making the white, Euro-American, educated, heterosexual, able-bodied man the ideal model of what it means to be human, humanism has served to label all those not included in this definition (women, Indigenous people, BAME and LGBTQI+ identities, disabled) as less rational, less able, closer to nature, and thereby less human. A political commitment to posthumanism means recasting difference, following Deleuze (2004), not as something negative but as positive and productive. It means focusing our stories on those who have been historically forgotten and excluded. This commitment to difference also underlies our need to focus on telling different, multiple, and diverse narratives about our past. It is a commitment to what Deleuze and Guattari (2014; see also Braidotti, 2011: 36–43) term the minoritarian. Embracing minoritarian narratives helps us shift from grand narrative to grand narrative*s*.

New materialist assemblages

Posthumanism and post-anthropocentrism are combined with new materialism in my approach to change. New materialism argues that all matter is in process. Matter is not static, dead, brute stuff awaiting the enlivening agency of a human to manipulate and change it. Rather, matter is viewed as lively, ever shifting, and full of potential. Rather than seeing humans as exceptional, they are relocated within new materialism as another form of matter alongside plants, materials, and animals. All matter is ever shifting: this has the effect of redistributing change across all materials. The properties and capacities of materials are not fixed and essential; instead they emerge from diverse relations. Our relational world of lively materials can be understood through the concept of 'assemblages'. Assemblages, drawn from the work of Deleuze and Guattari (2014; and as interpreted by Bennett, 2010; DeLanda, 2006; 2016), are relational, temporary gatherings of heterogeneous components. They exist at multiple scales, are always in process, and therefore historical and emergent. Assemblages have both material and expressive aspects, and as a result they can be analysed both in ways that concentrate on material processes and in ways that focus on meaning. Within assemblages cause and effect bleed into each other, meaning that singular explanations of change become impossible (Bennett, 2010).

Assemblages are post-anthropocentric and best understood from the position of a flat ontology where we do not decide in advance which components within will emerge as important or powerful. An assemblage approach is particularly appealing for archaeology for three key reasons: it allows us to move beyond dualisms, it has a concept of change at its heart, and it copes well with the diverse data of our discipline. Assemblages allows us to combine the many different forms of data that our discipline produces (from isotopes to ceramics) and does not suggest that there is a correct scale at which to work or a particular kind of data that should be privileged.

In Chapter 8 I offer an extended case study where I apply my approach to change to what has been considered one of the key transitions in the European past: the emergence of metalworking. Focusing on Britain and Ireland, current debates centre on the role of migration in the emergence of the Bronze Age. I shift the narrative by focusing on telling material histories of copper and bronze from c.2500 to 1700 cal BC. I explore how different and multiple understandings of copper and bronze emerged and transformed over time.

An emerging approach

This approach is not without its problems and I want to offer some critical reflection on these now. I know that for many people avoiding singular explanations of change will be deeply unsatisfying. My commitment to appreciating the complexity of causality means that I avoid reductive singular explanations. Instead I focus on describing the complexity and multiplicity of change and looking at how cause and effect bleed together. This is not about saying that there are not causes of change, but instead about saying that the nature of relational assemblages means that identifying anything as a simple singular cause is not possible, and thereby offering reductive cause-and-effect style explanations for change is always going to be unsatisfactory. A key related point here is that this does not mean that we avoid responsibility for our actions. As I argued in Chapter 7, we can still blame people for unethical or damaging behaviour: we are not diluting culpability. What I would suggest, though, is that when looking to find solutions to damaging behaviours we need to always consider wider assemblages of causation that bring about events, practices, or change – the solutions to our problems lie in working on whole assemblages (of both humans and non-humans), as well as holding humans responsible for their wrongdoing.

The position I adopt in relation to causation (that it is always complex and that cause and effect bleed together), combined with the commitment to seeing change as constant and ongoing, could be seen to lead to a view of the past as an undifferentiated flow of constant change[1] – effectively a soup of constant change. As I argued in Chapter 7, change has many different scales and tempos, and by using concepts such as phase transitions I think we can very effectively highlight that. We can identify moments of more rapid catalytic change and we can contrast these with periods where change is being directed towards creating stasis. Change in different materials occurs at different speeds: I cannot see mountains changing, but geology reveals them to be changing. It is important that we allow change in different materials and change of different tempos, scales, and characters to emerge.

Moving beyond block-time approaches is one of the biggest challenges we face as archaeologists. I do not think this is an easy task at all; it will not be quickly achieved. I am particularly aware that my use of Needham's (1996) metalwork assemblages to provide the chronological framework for some of my discussion in Chapter 8 could be viewed as effectively imposing a block-time model of change on my analysis. I counter this argument by suggesting that what I have tried to do is to focus on what we could take as a single block of time – 'the time of the flat axe' – and show the ongoing change within that period. More importantly, my assemblage approach necessarily paints a more complex picture as I look for components within assemblages that are changing at different rates, and I explore how older assemblages shape the ways new components emerge. To be more concrete, metal emerges as a new material physically, but how it emerges is shaped by pre-existing stone assemblages; as a result, the earliest metals in Britain and Ireland are effectively stoney materials, which transform through the period, slowly, in a series of different (but connected) ways, to become more metallic. The idea then is to open up the period block and show both aspects of stasis and change throughout in order to create a textured picture of change through time. This is not easy, and I think it takes a lot of work to avoid falling back on a block-time approach, particularly where we might struggle with issues of chronological and archaeological resolution.

This leads me on to my next issue for critical reflection: how do we know where assemblages start and end? Where do we cut the network (cf. Strathern, 1996)? How do we know where to stop our analyses? Does a relational approach mean that I can keep mapping relations and looking for connections between assemblages infinitely? If I am studying a cremation assemblage, do I need to map all the processes that created the cremated remains, consider all the materials that went into the cremation? Do I go further and consider the history of fire itself? How do we know where to cut off our assemblages, and the narratives that emerge from them, chronologically? In my own study of copper and bronze flat axes in Chapter 8 I reached back into the Late Neolithic, but at times I stretched further to consider axe production more broadly. Should I have reached even further backward and thought about the emergence of the axe as a form? This is a decision that we make as researchers. We focus on the bits of an assemblage (in both time and space) that are interesting to us and relevant to what we are trying to research (cf. Fowler, 2013). There are times when the archaeological record perhaps indicates to us a possible resting point in our analyses; in Chapter 8 my concern to explore the emergence of metal led me to flat axes and the resting point in my narrative comes with the emergence of palstaves. In a different narrative, this could merely have been a point of transition in a broader story.

This book has not engaged all that directly with issues of gender, identity, and power (but see Crellin, in prep). This is not (contrary to some critiques) because the theoretical frameworks of posthumanism and new materialism do not allow it, but rather a reflection of the material I have focused on in this book. As discussed in Chapter 7, the particular form of posthumanism I adopt, with its roots in feminism, is explicitly political and has much to say about gender, identity, and power. The commitment to posthumanism and post-anthropocentrism in this book is political to its core.

Perhaps the trickiest aspect of this book, more difficult even than avoiding block-time approaches to change, is my call to engage with the grand narrative. You may have noticed that I did not define grand narrative in Chapter 1: I simply took for granted that you would know what I meant. What is a grand narrative though? Does it have to stretch across a continent? Or a millennium? Does it have to deal with a fundamental aspect of human society? What would we define that as? Grand narratives are the stories we tell about where we have come from. The case study in Chapter 8 could be argued to eschew grand narrative – it engaged with a particular type of material culture and focused on mapping a material history. I want to suggest that this is not the case: at the close of the chapter I came back to what I see as the grand narrative of the Bronze Age – that metal is a superior technology that allowed the development of inequality and leadership and the emergence of chiefdoms. That is certainly a classic grand narrative. I offered an alternative story, one I would argue it is no less possible for us to cast as a story of the human past that we can share with the wider public and certainly one that seeks to disrupt and critique existing grand narrative. Tackling the grand narrative takes lots of small steps, lots of small stories. I am not suggesting each of us go and write our own version of a popular science history book that covers the whole sweep of human history in a few hundred pages,[2] rather that we draw on our expertise, our nuanced and complicated data, to begin to tell new stories that engage with grand narrative. By moving beyond a position where we expect there to be one single grand narrative, penned by one all-encompassing expert, we can sketch something new, where together, as a collective, we will be in a place to shout about the many different archaeological stories of our past.

On the plurality of relational approaches

This book advocates for a relational approach rooted in posthumanism; this is one of many relational approaches that emerge from a diversity of different times, places, and thinkers. Zoe Todd's (2016) critique of Latour and broader relational and posthumanist perspectives highlighted the overlaps between theoretical approaches that emphasise relations and critique anthropocentrism and Indigenous ontologies. Todd's critique is an important one, as Indigenous (and more broadly non-white) perspectives are frequently eclipsed and erased within academia. Similarly, Juanita Sundberg (2013) has considered how we might address the Euro-American-centrism in posthumanism. It is important to highlight that the anthropocentrism and humanism that are critiqued in this book are western perspectives that emerge from Euro-American ontologies: they are not universal (cf. Sundberg, 2013: 35). There are numerous Indigenous groups around the world who have relational and non-anthropocentric ontologies (for example, Deloria, 1973; Sundberg, 2013; Todd, 2016; Watts, 2013). In this book I have drawn on thinkers such as Bennett, Braidotti, DeLanda, Deleuze, and Guattari in the construction of my theoretical position and ontology. This has been a complex decision that I am still not completely satisfied with. The archaeology I do has its disciplinary, methodological, and philosophical roots in western-Cartesian philosophy. My archaeology is geographically located in Europe and chronologically situated in the Neolithic and Bronze Age. It has not, to date, involved working with Indigenous groups and I am not an expert in their ontologies. To begin to understand and appreciate Indigenous ontologies takes a sustained "serious engagement" (Sundberg, 2013: 40). There is no singular Indigenous ontology; rather, there are multiple Indigenous ontologies, each rooted in their own specific context and community. As Lindsay Montgomery (in prep) highlights, to talk of an Indigenous concept of agency, for example, erases the important differences between the ontologies of different Indigenous communities. Furthermore, Venessa Watts (2013: 32) argues that translating Indigenous cosmologies through a Euro-western process is an act of colonisation that does violence to the nature of key concepts. Euro-Americans must avoid mistranslating and misappropriating Indigenous ontologies. This has left me in a difficult position: I worry about the damage and exploitation I would do to Indigenous ontologies by translating them into my own work at present. On the other hand, I do not want to erase or fail to cite the Indigenous ontologies that deserve recognition.

The theoretical stance adopted in this book aims to be a positive contribution to redressing the violence and damage that comes in the wake of the dualistic and anthropocentric thinking dominant in Euro-American contexts. This emerges, particularly, from my own present context, where I am deeply concerned with the growing climate crisis and the rise of the far right. It is crucial to highlight that the post-anthropocentric, posthumanist, and new materialist ontology in this book is **not** the only ontology that offers this: many Indigenous ontologies offer such an approach. We should highlight these alternative ontologies and recognise their importance without appropriating them. My call to abandon progressive narratives is a serious one; doing so means that we can no longer assume that western practices, ontologies, and ways of being are superior. This makes space for us to recognise what has long been obvious to Indigenous communities: that western ontologies have led to damaging relationships between humans, and between humans and non-humans. The ontology adopted in this book, drawn from Euro-American thinkers, aims to be a more positive ontology for westerners, one that does not appropriate Indigenous ideas but instead attempts to open up more shared ground between them to allow better appreciation of the multiplicity of positive alternative ways of understanding our world that exist.

On becoming theory

Deleuze and Guattari (2014) teach us that assemblages are always in a process of becoming. New materialism teaches us that materials are always in process (Coole and Frost, 2010). Archaeological theory and archaeological theorists are no different: they are always in the process of becoming. This book has been in a process of becoming for a number of years and there is the temptation to look forward to the moment I hold a copy of the book in my hand and see that as the end of the process. It will not be. There will be talks, lectures, conversations with colleagues, citations, and critiques to come. This book and the processes behind it will continue to change and transform. This book is not my last word on change: it is an assemblage of ideas I have developed. I have drawn on the thinking of others, on my own experiences, and on conversations with colleagues, friends, and strangers to shape my thinking. I am proud of this book, though there are also parts of it I would have liked to keep mulling over and developing before letting them loose into the world. The assemblage of ideas is not fixed; you, the reader, will interpret them in your own way and choose to take them in different directions. I too will continue to think with it, be challenged in my thinking, and my own ideas will change.

This book outlines an approach that aims to be politically and ethically situated. I understand our world to be deeply relational, always emerging and changing, and therefore always historical. This leads to a position where I always try to consider the wider assemblage when making decisions about what are the most positive stories to tell about the past. We cannot make political and ethical decisions outside our historical assemblages and relations. This is a book that is embedded in a European context and actively seeks to critique western ontologies. I developed the ideas in this book embedded in my own assemblages, which are primarily geographically located within Britain, shaped by my research into the Neolithic and Bronze Age of Britain and Ireland, experienced through a gendered body, and embedded in late capitalism and the climate crisis: these wider assemblages have necessarily shaped my views.

All theory emerges from its context and is 'of its time': it is embedded within complex historical assemblages. This is not a justification for future changes to my thinking, or an excuse for ideas that later seem mistaken. Instead it is a call to think in an assemblage fashion – there are clearly negative and positive confederations of relations we can enter into, and there are many more complex assemblages of relations where right and wrong are not black and white but caught in myriad shades of grey. Navigating which theories, ideas, and narratives are the most positive responses to the shades of grey we live within is never easy and it is not static.

We need posthumanism and post-anthropocentrism now more than ever

Posthumanism and post-anthropocentrism are controversial. These are not ideas that are openly embraced by everyone. Despite this, it is my belief that now, more than ever, these are theoretical frameworks and ways of understanding our world that westerners need. As we begin to appreciate the true scope of our climate crisis and the current mass extinctions that are underway, it becomes increasingly clear that our anthropocentrism has allowed us to develop a deeply problematic relationship with non-humans and has, through colonialism, attempted to export this way of thinking across the world. Plants, animals, materials, things, and the environment have all become resources that westerners control, own, and shape for our own purposes. We think about what they can do for us and we think about ourselves as separate from them. We continue to give ourselves at least 50 per cent of the ontological space in this world (Harman, 2016: 31), relegating all the non-humans to a status of less-than (see Figure 7.1). We see ourselves as exceptional. This exceptionalism has led us to believe that we are the only beings endowed with rationality and education on earth; we've let ourselves believe that things are getting better, that progress is inevitable. Our humanism not only positions humans as exceptional but it also serves to make some of us more human than others. As Braidotti (2013; 2019) demonstrates, humanism's definition of the human excludes a great many who are presented as less rational, nearer to nature, and thereby less human. It presents difference as negative and allows the lives of some humans to be valued more than others. Our climate crisis is already affecting many communities who have been traditionally excluded by humanism more severely than those who have been enmeshed in some of the more damaging assemblages that have contributed to the crisis: climate justice is a posthumanist issue.

This is not, however, the only way to think about the world, it is not the only way to understand what it means to be human, and it is not the only way to think about our relationships with non-humans. There are a wide range of alternative ontologies, from those rooted in Indigenous communities across the world, to those developed by other philosophers. They show us other ways of being human and other ways of thinking about our relationships with the rest of the world. A relational perspective teaches us that we are not isolated and separate from the world but embedded in it. We are embedded in the problems we have created, and we need to be embedded in their solutions. Change is what we need and, as this book has argued, it is inevitable. What is not certain at present is what change will emerge. We are not powerless in the assemblages that we are embedded within, we have the capacity to act, and we act most effectively in heterogeneous assemblages of humans and non-humans. As archaeologists we also have the ability to shape the stories that we tell each other about the past, pasts where different ontologies and ways of life flourished. We tell stories about what it means to be human and how that always changes.

Notes

1 Some of the peer review for Crellin, 2017 suggested just this.
2 I wonder if one has to have had a long enough career and accumulated enough knowledge to be in a position to do this effectively.

Bibliography

Bennett, J. 2010. *Vibrant Matter: A Political Ecology of Things*. London: Duke University Press.
Braidotti, R. 2011. *Nomadic Theory: The Portable Rosi Braidotti*. New York: Columbia University Press.
Braidotti, R. 2013. *The Posthuman*. London: Polity.
Braidotti, R. 2019. A theoretical framework for the critical posthumanities. *Theory, Culture and Society* 36(6): 31–61.
Coole, D., and Frost, S. 2010. Introducing the new materialisms, in Coole, D. and Frost, S. (eds), *New Materialisms: Ontology, Agency and Politics*. Durham, NC: Duke University Press: pp. 1–43.
Crellin, R.J. 2017. Changing assemblages: vibrant matter in burial assemblages. *Cambridge Archaeological Journal* 27(1): 111–125.
Crellin, R.J. in prep. Posthumanist power, in Crellin, R.J., Cipolla, C., Montgomery, L., Harris, O.J.T. and Moore, S., *Archaeological Theory in Dialogue: Situating Relationality, Ontology, and Posthumanism*. London: Routledge.
DeLanda, M. 2006. *A New Philosophy of Society: Assemblage Theory and Social Complexity*. London: Continuum.
DeLanda, M. 2016. *Assemblage Theory*. Edinburgh: Edinburgh University Press.

Deleuze, G. 2004. *Difference and Repetition*. London: Bloomsbury.

Deleuze, G. and Guattari, F. 2014. *A Thousand Plateaus: Capitalism and Schizophrenia*. London: Bloomsbury.

DeloriaJr., V. 1973. *God is Red: A Native View of Religion*. New York: Putnam.

Fowler, C. 2013. *The Emergent Past: A Relational Realist Archaeology of Early Bronze Age Mortuary Practices*. Oxford: Oxford University Press.

Harman, G. 2016. On behalf of form: the view from archaeology and architecture, in Bille, M. and Sørensen, T.F. (eds), *Elements of Architecture: Assembling Archaeology, Atmosphere and the Performance of Building Spaces*. London: Routledge: pp. 30–46.

Harris, O.J.T. 2018. More than representation: multiscalar assemblages and the Deleuzian challenge to archaeology. *History of the Human Sciences* 31(3): 83–104.

Harris, O.J.T. and Cipolla, C. 2017. *Archaeological Theory in the New Millennium: Introducing Current Perspectives*. London: Routledge.

Montgomery, L. in prep. Indigenous alterity as archaeological practice, in Crellin, R.J., Cipolla, C., Montgomery, L., Harris, O.J.T. and Moore, S., *Archaeological Theory in Dialogue: Situating Relationality, Ontology, and Posthumanism*. London: Routledge.

Needham, S. 1996. Chronology and periodisation in the British Bronze Age. *Acta Archaeologia* 67: 121–140.

Robb, J. and Pauketat, T. 2013. From moments to millennia: theorising scale and change in human history, in Robb, J. and Pauketat, T.R. (eds), *Big Histories, Human Lives*. Santa Fe: SAR Press: pp. 3–33.

Strathern, M. 1996. Cutting the network. *Journal of the Royal Anthropological Institute* 2(3): 517–535.

Sundberg, J. 2013. Decolonizing posthumanist geographies. *Cultural Geographies* 21(1): 33–47.

Todd, Z. 2016. An Indigenous feminist's take on the Ontological Turn: 'ontology' is just another word for colonialism. *Journal of Historical Sociology* 29(1): 4–22.

Watts, V. 2013. Indigenous place-thought and agency amongst humans and non-humans (First Woman and Sky Woman go on a European world tour!). *Decolonization: Indigeneity, Education and Society* 2(1): 20–34.

INDEX

T - #0085 - 240125 - C0 - 234/156/12 - PB - 9781138292536 - Matt Lamination